Dreamweaver® UltraD[ev] For Dummies®

Mini-Glossary of Dreamweaver and UltraDev Terms

Anchor: Small icon that enables you to select a page element in the document window when the element itself may not be clickable (a hidden layer, for example).

Assets: Customizable collections of often-used site resources such as images or colors that can be previewed and deployed from a special palette.

Data binding: Association between data elements like recordset fields and page elements such as text fields or form elements.

Data connection: Definition of a connection to a DSN or other data source made from UltraDev. The definition is site-specific and held in a small file in a special subfolder called Connections.

Design Note: Electronic note that can be attached to an UltraDev file for private circulation among a workgroup.

Design time: Presentation of a Web page or Web site within UltraDev. Contrast with **Browse time,** which is presentation in a Web browser as the eventual user will see it. Differences between the two presentations vary from trivial to very widespread, depending on the content.

Document window: Main composition window in which you create your UltraDev Web page layouts.

Dynamic page or Dynamic site: Web page or Web site whose exact content cannot be precisely predicted at design time because some part of the content will vary according to the position of a data cursor.

Field: One coherent detail (column) of a data table, common to all records.

Launcher: Customizable palette of UltraDev features that you like to have close at hand. The Launcher typically displays the Site window, Data Bindings inspector, Server Behaviors inspector, and HTML Code view, but any of 14 features can be placed on the Launcher using a simple preferences editor.

Live Data View: Special UltraDev document window mode in which actual data is seen rather than placeholders, permitting design tasks to continue.

Live Object: Special type of object in one panel of the Objects Palette that prepackages collections of server behaviors.

Objects palette: Eight-panel palette containing HTML or server-side elements that you can easily deploy in the document window.

Placeholder: Code fragment placed in the document window to represent data bound to the page when no actual data is available for display.

Property inspector: Palette that displays the attributes of whatever element is currently selected in the document window. Most attributes are directly editable in this inspector.

Record: One complete element (row) of a data table.

Recordset: Representation of some part of a database that you need to have available to deploy on a Web page.

Site: The complete collection of files that UltraDev holds in its Local Folder at any one time, plus all subfolders.

Site definition: Complex information set about an UltraDev site, which includes locations of the local and remote folders, server technology, URL prefix, and so on.

Site window: Informational window depicting an entire UltraDev site and enabling creation of new files, exchange of files between the local folder and the server, and other functions.

Server behaviors: Prepackaged server functions that are frequently needed in dynamic Web sites, such as navigation through a data table, record insert/update/delete, and so on.

Server object: Packet of information held on the server and exchangeable with all pages in a Web site. A cookie is one example, but it's not a typical example because it can exist as either of two types of server object, the *request object* or the *response object*. It can (by definition) also exist on the user's client machine.

Template: Partial Web page having defined areas for custom design. Intended to help create a series of pages having some common design elements.

For Dummies®: Bestselling Book Series for Beginners

Dreamweaver® UltraDev™ 4 For Dummies®

Cheat Sheet

Document Window Shortcuts

Task	Shortcut
Insert <P>	Enter (or Return)
Insert 	Shift+Enter (or Return)
Insert a non-breaking space	Shift+Ctrl+Space
Begin a find and replace	Ctrl+F
Open page properties	Ctrl+J
Make a link	Ctrl+L
To refresh the LDV	Ctrl+R
Toggle LDV on and off	Shift+Ctrl+R
Save document	Ctrl+S
Open UltraDev Help	F1
Layers inspector (toggle)	F2
Objects palette (toggle)	Ctrl+F2
Frames inspector (toggle)	Shift+F2
Find next instance of last Find	F3 (not on Macintosh)
Property inspector (toggle)	Ctrl+F3
Behaviors inspector (toggle)	Shift+F3
Toggle all open floating palettes	F4
Minimize everything	Shift+F4 (not on Macintosh)
Site window (toggle)	F8
Source Code inspector (toggle)	F10
History inspector (toggle)	Shift+F10
Data Bindings inspector (toggle)	Ctrl+F10
Assets panel (toggle)	F11
Server Behaviors inspector (toggle)	Ctrl+F11
CSS Style Sheet inspector (toggle)	Shift+F11

Site Window Shortcuts

Task	Shortcut
Open selected page	Enter (not on Mac)
Open new document	Ctrl+N
Site files (toggle)	F8
Display Site map	Alt+F8
Open Assets panel	F11

UltraDev Shortcuts

Task	Shortcut
Open new document	Ctrl+N
Open existing document	Ctrl+O
Exit application	Ctrl+Q
Close file	Ctrl+W
Preview page in browser	F12
Preview page in secondary browser	Ctrl+F12

Acronym Corner

ASP: Active Server Pages

DBMS: DataBase Management System

DSN: Data Source Name

JDBC: Java DataBase Connectivity

JSP: Java Server Pages

LDV: Live Data View

ODBC: Open DataBase Connectivity

SQL: Structured Query Language

Copyright © 2001 IDG Books Worldwide, Inc. All rights reserved.
Cheat Sheet $2.95 value. Item 0797-4.
For more information about IDG Books, call 1-800-762-2974.

For Dummies®: Bestselling Book Series for Beginners

...For Dummies™: *References for the Rest of Us*®

BESTSELLING BOOK SERIES

Are you intimidated and confused by computers? Do you find that traditional manuals are overloaded with technical details you'll never use? Do your friends and family always call you to fix simple problems on their PCs? Then the *...For Dummies*® computer book series from IDG Books Worldwide is for you.

...For Dummies books are written for those frustrated computer users who know they aren't really dumb but find that PC hardware, software, and indeed the unique vocabulary of computing make them feel helpless. *...For Dummies* books use a lighthearted approach, a down-to-earth style, and even cartoons and humorous icons to dispel computer novices' fears and build their confidence. Lighthearted but not lightweight, these books are a perfect survival guide for anyone forced to use a computer.

> "I like my copy so much I told friends; now they bought copies."
> — Irene C., Orwell, Ohio

> "Quick, concise, nontechnical, and humorous."
> — Jay A., Elburn, Illinois

> "Thanks, I needed this book. Now I can sleep at night."
> — Robin F., British Columbia, Canada

Already, millions of satisfied readers agree. They have made *...For Dummies* books the #1 introductory level computer book series and have written asking for more. So, if you're looking for the most fun and easy way to learn about computers, look to *...For Dummies* books to give you a helping hand.

IDG BOOKS WORLDWIDE®

Dreamweaver® UltraDev™ 4 FOR DUMMIES®

by Stuart Harris

IDG BOOKS WORLDWIDE

IDG Books Worldwide, Inc.
An International Data Group Company

Foster City, CA ◆ Chicago, IL ◆ Indianapolis, IN ◆ New York, NY

Dreamweaver® UltraDev™ 4 For Dummies®

Published by
IDG Books Worldwide, Inc.
An International Data Group Company
919 E. Hillsdale Blvd.
Suite 300
Foster City, CA 94404
www.idgbooks.com (IDG Books Worldwide Web site)
www.dummies.com (Dummies Press Web site)

Copyright © 2001 IDG Books Worldwide, Inc. All rights reserved. No part of this book, including interior design, cover design, and icons, may be reproduced or transmitted in any form, by any means (electronic, photocopying, recording, or otherwise) without the prior written permission of the publisher.

Library of Congress Control Number: 00-109069

ISBN: 0-7645-0797-4

Printed in the United States of America

10 9 8 7 6 5 4 3 2 1

1O/SW/QS/QR/IN

Distributed in the United States by IDG Books Worldwide, Inc.

Distributed by CDG Books Canada Inc. for Canada; by Transworld Publishers Limited in the United Kingdom; by IDG Norge Books for Norway; by IDG Sweden Books for Sweden; by IDG Books Australia Publishing Corporation Pty. Ltd. for Australia and New Zealand; by TransQuest Publishers Pte Ltd. for Singapore, Malaysia, Thailand, Indonesia, and Hong Kong; by Gotop Information Inc. for Taiwan; by ICG Muse, Inc. for Japan; by Intersoft for South Africa; by Eyrolles for France; by International Thomson Publishing for Germany, Austria and Switzerland; by Distribuidora Cuspide for Argentina; by LR International for Brazil; by Galileo Libros for Chile; by Ediciones ZETA S.C.R. Ltda. for Peru; by WS Computer Publishing Corporation, Inc., for the Philippines; by Contemporanea de Ediciones for Venezuela; by Express Computer Distributors for the Caribbean and West Indies; by Micronesia Media Distributor, Inc. for Micronesia; by Chips Computadoras S.A. de C.V. for Mexico; by Editorial Norma de Panama S.A. for Panama; by American Bookshops for Finland.

For general information on IDG Books Worldwide's books in the U.S., please call our Consumer Customer Service department at 800-762-2974. For reseller information, including discounts and premium sales, please call our Reseller Customer Service department at 800-434-3422.

For information on where to purchase IDG Books Worldwide's books outside the U.S., please contact our International Sales department at 317-572-3993 or fax 317-572-4002.

For consumer information on foreign language translations, please contact our Customer Service department at 1-800-434-3422, fax 317-572-4002, or e-mail rights@idgbooks.com.

For information on licensing foreign or domestic rights, please phone +1-650-653-7098.

For sales inquiries and special prices for bulk quantities, please contact our Order Services department at 800-434-3422 or write to the address above.

For information on using IDG Books Worldwide's books in the classroom or for ordering examination copies, please contact our Educational Sales department at 800-434-2086 or fax 317-572-4005.

For press review copies, author interviews, or other publicity information, please contact our Public Relations department at 650-653-7000 or fax 650-653-7500.

For authorization to photocopy items for corporate, personal, or educational use, please contact Copyright Clearance Center, 222 Rosewood Drive, Danvers, MA 01923, or fax 978-750-4470.

LIMIT OF LIABILITY/DISCLAIMER OF WARRANTY: THE PUBLISHER AND AUTHOR HAVE USED THEIR BEST EFFORTS IN PREPARING THIS BOOK. THE PUBLISHER AND AUTHOR MAKE NO REPRESENTATIONS OR WARRANTIES WITH RESPECT TO THE ACCURACY OR COMPLETENESS OF THE CONTENTS OF THIS BOOK AND SPECIFICALLY DISCLAIM ANY IMPLIED WARRANTIES OF MERCHANTABILITY OR FITNESS FOR A PARTICULAR PURPOSE. THERE ARE NO WARRANTIES THAT EXTEND BEYOND THE DESCRIPTIONS CONTAINED IN THIS PARAGRAPH. NO WARRANTY MAY BE CREATED OR EXTENDED BY SALES REPRESENTATIVES OR WRITTEN SALES MATERIALS. THE ACCURACY AND COMPLETENESS OF THE INFORMATION PROVIDED HEREIN AND THE OPINIONS STATED HEREIN ARE NOT GUARANTEED OR WARRANTED TO PRODUCE ANY PARTICULAR RESULTS, AND THE ADVICE AND STRATEGIES CONTAINED HEREIN MAY NOT BE SUITABLE FOR EVERY INDIVIDUAL. NEITHER THE PUBLISHER NOR AUTHOR SHALL BE LIABLE FOR ANY LOSS OF PROFIT OR ANY OTHER COMMERCIAL DAMAGES, INCLUDING BUT NOT LIMITED TO SPECIAL, INCIDENTAL, CONSEQUENTIAL, OR OTHER DAMAGES.

Macromedia Fireworks 4 and Macromedia UltraDev 4 software by Macromedia, Inc. Copyright (c) 1998-2000 Macromedia, Inc., 600 Townsend Street, San Francisco, CA 94103 USA. All rights reserved. Macromedia, Fireworks, and UltraDev are trademarks or registered trademarks of Macromedia,Inc.

Netscape Communications Corporation has not authorized, sponsored, endorsed, or approved this publication and is not responsible for its content. Netscape and the Netscape Communications Corporate Logos, are trademarks and trade names of Netscape Communications Corporation. All other product names and/or logos are trademarks of their respective owners.

Trademarks: For Dummies, Dummies Man, A Reference for the Rest of Us!, The Dummies Way, Dummies Daily, and related trade dress are registered trademarks or trademarks of IDG Books Worldwide, Inc. in the United States and other countries, and may not be used without written permission. Dreamweaver is a registered trademark and UltraDev is a trademark of Macromedia, Inc. in the United States or other countries. All other trademarks are the property of their respective owners. IDG Books Worldwide is not associated with any product or vendor mentioned in this book.

IDG BOOKS WORLDWIDE is a registered trademark under exclusive license to IDG Books Worldwide, Inc., from International Data Group, Inc.

About the Author

Stuart Harris is an Internet consultant and author and, somewhere in his past, a Shakespearean actor and BBC TV documentary producer. He is an expert in HTML, dHTML, JavaScript, and Perl and proficient in other languages, of both computer and human varieties. He was an UltraDev beta tester and devised training courses for UltraDev under contract to Macromedia.

Harris's first computer book was *The IRC Survival Guide* (Addison-Wesley Trade Books, 1994). He followed up with IRC-related chapters for *Cyberlife!* (Sams, 1994) and *Internet Secrets* (IDG Books Worldwide, Inc., 1995 and 2000).

As a team with Gayle Kidder, Harris has authored numerous computer books since 1994, when their first book on accessing the newfangled technology of the World Wide Web with an out-of-left-field product called Netscape hit the bookstores. Since then, they have worn out several keyboards writing about the Internet and the Web. Their book-length ramblings have included *HTML Publishing for Netscape*, *Official Netscape Dynamic HTML Developer's Guide*, *HTML Publishing With Internet Assistant* (all Ventana Press), and *Drumbeat 2000 For Dummies* (IDG Books Worldwide, Inc.).

ABOUT IDG BOOKS WORLDWIDE

Welcome to the world of IDG Books Worldwide.

IDG Books Worldwide, Inc., is a subsidiary of International Data Group, the world's largest publisher of computer-related information and the leading global provider of information services on information technology. IDG was founded more than 30 years ago by Patrick J. McGovern and now employs more than 9,000 people worldwide. IDG publishes more than 290 computer publications in over 75 countries. More than 90 million people read one or more IDG publications each month.

Launched in 1990, IDG Books Worldwide is today the #1 publisher of best-selling computer books in the United States. We are proud to have received eight awards from the Computer Press Association in recognition of editorial excellence and three from Computer Currents' First Annual Readers' Choice Awards. Our best-selling ...For Dummies® series has more than 50 million copies in print with translations in 31 languages. IDG Books Worldwide, through a joint venture with IDG's Hi-Tech Beijing, became the first U.S. publisher to publish a computer book in the People's Republic of China. In record time, IDG Books Worldwide has become the first choice for millions of readers around the world who want to learn how to better manage their businesses.

Our mission is simple: Every one of our books is designed to bring extra value and skill-building instructions to the reader. Our books are written by experts who understand and care about our readers. The knowledge base of our editorial staff comes from years of experience in publishing, education, and journalism — experience we use to produce books to carry us into the new millennium. In short, we care about books, so we attract the best people. We devote special attention to details such as audience, interior design, use of icons, and illustrations. And because we use an efficient process of authoring, editing, and desktop publishing our books electronically, we can spend more time ensuring superior content and less time on the technicalities of making books.

You can count on our commitment to deliver high-quality books at competitive prices on topics you want to read about. At IDG Books Worldwide, we continue in the IDG tradition of delivering quality for more than 30 years. You'll find no better book on a subject than one from IDG Books Worldwide.

John Kilcullen
Chairman and CEO
IDG Books Worldwide, Inc.

Eighth Annual Computer Press Awards ≥1992

Ninth Annual Computer Press Awards ≥1993

Tenth Annual Computer Press Awards ≥1994

Eleventh Annual Computer Press Awards ≥1995

IDG is the world's leading IT media, research and exposition company. Founded in 1964, IDG had 1997 revenues of $2.05 billion and has more than 9,000 employees worldwide. IDG offers the widest range of media options that reach IT buyers in 75 countries representing 95% of worldwide IT spending. IDG's diverse product and services portfolio spans six key areas including print publishing, online publishing, expositions and conferences, market research, education and training, and global marketing services. More than 90 million people read one or more of IDG's 290 magazines and newspapers, including IDG's leading global brands — Computerworld, PC World, Network World, Macworld and the Channel World family of publications. IDG Books Worldwide is one of the fastest-growing computer book publishers in the world, with more than 700 titles in 36 languages. The "...For Dummies®" series alone has more than 50 million copies in print. IDG offers online users the largest network of technology-specific Web sites around the world through IDG.net (http://www.idg.net), which comprises more than 225 targeted Web sites in 55 countries worldwide. International Data Corporation (IDC) is the world's largest provider of information technology data, analysis and consulting, with research centers in over 41 countries and more than 400 research analysts worldwide. IDG World Expo is a leading producer of more than 168 globally branded conferences and expositions in 35 countries including E3 (Electronic Entertainment Expo), Macworld Expo, ComNet, Windows World Expo, ICE (Internet Commerce Expo), Agenda, DEMO, and Spotlight. IDG's training subsidiary, ExecuTrain, is the world's largest computer training company, with more than 230 locations worldwide and 785 training courses. IDG Marketing Services helps industry-leading IT companies build international brand recognition by developing global integrated marketing programs via IDG's print, online and exposition products worldwide. Further information about the company can be found at www.idg.com.

1/26/00

Acknowledgments

Now that my partner and erstwhile coauthor, Gayle Kidder, has got herself a fancy day job in a one-person cubicle, I've been forced belatedly to appreciate the load she used to carry, dealing with the administrative aspects of authoring as well as doing her share of the creative bits. She also deserves first acknowledgment, as a genuine e-commerce guru, for drafting Chapter 11 of this book and consulting on Chapter 12. As I finish the book, I can only hope that Gayle commits some appalling faux pas in the high-tech industry of Southern California and gets told she'll never work in this town again. That way, she'll be forced to rejoin the ranks of independent book authors.

Although I pride myself on thinking up interesting, instructive, and utterly fictitious Web sites to use as examples in my books, I'm not that hot at Web graphics. So I'm proud to acknowledge and thank Joey Large and Alexandra Rapp as the graphic artists behind most of the example Web sites that you find in this book, both on the printed pages and on the CD. Two other artists who demanded no payment more serious than a few candy kisses are Zachary and Jovana McCreary, the "Kid Picassos" featured in Chapters 1 and 2. The ceramics sold by the fictitious company Down To Earth in Chapter 4 are actually the work of the talented San Diego ceramic artist, Roberta Klein (robertaklein@earthlink.net).

On the technical side, thanks to Rick Crawford of Powerclimb — the author of the UltraDev Shopping Cart and other goodies — and John Darwell of IBM, my unofficial JSP consultant. Rick and John are both "alumni" of Elemental Software, where Drumbeat was born and raised. Thanks also to Tom Muck, author of a rival book, for good advice on server behavior extensions and some behind-the-scenes help with ColdFusion. The simple login validation routine in Chapter 8 was somewhat inspired by Hiran de Silva's fine tutorial at www.hiran.desilva.com/ultradev/.

Another of my failings is in the world of the Macintosh. I recognize that the Apple is an important technology with lots to offer creative designers. To me, however, a Mac is just an article of rainwear, and I struggled mightily with the Mac version of UltraDev until I discovered free help from Larry McLister of Macromedia, Ian Sokoloff of Interworks, and my old pal Ted Coombs of Science.org. The Mac-oriented sections of this book are now okay, and I hope Ted's NT Server recovers some day.

At Macromedia, thanks to all the UltraDev team, but especially Julie Thompson, Kevin Derby, David George, and Noah Hoffman.

Lastly, thanks to all the friendly folk who inhabit the Magicbeat mail lists where all we UltraDevians help each other out and boost each others' morale on a daily basis, and especially the authors of the UltraDev extensions who graciously allowed me to include their work in Chapter 14 and on the CD.

Publisher's Acknowledgments

We're proud of this book; please register your comments through our IDG Books Worldwide Online Registration Form located at www.dummies.com.

Some of the people who helped bring this book to market include the following:

Acquisitions, Editorial, and Media Development

Senior Project Editor: Jodi Jensen

Acquisitions Manager: Gregory S. Croy

Copy Editor: Jeremy Zucker

Proof Editors: Mary SeRine, Sarah Shupert

Technical Editors: Rob Turnbull, Max Hazelhurst

Senior Permissions Editor: Carmen Krikorian

Media Development Specialist: Jamie Hastings-Smith

Media Development Coordinator: Marisa E. Pearman

Editorial Manager: Kyle Looper

Editorial Assistant: Jean Rogers

Production

Project Coordinator: Jennifer Bingham

Layout and Graphics: Amy Adrian, Gabriele McCann, Kristin Pickett, Kendra Span, Brian Torwelle, Julie Trippetti, Jeremey Unger, Erin Zeltner

Proofreaders: Laura Albert, Valerie Bourke, Andy Hollandbeck, Dwight Ramsey, York Production Services, Inc.

Indexer: York Production Services, Inc.

General and Administrative

IDG Books Worldwide, Inc.: John Kilcullen, CEO; Bill Barry, President and COO; John Ball, Executive VP, Operations & Administration; John Harris, CFO

IDG Books Technology Publishing Group: Richard Swadley, Senior Vice President and Publisher; Mary Bednarek, Vice President and Publisher; Walter R. Bruce III, Vice President and Publisher; Joseph Wikert, Vice President and Publisher; Mary C. Corder, Editorial Director; Andy Cummings, Publishing Director, General User Group; Barry Pruett, Publishing Director

IDG Books Manufacturing: Ivor Parker, Vice President, Manufacturing

IDG Books Marketing: John Helmus, Assistant Vice President, Director of Marketing

IDG Books Online Management: Brenda McLaughlin, Executive Vice President, Chief Internet Officer; Gary Millrood, Executive Vice President of Business Development, Sales and Marketing

IDG Books Packaging: Marc J. Mikulich, Vice President, Brand Strategy and Research

IDG Books Production for Branded Press: Debbie Stailey, Production Director

IDG Books Sales: Roland Elgey, Senior Vice President, Sales and Marketing; Michael Violano, Vice President, International Sales and Sub Rights

◆

The publisher would like to give special thanks to Patrick J. McGovern, without whom this book would not have been possible.

◆

Contents at a Glance

Introduction 1

Part I: Basic UltraDev 7
Chapter 1: Putting Together a Quick Web Page with UltraDev 9
Chapter 2: Romping in the Dreamweaver Playground 35

Part II: Bringing Data to Your Pages 53
Chapter 3: Connecting to Your Data 55
Chapter 4: Recordsets and What They Offer 75
Chapter 5: Making Server Behaviors Work for You 101
Chapter 6: Live Data View 137

Part III: Advanced UltraDev 149
Chapter 7: SQL Variables: The Answer to Problems of Many Sorts 151
Chapter 8: Server Objects and Cookies 175
Chapter 9: UltraDev Extensions and Tricks 201
Chapter 10: The UltraDev View of Site Security 215

Part IV: E-commerce with UltraDev 231
Chapter 11: Setting Up Shop with UltraDev 233
Chapter 12: The Almost Complete E-store 251

Part V: The Part of Tens 273
Chapter 13: Ten Cute Things UltraDev Can Do 275
Chapter 14: Ten Extension Objects Worth Your Time 285

Part VI: Appendixes 291
Appendix A: Installing UltraDev for Windows 293
Appendix B: Installing UltraDev for Macintosh 295
Appendix C: Source Code Translations 305
Appendix D: About the CD 313

Index 321

IDG Books Worldwide End-User License Agreement 337

Installation Instructions 339

Book Registration Information .... *Back of Book*

Cartoons at a Glance

By Rich Tennant

page 7

page 53

page 149

page 291

page 231

page 273

Cartoon Information:
Fax: 978-546-7747
E-Mail: richtennant@the5thwave.com
World Wide Web: www.the5thwave.com

Table of Contents

Introduction *1*

What Is UltraDev? 1
How This Book Is Organized 1
    Part I: Basic UltraDev 2
    Part II: Bringing Data to Your Pages 2
    Part III: Advanced UltraDev 2
    Part IV: E-commerce with UltraDev 3
    Part V: The Part of Tens 3
Who You Are and Why You're Here 4
Conventions 4
    Platforms and server technologies 5
    Interpretations and timesavers 5
Icons Used in This Book 6

Part 1: Basic UltraDev *7*

Chapter 1: Putting Together a Quick Web Page with UltraDev 9

Taking the Quick Tour 9
    The floating palettes 10
    Floating palettes can form alliances 13
    The Launcher and Mini-launcher 14
    What's all this about data bindings and server behaviors? 15
    The Site window 16
Defining Your Site 18
    Preparing for a new site 18
    Six degrees of site definition 19
Making a First Page 28
    The document toolbar is your friend 29
    Use layers for easy page design 30
    Use text formats for page impact 33

Chapter 2: Romping in the Dreamweaver Playground 35

Working with Templates 35
    Making a new template 36
    Declaring editable regions in templates 38
    Modifying a template 38
    Using a template 40
    Adding content to a template 41

Building Your Own Sandcastles: Customizing UltraDev 43
    Guidelines and dots 43
    Rulers 44
    Preferences 44
    Extending UltraDev 45
Icing on the Cake: Defining Styles with CSS 45
    Page-by-page CSS 46
    Applying a CSS style 47
    Creating an external style sheet 48
    Editing an external style sheet 49
    Linking an external style sheet to another page 50
    Editing a style 51

Part II: Bringing Data to Your Pages 53

Chapter 3: Connecting to Your Data 55

Database Basics 55
    Rows and columns, records and fields 56
    ODBC: A common language 57
    A server of your own 57
Creating a Data Connection for an ASP Server 58
    Making a DSN 59
    Getting connected the easy way 61
Creating a Data Source Name for a ColdFusion Server 63
Creating a Data Hookup with JSP — Not for Amateurs 66
    Bridge to ODBC 67
    Doing it with pure JDBC 68
Setting Up Your Mac 70
    Connecting to a DSN 71
    Connecting to a ColdFusion data source 72
    Connecting to a JDBC data source 73

Chapter 4: Recordsets and What They Offer 75

Recordset Basics 76
    Making data available to a Web page 76
    Flowing data from a recordset to a page 79
    Making a repetitive list from ten data records 81
    Alpha-sorting a recordset 82
Pushbutton SQL 84
    Using the Advanced mode of the Recordset Builder 85
    Something about SQL 86
Data Filtering by Using the Recordset Builder 88
    Filtering in the Simple mode of the Recordset Builder 88
    Filtering in the Advanced Recordset Builder 89
Formatting Your Data 92

Dynamic Images 94
    Binding an image to a recordset 95
    Binding other attributes of the <IMG> tag 96
    Offbeat data bindings 97

Chapter 5: Making Server Behaviors Work for You 101

This Is What Your Site Looks Like — Well, Maybe 102
Binding Form Elements to Your Data 103
    Text elements bound, for update 104
    Text elements unbound, for insert 106
    Dynamic check boxes 107
    Making radio buttons dynamic 109
    Dynamic list and menu elements 110
    Hidden form fields 113
Insert (New Stuff) and Update (Old Stuff) 113
    Hand-crafting the Insert/Update server behaviors 114
    Live objects short cuts 116
Making a Repeat Region 120
Linking to a Detail Page 123
    Setting up the hyperlink source 123
    What happens on the other side? 124
    Doing it on autopilot with a Live object 125
Using Server Behaviors for Navigation 128
    Moving around the recordset, one behavior at a time 128
    Instant navigation with a Live object 129
    Record signposting 130
    Hide-and-seek buttons 132
Trash This! 134

Chapter 6: Live Data View 137

Designing in the Browser: They Said It Couldn't Be Done 137
So How Good Is Live Data View? 139
Adding the Query 142
Modifying LDV Settings 146

Part III: Advanced UltraDev 149

Chapter 7: SQL Variables: The Answer to Problems of Many Sorts 151

Giving Your Users a Way to Search 152
    Setting up a simple search page 152
    The results page — a bit more demanding 153
    What if the search comes up empty? 157
    Searching by category 159

Double Your Fun: Searching by Two Criteria 163
Filtering Multidimensional Searches with Static
  Options and Wild Cards 167
    What if nothing matches the user's search criteria? 169
    Reminding your users what they're looking for 170

Chapter 8: Server Objects and Cookies 175

Using the Request Object 176
  Making a page for listing approval 176
  Revising a listing 181
  Searching for keypals — or anything else 181
  Server variables 182
Cookies: Request Objects and Response Objects 184
  Who put the cookie in the jar? 185
  Letting keypals (or other users) put their passwords
    in the cookie jar 186
  More Response Objects 188
Using the Session Object 189
  Session variables in UltraDev 190
  Using session objects to set user access levels 191
  Personalizing your pages using session objects 192
  Using Session Objects to create a simple login
    validation technique 193
Doing it All in Live Data View 196
  Session variables in Live Data View 197
  Cookies in Live Data View 198
ColdFusion Specials 200

Chapter 9: UltraDev Extensions and Tricks 201

Customizing the Objects Palette 201
  Regrouping the Objects palette 203
  Making your own simple objects 203
  Making your own parameterized (how do you
    like that word?) objects 204
  The server behavior builder 206
Using the Macromedia Exchange 207
Mastering the Extension Manager 208
Cooking Up Your Own Insert Menu 210
Absolute Positioning à la Drumbeat 212
Extensionology Resources 214

Chapter 10: The UltraDev View of Site Security 215

What You Need to Know about Your Users 215
How to Get Information from Your Users 218
  New user registration 218
  UltraDev's Check New Username server behavior 220

Table of Contents   xvii

Keep Out! 223
    Setting up user access levels 223
    Identifying the user's access level at login 224
    Setting up the checkpoint on a restricted page 226
    Lackadaisical security 228
    Logging out 228

Part IV: E-commerce with UltraDev 231

Chapter 11: Setting Up Shop with UltraDev 233

Unwrapping the Cart Extension 234
Defining the Shopping Cart 236
Look Ma! No Database! 237
    Setting up the display page 237
    Adding the Buy Me button 239
    Testing the cart 241
Going Big-Time: Bring That Database Right Over Here 242
    What you need in the database 243
    Hooking up the database 244
    Creating the catalog 245
    Putting the goods on display 245
    Flippin' through the catalog 246
    Feeding the buy impulse 247

Chapter 12: The Almost Complete E-store 251

What Your E-store Looks Like 251
E-store Preliminaries 252
The Shopping Cart Display Page 253
    Using the special repeat region server behavior 255
    Updating the cart 256
    Proceeding to checkout 258
Closing the Deal 259
    Building the order confirm page 259
    Transferring the contents of a shopping cart to a database 260
E-mail Notification of Orders 265
    Configuring your NT server 266
    Using the CDO Mail server behavior extension 268

Part V: The Part of Tens 273

Chapter 13: Ten Cute Things UltraDev Can Do 275

Using Layout View 275
Converting Tables to Layers (And Layers to Tables) 277

Dreamweaver UltraDev 4 For Dummies

    Aligning and Sizing 278
    Binding a Recordset Field to Attributes of a DIV 278
    Adding a Color Attribute to the Horizontal Rule Tag 280
    Defaulting CSS Attachments and Other Stuff 281
    Fooling Your Computer 282
    The Poor Man's Database 282
    Turning Read-Only Attributes On and Off 284
    I Changed My Mind! 284

Chapter 14: Ten Extension Objects Worth Your Time 285

    UltraDev Shopping Cart 286
    CDO Mail 286
    Footnote 287
    Form Button Fever! 287
    Right-Click Menu Builder 288
    Horizontal Looper 288
    Banner Builder 289
    Redirect if Cookie Exists 289
    Guest Book 289
    Upload File from Page 290

Part VI: Appendixes 291

Appendix A: Installing UltraDev for Windows 293

    Technical Requirements Checklist 293
    The Simplest Installation You Ever Did 294

Appendix B: Installing UltraDev for Macintosh 295

    Technical Requirements Checklist 295
    Why Do I Need All This Setup? 295
    Installing UltraDev 297
    Configuring the NT Server 297
        Pre-flight checklist 297
        Hosting the Mac 298
    Meanwhile, Back on the Mac. 301

Appendix C: Source Code Translations 305

Appendix D: About the CD 313

    System Requirements 313
    Using the CD with Microsoft Windows 314
    Using the CD with the Mac OS 315

Table of Contents

Software on the CD-ROM 315
    Web-authoring software 316
    Web servers 316
    Graphics program 316
    Web browsers 317
    Server behavior extensions 317
    Template sets 318
    Files from the author 318
If You've Got Problems (Of the CD Kind) 319

Index 321

IDG Books Worldwide End-User License Agreement 337

Installation Instructions 339

Book Registration Information .... Back of Book

Introduction

I'm under no illusion that you opened this book yelling, "Wow! A book by Stu Harris! This has gotta be a great read!" I know, I know — it was that yellow and black cover, wasn't it? Plus curiosity about Dreamweaver UltraDev, probably.

It's both a privilege and a challenge for an author to write for such a high-profile series of books as *For Dummies*. I hope I can satisfy all your curiosities about this complex piece of software, in the style you have a right to expect from the colors of the cover.

I'll start with the obvious first question. . . .

What Is UltraDev?

UltraDev is a Macromedia software product that resulted from merging the features of Dreamweaver, already a highly successful Web publishing tool, and Drumbeat, an independent application acquired from Elemental Software.

Drumbeat's great strength lies in its ability to interact with database tables, creating pages on the fly according to what the data dictates. When the two products merged as Dreamweaver UltraDev in June 2000, Drumbeat's talents went under the hood, managing the data interface somewhat unobtrusively.

The result is a product that looks almost entirely like Dreamweaver but with some of the power and ingenuity of Drumbeat when the time comes to connect to data. UltraDev is the most capable tool available for building modern Web sites.

How This Book Is Organized

A consistent feature of *For Dummies* books is that you don't have to read them sequentially, as you might *Moby Dick* or *A Tale of Two Cities* (that's why they don't need to begin intriguingly with "Call me Ishmael" or "It was the best of times, it was the worst of times"). Cynics may say that the most useful part of the book is the part I *didn't* write — the index. Flip through that, or browse the table of contents, find what you need, read it, and get back to work. Grab one of my demo databases off the CD if you think it'll help.

Nevertheless, I tried to keep in mind the kind of learning curve readers would face as I planned and then wrote, this book. Dreamweaver, Drumbeat, and UltraDev are all so new that it's no problem remembering how I felt as I grappled with the concepts, trying to read the minds of the people who created these applications and hoping to develop proficiency as quickly as possible. So here's a sequential guide to the book's organization. Read this out of order, too, if you like.

Part I: Basic UltraDev

This first section of the book is really about Dreamweaver. Ninety percent of the material in this section could apply to the current version of Dreamweaver, anyway. I felt it was important to lay this foundation rather than assume that all readers already knew about Dreamweaver and just wanted to know what makes it into UltraDev. The section is far from being a comprehensive Dreamweaver manual. Chapter 1 is the crash course allowing you to define a site and get going, and Chapter 2 simply presents three of Dreamweaver's many features — the three I think you most need in order to get beyond the elementary stuff.

Part II: Bringing Data to Your Pages

I hope I've written this section so that it's accessible to readers who start off completely clueless about databases. That was certainly my intention.

As a matter of fact, the database management concepts you need to grasp in order to understand how UltraDev relates to data are not at all advanced. My central focus in this part is the practical question of what you have to understand within the UltraDev application itself — *recordsets* and *server behaviors*. They are the subjects of two meaty chapters, preceded by an essential preliminary chapter on data connections, and followed by a short chapter on UltraDev's very useful Live Data View mode.

Read this section, and I guarantee that you'll be able to build a database-driven Web site even if you knew nothing when you started.

Part III: Advanced UltraDev

It's obvious that the principal market that Macromedia sees for UltraDev is professional Web publishers working in a corporate environment. A steady look at the list of server behaviors reveals certain built-in assumptions about the logical flow of the overall site.

My goal in this part is to go along with Macromedia's assumptions in so far as it helps to understand the application, but to resist adopting the corporate mentality completely. I believe that if you're reading this book to better understand UltraDev, you need to know about search strategies, server variables, and extension objects whether or not you work in a corporate cubicle — whether you even think of yourself as a professional at this business.

I've chosen examples that are hopefully more interesting than what sellers of widgets may need in their daily grind, and I tried to keep this stuff as light as possible. There's no question, though, that the training wheels are off in this part; you'll get along best if you have some of the mentality of a programmer. By no means do you need to be an expert at the active server technologies, but it simply isn't possible to explain the cool features of UltraDev without introducing a few fragments of source code into the conversation.

Part IV: E-commerce with UltraDev

E-commerce is not a built-in feature of UltraDev, despite what some of the Macromedia press releases say. So what are two whole chapters about e-commerce doing in this book?

Well, e-commerce is the supreme example of UltraDev's policy of allowing itself to be extended in any direction that the imaginations of programmers tend to flow. The underlying concepts behind UltraDev extensions are covered thoroughly in Part III. In this part, I deal with a sophisticated extension package that was created, not by Macromedia per se, but by a small independent team under contract (a team in which I played a small role, in fact).

E-commerce is unquestionably what many clients of Web designers are screaming for today. The UltraDev Shopping Cart extension that I talk about in Chapter 11 doesn't claim to be a complete e-commerce solution. That's a blessing, in fact — it enables me to cover all the essential features of a shopping cart Web site without getting into the really complicated stuff about sales tax and shipping calculations.

In this part, I'm happy to settle for taking you all through the process — from creating a catalog of goodies to entice your shoppers to writing out the final order in your database. I even throw in an extra UltraDev extension that automatically sends an e-mail to the retailer when an order arrives.

Part V: The Part of Tens

Extensions to UltraDev really are an important topic. So not only do I talk about UltraDev extensions in Parts III and IV, but I also selected ten miscellaneous extension packages to tempt you with in this part — and *miscellaneous* is not a synonym for "cute but useless."

The other chapter in this part offers you a look at some other interesting UltraDev features.

Who You Are and Why You're Here

Here's what I know about you:

- You know HTML and you know basically how to make a Web page.
- You aren't scared by the idea of copying working files to a server folder — `C:\Inetpub\wwwroot`, most likely.
- Even if you've never used Dreamweaver, you can figure out how to deploy standard page elements from an Objects palette into a document window. You can find some guidance on this in Chapter 1, but I didn't have the space to illustrate how to use all 65 objects.
- You have given some thought to linking a database to a Web site, and you have access to a server capable of hosting a data-linked Web site.

As I was writing this book I had three groups of readers in mind, all of which I thought were entitled to expect to get satisfaction from my work:

Drummies are those of you who have used Drumbeat to some extent. You know what recordsets and templates are. You're about to suffer severe separation anxiety when you don't find your Interactions Center.

Dreamies are those who already know Dreamweaver. You know what behaviors and style sheets are. Now you're wondering if you need to get involved with this new concept, database connection. You probably do. If you know Dreamweaver really well, you'll very likely skip Part I.

Newbies don't know either of UltraDev's forerunners. This book is every bit as much for you as it is for the Drummies and Dreamies. Just don't expect me to teach you HTML — other than that, the necessary smatterings of knowledge are all between these covers.

At various points throughout the book, you'll see those whimsical icons, drawing your attention to paragraphs of particular interest to one or another reader group.

Conventions

I follow the typographical conventions of the *For Dummies* series by using *italics* when a new word or phrase is used for the first time and defined in the text. I use **bold** type for words or phrases that you're expected to type and `monofont` to identify source code, screen messages, and URLs.

Platforms and server technologies

UltraDev is equally good for both Windows and Mac platforms, and for four server models: ASP/JavaScript, ASP/VBScript, JSP, and ColdFusion.

I decided early on that that this book would become unreadable if I mentioned every possible setup at every stage. So here's how I decided to handle the problem:

- File extensions are not used at all. Mentally add on your `.asp`, `.jsp`, or `.cfm`.
- Although I may occasionally give control key combinations both ways — Ctrl+S (Windows) or ⌘+S (Mac) — most of the time I just mention the Windows key combo and figure the Mac jockeys will understand.
- On the (not very frequent) occasions when I feel inspired to write out source code, ASP/JavaScript is the only version you'll actually find in the chapter. Each source code sample is numbered and you can turn to Appendix C to find the code for the other versions (ASP/VBScript, JSP, and ColdFusion).

Interpretations and timesavers

Every time I describe how to use an UltraDev dialog box (and that's a *lot* of boxes!) the final step in the process is to click an OK button. Can I just say that once right now, please? We'd both get crabby, I think, if I wrote that out every time.

The two rival HTML tags, `LAYER` and `DIV`, can cause semantic problems in books like this. `LAYER` was Netscape's proposal for the HTML 3.0 standard for absolute positioning on a Web page. Microsoft went for `DIV`. Since the `DIV` tag already existed, the standards authority backed Microsoft. Netscape sighed (presumably) and made `DIV` work in its next version. Now `DIV` works in both browsers; `LAYER` and `ILAYER` work only in Netscape. The semantic problem is that *layer* is a proper English word and *div* ain't. Isn't. So if you find me (and other computer book authors) writing sentences like "Place a layer on the page at x=20, y=220," we probably mean a `DIV`. Personally, I wish Netscape had won the Great Layer Wars. You find out more about this in Chapter 13.

I've adopted the programmers' habit of talking about *design-time* and *browse-time* views of a Web page. There's a very important difference when you're dealing with pages derived from a database. When you design the page, you aren't generally dealing with all the actual words and images that will inhabit the page. Some of them are variable, depending on the position of the data cursor. They're called *dynamic* elements. So the *design-time view* is what you see in the UltraDev document window, using temporary placeholders for the dynamic items. The *browse-time view* is what the user of the page sees in his or her browser, after the Web server has replaced the placeholders with real data.

Icons Used in This Book

In addition to the Drummies and Dreamies margin icons shown earlier, you'll find the following standard ones:

Extra info that isn't essential to running UltraDev but that I think you'll find useful.

You won't find many of these, fortunately. But no modern software is entirely without traps, and I try to point them out with this icon. A typical reason for a warning is that you're about to do something that will be difficult or impossible to undo.

This icon points out optional (extra) info for programmers or advanced users. I promise the non-techies that no harm can possibly come to them if they ignore all these.

I use this icon when I'm reiterating something that I wrote in another section. Because you may not be reading the book in sequence, this is sometimes simpler than putting in a cross-reference.

This icon highlights pointers to content on the accompanying CD that's relevant to what's on this page or in this chapter.

You'll see this icon when I refer to other *For Dummies* books that you might want to check out for more information about a related topic.

Part I
Basic UltraDev

In this part . . .

A great deal of what's in these two chapters applies to UltraDev and Dreamweaver equally. Coping with the floating palettes in Chapter 1 and the templates and styles in Chapter 2 — these are topics of equal interest to users of both applications. I hope that readers with no Dreamweaver experience — those I call "newbies" in this book — find enough here to get comfortable with the user interface. But if you have any notion that these two chapters are the definitive guide to Dreamweaver, I can only say, "In your Dreamweavers!"

Dreamweaver experts — Dreamies — shouldn't be in too much of a hurry to skip to Part II. There's gold in them thar chapters and it doesn't take much finding. UltraDev's powerful interfacing with external data sources makes it inevitable that the site definition process gets into some unfamiliar territory. You also get to know one new toolbar and two completely new inspectors.

So whether you think you know it all or not, read this part!

Chapter 1

Putting Together a Quick Web Page with UltraDev

In This Chapter

▶ Tour the UltraDev screen

▶ Define an UltraDev Site

▶ Design a quick Web page

*T*his chapter is mostly a crash course in Dreamweaver. Much of its content applies to the latest Dreamweaver release, certainly. Server behaviors and data bindings, on the other hand, are specific to UltraDev, and important parts of the site-definition process are concerned with Web server technologies, which have much more importance in UltraDev than they do in "vanilla" Dreamweaver.

Read on to find out more about all this amazing jargon. Tomorrow, you can impress your friends . . . or lose them.

Taking the Quick Tour

The very first time that you start UltraDev after installation, you see a nice little welcome window (see Figure 1-1) offering four possible answers to the question "All right — now what?" (See Appendix A or B if you need help with installation.) Both the guided tour and the tutorial are worth doing, and the other two options lead you to parts of the UltraDev Help system.

All four options open browser windows, with UltraDev standing pat in the background. Once you have (or maybe have not) taken a look at these goodies, close the welcome window and kiss it goodbye forever.

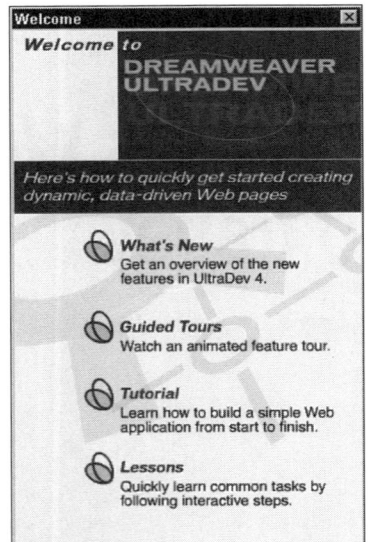

Figure 1-1: Welcome to UltraDev!

The floating palettes

Figure 1-2 shows the UltraDev screen that you're left with when you dismiss the cheery welcome screen. Drummies, and perhaps Newbies too, may find that Dreamweaver's floating palettes concept takes some getting used to. Might as well get it over with — go on, practice pushing those disembodied bits and pieces around your screen by grabbing their title bars in the usual way. Then press F4 a few times and see everything except the document window blink on and off. Press Shift+F4 to minimize all the bits and pieces at once. (Two very good key combos to know, those F4s.) Now introduce yourself to the art of selecting things to fill your screen by using the handy-dandy Table 1-1.

The two-monitor way of life

Some people who work with UltraDev professionally keep so many palettes and inspectors active that they find it's too much trouble to keep pushing them around their screen. They separate the document window onto a monitor of its own by using a graphics card with dual-monitor support (or two PCI video cards) and a double-wide screen resolution of 2048 x 768 (you might call it computer CinemaScope). Then they adjust Monitor A to show only the screen area with the document window, and Monitor B to show the other half where all the palettes live.

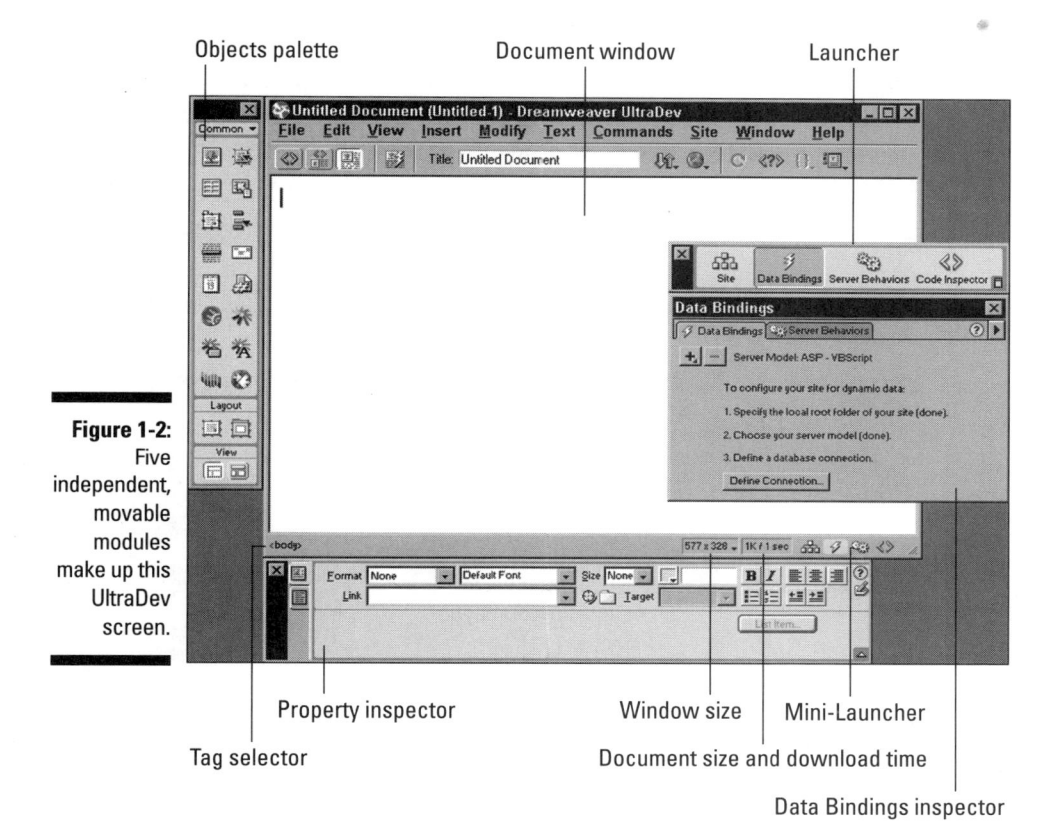

Figure 1-2: Five independent, movable modules make up this UltraDev screen.

Callouts: Objects palette, Document window, Launcher, Tag selector, Property inspector, Window size, Mini-Launcher, Document size and download time, Data Bindings inspector

Table 1-1	Screen Customization Guide	
Element	*What It Does*	*How to Toggle It On and Off*
Objects palette	Provides 65 things that you can put on a page	Window➪Objects or Ctrl+F2
Property inspector	Lets you edit the attributes of whatever element is currently selected on the page	Window➪Properties or Ctrl+F3
Launcher	Provides instant-click access to all other palettes	Window➪Launcher or F2
Site window	Lets you stand back and see your entire site	Window➪Site Files or F8

(continued)

Part I: Basic UltraDev

Table 1-1 *(continued)*

Element	What It Does	How to Toggle It On and Off
Data Bindings inspector	Lets you control data sources	Window⇨Data Bindings or Ctrl+F10
Server Behaviors inspector	Lets you control server functions	Window⇨Server Behaviors or Ctrl+F11
HTML Source Code inspector	Lets you see and edit your source code	Window⇨Code Inspector or F10
Assets Panel	Groups nine categories of site assets (images, colors, templates, etc.) for easy access	Window⇨Assets or F11
Behaviors inspector	Provides a grab-bag of dynamic HTML stuff	Window⇨Behaviors or Shift+F3
History inspector	Lets you replay and reconsider your layout activities	Window⇨History or Shift+F10
Frames inspector	Lets you select frames for design activity	Window⇨Frames or Shift+F2
Layers	Lets you inspect and edit layers	Window⇨Layers or F2
Library	Lets you store anything you want to reuse	Window⇨Library
CSS Styles	Lets you create, edit, and import CSS styles	Window⇨CSS Styles or Shift+F11
HTML Styles	Lets you edit standard HTML styles	Window⇨HTML Styles
Timelines	Create and edit animations	Window⇨Timelines or Shift+F9
Templates	Lets you manage page templates	Window⇨Templates

TIP

If at any time you can't find a floating palette, you can reset the visible palettes by choosing Window⇨Arrange Floating Palettes. Resetting the palettes is a satisfying experience — must be like being a sergeant major getting troops to form lines. The Launcher flies to the top-right, the Objects palette sails to the top-left, and the Property inspector scampers down to the bottom. The palettes all stand at attention and salute. Don't forget, too, that you can toggle them all on and off by pressing F4.

Chapter 1: Putting Together a Quick Web Page with UltraDev

Floating palettes can form alliances

You simply can't make the floating palettes attach to the document window (much to the chagrin of some dedicated Drummies I could name). You can, however, make subgroups of palettes get into bed together, as it were. Actually, if you look closely at the Data Bindings inspector, you see that it's already in bed with the Server Behaviors inspector. By default, they're on different tabs of the same window. You can marry and divorce palettes by dragging and dropping their tabs. To separate the Data Bindings and Server Behaviors tabs, click the Data Bindings tab and drag it out of its shared window. While the tab is on the move it's just an outline (see Figure 1-3), but as soon as you drop it outside, it forms a window of its own (see Figure 1-4).

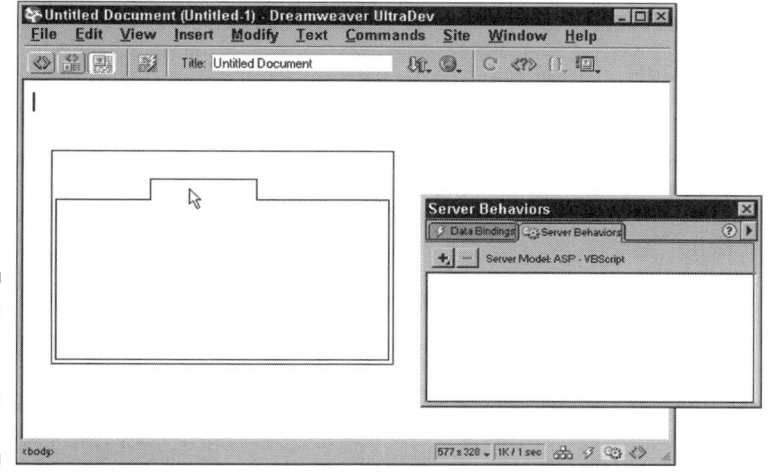

Figure 1-3: The Data Bindings tab on the move.

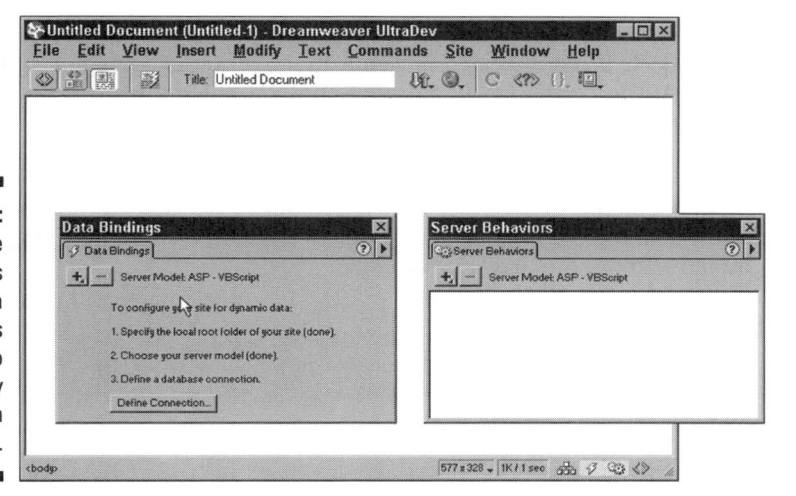

Figure 1-4: Dropping the tab causes the Data Bindings inspector to automatically form its own palette.

To put Data Bindings back into the shared window, click the tab area and drag its outline until its tab overlaps the tab area of the Server Behaviors palette. Then drop it again.

By default, History, Frames, Layers, and Behaviors live together in a shared window, but it's in your power to make any of them leave home and set up housekeeping on their own.

You can't make the Objects palette go and live in another window, but you can make it accept bedfellows in its own home. Just click and drag any tab into the Objects palette and drop it there. After you do that, you probably want to undo it because it isn't a very practical arrangement.

The Launcher and Mini-launcher

The Launcher is intended to be a lightning-quick way to summon and dismiss features that you use often. By default, the Launcher comes equipped with buttons to launch the Site window, the Data Bindings inspector, the Server Behaviors inspector, and the HTML Source window (refer to Figure 1-2). But there's no reason why you should be content with that. You can choose from a grab bag of 15 possible palettes and inspectors to customize your Launcher.

To customize your Launcher, follow these steps:

1. **Choose Edit⇨Preferences.**

    The Preferences dialog box opens with a list of 16 configurable things to choose from — enough to keep you busy for at least one rainy day.

2. **From the Category box on the left, click Floating Palettes (see Figure 1-5).**

3. **Add items to the Launcher by clicking the plus (+) button and selecting them from the pop-up menu. Remove items by selecting them in the list and clicking the minus (-) button. Customize the order of items in the Launcher using the up and down arrow buttons.**

Whatever you decide to put on your Launcher also appears on your Mini-launcher, which is embedded in the bottom-right corner of the document window frame (see Figure 1-2). Whatever the Launcher can do, the Mini-launcher can do, too. It's your choice.

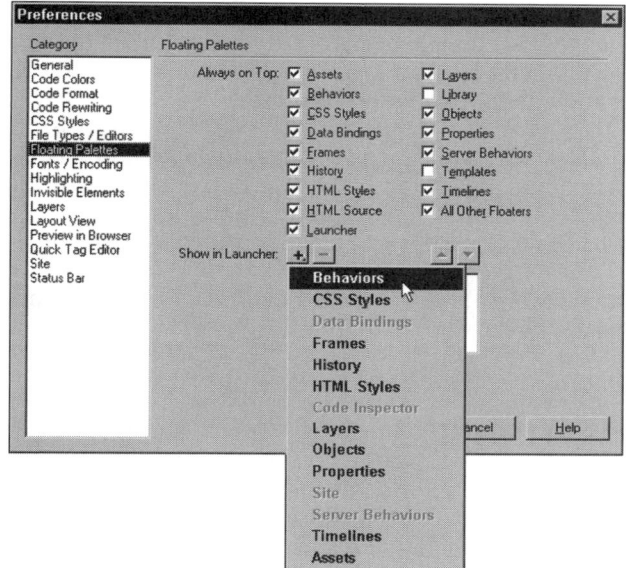

Figure 1-5: A rainy day activity — messing around with the contents of your Launcher.

What's all this about data bindings and server behaviors?

Server behavior normally refers to the penchant that Los Angeles waitresses have for introducing themselves, explaining that they look this tired because they were on a movie set at 4 a.m., and reciting the daily specials laconically without any reference to the prices.

In UltraDev, however, *server behavior* does not have this traditional meaning (surprise, surprise!). Server behaviors, together with *data bindings,* put the *Ultra* in UltraDev. Neither feature is needed in the straight Dreamweaver application.

What makes UltraDev different is that some of the page content can come from a database, and is not precisely known at design time. Pages that are supplied with content from a database are known as *dynamic pages,* which are distinct from normal *static pages* in that the content is completely defined at design time. Static pages have the file extension .html or .htm and can be viewed immediately in a browser. Dynamic pages have file extensions .asp, .jsp, or .cfm and must pass through a server before they can be browsed.

To create a line of text — or an image or form field — on a page that changes as the data changes, the text, image, or form field is linked to the database in a process known as *data binding*. UltraDev makes this pretty much a point-and-click operation using an on-screen palette.

Data binding makes it possible for you to create pages that navigate through a catalog, and that add, delete, and edit your database records. Navigation, addition, deletion, and update functions are examples of the server behaviors that UltraDev brings to your design screen in another special palette.

You find out much more about server behaviors in Chapter 5, and the details of data binding are covered in Chapter 4.

The Site window

You use the Site window after you fully define a Web site in UltraDev. *Defining* a site is simply the process of establishing your site structure for UltraDev so that it can organize all the necessary files both in your working folder and on the server. (See "Defining Your Site" later in this chapter.)

Even if you haven't defined a site yet, you can still click the Site button on the Launcher to open the Site window (see Figure 1-6). The Site window holds the not-really-quite-defined site for the UltraDev tutorial, and it's a good place to begin getting familiar with the following features of the Site window:

- **Site Files view:** In this default view, working files that are needed for this site are listed in the right pane. For any file that your mouse pointer is hovering over, details appear on the bottom border of the Site window. You open a file (a Web page, normally) either by double-clicking it from the list in the right pane or by selecting it and pressing Enter. Files published to the server are listed in the left pane. No files are listed in the left pane of the tutorial site shown in Figure 1-6 because no server has been defined for the site.

- **Shutter arrow:** You can make the left pane vanish and reappear by clicking the arrow at the extreme left end of the bottom border of the window.

- **Site Map view:** You can change to this view by clicking the Site Map View button (the third button from the left under the menu bar). The Site Map view, shown in Figure 1-7, depicts the link relationships between the pages of your site — but only if you've designated one page as the *home* page. (You find out how to designate the home page in the

Chapter 1: Putting Together a Quick Web Page with UltraDev *17*

"#5: Site Map Layout" section later in this chapter.) The site map appears in the left pane and steals space from the right pane — up to 100 percent of it, if necessary. To return to the Site Files view, click the leftmost button on the toolbar.

- **Get and Put:** You use these buttons to transfer files between your local working folder and the server holding your Web site. These functions are repeated in a button on the toolbar of the document window, which is where they're normally most useful for transferring the current page to the server.
- **Sites drop-down list:** You use this list to switch between the sites you've defined.
- **FTP Connect/Disconnect:** When you're working with a remote server and transferring files back and forth by *File Transfer Protocol* (FTP), you may need to go offline while you fuss over some design problem and then reconnect when you're ready to talk to the server again. This button is your friend in such situations.

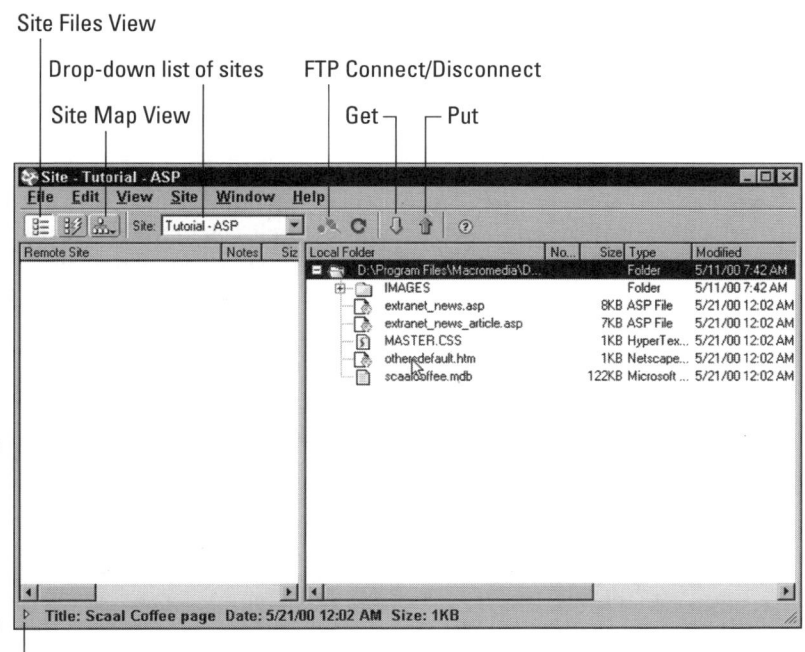

Figure 1-6: A Site window in Site Files view.

Site Files View
Drop-down list of sites
Site Map View
FTP Connect/Disconnect
Get
Put
Vanish left pane

Part I: Basic UltraDev

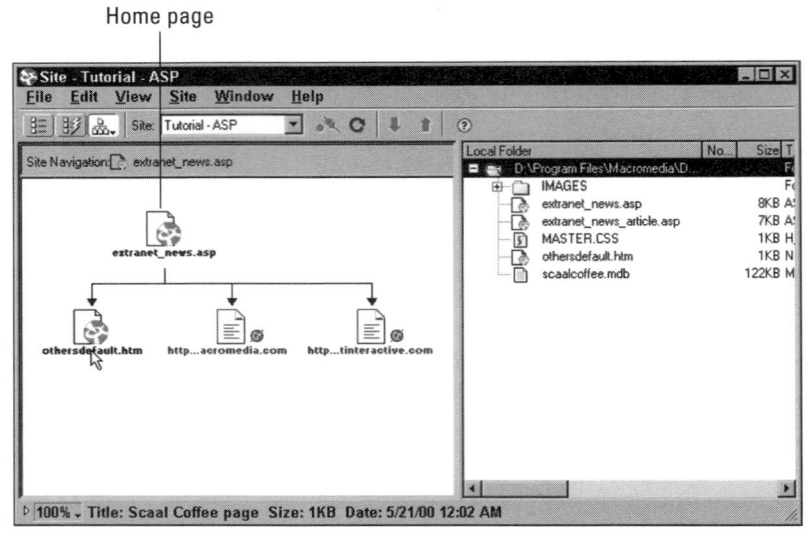

Figure 1-7: A Site window in Site Map view.

Home page

Defining Your Site

Drummies, as well as Dreamies, will be familiar with the concept of a site in the parlance of Web-design applications. But Newbies may need a little more explanation. A *site* is simply a coherent collection of files. HTML source code, media files of all kinds — everything that belongs in the root directory plus all of its subdirectories. In UltraDev and also in Drumbeat, a site definition includes a lot more than just pointing to the files and saying "that's the site." I go into more detail later in this chapter.

UltraDev's site definition process is roughly equivalent to all of Drumbeat's publish settings, some of Drumbeat's site preferences, plus two extra features: File Check In/Out for working as a team and private Design Notes. You find out about these features a little later in the section "Six degrees of site definition."

Every working file in UltraDev must be part of a site. In general, the same set of files exists on the server as in your local working directory. The server may be on the same machine as your local files, on a different machine accessed by file sharing, or on a remote machine accessed by FTP (File Transfer Protocol).

Preparing for a new site

Suppose that you want to create a Web site called KidPicassos that's a gallery of children's art (this is *not* kidpicasso.com, which is a registered domain).

Chapter 1: Putting Together a Quick Web Page with UltraDev

The first thing you need to do is create a fresh working folder. For the KidPicassos example, the path to the working folder is likely to be similar to one of the following:

WINDOWS: `C:\Ultradev sites\KidPicassos`

MAC: `Macintosh HD:Applications:Dreamweaver UltraDev:KidPicassos`

Gather together all the images that you want to include on the Web site and place them in a subfolder named `images` (or whatever other name you want to use) that is one level below the working `KidPicassos` folder. If you also want to include audio and/or video files on the site, you can either make separate folders for them or, if you have only a few, you can create one folder called `media` for everything binary.

As you proceed to define your site, you'll soon need to understand the file structure on the server side as well. That's what eventually appears in the left pane of the Site window.

You don't need to create server-side folders ahead of time, though.

Six degrees of site definition

To start the sequence of dialog boxes that add up to a complete site definition, choose Site⇨New Site. You're now looking at the first of six site-definition pages (see Figure 1-8).

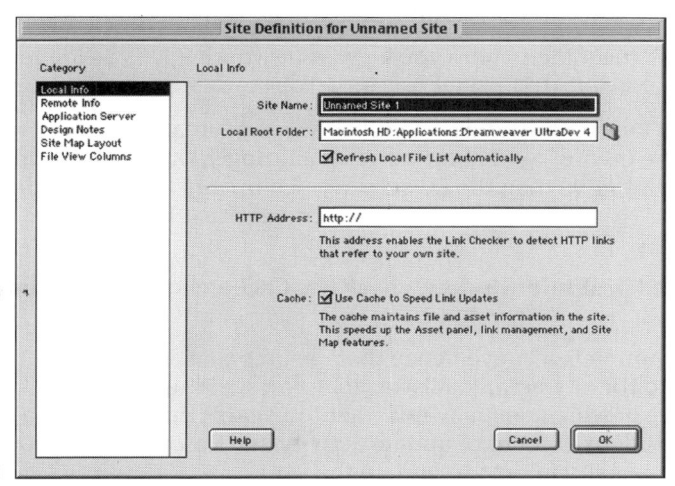

Figure 1-8: The first site definition category: Local Info.

All six pages have an OK button, which brings the curtain down on the entire six-part saga. So don't click that OK button until all aspects of your site definition are complete. Okay?

Like everything in UltraDev, however, a site definition is not irrevocable. You can review and re-edit any previously defined site by choosing Site➪Define Sites. The Define Sites dialog box opens, listing all your defined sites (see Figure 1-9). Select a site and click Edit to run through any or all of the site definition categories again.

Figure 1-9: The Define Sites dialog box lists all current sites.

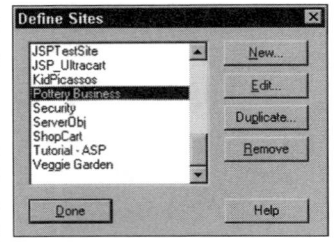

#1: Local Info

Follow these steps in the Local Info site definition category:

1. **In the Site Name text box, type the name of the new site.**

    In this example, the name of the site is KidPicassos.

2. **To register the local root folder, click the folder icon to the right of the Local Root Folder text box and drill down through the folder levels to the working folder that you already prudently created.**

    This is the folder where you keep your working files — in the example, the path is `D:\UltraDev sites\kidpicassos\`.

    If you imprudently didn't create it, you can create it right now by clicking the Create New Folder button. Amazingly, the Mac screen makes this more intuitive than the PC screen — compare Figures 1-10 and 1-11. On the PC (Figure 1-10) you have to recognize that button to see the ToolTip.

3. **In the Local Info window, check the Cache check box to enable the cache.**

    This option is a convenience that ensures that any time you copy new files to the site area, the listing that you see is updated. The only circumstance in which you may not want to use this option is if you expect a tremendous amount of update activity and you don't want to pay the slight penalty in time to update the list.

Chapter 1: Putting Together a Quick Web Page with UltraDev   21

Link management is an option that you're less likely to need. UltraDev can easily check the integrity of internal hyperlinks within your site if you choose File➪Check Links or Shift+F8. If you want UltraDev to also verify links on the server, however, you must supply a URL in the HTTP Address text box. The URL will often begin `http://localhost/` because that's how a Web browser finds a page that comes from a server on the same machine.

Figure 1-10: Use the Create New Folder button in the Windows dialog box — if you can find it.

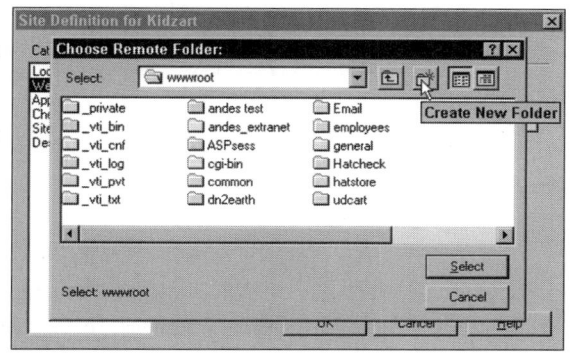

Figure 1-11: On the Mac, the Create button is labeled in plain English.

A completed Local Info category page of a site definition is shown in Figure 1-12.

#2: Remote Info

In this category you define how to transfer working files to the server, if any. Why might you not have a server? If you are using UltraDev's Web page authoring capabilities only and have no need for any page parsing by a server.

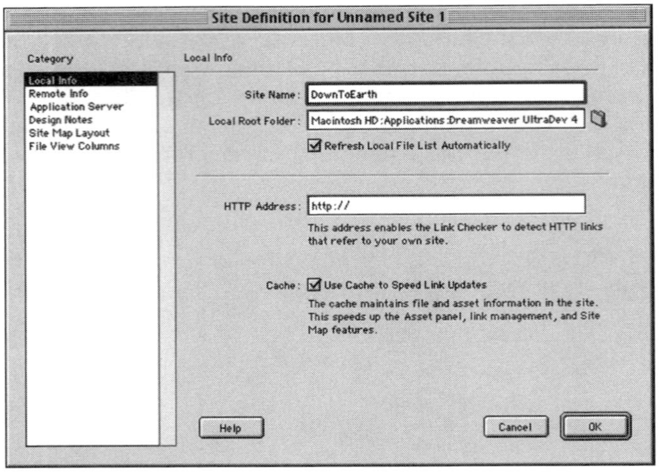

Figure 1-12:
A completed Local Info page of the Site Definition dialog box.

Parsing is what goes on when an ASP, JSP, or ColdFusion server takes your Web page and interprets embedded logical code before serving it to the user. If you create dynamic pages, they cannot be simply viewed directly in a browser but must be first parsed by a server. Using UltraDev without parsing by the server is essentially the same as using Dreamweaver.

If that's your situation, you can leave the Access drop-down list set at None and skip ahead to the Design Notes category.

Most of the time, if your operating system is Windows, you select Local/Network from the Access drop-down list, click the folder icon, and navigate to the remote folder where you plan to stash your published files.

The folder needed here is the one used by the Web server either on your own machine or on another machine in your LAN. The folder is normally a subfolder of one known as wwwroot. One common situation is that you're working with a Personal Web Server on your own machine. In that case the path to, say, a kidpicassos folder is probably C:\Inetpub\wwwroot\kidpicassos. Another common situation is that you're working with an NT server mapped to your J: drive. In that case, the path would be J:\Inetpub\wwwroot\kidpicassos. If you aren't sure where your server is, you'll have to find a systems administrator to consult.

You can either create the subfolder below wwwroot using your Windows Explorer or use the Create New Folder option in the file finder dialog box when you get that far.

As on the Local Info page, there's an option to auto-refresh your file list, which you should take.

Chapter 1: Putting Together a Quick Web Page with UltraDev

Figure 1-13 shows the completed setup for Local/Network access.

Another option on the Access drop-down list is to transfer files to the server by FTP. If you're working direct to a remote server connected by dial-up, for instance. Or if you're designing on a Mac but using a network Windows server — server administrators sometimes recommend transferring files by FTP rather than via an AppleTalk connection (and if the Mac is networked to a Windows 9x machine, you have no choice).

For FTP hosting, select FTP from the Server Access drop-down list and fill out the following details:

1. **FTP Host.** This is the Internet address of the FTP server that's hosting you. It may very well be a numerical IP address.
2. **Host Directory.** This is the path to the folder where your published files are stashed, from the FTP root of the remote server.
3. **Login/Password.** You pretty much always need a login and password for this type of Web publishing. Decide whether you want these details stored in the system and, if you do, check Save.
4. **Security options.** Check for Passive FTP or Firewall options if required. The systems administrator of the hosting server can tell you if either option is appropriate.

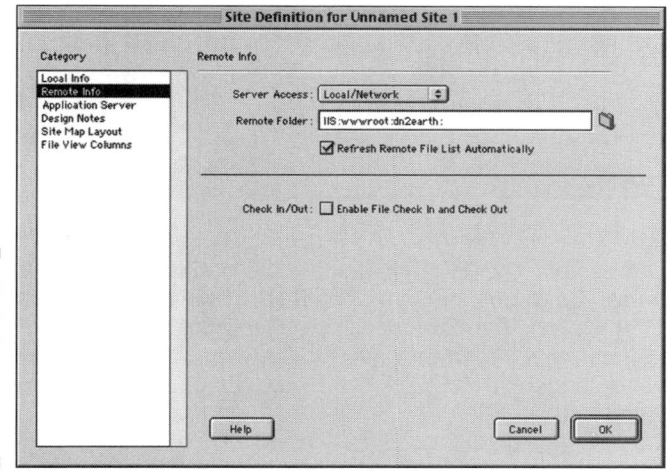

Figure 1-13: Remote Info category page for a typical Local Web server.

The other options on the Access drop-down list, SourceSafe Database and WebDAV, are specialized connection types for distributed Web site management and are not covered in this book.

The lower half of the Remote Info category page is concerned with UltraDev's File Check In/Check Out feature, which is disabled by default.

If you work on your own, you can ignore this feature. It's a useful option, though, if you work in collaboration with other people and share a set of working files. In that situation, there's always the danger of accidentally overwriting somebody else's work.

If you enable Check In/Out, some additional text boxes and check boxes appear. You must choose a Check Out nickname and enter your e-mail address (see Figure 1-14). When you have a file checked out, other members of the group see a red check mark beside the file in the Site window and can identify you by your nickname. The file is set as read-only (*locked* in Mac terminology), so others can open the file but can't make changes to it.

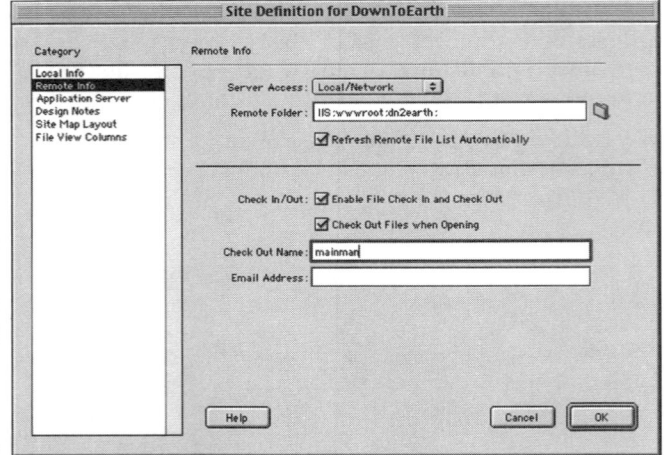

Figure 1-14: If you want checkout privileges, choose a nickname.

Check In/Out has two modes. By default, a file is marked as checked out by you as soon as you double-click to open it (but *not* when you open it by choosing File⇨Open). If you uncheck the Check Out Files When Opening box, a file is no longer checked out automatically when you double-click to open it. You have to choose Site⇨Check Out in the document window to mark the file as checked out.

#3: Application Server

In this category page you define the characteristics of the server and set up for viewing your pages as the server dishes them up to a browser.

This dialog is fairly complicated, and you have to get it absolutely right. The info you supply to this page is essential for creating and previewing your pages. So follow these steps carefully, okay?

1. **Select ASP, JSP, or Cold Fusion as your server model.**

   ASP, JSP, and Cold Fusion all do the same thing, but using different conventions. They make it possible for logic to be embedded in an HTML page, delimited by agreed symbols (in ASP the delimiters are <%> and <%>). The server interprets (parses) the logic and executes any instructions, including instructions to fetch information from a database, before serving the page.

   The final result is the same regardless of the server technology. Your choice is purely a matter of what is available to you.

   If you select ASP, you also have a choice between JavaScript and VBScript as the default scripting language. The only reason to choose one or other is if you intend to poke about in the source code and one of the languages comes more naturally to you. Functionally they're identical, and you could use UltraDev effectively for a decade without ever seeing, let alone editing, ASP source code.

2. **Choose a language and set the Scripting Language drop-down list.**

3. **The default page extension is normally .asp for an ASP server site.**

   You'll notice that the same Remote access options are on this page as on the Remote Info page. That's because it's possible to use UltraDev in a distributed management mode (the SourceSafe and WebDAV options in the Remote Info page). In that case the Remote server and the Application server could be two different machines. In normal use, you should just make sure that the access options default to the same as those on the Remote info page.

4. **Set the URL prefix to direct your browser(s) to the pages published for this site.**

   This step requires the path to your pages as seen by a browser to which the pages are served. It's completely different from the path defined in the Local Info site definition category, which is concerned with copying your files to the right folder for publishing. This path must be a fully-qualified Internet address, and your local Web server is normally addressed as localhost.

   In a Windows setting, the URL prefix is typically `http://localhost/` followed by the local path, but it could also be an IP address followed by a local path, as in Figure 1-15 (which is for a networked Mac). Note that the prefix must end in a forward slash.

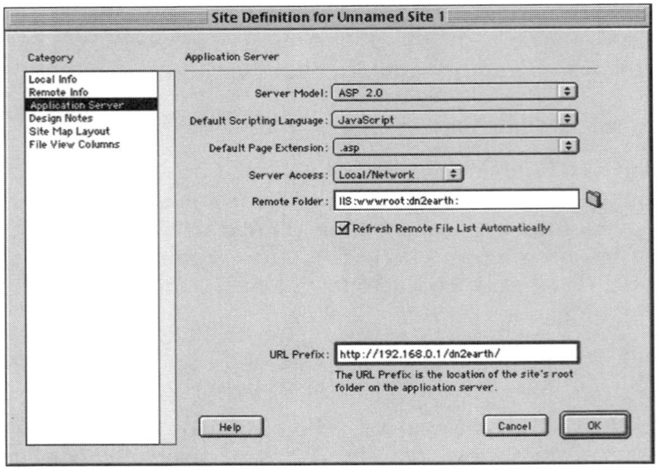

Figure 1-15: Completed App Server Info for KidPicassos.

#4: Design Notes

Design notes are subsidiary text files, loosely associated with your working files, which contain information that you want to record about the file but that you don't want to insert in the file itself. You can access design notes from the document window by choosing File➪Design Notes. An example of a design note is shown in Figure 1-16.

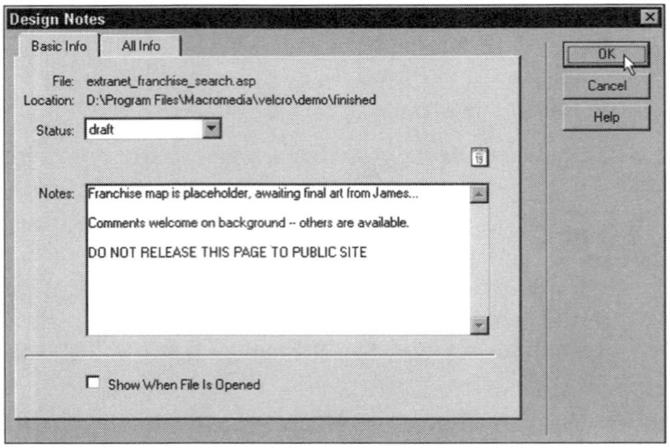

Figure 1-16: Example of a Design Note.

Design notes can never be seen by users browsing the site, so you may want to use them to record confidential or proprietary information. They can be shared with a collaborative group if Upload Design Notes for Sharing is checked on this page.

#5: Site Map Layout

You probably won't have to worry about most of the options on the Site Map Layout page. It's important, however, to declare here which page of your site you consider the home page. To define the home page, click the folder icon next to the Home Page text box and navigate to the page that you want to designate as "home." The path for that page then appears in the Home Page text box.

If you have no home page, you don't get the advantage of a nice pictorial view of your site (see Figure 1-17). You display that by clicking the Site Map View button.

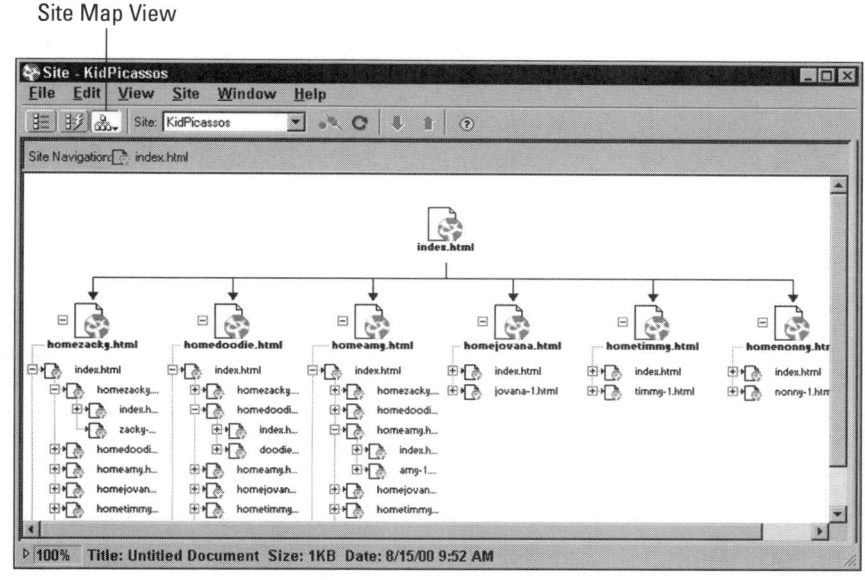

Figure 1-17: KidPicassos site tree, showing hyperlink cascade.

Figure 1-18 shows this dialog box completed.

All done

When you're finally satisfied — or think you're satisfied — or you're pretty sure you've left something out but you want to get going anyway — click OK. Provided you checked Enable Cache in the Local Info dialog box, you'll see a little dialog box telling you that UltraDev is about to create a site cache. Just click OK.

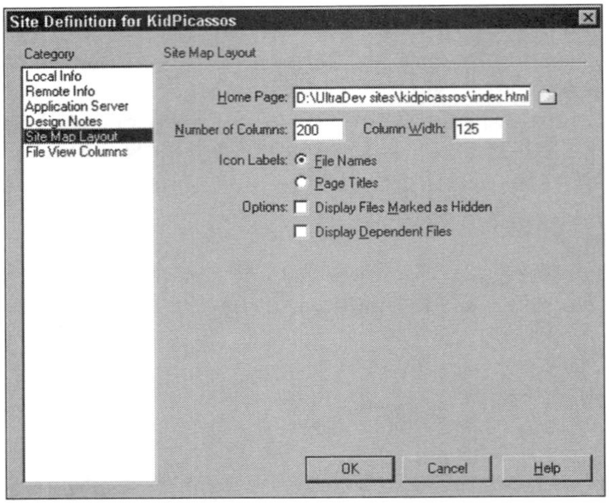

Figure 1-18: A completed Site Map Layout dialog box.

Making a First Page

When you finish defining a new site in UltraDev, you're generally left gazing at an empty Site window. The left side of the window lists files in the server-side site folder — it's probably empty. The right side lists files in your working folder as you defined it in the Local Info page of the site definition. That's probably empty as well, although any content that you've previously gathered, such as media files, style sheets, and so on, is listed there.

One immediate housekeeping task is to select any files or directories that will be needed on the server and use the Put button to transfer them there. They then show up in the left side of the Site window.

No doubt, you're impatient to make a page. Fine. To get started, follow these steps:

1. **In the Site window, choose File➪New File.**

    A phantom new file appears in the list on the right side of the Site window with a default file name and extension, and an active cursor.

2. **Name the file, not forgetting the extension appropriate to your chosen server technology (.html, .htm, .asp, .jsp, or .cfm).**

3. **Select the file and press Enter.**

    A document window opens representing this new page.

Chapter 1: Putting Together a Quick Web Page with UltraDev   29

4. **Enter a title for the page in the title box in the middle of the document toolbar (see Figure 1-19).**

    The *title* is quite different from the *filename,* which you assigned in Step 1. The title is visible in the title bar of a browser; the filename becomes the last part of the page's URL.

I often begin a site by making a whole set of pages, just doing filenames and titles. Watching your list of files grow in the Site window is an extremely rapid way of making yourself believe you've made lots of progress.

The example site of kids' artwork, KidPicassos, needs some peripheral pages but the general design is artwork and comments contributed by kids with whom you're acquainted. Maybe six pages per kid, six to ten kids. Each kid gets a simple "about me" page. Refer back to Figure 1-17 to see part of the site tree.

The document toolbar is your friend

Figure 1-19 should help you understand how to use the document toolbar.

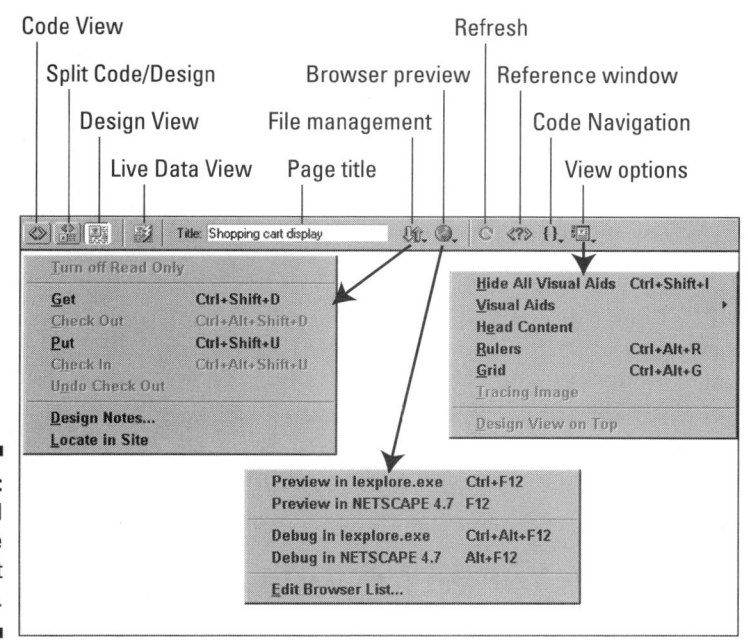

Figure 1-19: Exploded view of the document toolbar.

At the left end of the document toolbar is a sequence of four buttons allowing you to choose how to use your document window. From left to right, they are:

- **Code View:** Fills the document window with HTML/JavaScript source code.

  This is subtly different from opening the HTML Code inspector by clicking the Launcher. The Code inspector opens in a separate window, whereas Code View displays HTML and JavaScript in the document window itself.

- **Code and Design Views:** Splits the document window horizontally between Code (upper pane) and Design (lower pane).

- **Design View:** The normal view of your design-time page.

- **Live Data View (LDV):** A view in which sample data from a database is brought into the page. A new toolbar appears to control LDV characteristics. See Chapter 6 to find out what LDV is all about.

Other important features of the document toolbar are as follows:

- **The Title text box:** The box to the right of the LDV button in which you enter and edit the page title.

- **The File Management button:** Clicking this button drops down a useful list of functions. The one that you use all the time is *Put,* which transfers this page to the server.

- **The Preview/Debug in Browser button:** Enables you to edit your list of installed browsers and to open the current page in any browser, either in ordinary preview mode or in a special mode designed to allow easy debugging of client-side JavaScript. If you don't intend to write JavaScript functions, you won't need this mode.

- **The Refresh Design View button:** This button is only available while you're editing JavaScript functions in Code View.

- **The Reference button:** Opens the context-sensitive Reference window.

- **The Code Navigation button:** This button is only available while you're editing JavaScript functions in Code View. Clicking this button causes a pop-up menu to appear with a list of all your JavaScript functions so that you can select one and instantly locate it in the Code View.

- **The View Options button:** Deploys a drop-down menu of options concerned with visual aids.

Use layers for easy page design

A typical page in the example KidPicassos site has these elements:

- Site banner (.gif)
- Name of kid (headline text)

Chapter 1: Putting Together a Quick Web Page with UltraDev   31

- ✓ The artwork (.gif or .jpg)
- ✓ Kid comments (funky text)
- ✓ Navigation (text or .gifs)

All those elements can conveniently be placed on layers, so as to have absolute control over their placing on the page and to make it possible to overlap them. You don't have to use the same layout on every page — you can vary things according to the size of the art and the length of the kid name.

The two most important page elements that you need — layers and images — are UltraDev *objects,* available on the Common panel of the Objects palette.

So choose Window⇨Objects (or press Ctrl+F2) to open the Objects palette if it's not already open.

If the palette is open but not showing the Common panel, click in the Objects header and choose Common from the pop-up menu (see Figure 1-20).

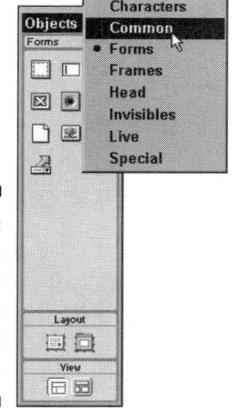

Figure 1-20: Selecting the Common panel of the Objects Palette.

The Objects palette is a floating palette with buttons representing 65 objects in 8 categories. Clicking the header area displays these six categories, and clicking one of the categories from the pop-up menu displays the panel relevant to that category. If you hover your mouse over any of the buttons on any subpalette, a ToolTip appears that tells you the purpose of the button. These objects can be placed in the current document but not all of them are visible on the page (the objects in the Head category, for instance, go directly into HTML source code).

To make a layer to hold a banner image, click the Layer button on the Common panel of the Objects palette; then move your cursor into the document window.

Part I: Basic UltraDev

The cursor has a special layer-drawing appearance. Use it to sweep out an area roughly where you want your banner to appear. It doesn't have to be exact. When you release the mouse button, the layer is set and (provided that you have preferences set to see invisible elements) a small icon called a *layer anchor* appears at top-left of the document window. This is to help you to select the layer later, when its edges may overlap with other layers.

TIP

If you want your layers to be placed accurately, turn on the pixel rulers by choosing View⇔Rulers⇔Show or using the View Options toolbar button. You can then keep track of the cursor's x, y coordinates.

To place an image on a layer, make sure a blinking cursor is in the top-left corner of the layer and follow these steps:

1. **In the Common Objects Palette, click the Image button to open the Select Image Source dialog box.**
2. **Browse the folders until you find the image that you want to place on your page and then double-click.**

   The image flows into the layer that you created for it (Figure 1-21 shows the banner art for my KidPicassos page). The image is permitted to go beyond the boundary of the layer, but if the layer is quite a bit larger than the image, it's worth shrinking it. Drift your mouse pointer to any edge of the layer until it changes to a "move" pointer. Click, and the layer acquires resizing handles. While the cursor has the "move" appearance it, you can use it to move the layer bodily around the page.

3. **Repeat Steps 1 and 2 to add any other artwork to the page.**

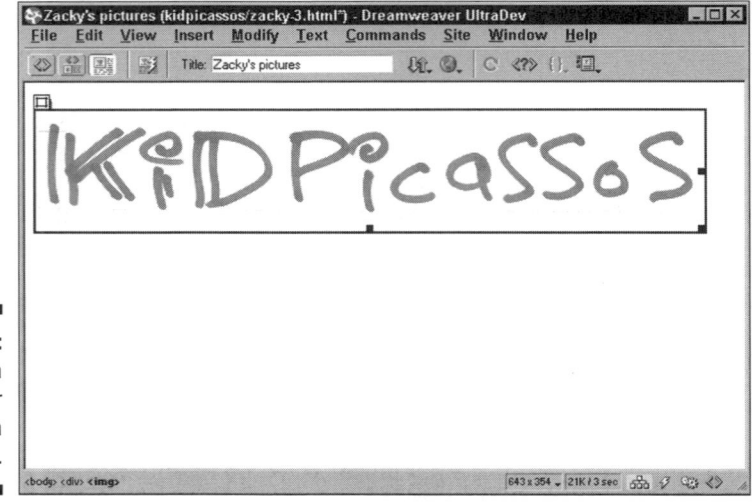

Figure 1-21: Flowing a banner image into a layer.

Use text formats for page impact

When you insert text into an UltraDev page, you can control the font family, weight, size, color, and alignment from the Property inspector.

The Property inspector is another floating palette that displays all the attributes of whatever layout element is currently selected. You can edit virtually all of the attributes — positioning, size, z-index, alignment, and so on — in the Property inspector. Drummies will recognize this as an Attributes Sheet in disguise.

Continue your page (KidPicassos in this example) as follows:

1. **In the Common Objects palette, click the Layer button and then click and drag a layer box in a suitable position for a headline.**

2. **If the Property inspector is not already open, open it with Window⇨ Properties.**

   Alternatively, you can press Control+F3.

3. **Use the text controllers in the Property inspector to choose a font, size, and color (or an HTML header format) and then type your text.**

   Figure 1-22 shows the selection of Comic Sans Bold, size 6, in a blue color #3333FF, centered. You can also see the headline "Zacky #3" in this font.

Figure 1-22: Using the Property inspector to define text style.

Part I: Basic UltraDev

Figure 1-23 shows my Zacky #3 page pretty much complete. Assuming you have all the art and text gathered together and ready to go, you can put together a Web page like this in about five minutes.

Chapter 2 presents some ideas for labor-saving ideas on your site.

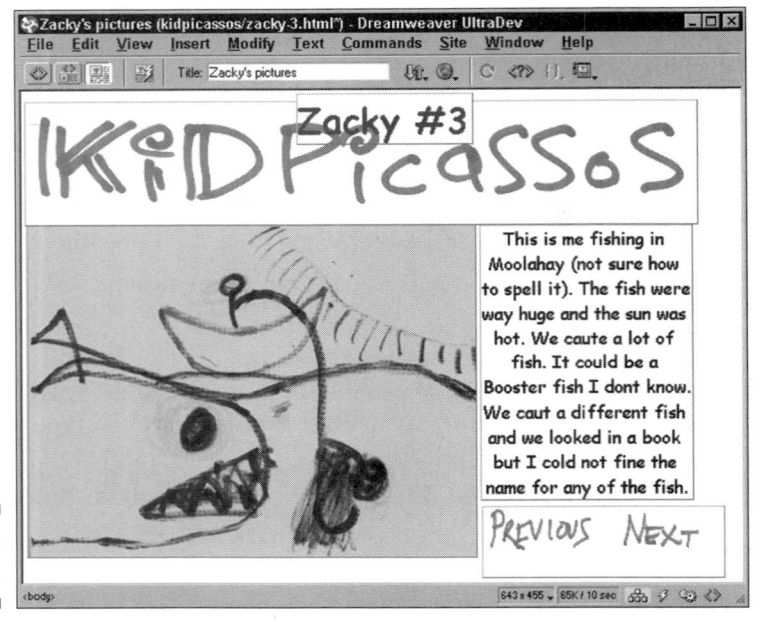

Figure 1-23:
All done.

Chapter 2

Romping in the Dreamweaver Playground

In This Chapter
▶ Templates
▶ Preferences
▶ Cascading Style Sheets

From Chapter 3 of this book to the end, I write mostly about what turned Dreamweaver into Dreamweaver UltraDev — data connections. But of course, Dreamweaver was already a highly successful and full-featured application for Windows and Macintosh before it was ever UltraDev'd. *Dreamweaver 3 For Dummies* by Janine Warner and Paul Vachier (published by IDG Books Worldwide, Inc.) fills 400 pages and specifically focuses on Dreamweaver features. You can think of that book as a companion volume — I don't have the space to compete even if I wanted to. But to bring Drummies and Newbies up to speed, this chapter is my personal take on what makes Dreamweaver cool.

I chose three features of Dreamweaver that I like a lot and that ought to be in any user's list of top ten great features: Templates, Customization, and Cascading Style Sheets (CSS). This chapter is just a goody-bag — reach in and grab what you think you need.

Working with Templates

In Chapter 1, I describe a mythical children's art gallery site called KidPicassos. A typical KidPicassos page consists of a banner, a kid's name, artwork, a comment, and some navigation elements. Even though the properties of the page may vary quite a bit — the pixel dimensions of the art, the length of the comment, and even the kid's name — a combination of layers and templates can be quite a labor-saver for a site like this in which the fundamental page design stays the same.

A *template* is a partial Web page, representing the elements that a series of pages have in common, plus at least one *editable region* that can accept unique content. You can create a new page in a series by using the template as a starting point and adding just the features that are unique to that page.

Dreamweaver templates and Drumbeat templates are two very different animals. Unlike Drumbeat, Dreamweaver doesn't let you nest templates or drag pages into and out of templates. The most important difference of all, however, is that in Dreamweaver templates, only certain regions of a template page are declared *editable*. Noneditable regions are *locked,* which means that they can hold only the template content.

Making a new template

UltraDev considers templates as site assets, along with images, colors, links, and various libraries of more exotic objects. Site assets are displayed in a multitab panel called the Assets panel.

I recommend keeping the Assets panel on your Launcher, for ease of deployment, although you can also open it by choosing Window⇨Assets or pressing F11. Add the Assets panel to the Launcher like this:

1. **Choose Edit⇨Preferences or press Ctrl+U.**

    The Preferences dialog box opens.

2. **In the Category panel on the left side of the dialog box, select Floating Palettes.**

3. **Click the plus (+) button beside the words Show in Launcher and choose Assets from the pop-up menu.**

4. **Close the Preferences dialog box.**

From now on, I assume that you have the Assets panel available on your Launcher.

To make a template, you have two choices. You can either add a new template to the Assets panel, or you can build a page and then save it as a template.

Adding a new template to the Assets panel

Here's how to add a new template to the Assets panel:

1. **Launch the Assets panel and click the Template icon in the left margin.**

2. **Click the New Template button in the lower-right margin.**

    A new untitled template appears in the template list, and a helpful message appears in the Templates preview window (see Figure 2-1).

Chapter 2: Romping in the Dreamweaver Playground 37

3. **Type a name for the new template.**

4. **Click the Edit Template button in the lower-right corner.**

   The template opens as a document window. Build your template and save it. By default, templates save to their own folder, one level below the main site document files.

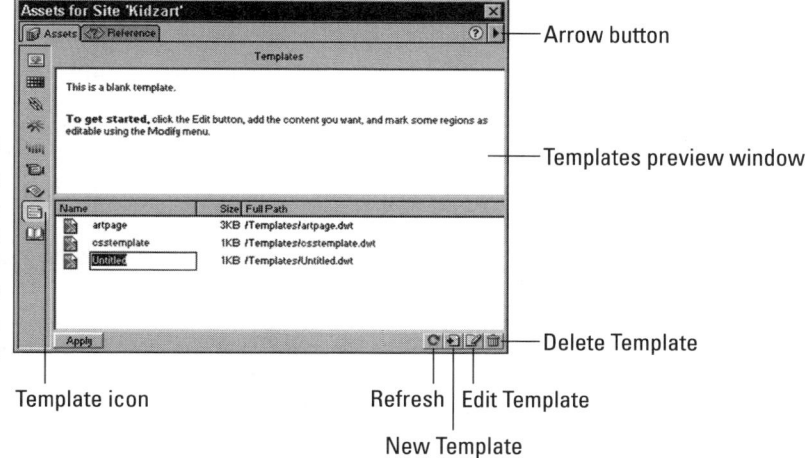

Figure 2-1: Creating a template in the UltraDev Assets panel.

Arrow button
Templates preview window
Delete Template
Template icon   Refresh | Edit Template
New Template

Notice the little arrow button in the top-right corner of the Assets panel? Clicking that button pops up a useful menu of things that you might want to do in managing your assets, including templates. The option Copy to Site allows you to transfer a template to any site that you've defined.

After you make a few templates, you may also notice that the Templates preview window shows whatever template is selected in the list under the Preview window. The window can look a bit silly in a small panel, but you can drag the edges and the horizontal divider of the panel around, making it much bigger and more useful as a preview if that's what you need.

Building a page and saving it as a template

Here's how to make a template from a page:

1. **Open a new page by choosing File➪New or by pressing Ctrl+N.**

   A fresh document window opens.

2. **Build whatever elements you want, using the full range of the UltraDev page composition aids.**

3. **When you finish, choose File⇨Save as Template.**

   The Save As Template dialog box opens. The box includes a drop-down list of all your defined UltraDev sites and a list of all your existing templates.

4. **Reset the Sites drop-down list, if necessary, and type a name for the template.**

5. **Create at least one editable region (see the next section).**

6. **Click Save.**

The page is now a template, with the DWT file extension, and behaves exactly the same as if it had been created as a template from scratch. Note that if you first save the page as a page and then save it as a template, both documents exist.

Declaring editable regions in templates

A template is meaningless unless it has at least one editable region — although it's possible to create a noneditable template (UltraDev grumbles but allows it). Typical containers for editable regions are layers and table cells, but even simple text paragraphs can be editable. To declare an editable region, place your cursor in the region, choose Modify⇨Templates⇨New Editable Region, and type a name for the region in the dialog box. You can also invoke the New Editable Region dialog box by pressing Ctrl+Alt+V.

Figure 2-2 shows a template I created for the KidPicassos site. It has these elements, including four editable regions:

- A layer containing the banner — not editable
- A layer overlapping the banner where the kid's name can be placed — an editable region called `kidname`
- A layer for the picture — a blank editable region called `kidart`
- A layer for the comment — a blank editable region called `kidcomment`
- A layer for navigation that includes two images — an editable region called `kidnav`

Modifying a template

You can modify a template at any time by launching the Assets panel and either double-clicking the template in the list or selecting it and clicking the Edit Template button.

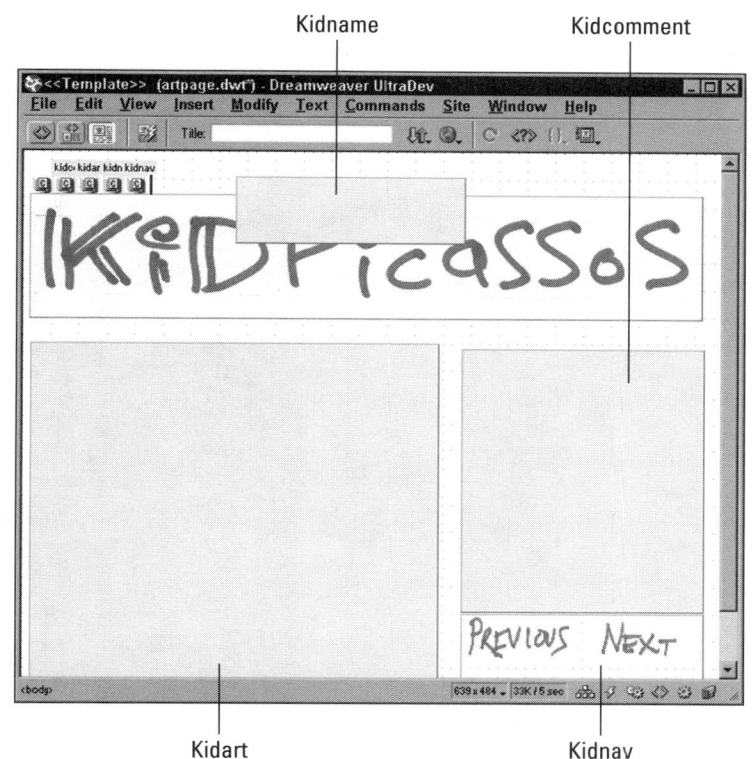

Chapter 2: Romping in the Dreamweaver Playground 39

Figure 2-2: A template with four editable regions. (Labels: Kidname, Kidcomment, Kidart, Kidnav)

Template files also appear in a special folder in the site window. As long as the Templates folder is expanded, you can double-click a template to reopen it for modification.

Figure 2-3 shows the menus associated with template options when you choose Modify⇨Templates. The artwork layer is selected in the document window and it's just about to be defined as an editable region.

TIP You can arrange for the font style in a layer to be preset in a template. Set up the font style and type a word in that style. Then use your Launcher to open the HTML Source window. Locate the word that you just typed and delete it carefully, making sure that the `<font>` and `</font>` tags don't get deleted.

If you make a change to a template that already has dependent pages, UltraDev is clever enough to know that those pages may need updating. An Update Template Files dialog box appears (see Figure 2-4) and gives you the option of bringing dependent pages into conformity or leaving them as they are.

Part I: Basic UltraDev

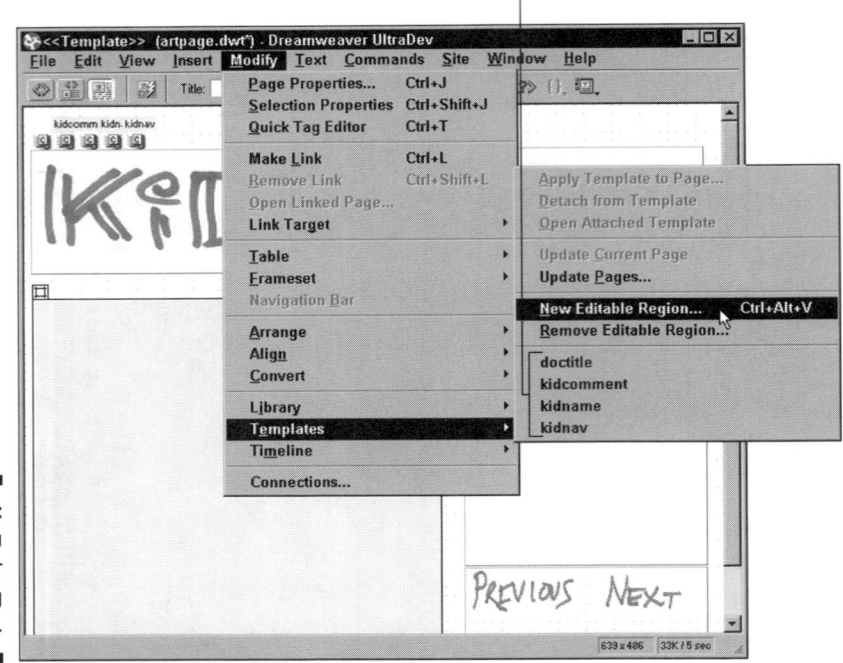

Figure 2-3: Menu options for managing templates.

Editable regions added so far

Figure 2-4: Updating pages already connected to a template.

Using a template

Using a template is extremely simple. Just choose File➪New From Template, select the appropriate template from the Select Template dialog box, and click the Select button. The new page opens in the document window with all the template elements already in place.

Note that anything on the template that's not designated as an editable region — like the banner in the KidPicassos example — is locked. You can neither change it nor delete it. You can work only within the editable regions. Figure 2-5 shows a comment being inserted (in a preset font) on the KidPicassos template. Note the template label in the top-right corner of the window and the labeled layers in the top-left corner.

Figure 2-5: Adding unique material to a template.

You're free to change the dimensions and positioning of layers in a template-derived page as long as the layers are defined as editable regions. That's what makes layers suitable for template work.

Adding content to a template

Template content is by no means restricted to layers. A simple block of text can be either editable or locked. An image can also be either editable or locked. Figure 2-6 shows a template created for a Macromedia tutorial by JUXT Interactive. It's a template for an e-zine page that includes both locked and editable regions. The page has been created entirely with a table.

Part I: Basic UltraDev

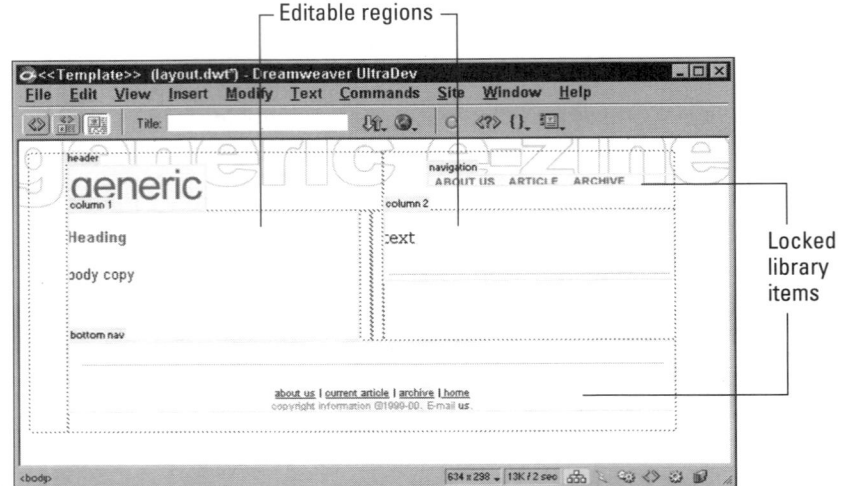

Figure 2-6: A generic e-zine template.

Figure 2-7 shows a page created from this elegant template.

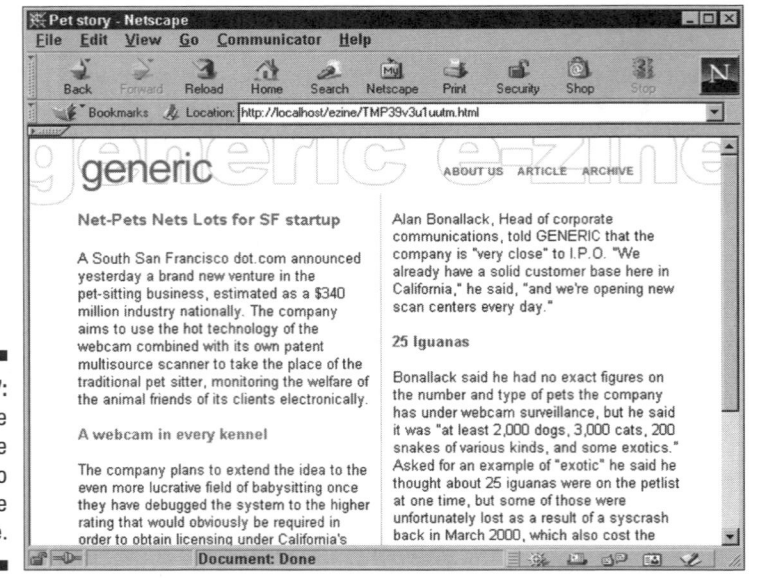

Figure 2-7: The e-zine template used to make a live page.

The generic e-zine fileset is on the CD that accompanies this book, in the folder `\Extensions\Templates\Ezine`. The CD also includes two other Macromedia tutorial sets: Club, which is a skeleton site for a music venue, and Design, an advertising art service. You find eight templates in all.

Building Your Own Sandcastles: Customizing UltraDev

You can customize UltraDev in many ways. Not only can you put together your UltraDev screen from over a dozen palettes and inspectors, but you can also place those elements the way you like, dock them together, expand and shrink them to suit your mood, or perform whatever intricate operation that you're attempting.

Besides that, customization options pop up in all sorts of places. The following sections highlight just a few UltraDev customization options.

Guidelines and dots

For precision in placing page layout elements, most modern Web-building applications offer an optional and editable guide pattern — typically a dot grid, ten pixels square. That means dots placed at the intersection of imaginary sets of horizontal and vertical lines ten pixels apart. UltraDev is no exception.

Choose View➪Grid➪Edit Grid to open up the Grid Settings dialog box shown in Figure 2-8. You can use this dialog box to customize guidelines or guidedots in the document window. You can also control the color, spacing, and rendering of the guides.

Figure 2-8:
Grid Settings dialog box.

Although "snapping to guides" may sound like the reaction of a party of weary mountaineers when told they have to climb another 1,000 feet before lunch, it's actually a highly useful aid for aligning movable objects, like layers. With snapping enabled, a layer can settle only when aligned with the guide grid. Drummies are familiar with this idea because Drumbeat has a ten-pixel dot grid by default.

You can toggle snapping on and off by choosing View➪Grid➪Snap To Grid.

You can toggle the whole grid on and off by choosing View⇨Grid⇨Show Grid. The Options menu that drops down from the far-right icon on the toolbar also offers on/off toggles for all visual aids including the guide grid.

Rulers

Choose View⇨Rulers⇨Show to add horizontal and vertical rulers to the document window. The submenu you see by choosing View⇨Rulers offers options for having the rulers marked in pixels, inches, or centimeters, and for resetting the zero points to the current position of the top-left corner of the window.

The Options menu that drops down from the far-right icon on the toolbar also offers an on/off toggle for either the rulers or all visual aids.

Preferences

Choose Edit⇨Preferences to browse the 16-category Preferences dialog box. The preferences for some categories, such as CSS Styles, and Code Rewriting, are pretty obscure. Others are really worth taking a look at. By playing with the options in the Fonts and Highlighting categories (see Figure 2-9), for example, you can make a significant difference in your UltraDev work environment.

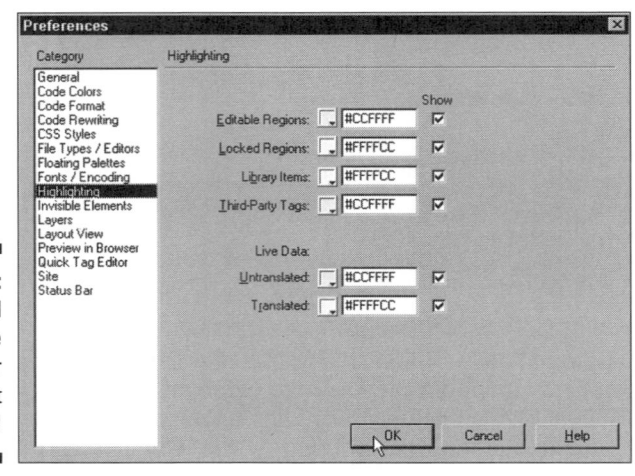

Figure 2-9: Look at all those options for highlight colors!

Some preferences that you may think are of no interest have hidden gems. Buried in the Site dialog box, for example, is a Save Files Before Putting check box. I like that one because when I'm developing a complex page that needs to be interpreted by a Web server, I constantly need to save the page, open the site window, click the Put button to transfer it to the server, and then

Chapter 2: Romping in the Dreamweaver Playground

press F12 to view my page in the default browser. With Save Files Before Putting checked, my pages are automatically saved as part of the Put operation. Saves wear on the *S* of my keyboard.

Extending UltraDev

Dreamweaver extensions and UltraDev server behavior extensions offer even more radical customization options. Turn to Chapter 9 to find out more about how to customize these extensions and how to transform your Objects palette.

Icing on the Cake: Defining Styles with CSS

Back in the bad old days of HTML 1, there was no such thing as typographical style. You chose between whatever the browser offered (hands up, who remembers Mosaic) as its interpretation of the <H1>, <H2>, <H3>, <H4>, and <P> tags. Third generation browsers eventually began accepting tags such as <FONT FACE="Helvetica" COLOR="#ff0000"> — what a new dawn that was. Then along came Cascading Style Sheets (CSS), and the Web went for style in a big way.

Cascading Style Sheets were developed and vigorously promoted by the World Wide Web Consortium (W3C) — an international body that attempts to mediate in the browser wars and impose some accepted standards on the HTML community. The CSS standard is one of their success stories.

Style sheets allow you, as the site author, to define an unlimited number of typographical styles by controlling these properties, among others:

- Font family (Times Roman, Helvetica, and so on)
- Font size in points, pixels, or other units
- Font weight (boldness)
- Font style (normal or italic)
- Font variant (normal or smallcaps)
- Color
- Font decoration (underline, blink, and so on)
- Background color, image, repeat
- Horizontal and vertical alignment
- Box properties, including border style and color, background color, padding, and margin

Part I: Basic UltraDev

You give each style a name, which can then be attached to any piece of text on a page. Better still, you can define CSS styles in a completely separate document that can then be attached to any or all of the pages on your site. If you later make a change to an external style sheet — as a result of corporate or artistic rethinking, perhaps — the change ripples through your site like quicksilver. Amazing.

Page-by-page CSS

For creating a new style, UltraDev leads you through an eight-category Style Definition dialog box. This dialog box includes more options than you would ever need to specify about a style — more than UltraDev is even capable of displaying.

Here's how you create a style:

1. **Open the page that you want to create a style for and choose Window⇨CSS Styles (or press Shift+F11).**

   The CSS Styles palette opens (see Figure 2-10).

Figure 2-10: CSS Styles palette.

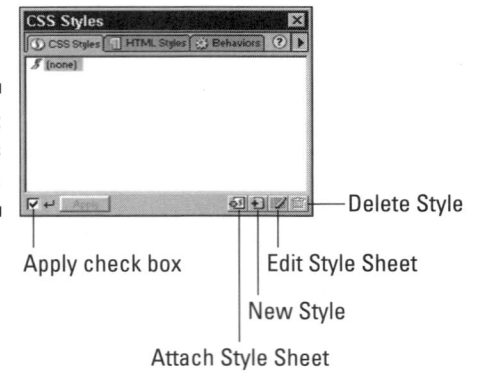

- Delete Style
- Edit Style Sheet
- New Style
- Attach Style Sheet
- Apply check box

2. **Click the New Style button (the one that resembles a plus sign in the lower-right corner of the dialog box).**

   The New Style dialog box opens. Leave the Type radio button set to the default, Make Custom Style (class).

3. **In the Define In section of the dialog box, click the radio button for This Document Only.**

4. **Type a name for the style in the Name text box.**

   Style names begin with a period, but UltraDev sticks one on for you if you forget.

Chapter 2: Romping in the Dreamweaver Playground

5. **Click OK.**

    The eight-category Style Definition dialog box opens, set for the first category (see Figure 2-11). The Type category lets you determine font family, style, weight, size, and so on.

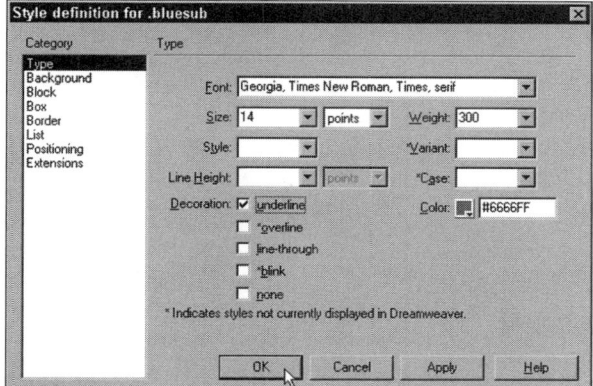

Figure 2-11: A comprehensive Style Definition dialog box.

6. **Create whatever font style that you want by using the drop-down lists, check boxes, and color picker.**
7. **Choose any other category from the Categories list and continue to choose options until you've created a complete style.**

    Note that options marked with an asterisk (*) don't display in UltraDev, but they do generally appear in up-to-date browsers.

8. **Click OK.**

    The new style that you created appears in the CSS Styles palette, but it's available for the current page only. The new style isn't available on other pages in your site or in other sites. The upcoming "Creating an external style sheet" section tells you how to create styles that are available throughout your site.

Applying a CSS style

You can apply a CSS style to text in two ways:

- Outline the text words you wish to impose the style on and select the style name in the CSS Styles palette.
- Place your cursor anywhere within a paragraph and select the style name in the CSS Styles palette. The style is imposed on the whole paragraph.

Figure 2-12 shows a subhead style being imposed effortlessly on an e-zine article by using the first method.

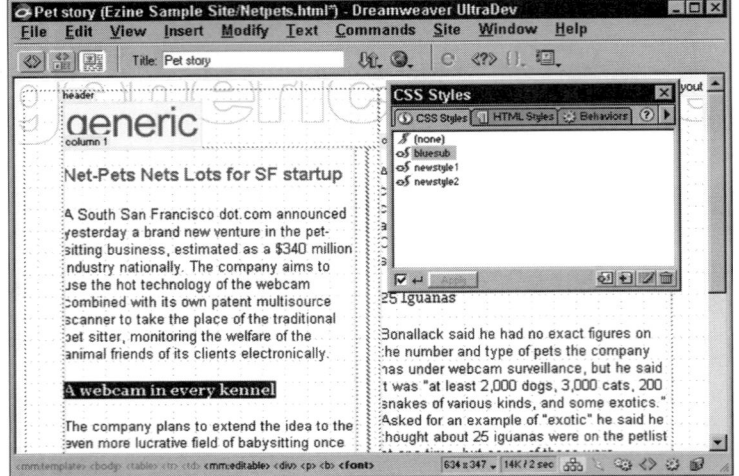

Figure 2-12: Imposing the .bluesub style on an e-zine subhead.

If you uncheck the Apply check box in the lower-left corner of the CSS Styles palette, style imposition is inhibited by either of the methods described earlier. To remove all styles, choose (none) at the top of the CSS Styles palette.

Drummies are sure to lament the fact that, unlike Drumbeat's somewhat similar style creation dialog boxes, no style preview pane is present in the UltraDev version. This feature has been requested for a future release. Drummies may also get a slight shock when they realize that styles are not automatically available site-wide — for more on that, see the next two sections.

Creating an external style sheet

Page-by-page CSS styles are strictly associated with the page on which you create them and aren't available to any other page (unless you use the fairly distasteful process of copying and pasting from the HTML Source of the page in which they are defined).

It's much more in the spirit of CSS to create styles in an external file so that the styles are then accessible to any page that you create.

To create an external CSS style sheet, follow these steps:

1. **With any page open, choose Window⇨CSS Styles (or press Shift+F11).**

    The CSS Styles palette opens.

2. **Click the New Style button.**

    The New Style dialog box opens. Leave the Type radio button set to the default, Make Custom Style (class).

 3. **In the Define In section of the dialog box, the drop-down list defaults to New Style Sheet File unless any CSS style sheets are already attached to this page.**

 4. **Type a name for the style in the Name field.**

    Style names begin with a period, but UltraDev sticks one on for you if you forget.

 5. **Click OK.**

    The File Saver dialog box opens. Inspect the path to make sure that the file will be saved in the folder that you expect.

 6. **Type a name for your new style sheet, using the file extension .css, and click the Save button.**

    The Style Definition dialog box opens.

 7. **Create whatever font style you want by using the drop-down lists, check boxes, and color picker.**

 8. **Choose any other category from the Categories list and continue to choose options until you've created a complete style.**

    Note that options marked with an asterisk (*) don't display in UltraDev, but they do generally appear in up-to-date browsers.

 9. **Click OK.**

    The new style that you created appears in the CSS Styles palette.

Now when you save your style definition, it saves to the external style sheet that you named in Step 6. You can add more styles to that style sheet, attach it to other pages in the site, or edit it.

Editing an external style sheet

One of the great virtues of CSS is that style changes need to be made only once to apply to an entire site. A CSS style sheet must be easily editable in order to be useful. You have two choices when editing an external style sheet:

- In the CSS Styles palette, click the Edit Style Sheet button, select the style sheet in the Edit Style Sheet dialog box, and then click the Edit button.
- In the Site window, double-click the CSS style sheet filename.

In either case, the style sheet's edit window opens (see Figure 2-13).

Figure 2-13: Edit window of a CSS style sheet.

In the style sheet's edit window, you can use the New, Edit, Duplicate, and Remove buttons to create and edit as many styles as you want, following the same steps provided earlier for creating a single-page style or for creating an external style sheet.

When you have made all the necessary changes to the style sheet, click the Save button.

If any page in a site references an external CSS style sheet, the CSS file must be transferred to the server. In the Site window, select the CSS file and click the Put button to send it to the server.

Linking an external style sheet to another page

Even though a CSS file may reside in your local site root folder, it still isn't automatically attached to every page that you create. Here's how to link an external style sheet to a new page:

1. **In the CSS Styles palette, click the Attach Style Sheet button.**
2. **Browse to select the CSS file that you want to attach to the page.**
3. **Click OK and then click Done.**

    The styles in the linked style sheet become available in the palette.

If you know that you're going to need to link a CSS style sheet to many pages in a site, it's worth creating a template whose entire document area is an editable region (see the "Working with Templates" section earlier in this chapter). After creating such a template, link the CSS style sheet to the template and give the template a name that you'll remember. Then every time you need a fresh page, create it by choosing File➪New From Template, instead of just File➪New.

Chapter 13 covers another, more radical, suggestion for attaching a CSS style sheet to every page that you create. Drummies may love this one!

Editing a style

You can return to the Style Definition dialog box of an existing style at any time to modify it. If the style is defined in an external style sheet, you can open the style sheet to which the style belongs and edit as described in the section, "Editing an external style sheet," in this chapter.

If the style is a *local* style defined only for the current page, it appears in the Edit Style Sheet dialog box for that page.

Much quicker, however, is to open the CSS Styles palette (press Shift+F11) and double-click the style name.

You can invoke a pop-up menu offering most of the CSS style sheet functions by right-clicking in the CSS Styles palette or by using the arrow button in the top-right corner.

TIP

If a page has both local styles and external style sheet styles available, you can tell which are local and which are external by the different margin icons in the CSS Styles palette (see Figure 2-14).

Figure 2-14: CSS Styles palette containing local and external styles.

TIP

A CSS reference is built in to UltraDev. Click the reference icon (<?>) on the UltraDev toolbar and select O'REILLY CSS Reference. By default, the reference is in the same palette as the Assets panel.

Part II
Bringing Data to Your Pages

The 5th Wave   By Rich Tennant

"What I'm looking for are dynamic Web applications and content, not Web innuendoes and intent."

In this part . . .

Part II strongly focuses on what makes UltraDev different from Dreamweaver. The difference can be highlighted with just one word — data.

In growing Dreamweaver into UltraDev (and borrowing from Drumbeat along the way), Macromedia wisely recognized a fact of life on the Web of the 21st century — pretty much everybody has some data to present. Once you have more than a small amount of data in the back end of your Web site, HTML loses interest and even client-side JavaScript fails you. You have no alternative but to come to grips with a server technology of one kind or another. UltraDev is the response to a clear need for an interface that makes the complexities of active server pages accessible, understandable, and even convenient.

Through Chapters 3, 4, and 5, I follow a perfectly logical flow as a database is made available first to your system as a whole, then to UltraDev, and, finally, to a specific site and a specific page. In Chapter 5, you also find out what part the database plays in the server behaviors that make your pages respond dynamically to the underlying data. If you're new to all this, you may find it hard to believe, but if you read this part, you'll soon be prattling on about SQL, ODBC, ASP, recordset filtering, and data binding just like a real geek. Have fun with it.

Chapter 3
Connecting to Your Data

In This Chapter
- Exploring database basics
- Making a data connection for an ASP server
- Getting connected with ColdFusion
- Connecting to your data using JSP
- Preparing to set up your Mac

*P*art I of this book is not really about UltraDev — it's more of an exercise in making sure that you're familiar with the Dreamweaver way of working. The very essence of UltraDev is that it makes it easy for you to connect your Web site to a database and have the pages respond to the information flow just as it comes — making your Web site a user-friendly extension of the database. That's the extra functionality that turns Dreamweaver into UltraDev.

UltraDev makes it easy, yes, but there's still some essential setup required. This chapter takes you through the process of making a database available as you design pages and as your users interact with them.

Database Basics

The first step in bringing data to your pages is to get some data. Duh! Well, it's true — there's no point in setting out to make a data-driven Web site unless you have data worth looking at.

The word *data* covers a multitude of sins and graces. It could mean anything from a list of your 18 music CDs to a 20-gigabyte relational database of every part required to make every automobile General Motors has manufactured since 1960.

It's a fairly safe bet that you wouldn't be reading this book if you weren't interested in connecting a database to a Web site. Perhaps you already have a database that you need to plug in to the Web; perhaps you are merely wondering what advantages it might have for you. What's certain is that in deciding to drive your Web site with a data engine, you're right with the trend. These days, databases are everywhere on the Web. Virtually every e-commerce site, absolutely every auction site, most pen pal and key-pal sites and city guides, and all the most interesting science sites — all are examples of data-driven sites. To pull off this trick, you don't need to be a database guru. You just need to be familiar with some of the fundamental concepts — UltraDev does the rest.

Rows and columns, records and fields

The bottom-line minimum requirement for a database is that the data must be organized in rows and columns. Each *row* describes one item in the database; each *column* describes one component of that description. In database terminology, each row is a *record,* and each column is a *field.*

The classic example of a simple database is a listing of your business or personal contacts. As you transfer your Rolodex into the computer, each Rolodex card becomes a data record, and each component — such as name, city, state, phone, and fax — becomes a field.

A database almost invariably ends up as a file somewhere in your computer system. As to the format of the file, that depends on how you choose to manage your database. It's actually quite possible for a database file to be perfectly readable text. But that type of database is suitable only for a fairly simple list, such as one containing your 18 music CDs. Anything more complex would be extremely irksome to maintain and edit as a text file.

Much more likely, you're going to choose a software application designed for data manipulation. Database management software offers very significant services, such as automatic generation of sequential ID numbers, sorting the data in various ways, and controlling the type of data (text, numeric, date/time, and binary are examples of data types).

Microsoft Access is the most widely used database application at present, and it offers all the features just mentioned. More powerful applications, such as Oracle and Paradox, are also very common in the business world. But the point to bear in mind is that once you decide on a database application, you're kind of committed. A database created in Paradox can't be edited in Oracle, and vice versa. Open an Access file in an ordinary text editor, and you see something like Figure 3-1 in which only a couple of words are recognizable. The rest of the file is binary gibberish, and what it all actually means is kind of a trade secret. Fortunately, you don't need to have the slightest curiosity about this file, thanks to a standard known as *Open Database Connectivity* (ODBC).

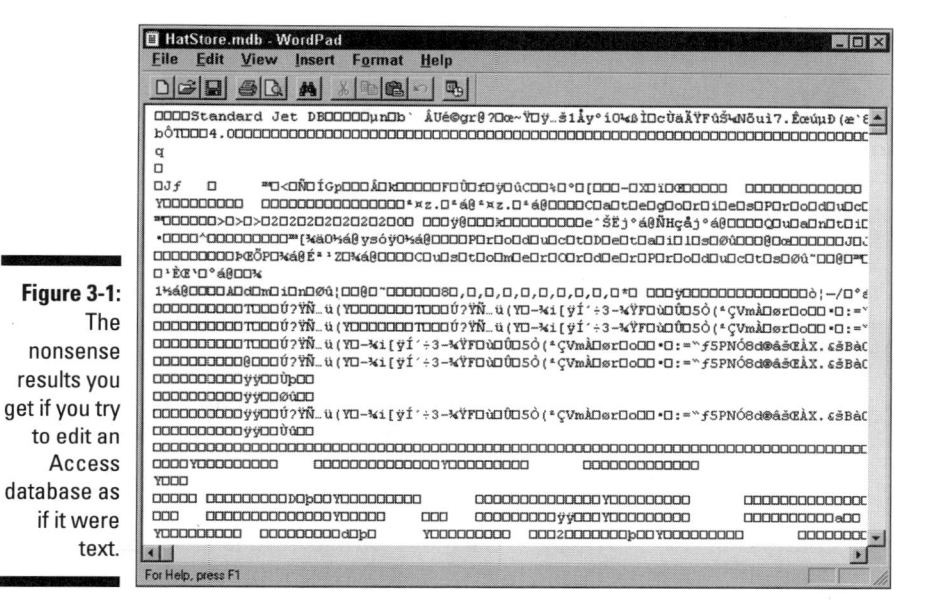

Figure 3-1: The nonsense results you get if you try to edit an Access database as if it were text.

ODBC: A common language

The ODBC standard permits other applications to read data formatted in proprietary ways via an intermediary called a *driver*. Access, Oracle, Paradox, FoxPro, and the rest of the database applications all have fancy ways of storing your data. But after the data passes through an ODBC driver, it all comes out looking the same — kind of like a sausage machine. Generally, a driver is included when you buy a database application, but many database drivers are also downloadable from the Internet at no cost.

ODBC and similar standards make it possible for a user of your data-enabled Web site to read formatted data without having any rights whatsoever to the application that created the database in the first place. As you discover in the following sections, ODBC plays a crucial role in bringing data to your UltraDev Web site.

A server of your own

In creating static Web sites — and I expect you're pretty good at that — you're used to the idea of just making up a page, checking it in your local browser (*several* local browsers, if you're fastidious) and leaving the question of posting it to a Web server for some other time.

When you move into the world of dynamic pages, however, you absolutely *must* have a local Web server to test your pages on — even if that's not where your pages will finally be published. UltraDev embeds special source code in your pages in order to manage the data flow. This special code is *not* HTML, so your browser can't interpret it. Consequently, this source code must first pass through a server for processing. The server consults the database and, in a process called server *parsing,* replaces the embedded code with appropriate HTML before presenting the page to a browser.

UltraDev supports three different server technologies that serve those so-called *active pages* — meaning that they are designed to work with dynamic content — in their own ways:

- **Active Server Pages (ASP):** A Microsoft technology supported by the Personal Web Server (PWS) and the Internet Information Server (IIS).
- **Java Server Pages (JSP):** A Sun Microsystems technology supported by the IBM WebSphere and Allaire JRun servers.
- **ColdFusion (CF):** An Allaire technology with its own language and server.

If your server uses ASP, the following section provides the steps for connecting to your data. If your server uses ColdFusion or Java Server Pages (JSP), it's not quite so simple. ColdFusion uses ODBC in its own way, and JSP has its own standard called JDBC. (See "Creating a Data Source Name for a ColdFusion Server" or "Creating a Data Hookup with JSP — Not for Amateurs" a little later in this chapter if you're working with either one of those server technologies.) And Mac users, sorry to have to break this to you, but you're in for a fairly complex one-time setup (described in Appendix B).

If you need to know more about database management, IDG Books offers a number of books that can help you. *Database Development For Dummies* covers general database management. Specific database applications are covered in books such as *Access 97 For Windows For Dummies, Access 2000 For Windows For Dummies,* and *Oracle8 For Dummies.* Books in the *For Dummies* series also deal with server technologies such as ASP and ColdFusion in far more detail than this book can find room for.

Creating a Data Connection for an ASP Server

If you're a Windows user, setting up a data connection with Active Server Pages (ASP) is easier than with the other server technologies, simply because all the bits and pieces are native to your operating system. You can easily obtain the servers that support ASP — the Internet Information Server (IIS) and the

Personal Web Server (PWS). IIS comes as part of NT Server and Windows 2000 Server; PWS is on the Windows 98 CD, or you download it for free from a Microsoft Web site.

After you've installed either IIS or PWS, you can do the UltraDev data hookup in the time it takes you to drink a cup of hot coffee. Basically, it's a straight-through connection to whatever flavor of ODBC driver you have. There's only one little problem, and it arises from a fact of life for a Web designer (that's you): the machine that you work on every day to create your stunning Web page designs probably isn't the same machine that your pages are displayed on when it's time to throw them open to the public.

You're quite used to the idea that dependent files, such as images and style sheets, must have the same relationship to the HTML files on the server as they had on the design machine. Well, that same principle applies to the database that runs a data-driven Web site. The problem is that you may not be in control of the path to the data. Your ISP may decide next Tuesday to put the actual database on a completely different machine or change its location on the Web server.

The Microsoft solution to elusive data is something called a *Data Source Name* (DSN). A DSN is really nothing more than a fancy nickname for the path to the database. Connecting to your data via a DSN allows the actual path to change in any unpredictable and bizarre way as long as the DSN knows about it. You have to create a DSN before you can actually connect to your data, and the following section tells you how to do this.

Making a DSN

Creating a DSN has a lot to do with Microsoft but nothing to do with UltraDev. The process is entirely external to UltraDev, but UltraDev won't connect to your data until the DSN is in place. In the following steps, I show you how to set up a DSN. It works the same for any ODBC-compatible database, but the actual example I use references an Access 2000 database that I have stored on my hard drive at `C:\databases\newhatstore.mdb`:

1. **Click the Start button and choose Settings⇨Control Panel.**

    The Control Panel appears.

2. **In the Control Panel, double-click ODBC Data Sources (it may also say 32bit).**

    The ODBC Data Source Administrator appears.

Part II: Bringing Data to Your Pages

3. **Click the System DSN tab (make sure that you click *System* DSN and not *User* DSN) and then click the Add button.**

   Be particularly careful in choosing the correct tab here. Choosing the User DSN tab at this point will drive you crazy later because UltraDev won't find it.

   The Create New Data Source panel opens, as shown in Figure 3-2. This figure shows this panel on my Windows 95 machine, and you can see that I have quite a selection of database drivers available. Hmmm, don't remember buying that Paradox driver — or ever using it, come to think of it.

   Figure 3-2:
   The Create New Data Source panel is one stage in creating a DSN.

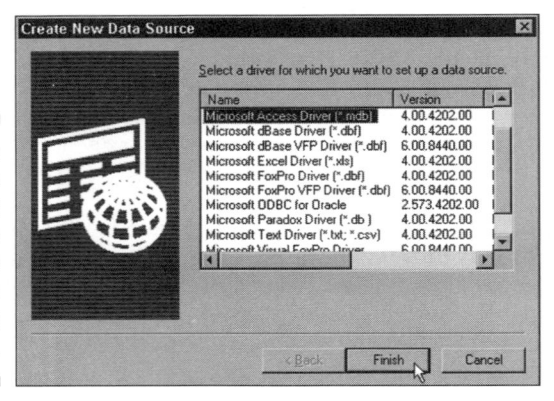

4. **Click Microsoft Access Driver (*.mdb) and then click the Finish button.**

   The ODBC Microsoft Access Setup dialog box opens.

5. **In the Data Source Name text box, type a name for the data source.**

   For this example, I used **hatstore** for the data source name.

6. **Click the Select button.**

   The Select Database dialog box opens.

7. **Navigate to the directory in which your database is stored and click OK.**

   For this example, I went to `C:\databases\newhatstore.mdb`. The path appears in the Database section of the ODBC Microsoft Access Setup dialog box (see Figure 3-3). If you don't see the correct path here, you need to click the Select button and again navigate to your database. Make sure that the filename is actually selected in the file-finder.

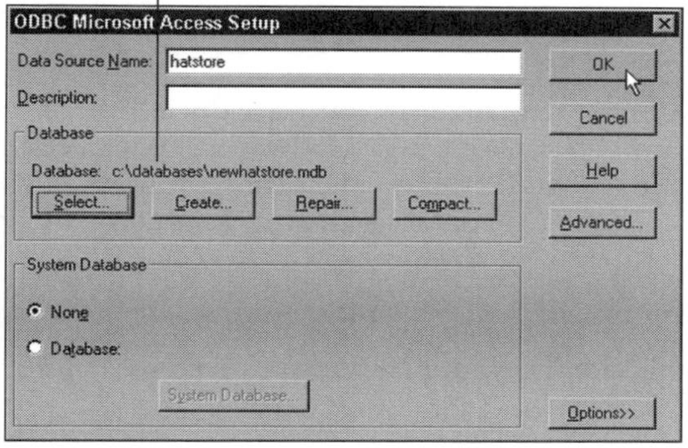

Figure 3-3: DSN setup finished, except for clicking a few OKs.

8. **(Optional) You can type something in the Description text box if you like, but UltraDev never reads your golden words (and no literary prizes are given for database descriptions in this cruel world).**

9. **If your database requires a login name and password, click the Advanced button and fill out the authorization panel.**

10. **Click OK three times to close the ODBC Microsoft Access Setup dialog box, the ODBC Data Source Administrator, and the Control Panel.**

    Is that cup of coffee cold yet?

The final step (Step 10A?) is to send e-mail to whomever runs your server informing them of what DSN you've chosen and earnestly entreating them to set up the same DSN on the server. If the person who runs the server is you, send an e-mail to yourself so that you have a paper trail in case one of you screws up.

Getting connected the easy way

Okay, now you can fire up UltraDev and take the next step, which is to create a data connection:

1. **Open any UltraDev page and choose Modify⇨Connections.**

    The Connections list opens. It contains a list of data connections that already exist (if any), and you're given the option of editing, duplicating, or removing them.

Part II: Bringing Data to Your Pages

2. **Click the New button.**

   A pop-up menu appears offering the choice of a connection via Custom Connection String, Custom Connection String with Server.MapPath( ), or DSN.

   Note: Certain database management software doesn't subscribe to the ODBC/DSN club and can only be accessed with a special *connection string*, so that's the reason UltraDev offers those choices. If you happen to be using one of those rare databases, only your software documentation can initiate you into the mysteries of data connection strings.

3. **I assume that you're using a DSN connection, so click that option.**

   The Data Source Name (DSN) dialog box appears (see Figure 3-4).

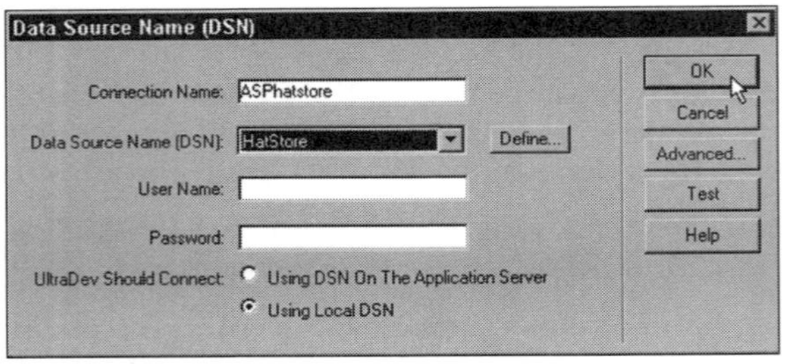

Figure 3-4:
The DSN dialog box.

4. **Type a name for your data connection in the Name text box.**

   Spaces are not allowed in data connection names, and you cannot edit them later.

5. **Select a DSN from the DSN drop-down list, which contains all System DSNs that you have defined.**

   If you suddenly realize that you forgot to create a System DSN, the ODBC button in this dialog box is a shortcut back to the Data Source Administrator.

6. **Type a username and password if your database requires them.**

7. **Choose whether you want to connect to a Local DSN (on the design machine) or the DSN on the Application server, and click the appropriate radio button to register your choice.**

   Here's the deal on this choice: In many cases you're working with only one DSN on only one machine; in that case pick Local. If you're networked, and the DSN is only on the server, make the other choice.

Chapter 3: Connecting to Your Data 63

Sometimes a DSN can be defined on both the local machine and also on the server — if, for example, the server-side database is really gigantic and you like to work with a small-scale version during design. In that case it's perfectly possible to choose Local DSN for design and then return to this dialog box and change it when the site's finalized.

If you transfer the finished site to an ISP, the choice may also need to be revised. It entirely depends on how you define your site (see Chapter 1).

8. **Click the Test button.**

   You should see the message `Connection was made successfully`.

9. **Click OK to close the DSN dialog box and then click Done to close the Connections list.**

If ASP is your game, you're all done. You can skip to Chapter 4 and start making recordsets.

Creating a Data Source Name for a ColdFusion Server

ColdFusion (CF) is the technology from Allaire Corporation for serving active pages. Whereas ASP uses for its logic the pre-existing languages JavaScript and VBScript, enclosed in the ASP wrappers `<% ... %>`, ColdFusion is a "language" all its own, enclosed in meta-tags such as `<CFOUTPUT> ... </CFOUTPUT>`. The end result is the same. Your Web site users would have to examine the file extensions to even be aware of what server technology you are using.

The server for ColdFusion is not a standalone application. It must be loaded into a machine that already has a Web server such as PWS or IIS installed. A ColdFusion server is included on the UltraDev CD and also on the CD that accompanies this book.

If ColdFusion is your choice, you can be nearly as lah-di-dah about data connections as ASP devotees because the idea of a DSN applies to ColdFusion just as it does to ASP. The data source that you create for CF ends up in the Data Source Administrator of your Windows machine looking no different than if you had created it with Windows' own Data Source Administrator. The trick, however, is that you need to create the data source within the *CF Administrator* (see Figure 3-5) — or at least register the DSN in the Administrator.

Part II: Bringing Data to Your Pages

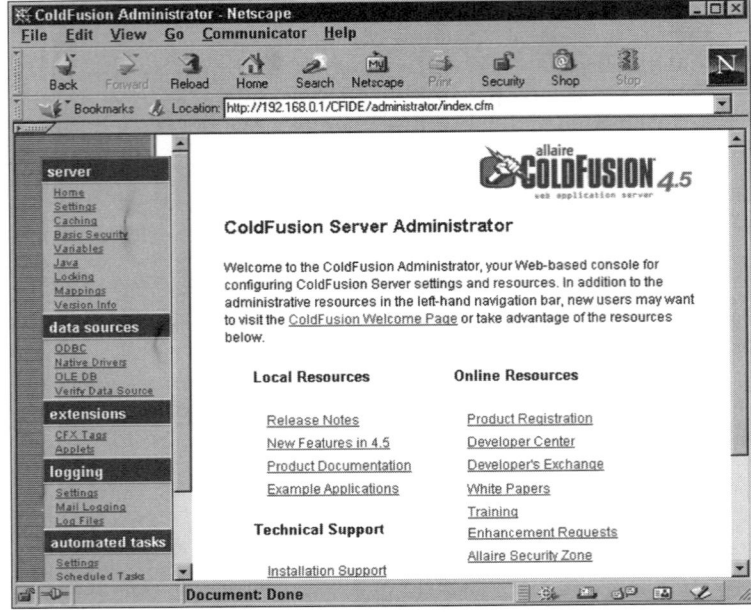

Figure 3-5:
The ColdFusion Server Administrator.

To make a DSN that is acceptable to ColdFusion, follow these steps:

1. **Open your ColdFusion Server Administrator (the local address is probably something similar to the one shown in Figure 3-5).**
2. **Click the ODBC link under Data Sources in the left pane.**

    The list of your available ODBC data sources appears in the right pane.

3. **Select the correct driver from the ODBC Driver drop-down list and click the Add button.**

    The Create ODBC Data Source page opens.

4. **In the Data Source Name box, type a name for the DSN.**

    Optionally (and uselessly), you can also add a description.

5. **Type the path to the database file in the Database File text box or click the Browse Server button to navigate to the file.**
6. **Type any needed username and password information and click the Create button.**

    You're returned to the list of data sources with the new data source now added (see Figure 3-6).

7. **Click the Verify link next to the data source for which you want to confirm a connection.**

    With any luck, you see the screen shown in Figure 3-7.

Chapter 3: Connecting to Your Data

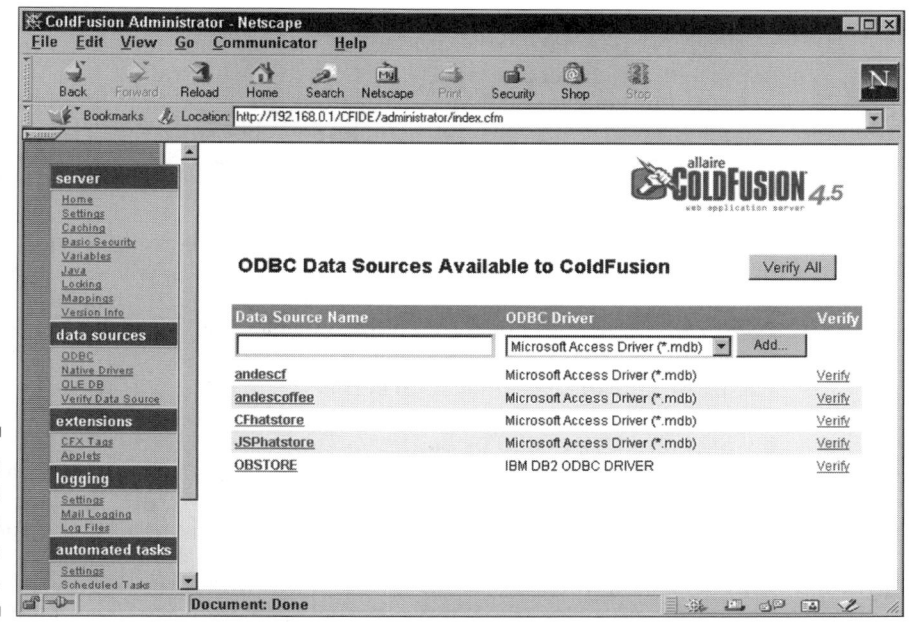

Figure 3-6: The updated ColdFusion data source list.

Figure 3-7: ColdFusion data source success.

WARNING! One reason that the data source verification may fail is that you don't have a sufficiently up-to-date driver. MDAC (Microsoft Data Access Components) version 2.1 or higher is required for both CF and UltraDev. If you can't remember whether you installed MDAC 2.1, open the ODBC Data Sources Administrator from your Control Panel and click the Drivers tab. If the version number of your Microsoft Access driver begins with *3,* you need the upgrade. See Appendix A for details.

After you've successfully made a DSN that ColdFusion can recognize, you can make the UltraDev data connection almost exactly as you would for an ASP server. See "Getting connected the easy way" earlier in this chapter. Choose DSN from the pop-up menu that appears when you click New in the Connections list. Be ready to answer the question whether the DSN is on the Local machine or the Application server.

If you connect to a ColdFusion Data Source on a machine other than the one running UltraDev, you'll be asked to log on with a username and password for the ColdFusion Remote Development Services (RDS). RDS is simply a method of making a data connection, and if you have not configured any special security from the data source you're connecting to, the administrator password will do for both the RDS username and password. After you register the RDS username and password, UltraDev should remember them and not bother you for them again.

TIP You can read much more about RDS and data security in Chapter 9 of the ColdFusion server documentation. The relative path is `/cfdocs/Administering_ColdFusion_Server/09_Configuring_Basic_Security/admin094.htm`.

Creating a Data Hookup with JSP — Not for Amateurs

Java Server Pages (JSP) is a rival to ASP, developed by Sun Microsystems and supported by IBM's WebSphere server and Allaire's JRun.

If you choose JSP as your server technology, you're in for a whole different ballgame. JSP has its own convention for reading proprietary databases, called JDBC (Java Database Connectivity), and hooking up to your data when your server uses JSP is not quite as simple as connecting with ASP or ColdFusion. But if you use JSP, that's the game you need to learn to play if you don't play it already. Read on for more information.

Bridge to ODBC

Sun Microsystems and its development partners, Javasoft and Intersolv, offer a JDBC-ODBC translator known as a *bridge,* which enables you to access an ODBC data source using JSP. As I write this, however, the bridge is officially considered only a transitional solution. In my experience, the bridge isn't well supported and doesn't function very reliably.

In principle, though, the bridge is a good and simple idea. It allows you to access the database via a DSN, even though you are using a theoretically incompatible convention — JDBC. There are many possible configurations for working with JDBC, but a typical situation is that you design on your own Windows machine (the "design machine") that is networked to a server running WebSphere or JRun. The server almost certainly has the JDBC-ODBC bridge already available, defined as a driver in the class `sun.jdbc.odbc.JdbcOdbcDriver`. In the unlikely event that the server doesn't have any version of the Java Development Kit (JDK) installed, you can download it from `http://java.sun.com/products/jdk/1.1/download-jdk-windows.html`.

You may think of a *class* as something that you take to gain academic credits — or if you're British you think of it as a quality *other* people have — but in Java, it simply means a prepackaged module of Java code.

To set up a data connection using the JDBC-ODBC bridge, first create a DSN on the server (see "Making a DSN" earlier in this chapter). Then, with any UltraDev page open, choose Modify⇨Connections. The Connections list opens. Click New and choose ODBC Database (Sun JDBC-ODBC Driver) from the pop-up menu. The connection dialog box opens. Now proceed:

1. **Type a name for this connection in the Connection Name text box.**

    Spaces are not allowed in data connection names, and you cannot edit them later.

2. **The Driver text box defaults to the correct driver class,** `sun.jdbc.odbc.JdbcOdbcDriver`.

3. **The URL text box shows** `jdbc:odbc:[odbc dsn]`. **Simply replace the** `[odbc dsn]` **token with the actual DSN on the server.**

4. **Type any required username and password information.**

5. **Check that the radio button for using the DSN on the Application server is selected, as it should be by default.**

    A completed run-time tab for `JDBC-ODBC`, accessing a DSN named stamps, is shown in Figure 3-8.

Figure 3-8: A completed data connection using the JDBC-ODBC bridge.

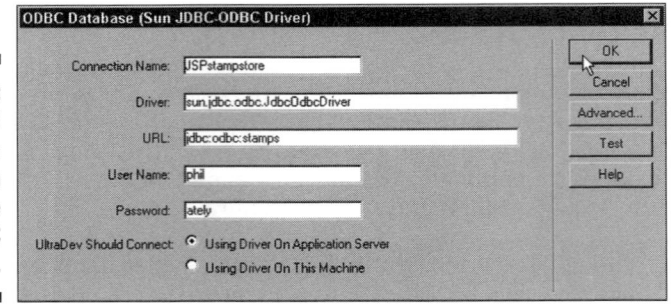

The next section describes a pure JDBC setup, which you'll probably prefer if you're a Java guru.

Doing it with pure JDBC

If your Web server is IBM WebSphere or Allaire JRun, you should definitely consider going the whole JDBC hog, using a fully JDBC-compatible database, such as IBM's DB2. The decision may well not be yours in any case — your work situation may require you to make UltraDev function in an all-JDBC setup. DB2 may seem impenetrable to those of us who are used to actually seeing and manipulating our data, but DB2 and WebSphere talk to each other just as naturally as old friends. It's the IBM view of the computer universe as opposed to the Microsoft view — neither more nor less valid but definitely not for amateurs.

You can find evaluation versions of DB2, WebSphere, and JRun on the CD that accompanies this book.

DB2 installs its own JDBC driver, whose class is `COM.ibm.db2.jdbc.app.DB2Driver`, if the database and the server are on the same machine. If they're on different machines in the same LAN, the class is `COM.ibm.db2.jdbc.net.DB2Driver`. The archive files `db2java.zip` and `runtime.zip` need to be in the CLASSPATH environment variable of the NT server for the drivers to be accessible. The archive files are normally at `C:\SQLLIB\java\`. Macromedia also recommends that you copy these archives into the configuration folder `\Dreamweaver Ultradev\Configuration\JDBCDrivers`.

Setting a `CLASSPATH` environment variable makes JDBC classes (of which drivers are one example) accessible from anywhere in the machine, just as setting a `PATH` environment variable in the DOS environment allows you to run applications that are in the path regardless of which directory is actually open at the time.

To set a `CLASSPATH` environment variable on an NT server, right-click the My Computer icon and select Properties from the pop-up menu. Click the

Environment tab and select `CLASSPATH` in the Variables list. The current value of `CLASSPATH` appears in the Value box at the bottom. Append to the existing value a semicolon followed by the path to the archive files, typically `;C:\SQLLIB\java`.

To set up a run-time JSP connection for a DB2 database residing on an NT server, follow these steps:

1. **Open any UltraDev page and choose Modify➪Connections.**

    The Connections list appears.

2. **Click New and choose either IBM DB2 App Driver or IBM DB2 Net Driver from the pop-up menu, depending on whether your database is on the same machine as the JSP server (App) or on a different machine (Net).**

    The Define Connection dialog box appears.

3. **In the Connection Name box, type a name for this connection.**

    Spaces are not allowed in data connection names, and you cannot edit them later.

4. **The Driver box defaults to the correct driver class.**

5. **The URL text box shows** `jdbc:db2:[database name]`. **Simply replace the placeholder token** `[database name]` **with the actual DB2 data name.**

6. **Type the username and password associated with the database to which you're connecting.**

    DB2 databases *always* need passwords for access — they're fussy about security.

7. **Check that the radio button for using the DSN on the Application server is selected, as it should be by default.**

8. **Click the Test button to test the connection.**

    You should see the message `Connection was made successfully`.

    A completed DB2 Connection dialog box is shown in Figure 3-9.

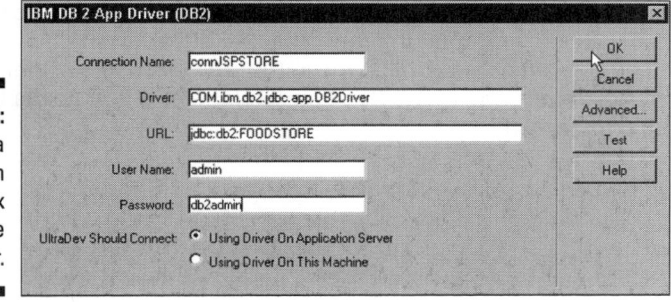

Figure 3-9: Data connection dialog box using the DB2 driver.

Setting Up Your Mac

The fundamental problem of building database-driven Web sites on your Mac can be stated simply: The database itself is highly unlikely to reside on the Mac when the site is fully deployed. It therefore makes little sense to develop your site entirely within a Mac environment. The recommended solution is to keep the database on a networked NT server and force the two rival machines to declare enough of a truce to cooperate in the matter of data exchange.

The setup, admittedly, is tricky — the compensation is that all the most difficult steps have to be completed once only, as the initial setup. Once the Mac and the networked NT are configured, though, the data connection process is hardly any different from the other configurations described in this chapter.

So hook your Mac up to an NT server, open up Appendix B of this book, and follow its steps carefully and as calmly as possible. Here's a checklist of what you should have achieved at the end of the day:

On the Mac:

- Configured the TCP/IP settings
- Made an AppleTalk connection to the NT server (unless you opt to transfer files by FTP — see Appendix B)

On the Server:

- Set up the database itself, with permissions set for the Mac remote machine and the IIS server to access it
- Created a Data Source Name (DSN) for accessing the database
- Created a directory at server root for the UltraDev files, with permissions set for the Mac remote machine to access it
- Set up Macintosh Network Services
- Made a Macintosh Volume allowing direct access to the server directory for publishing files

Once you have the Mac-NT setup working, you can turn to the question of creating a specific data connection for a specific UltraDev site, and that's what this section is all about. Unlike the setup procedures in Appendix B (that you perform only one time), this connection definition needs to be done for every site you create.

Connecting to a DSN

The Mac has no understanding of ODBC — the Microsoft standard for communicating with DSNs — so a Mac-DSN connection is theoretically impossible. UltraDev makes the impossible possible by using an HTTP request to access the data. In a sense, when UltraDev executes its connection scripts, it's behaving as if it were a browser, and the server machine responds dumbly without realizing that it's giving data to a completely incompatible machine. Pretty clever idea, that.

So the steps to a DSN connection are just like the same steps on a Windows machine:

1. **Open any UltraDev page and choose Modify⇨Connections.**

    The Connections list opens. It contains a list of data connections that already exist (if any), and you're given the option of editing, duplicating, or removing them.

2. **Click the New button and choose DSN from the pop-up menu.**

    The DSN connection dialog box opens.

3. **Type a name for your data connection in the Connection Name text box.**

    Spaces are not allowed.

4. **Click the DSN button to see a list of all DSNs available on the server machine (see Figure 3-10).**

    If you see no DSN list, don't despair. The Mac-Windows connection can sometimes make this impossible. Just type in the DSN name.

5. **Select the DSN you need to connect to and click OK.**

6. **Back in the DSN connection dialog box, type any needed username and password, and click Test.**

    You should see the message `Connection was made successfully`. Again, though, testing through the Mac-Windows connection can be problematic. It's possible that the test may fail but recordsets may work fine.

7. **Click OK to close the DSN dialog box, and then click Done to close the Connections list.**

Part II: Bringing Data to Your Pages

Figure 3-10: Selection list of available DSNs on a remote server.

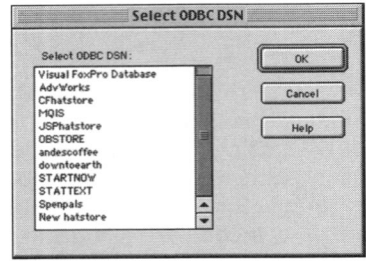

Figure 3-11 shows a completed Mac-DSN connection dialog box.

Figure 3-11: Data connection dialog box for a Mac-ODBC connection.

Connecting to a ColdFusion data source

The connection steps for a ColdFusion data source are essentially the same as for an ordinary DSN. The differences are:

- The pop-up menu that appears when you click the New button in the Connections list is different. Choose the ordinary "vanilla" DSN rather than the advanced, which requires installation of special drivers and further tortuous setups on both machines.

- The first time that you connect to a ColdFusion data source on the remote machine, you'll be asked to log on to the ColdFusion Remote Development Services (RDS). See the note about this in "Creating a Data Source Name for a ColdFusion Server" in this chapter. The same section gives detailed steps for making a ColdFusion data source.

Figure 3-12 shows a completed Mac-ColdFusion connection dialog box.

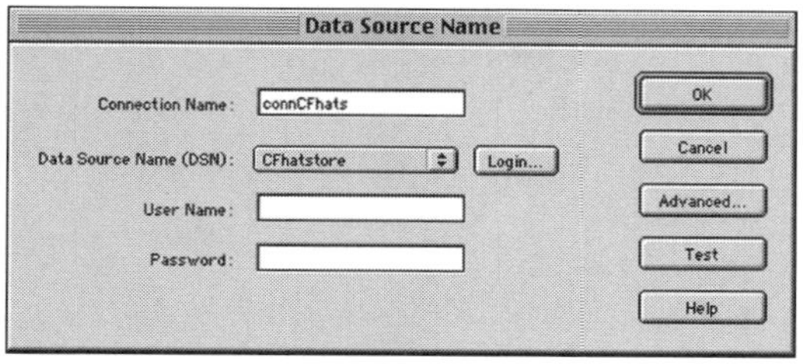

Figure 3-12: Data connection dialog box for a Mac-ColdFusion connection.

Connecting to a JDBC data source

The steps for connecting to a JDBC data source are exactly the same as for the Windows procedure described in "Bridge to ODBC" and "Doing it with pure JDBC" in this chapter. Figure 3-13 shows a completed Mac-JDBC connection dialog box.

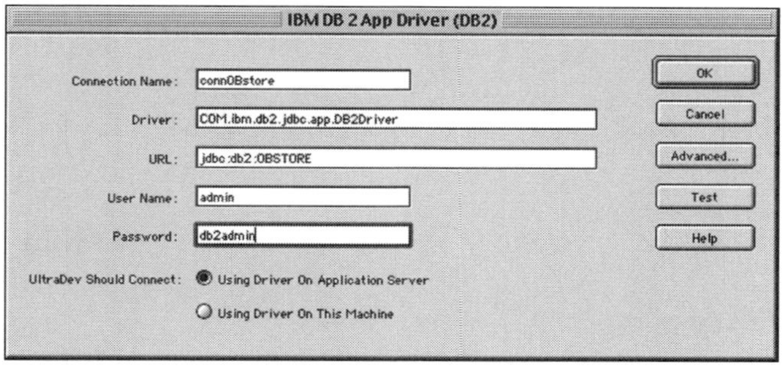

Figure 3-13: Data connection dialog box for a Mac-JDBC connection.

Note that for JDBC, unlike the other data connection types, you do have the option of connecting to a database driver actually on the Mac. This is the type of connection you'd use if the whole site, database and kitchen sink and all, was on the Mac.

Chapter 4
Recordsets and What They Offer

In This Chapter
- Creating recordsets
- Sorting recordsets
- Building advanced recordsets with SQL
- Filtering recordset data
- Formatting recordset data
- Binding images to recordset data

Databases contain far more stuff than you'd ever want to put on one Web page. A database usually consists of many different tables, and each table has many different columns, or *fields*. Very often, you are interested in only one table, and in only *some* of the fields in that table. You need to have some way to list those selected fields so that you can flow them onto the page in what seems like a sensible order.

For all these reasons, you need a way to display a representation of your data, called a *recordset* (or *resultset* if JSP is your server model). A recordset is very similar to a data query. In this chapter, I show you how to work efficiently with recordsets.

ON THE CD

A Microsoft Access database called DownToEarth.mdb is in the Demo sites\Databases folder on the accompanying CD. Down To Earth is the database of a fictitious pottery and fine art ceramics business. I supply this database so that you can, if you wish, create the same pages I use for demonstration in this chapter. If you want to follow along, you should create a DSN called downtoearth and a data connection called connDown2Earth. (See Chapter 3 if you need help with either of these tasks.) Next you must define a site called Pottery Business. (See Chapter 1 for more about defining a site.) I've also included a complete set of Web pages for the DownToEarth site, in both start and finished state, in the Demo sites\DownToEarth folder.

Part II: Bringing Data to Your Pages

> Drummies can skip the first section of this chapter, but on no account skip the whole thing. UltraDev doesn't deal with recordsets in the same way as Drumbeat. For one thing, they're page-specific rather than site-wide (which some people, including this author, think is a shame). For another thing . . . well, you'll see.

Recordset Basics

A recordset is even more abstract than most data structures. In a way you could say it doesn't really exist at all. It's nothing more sophisticated than a listing of whatever parts of a database you want to create when a Web page loads. The recordset vanishes like dew in the morn when the user moves on (although you may create it all over again on the next page). The exact content of a recordset at any moment is dependent on what's considered to be the current record — the one the *data cursor* is pointing to, in the jargon. But rather than trying to imagine what a recordset actually looks and feels like, it's more rewarding to think in the practical terms of how UltraDev makes it easy for you to create and use one.

Making data available to a Web page

Suppose that you have a data table called Customers that you want to use to make a listing on a Web page — for part of an intranet, perhaps. This table is a record of all the people who have bought stuff from your enterprise (plus maybe some hot prospects), and it contains their names, addresses, phone numbers, e-mail, and so on. Most important, every customer has a unique CustomerID, which you eventually use to relate this table to other tables.

The `DownToEarth.mdb` sample database has just such a data table that you can use if you don't have a homegrown one on hand. By the way, all these people are entirely fictitious, and any resemblance to real people is purely coincidental.

Here's how you make data available to a Web page:

1. **Make a fresh page (see Chapter 1 if you need help with this task).**

   In my example, the page is called Clients.

2. **In the Launcher, click Data Bindings.**

   The Data Bindings inspector appears. It's blank and grayed out.

3. **Click the plus (+) button and you see the menu shown in Figure 4-1.**

Chapter 4: Recordsets and What They Offer   77

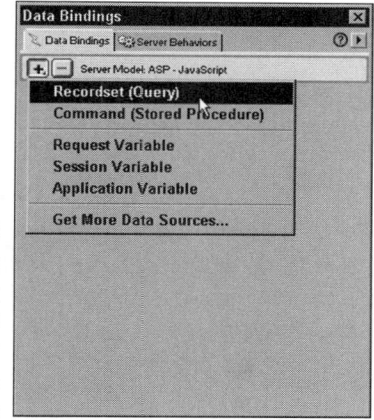

Figure 4-1: The Data Bindings inspector menu.

   4. **Select Recordset (Query) from the menu.**

      The Recordset Builder opens (see Figure 4-2).

Figure 4-2: The Simple mode of the Recordset Builder.

The Recordset Builder has two modes — Simple and Advanced. The version used last is the version that opens. If this is its first-ever outing, you see the Simple mode. If your Recordset Builder looks a lot more complicated than Figure 4-2, click the Simple button to uncomplicate it. The Simple button then becomes the Advanced button, as shown in the figure.

   5. **In the Name text box, type a name for the recordset.**

      In the example, I've entered **rsClients** (like many ASP hackers, I prefix recordset names rs and Connection names conn. It's purely a convention).

Part II: Bringing Data to Your Pages

6. **In the Connection drop-down list, select your data connection.**

   In the example, I chose the connection connDown2Earth.

   Notice the little Define button to the right of the Connection list? Clicking this button provides a shortcut to the Define Connection dialog box in case you have a "D'oh!" moment when you see the list.

   All the data tables in the database that you selected in the Connection list are now available in the Table drop-down list.

7. **In the Table drop-down list, select the table containing the data that you want to list on your page.**

   In the example, I selected the Customers table.

   After you choose a table, all the columns (fields) in that table are available in the Columns window.

8. **For this simple recordset, leave the Columns radio button set at All.**

   You can choose whether to include all columns in the recordset, or just selected columns. Clicking the All radio button kills the column list (you can see it's grayed out in the figure), but clicking the Selected radio button enables you to scroll through the complete list.

   Ignore everything below the Columns window for now.

9. **Click the Test button to test the connection.**

   The Test SQL Statement window appears (see Figure 4-3). All your data is there, ready to go to work. (If it isn't there, or if it's wrong, troubleshoot by backtracking to the Data Connection — which also has a test function — then to the DSN, and finally to the database itself.)

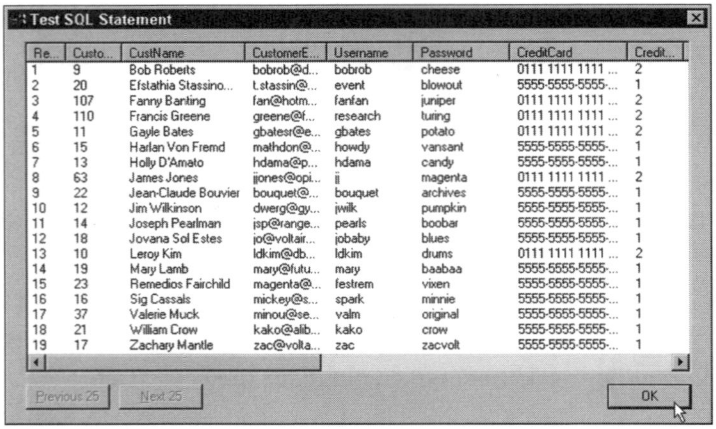

Figure 4-3: The Test SQL Statement window.

When you close the Recordset Builder, the recordset appears in the Data Bindings inspector. You can expand it by clicking the little plus box (arrow on the Mac) to see the individual data fields all in order (see Figure 4-4). The data is now available to be deployed onto a Web page.

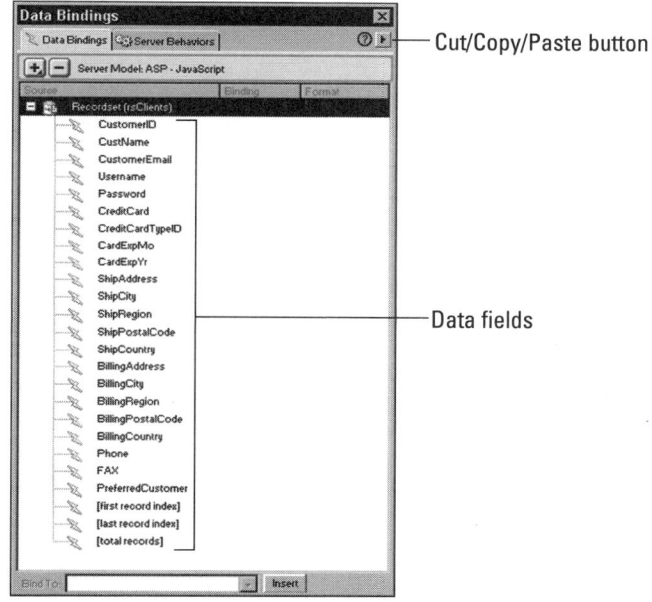

Figure 4-4: The Customers recordset represented in the Data Bindings inspector.

Any time that you need to copy a recordset from one page to another, you can use the teensy black Cut/Copy/Paste arrow at the upper-right corner of the Data Bindings or Server Behaviors inspector. Simply click the arrow, select Copy, open the destination page, click the arrow again, and then select Paste. The recordset inserts into the page immediately.

Flowing data from a recordset to a page

Figure 4-5 shows a pretty basic title-and-table setup ready to receive data — in this example, customer data from the DownToEarth database. You can easily insert a table by clicking the Table button on the Common panel of the Objects palette. For this example, I gave the table two rows and four columns, and I set the width at 100 percent and the vertical alignment at Top for the second table row.

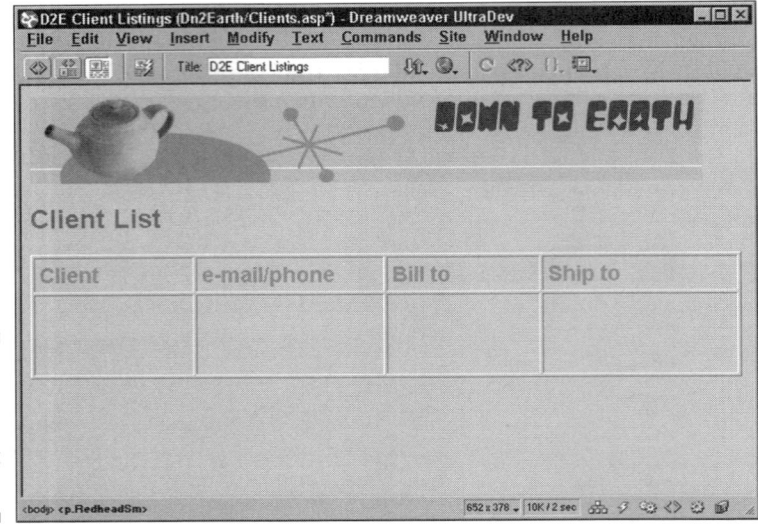

Figure 4-5: The table setup for the Client List Web page.

After you create a table, here's how you flow the data into it:

1. **Place a cursor in any table cell in which you expect to see data.**

   Using the DownToEarth example, the first cell is the lower-left cell, which expects to be filled with the client's name.

2. **Expand the recordset in the Data Bindings inspector and select the data field you want to see in the table cell.**

3. **In the Data Bindings inspector, click the Insert button embedded in the lower margin of the window.**

   A data placeholder appears in the cell at the cursor position. In the DownToEarth example, this placeholder reads **{rsClients.CustName}**. Don't worry if the table distorts — you can drag it back into shape later.

4. **Repeat Steps 1-3 for each data field that you want to flow onto the page.**

   In the DownToEarth example, I placed 12 data fields on the page to arrive at the situation shown in Figure 4-6. I used the CSS style sheet `pottery.css` (available on the CD-ROM) to add some text styles. CSS style sheets are explained in Chapter 2.

5. **If you need to readjust the widths of the table columns, just drag the column dividers.**

   Live Data View, explained in Chapter 6, is a godsend for this task and is sometimes the only practical way to adjust table column width.

The table is essentially done. You can save the page, transfer it to the server, and examine it in a browser (press F12 or use the Preview in Browser button on the UltraDev toolbar). You see the data associated with the first record in the data table.

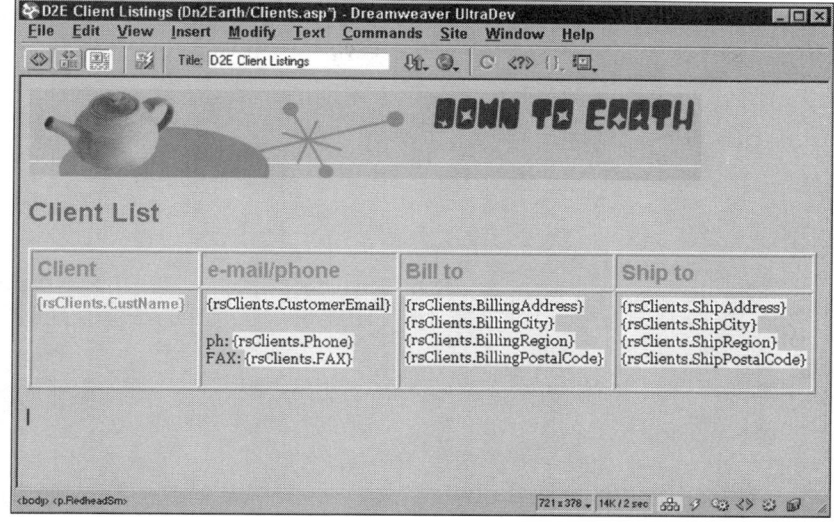

Figure 4-6: The DownTo Earth Client List table with dynamic data placeholders.

Making a repetitive list from ten data records

You may want to use a recordset to display not just a single data record but several records on a single page. In the DownToEarth example, and very likely in your own customer listings, it's highly desirable to list, say, ten customers at a time by using the same basic page layout that holds one sample record at design time.

Making one table row into many is a job for the Repeat Region server behavior. *Server behaviors* are explained in detail in Chapter 5, but there's no reason you can't use one right now, because it's very relevant to the general task of recordset management.

First, decide which table row you want to repeat and select the entire row. You can either find the appropriate `<tr>` tag in the tag selector in the lower-left corner of the Document window, or you can maneuver your cursor until it's an arrow pointing along the row (see Figure 4-7) and then click to select the row.

Click Server Behaviors in the Launcher to open the Server Behaviors inspector. Click the plus (+) button and select the first behavior on the list, Repeat Region. The Repeat Region dialog box opens (see Figure 4-8). In the Show section, simply change the default number of repeats from 5 to whatever number you fancy, and you're done.

Part II: Bringing Data to Your Pages

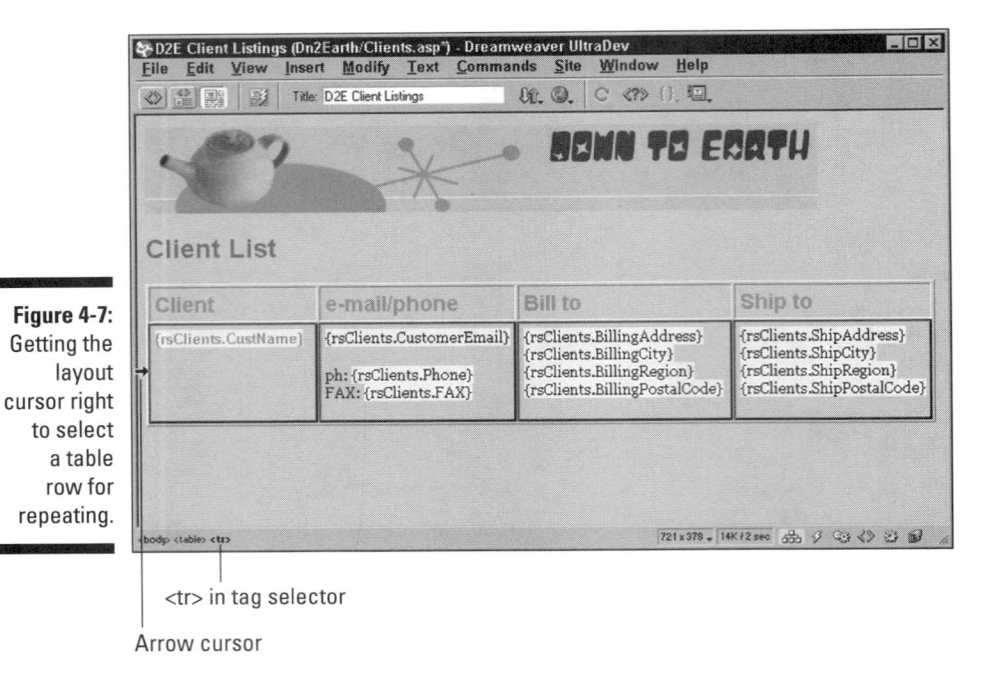

Figure 4-7: Getting the layout cursor right to select a table row for repeating.

Figure 4-8: The Repeat Region dialog box.

> *Repeat regions* are most often applied to table rows, but they don't have to be. A simple line of text — a product name, for example — can be iterated from the recordset as many times as you choose.

Alpha-sorting a recordset

You may want to list the contents of a recordset alphabetically. UltraDev makes it dead easy to do.

Open a recordset by double-clicking it in either the Data Bindings inspector or the Server Behaviors inspector. The Sort drop-down lists at the bottom of the dialog box (see Figure 4-9) enable you to choose which field to sort on. In this figure, the recordset will be sorted on the CustName field in ascending order.

Chapter 4: Recordsets and What They Offer

When you finish establishing the sort criteria, click OK to close the dialog box. Save the page and transfer it to the server. Figure 4-10 shows the DownToEarth Customers recordset sorted alphabetically on the CustName field.

Figure 4-9: Sorting a recordset.

Sort drop-down lists

Figure 4-10: An alphabetically sorted Customers list.

Pushbutton SQL

If you're interested, you can examine the server-side code that's created when you build a recordset. After you build your recordset, click the Code button at the left end of the toolbar and scroll to the top of the document. Using the example shown in the figures in this chapter, the ASP/JavaScript version is something like this:

```
<%
var rsClients = Server.CreateObject("ADODB.Recordset");
rsClients.ActiveConnection = "dsn=downtoearth;";
rsClients.Source = "SELECT * FROM Customers ORDER BY CustName ASC";
rsClients.CursorType = 0;
rsClients.CursorLocation = 2;
rsClients.LockType = 3;
rsClients.Open();
var rsClients_numRows = 0;
%>
```

In ASP/VBScript, it's this:

```
<%
set rsClients = Server.CreateObject("ADODB.Recordset")
rsClients.ActiveConnection = "dsn=downtoearth;"
rsClients.Source = "SELECT * FROM Customers ORDER BY CustName ASC"
rsClients.CursorType = 0
rsClients.CursorLocation = 2
rsClients.LockType = 3
rsClients.Open
rsClients_numRows = 0
%>
```

In Cold Fusion, it's this:

```
<cfquery name="rsClients" datasource="dsn= downtoearth;"  >
SELECT * FROM Customers ORDER BY CustName
</cfquery>
<cfset Hats_NumRows = 0>
<cfset Hats_Index = 1>
```

In JSP, the connection is not made via a DSN, and the recordset declaration gets all wrapped up with the data connection, like this:

```
<%
Driver DriverrsClients =
            (Driver)Class.forName("COM.ibm.db2.jdbc.app.DB2Driver").newInstan
            ce();
Connection ConnrsClients =
            DriverManager.getConnection("jdbc:db2:DOWNTOEARTH","admin","db2ad
            min");
PreparedStatement StatementrsClients = ConnrsClients.prepareCall("SELECT * FROM
            Customers ORDER BY CustName");
ResultSet rsClients = Statement rsClients.executeQuery();
boolean rsClients _isEmpty = !rsClients.next();
boolean rsClients _hasData = !rsClients _isEmpty;
Object rsClients _data;
int rsClients _numRows = 0;
%>
```

Whether you use ASP, JSP, or ColdFusion, the thing to note is that all three server models have one statement in common, and it's this one:

```
SELECT * FROM Customers ORDER BY CustName
```

This statement is a snippet of a common language called *Structured Query Language (SQL)*. Just like ODBC, which is introduced in Chapter 3, SQL is intended to be a lingua franca — a kind of Esperanto of databases (although it's a safe bet that more people are familiar with SQL than with Esperanto). You don't need the Microsoft SQL Server to interpret SQL — virtually all databases understand it.

`SELECT * FROM Customers ORDER BY CustName`, simply means "give me all fields from the Customers data table, sorted on the CustName field." Readers old enough to have worked in DOS will have no trouble recognizing that the asterisk means *everything*.

If you use the option to select columns in the Recordset Builder to, say, select only the CustName, Phone, and FAX fields, the SQL statement would be `SELECT CustName,Phone,FAX FROM Customers ORDER BY CustName`.

The Advanced mode of the Recordset Builder (discussed in more detail in the following section) expects you to create your own SQL statements to derive whatever you need from the data tables — but it does its very best to help you out. Pushbutton SQL is an ideal that the Recordset Builder strives for.

Using the Advanced mode of the Recordset Builder

A common requirement in commercial database management is to display a data table of orders that customers have placed. Even though the database application itself has perfectly good routines for designing this type of data view, real-life corporations often prefer the easy sharability of a database-driven Web page.

UltraDev's Recordset Builder is well capable of producing this more complicated data set. Typically, you need to build a table that displays — from left to right — the order number, order date, item ordered, quantity ordered, unit price, and then all the customer's shipping information.

The customer's shipping information gets you your instant ticket to the exciting new territory of the Advanced mode of the Recordset Builder. You see, the first five items all come from the same data table (Orders), but the customer shipping information is in a different data table. The two tables are related by the common CustomerID field. Welcome to the world of relational databases, where the Simple mode of the Recordset Builder cannot help you.

Something about SQL

You've already met this simple form of SQL:

```
SELECT [some fields] FROM [some table]
```

To make pages that pick out specific records or groups of records — like "show me all the customers who owe us money" — you need to extend your understanding of SQL a little to encompass the idea of data filtering. It's done like this:

```
SELECT [some fields] FROM [some table] WHERE [some condition is true]
```

Here's a simple example of filtering that you can use to find a particular customer:

```
SELECT * FROM Customers WHERE CustName = 'Joseph Pearlman'
```

There, that's not a whole lot different from plain English, is it?

Ready to generate an advanced recordset for orders? Okay — prepare a page that resembles the one shown in Figure 4-11. When your page is ready, follow these steps:

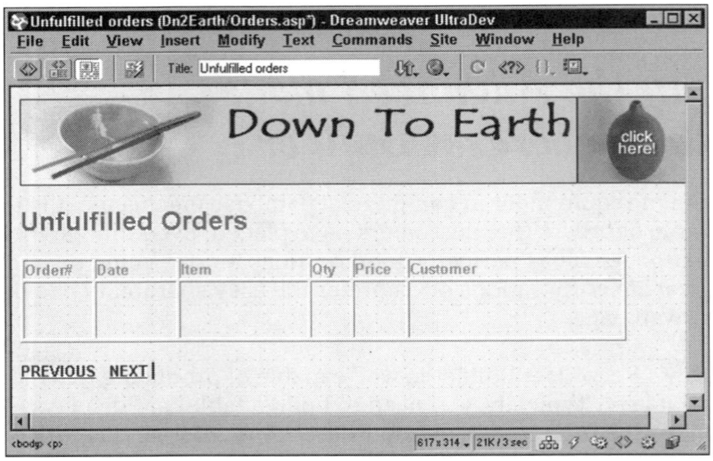

Figure 4-11: A skeleton layout for an orders page.

1. **In the Data Bindings inspector, click the plus (+) button and select Recordset (Query) from the menu.**

    The Recordset Builder opens in Simple mode.

2. **Click the Advanced button.**

Chapter 4: Recordsets and What They Offer

3. **Name the recordset in the Name text box and select your data connection in the Connection drop-down list.**

   In the DownToEarth example used in this section, I named the recordset rsUnfOrders, and the data connection is connDown2Earth.

   The Data Tables appear in the Database Items box, along with Views and Stored Procedures if any exist (there are none in my Down To Earth example).

4. **Expand the Orders table, locate and select the first field that you need.**

   If you have a standard sort of commercial orders data table, the first field is probably OrderID.

5. **Click the SELECT button to the right of the Database Items box.**

   The beginning of the SQL statement, SELECT OrderID FROM Orders, appears in the SQL box.

6. **Do the same with the other fields that you need from this table and watch the SQL statement build.**

   In this example, it would evetually become SELECT OrderID, ItemName, ItemPrice, Qty, Date FROM Orders.

7. **Close up the Orders table and open the Customers table.**

8. **Select the needed fields from the Customers table.**

   In the example, the SQL statement becomes SELECT OrderID, ItemName, ItemPrice, Qty, Date, LastName, FirstName, ShipAddress, ShipCity, ShipRegion, ShipPostalCode FROM Orders, Customers.

9. **Now select the CustomerID field in the Customers table and click the WHERE button.**

   The clause WHERE CustomerID is added to the SQL statement.

   You have to complete this statement by hand. The WHERE clause first relates the two tables like this: WHERE Orders.CustomerID = Customers.CustomerID. Those two fields have to be specified in that way because there are fields with identical names in both tables.

You have now retrieved every order, including the customer information that goes along with each one. You can test the SQL with the Test button, bringing all the data into the Test SQL Statement window. If there's a problem, the error message is probably not going to be very informative. SQL is not case sensitive but the syntax must be exact.

After you have your SQL performing correctly, you can use the same steps as in the section "Flowing data from a recordset to a page" earlier in this chapter to place the order information on your Web page.

Data Filtering by Using the Recordset Builder

Many data management tasks require you to select from a data table only those records that meet a certain criterion. You often have to examine the value of a certain recordset field to determine which records are okay and which are of no interest. For example, you may want to sort a data table of orders that customers have placed and select only those orders that are unfulfilled.

To determine which orders have not been filled, an order-fulfilled field is examined in the database. An order-fulfilled field is usually a *Boolean* field, otherwise known as *binary, yes/no, true/false,* or *1/0.* Records representing unfulfilled orders have that field set to false (in the original Access database, the field is a check box that remains unchecked for unfulfilled orders). UltraDev has the tools for filtering a recordset according to the state of this field.

Filtering in the Simple mode of the Recordset Builder

Filtering a recordset that's constructed in the Simple mode of the Recordset Builder is almost a point-and-click operation. First, you build a simple recordset from an Orders data table (for instructions, see "Recordset Basics" earlier in this chapter). You can use the Orders table from the Down2Earth database on the CD if you don't have one of your own.

Notice that the Filter area of the Recordset Builder is a block of four option elements — three drop-down lists and a text box (see Figure 4-12).

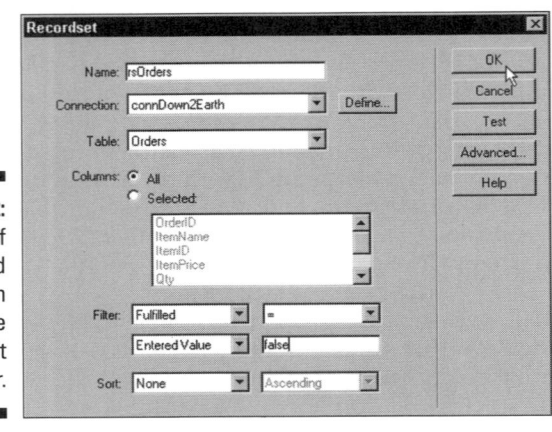

Figure 4-12: Example of a filtered recordset in the Simple recordset builder.

Here's how you use these four boxes:

- **The top-left** drop-down list enables you to select the recordset field to use for filtering.
- **The top-right** drop-down list enables you to select the mathematical operator needed for the filter operation.
- **The bottom-left** drop-down list enables you to select the type of parameter that will be used to impose the filter — an incoming URL parameter, for example, or a server object, such as a cookie. (See Chapter 8 to find out more about server objects and cookies.)
- **The bottom-right** text box contains the parameter value that you want to filter on.

Suppose that you want to filter your Orders data table to select only those records that are unfulfilled. In my Down To Earth example, that means that the Fulfilled field has a value of false. Here's how you filter a recordset:

1. **In the top-left Filter drop-down list, select the field that you need to filter on.**

   Fulfilled, in the example.

2. **In the top-right Filter drop-down list, select the mathematical operator appropriate for the select logic.**

   = (equals), in the example.

3. **In the bottom-left Filter drop-down list, select to the type of parameter that will do the filtering.**

   Entered Value means that you're going to supply the filter value manually in the dialog box.

4. **Type** false **in the bottom-right text box.**

Figure 4-13 shows the recordset builder set up for this filter. This recordset could produce a listing of unfulfilled orders similar to what you see later in Figure 4-16, but *without* the customer information, which comes from a separate data table.

Filtering in the Advanced Recordset Builder

Filtering a recordset in the Advanced mode of the Recordset Builder is just a matter of adding an additional filtering clause to the existing SQL statement.

Part II: Bringing Data to Your Pages

If you read the "Something about SQL" section earlier in this chapter, you can use the recordset you build there as a starting point. If not, find a data table of merchandise orders with a binary field for fulfilled/unfulfilled orders and make your own SQL statement. Then proceed with these steps to filter a recordset in the Advanced mode of the Recordset Builder:

1. **Expand the Tables and Fields in the Database Items box so that you can select the Fulfilled field.**

2. **Click the WHERE button.**

   The expression `AND Fulfilled` is appended to the existing SQL statement.

3. **Finish the line of SQL by typing** = false.

   The SQL statement is complete, and the Recordset Builder now looks like Figure 4-13.

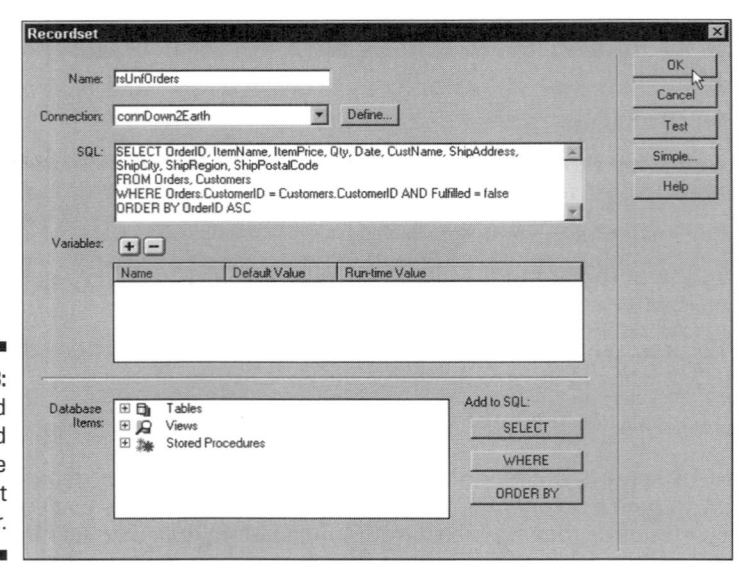

Figure 4-13: A completed Advanced mode of the Recordset Builder.

Figure 4-14 shows (most of) a page displaying unfulfilled orders, with data placeholders inserted, and Figure 4-15 shows the final result in a browser.

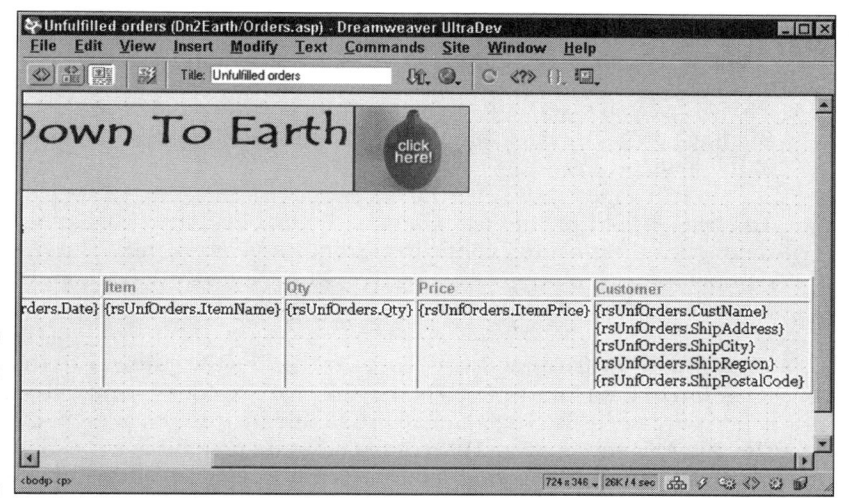

Figure 4-14:
A completed design-time page.

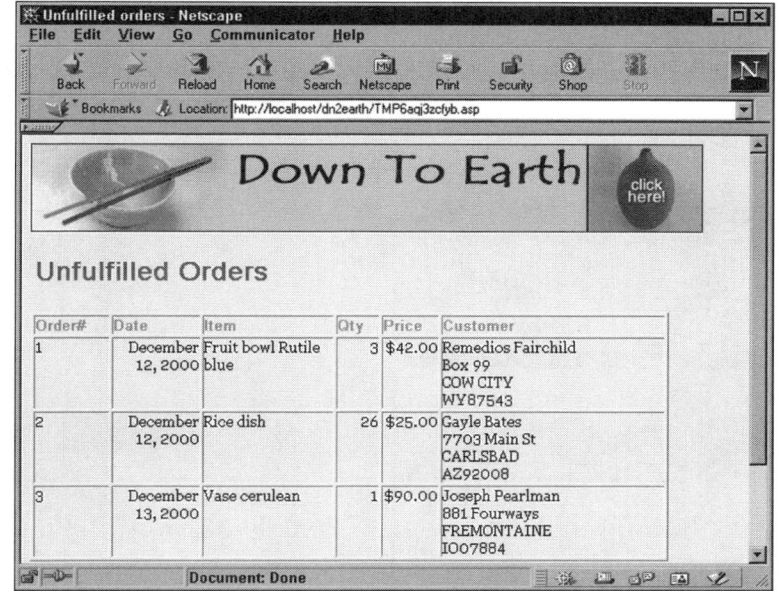

Figure 4-15:
The unfulfilled orders table in Netscape.

Formatting Your Data

Every time you insert dynamic data from an expanded recordset in the Data Bindings inspector, two additional columns — Binding and Format — pop up in the inspector window.

You can ignore the Binding column — it can become important when binding data to form elements, but it's irrelevant for inserting text. But the Format column is much more interesting. It's set to None by default, and there's a little drop-down arrow beside it (see Figure 4-16).

Click that little arrow and you discover that it's the gateway to the magic kingdom of data formatting. Figure 4-17 is an exploded form of the formatting menu cascade — no less than 56 possible data formats in eight categories (for the ASP server model), which is more than you'll ever need in a lifetime of UltraDev use. And if you're interested, you can select the last item on the menu, Edit Format List, and create your own fantasy format.

So what's this all about? Here's a practical example: In the Down To Earth example, the pottery prices don't automatically include the dollar sign or the extra decimal places. A price of $35 comes out as just 35 instead of $35.00 because *35* is exactly what the database contains. If you look at it in Microsoft Access, you see $35.00 because the data field is *formatted* as Currency, 2 Decimal Places. UltraDev offers you the opportunity to do this same kind of formatting as you insert or bind dynamic data.

Figure 4-16: The Data Bindings inspector with the Binding and Format columns.

Format column drop-down arrow

Chapter 4: Recordsets and What They Offer

Figure 4-17: All your formatting options.

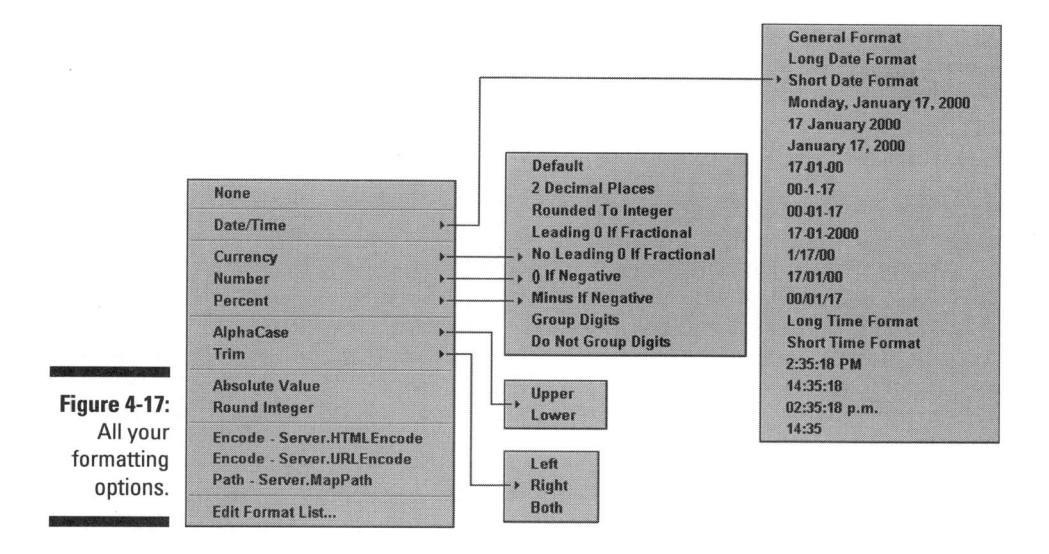

Suppose that on your page you want to insert dynamic data that represents the price of an item:

1. **Expand the recordset in the Data Bindings inspector.**

2. **Select the price field in the recordset, place your cursor where you want the price to appear in the document window, and then click the Insert button in the Data Bindings inspector.**

   The data placeholder appears on the page, and the Format drop-down arrow appears in the Data Bindings inspector.

3. **Click the drop-down arrow and choose Currency⇨2 Decimal Places from the menu cascade.**

4. **Save the page and transfer it to the server.**

   You'll see the amounts shown in dollars (or your local currency, if you don't use dollars).

If you want to play around with data formatting, the Data Bindings inspector offers plenty of opportunities. Dates are formatted by default as mm/dd/yy, but you can change them to any of 12 other formats. You can play around with turning text fields to all uppercase or all lowercase — you can have all kinds of formatting fun.

And don't forget, if you have too much fun and regret it (formatter's remorse?), you can always revert to the format at the top of the list — None.

Part II: Bringing Data to Your Pages

> **TIP:** To edit a data format later, select both the data placeholder in the document and the recordset field in the Data Bindings inspector, and the format drop-down arrow appears.

Dynamic Images

Perhaps the most straightforward use of a recordset is to create a product catalog page. Typically, the Products data table in a commercial database contains all the information needed for a catalog. Therefore, a recordset created for this purpose can be built using the Simple mode of the Recordset Builder, and the product name, description, price, and so on can be placed on a catalog page exactly as described in "Flowing data from a recordset onto a page" in this chapter.

This section describes how to enhance a catalog page — or any other dynamic page — with a dynamic image. In other words, you find out how to make your image change along with the other parts of the page as the user browses the catalog.

> **ON THE CD:** The `DownToEarth.mdb` database includes a table called Products, which describes a (small) selection of the merchandise. And in the `images` folder beneath the Demo sites\DownToEarth folder, you'll find a corresponding set of images.

To make a product catalog on the Web, just create a skeleton catalog page, make a recordset, and insert the data. Figure 4-18 shows an almost complete catalog page, using layers to space out the material and the `pottery.css` style sheet to give some coherent typographical style.

What's unfinished in Figure 4-18 is the image of the product. What you see there is merely a placeholder — one of the product images taken at random (nice, isn't it?) — something to design around. As things stand, the image isn't dynamic, so it won't change along with the rest of the information as the user browses the catalog.

As you'll see if you make a recordset from the Down2Earth Products data table and test it, the image information is contained in the data table as a path to the appropriate image — `images/bowl774.jpg`, for instance. The assumption is that the images are all stored in a folder called `images` one level below the page files on the server, just as they are in the local folder where the working files are stored. An essential first step in making dynamic images is to transfer all the images to the server by selecting the images folder in the Site window and clicking the Up arrow.

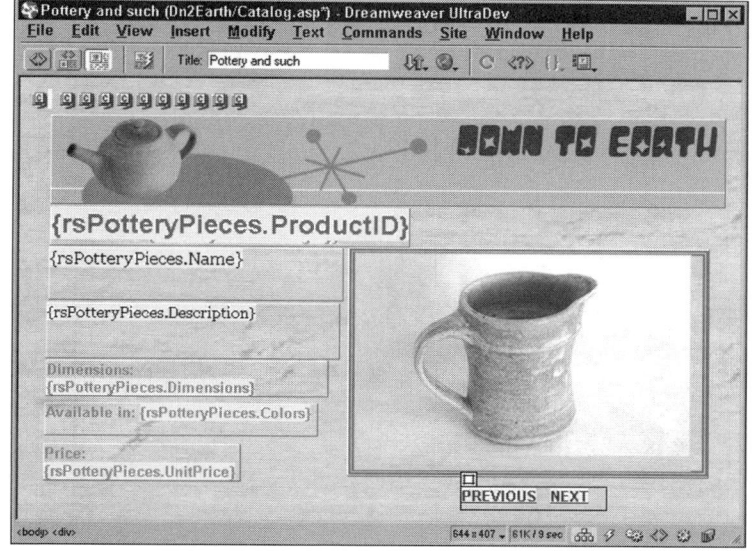

Figure 4-18: A not-quite-complete catalog page for Down To Earth Pottery.

Binding an image to a recordset

You can make an image dynamic by using either of the following methods.

Method #1 for making a dynamic image

1. Expand the recordset in the Data Bindings inspector.
2. Select the image in the Document window.
3. Select the Picture field in the recordset.
4. Click the Bind button embedded in the margin of the Data Bindings inspector (see Figure 4-19).

Method #2 for making a dynamic image

1. Select the image in the Document window.
2. In the Property inspector, click the file-folder icon to the right of the image Src box.

    The Select Image Source dialog box opens.

3. Next to Select File Name From at the top of the dialog box, click the Data Sources radio button.

    The expanded recordset opens in the Data Sources window (see Figure 4-20).

4. Select the Picture field and click OK.

Now the image changes along with most everything else on the page as the user navigates from piece to piece.

Part II: Bringing Data to Your Pages

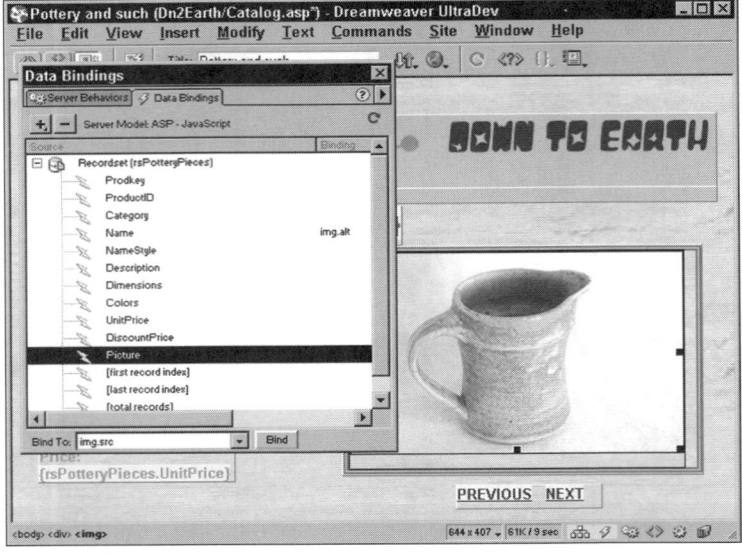

Figure 4-19: One way to bind an image to dynamic data.

Binding other attributes of the <IMG> tag

In the preceding section, I describe two ways that you can bind an image to a recordset. In the first method, you click the Bind button in the Data Bindings inspector (see Figure 4-19). Notice that `img.src` is displayed in the Bind To text box with a little drop-down arrow beside it. Clicking that down arrow uncovers 20 other attributes of <IMG> that you can hypothetically bind data fields to.

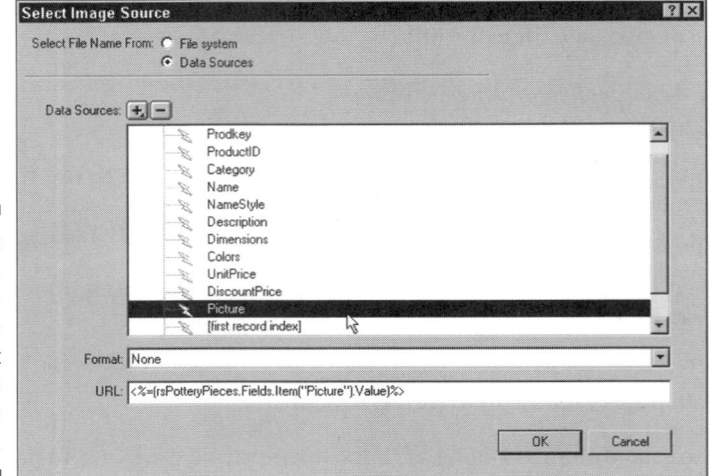

Figure 4-20: Selecting an image data field in the Select Image Source dialog box.

Some of the attributes seem extremely unlikely candidates for data binding, but others suggest possibilities. If the images your database refers to have highly variable geometry, you may consider controlling their display sizes by binding `WIDTH` and `HEIGHT` attributes to data fields inserted for that purpose.

To get the idea of how to bind other attributes to a field, try binding the `ALT` attribute of the image to the Name field of the recordset. The `ALT` attribute determines what appears in the tooltip when a user moves the mouse over the image. In addition — and perhaps more to the point — the `ALT` attribute determines what text appears in place of the image for users who don't see images, either because they're visually handicapped or because they're using antediluvian browsers.

Here's how to bind an attribute to a field:

1. **Expand the recordset in the Data Bindings inspector.**
2. **Select the image in layout.**
3. **Select the Name field in the recordset.**
4. **Click the Bind button embedded in the margin of the Data Bindings inspector.**
5. **When the Bind To drop-down arrow appears, click it and select** `img.alt` **from the pop-up menu of attributes.**
6. **Save the page and transfer it to the server; then open the page again and move your mouse over the image to check that the ToolTip shows the product name (see Figure 4-21).**

Offbeat data bindings

Images, of course, aren't the only HTML elements that can have their attributes bound to dynamic data. In fact, in principle you can bind *any* attribute of *any* element — though it may not always be sensible, and it may not always be straightforward.

Here's an unusual data binding that's sensible but definitely not straightforward. Suppose that you're making a catalog page, and you want to feature certain products in an eye-catching way. You want the name of the featured product to appear in a special style called SpecialOffer. You add this information to the data table, in a field called NameStyle. Now, on the face of it, what you're trying to do is impossible because a simple piece of text has no attributes that can be bound to data. However, if you place the product name on a layer, you can bind the style of the *layer* to data, which lets you achieve the desired result.

Part II: Bringing Data to Your Pages

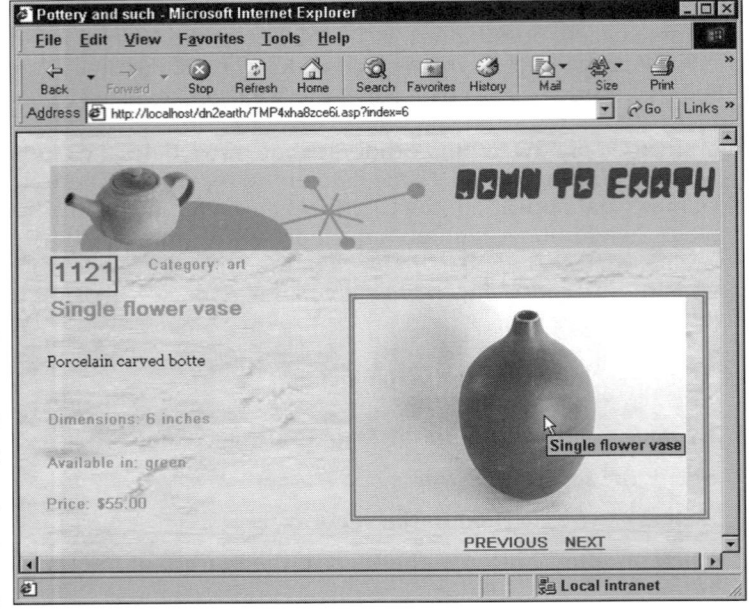

Figure 4-21: The ALT attribute of the product image correctly bound to its name.

But here's the snag in your plan. When you select the layer containing the name and the NameStyle field in the recordset, you find that you have no option to bind, only to insert. In that case, do this instead:

1. **Select the layer.**
2. **In the layer's Property inspector, click the List Mode tab at the left end of the inspector to turn the properties into list mode (see Figure 4-22).**
3. **In the property list, select the property *class* (you may have to use the drop-down arrow to add it to the list).**

   Click the little lightning bolt at the extreme right end of the line, and a Dynamic Data dialog box opens with the recordset already expanded.

4. **Select the NameStyle field, click OK, and you're all done.**

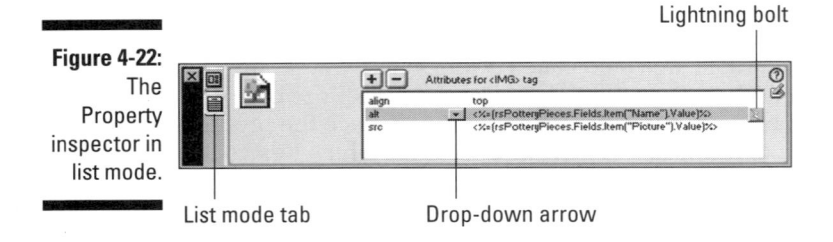

Figure 4-22: The Property inspector in list mode.

Chapter 4: Recordsets and What They Offer

Figure 4-23 shows an example from the Down To Earth pottery catalog — a splendid vase with the special style attached to its name.

You can also make phrases like

Look!   New!

pop up on cue for certain products by binding the visibility attribute of a LAYER to a field in the database. If the word in that field is *hide,* the layer is invisible for that data record. If the word is *show,* the layer pops into view.

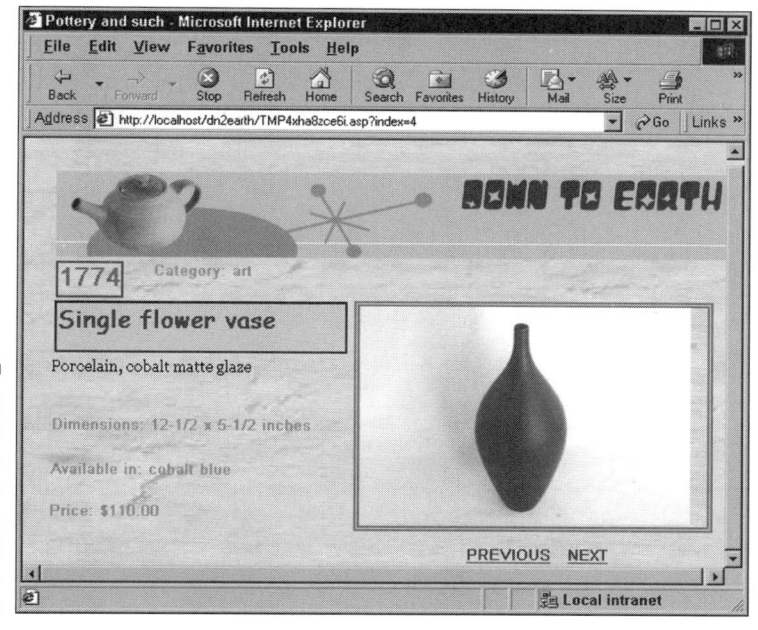

Figure 4-23: A featured piece gets the special typographical treatment.

That simple method, however, only works for a Netscape-style LAYER element. If you use the DIV element for layers, to make your pages valid for MSIE, this task becomes much trickier. Visibility, you see, is not an independent attribute but is simply one components of the style attribute of a DIV. You find out an interesting way of making a DIV behave like a LAYER in Chapter 13.

All the site files, images, and database tables for the Down To Earth site are on the accompanying CD, in ASP format.

Chapter 5

Making Server Behaviors Work for You

In This Chapter

▶ Figuring out what your site looks like
▶ Binding form elements
▶ Creating Update and Insert pages
▶ Repeating regions
▶ Using Go To Detail Page
▶ Getting around with server behaviors
▶ Using the Delete function

Server behaviors are, in many ways, the heart and soul of UltraDev. Databases, data connections, and recordsets bring the data to your pages. Form elements and text fields are the design molds into which the data is poured so that it comes out looking pretty. Server behaviors are what make it all happen when the time comes for a real, live user to browse your Web site.

A *server behavior* is simply an organized way for you to interact with your data. Adding a new record to the database, deleting an existing record, updating a record — these are three typical data tasks for which you depend on server behaviors. The delete and update behaviors require a recordset to be on the page, the insert (add record) behavior doesn't.

There are a couple dozen standard out-of-the-box server behaviors, as well as five so-called *Live objects* — prepackaged useful tasks built around server behaviors. Live objects occupy their own special panel in the Objects palette, and they all pop up dialog boxes of varying complexity to allow you to tell them what to do. In this chapter, I describe how to use all the Live objects and most of the server behaviors in the context of an example site that pretty much follows UltraDev's basic assumptions about the behaviors you'll find most useful.

When you click the plus (+) button in the Server Behaviors inspector, a menu of server behaviors opens. A few items on this menu aren't covered in this chapter. Recordsets are well covered in Chapter 4 and have no business on this menu anyway. Other items on the menu are for advanced users of UltraDev and are outside the scope of this book — that applies to Command, Edit Server Behavior, and New Server Behavior.

This Is What Your Site Looks Like — Well, Maybe

UltraDev knows what your Web site looks like. Well, of course it doesn't *really,* but it *thinks* it does. You can't blame UltraDev. When the Macromedia slaves (sorry, brilliant programmers) thought about what might be needed in the way of data manipulation, they had to make some assumptions. Figure 5-1 is a schematic view of what the programmers think your site looks like. The Macromedia assumption is that most sites follow a rather standard corporate intranet approach that includes administrative as well as user functions. So, if you don't find what you need on the basic list of server behaviors, it may be that your site doesn't quite follow the programmer's assumptions. (If that turns out to be the case, see Chapter 9 for information about how to add additional functionality.)

All the pages suggested in Figure 5-1 are active pages that somebody has to build to make the overall site function. In this chapter, I describe in some detail the UltraDev server behaviors that make these pages function as they do. Here's a thumbnail sketch of what each of these pages has to achieve:

- **Results page:** Provides brief details of records that match some search criteria input by a user, along with hyperlinks to a Detail page. Usually has several records per page.
- **Detail page:** Displays complete records, usually with browse navigation and links to Update/Delete/Insert. The links are commonly protected so that only users with administrator privileges can use them (see Chapters 8 and 10).
- **Update page:** Displays a complete record in form elements for editing.
- **Insert page:** Displays a blank form so that you can create a fresh record.
- **Delete page:** Displays a record so that you can delete it. A Delete page can be combined with an Update page.

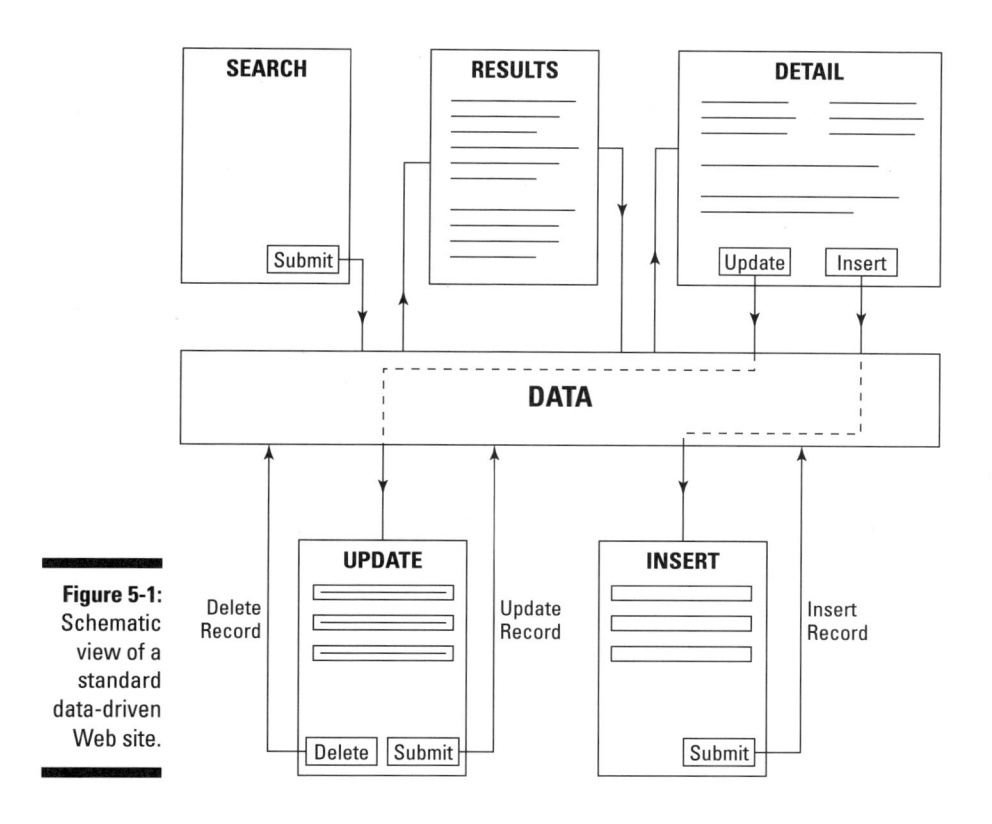

Figure 5-1: Schematic view of a standard data-driven Web site.

What's missing in this chapter is a page that allows the user to enter search criteria, which I describe in Chapter 7. The Update, Insert, and Delete pages are normally restricted so that only administrators can access them. The restrictions imply some sort of login page so that you can sort out who's an administrator. UltraDev offers four special User Authentication server behaviors that I deal with separately in Chapter 10.

Binding Form Elements to Your Data

In Chapter 4, I deal with the topic of *data binding* — in the sense of binding data to attributes of HTML tags, such as the SRC and ALT attributes of the <IMG> element, and the CLASS attribute of the <DIV> element. In this chapter, *data binding* has a different meaning: It refers exclusively to binding data to form elements.

You may need this variation of data binding when you want an online form to contain certain information when the page loads, but the information isn't completely *predictable*. It's information that derives from a database, and you can bind it to any type of form element that you like — a text box, a check box, a radio button, and so on. These elements then become *dynamic elements*.

Text elements bound, for update

Take a look at Figure 5-2. It's part of an online form used to update a database used by vegetable gardeners. The whole point of an update operation is that it streams the data as it currently exists on to the page and gives a user the opportunity to change some of it. The user can then click a button and have the old data overwritten with the new data.

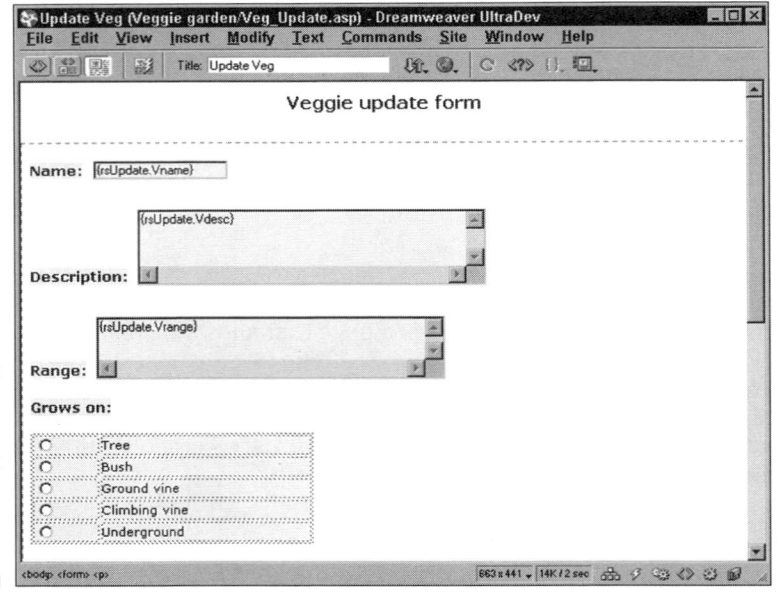

Figure 5-2: Design-time view of part of an Update page.

This is the design-time screen, not the browse-time view. Notice that the text boxes are filled with weird stuff like `{rsVegUpdate.Vname}`, `{rsVegUpdate.Vdesc}`, and so on. Although you can't see it in the black and white figure, the boxes are actually a pretty eggshell blue color.

This stuff isn't so weird when you think about it a bit. Fact is, the data is being grabbed from a recordset named `rsVegUpdate`, which has fields called Vname, Vdesc, and so on. The Name text box is bound to the Vname field, and the Description text box is bound to the Vdesc field. At browse-time, words like *beetroot* and *artichoke* are pulled from the recordset and appear in the text boxes in place of the field names. Here's how you make that data binding happen:

1. **Insert your recordset on the Update page.**

    You do this by clicking the plus (+) button in either the Data Bindings inspector or the Server Behaviors inspector and choosing Recordset from the pop-up menu. (You can find detailed instructions for creating and managing recordsets in Chapter 4.)

2. **Expand the recordset in the Data Bindings inspector so that you can see the actual fields that you need to bind (see Figure 5-3).**

    If the Data Bindings inspector isn't open, open it by clicking your Launcher or by pressing Ctrl+F10.

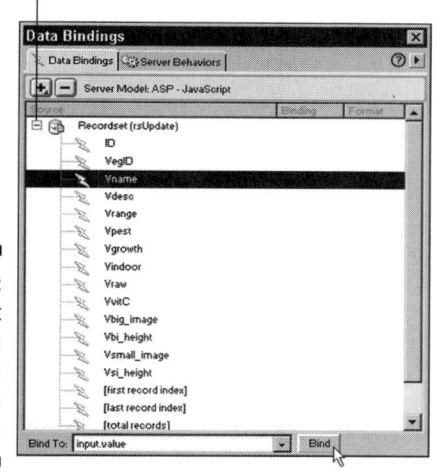

Figure 5-3: Recordset expanded in the Data Bindings inspector.

3. **On the Update page, select the first text box that you want to bind.**

    In my gardening example, it's the text box with the name of the vegetable.

4. **In the Data Bindings inspector, select the equivalent field and click the Bind button embedded in the lower margin of the inspector.**

    The placeholder text {rsVegUpdate.Vname} appears immediately in the text box.

    Note: The option that you can reach by clicking the plus (+) button in the Server Behaviors inspector and choosing Dynamic Elements⇨ Dynamic Text is *not* appropriate for this operation. Using this option replaces your text box with a text string — not what you want. You can use the Server Behaviors Dynamic Elements⇨Dynamic Text Field command, but using the Data Bindings inspector procedure described here is faster.

   5. **Repeat Steps 3 and 4 to continue binding all needed text boxes to their respective recordset fields.**

      Multiline text boxes are treated exactly the same — even password boxes, although the data ends up being shown as a row of asterisks on screen.

Text elements unbound, for insert

Take a look at Figure 5-4. It's part of an online form designed to insert a fresh record into a vegetable gardener's database — somebody needs to add a new fruit or vegetable plant to the collection.

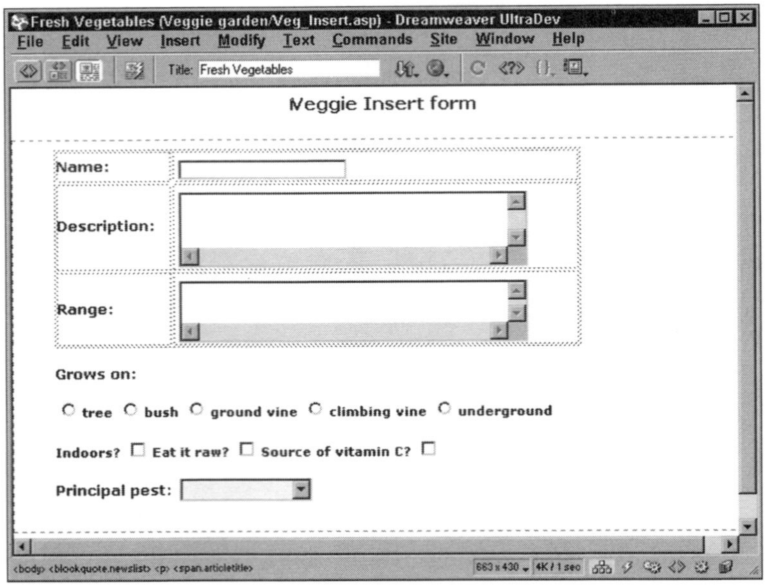

Figure 5-4: Time to add a new veggie — no data binding required.

In this case, no data binding to a master veggie recordset is required because the text boxes and other form elements are presented empty and waiting for fresh stuff, rather than filled with existing stuff that may not need to be changed much. That's the difference between *update* and *insert,* and in the "Insert (New Stuff) and Update (Old Stuff)" section later in this chapter, I lead you through the dialog boxes that UltraDev provides for completing the update and insert operations.

> **TIP:** On both Update and Insert pages, it's a good idea to give all your form elements the same names as the data fields they bind to. It isn't obligatory, but in the "Insert (New Stuff) and Update (Old Stuff)" section, it becomes obvious why this is recommendable.

Dynamic check boxes

Check boxes, as surely even your Great Aunt Bertha knows by now, are good for storing and displaying information that is binary — also known as On/Off, Yes/No, Y/N, 1/0, or even -1/0. In programming lingo, anything with only two possibilities is referred to as *binary*.

The veggie database example could include several binary fields, represented by check boxes, in the online forms for updating and inserting data. Here are a few possible binary fields:

- Can it be grown indoors?
- Can it be eaten raw?
- Does it contain Vitamin C?

Just as with a text element (text box), a check box on an Insert page doesn't need to be connected to the data until the time comes to submit the form. On an Update page, however, you really want all your check boxes to come up checked or unchecked according to the information in the database for the current record. If whoever made the database thinks pumpkins can be grown indoors, the Indoors? check box should appear checked when you bring the pumpkin record into the browser window for update. In that particular case, updating the data would be a very good idea!

Here's how to bind a check box on an update page to a binary data field in a recordset:

1. **If there's more than one check box on your page, select the one that you want to bind to data.**
2. **Open the Server Behaviors inspector and click the plus (+) button.**
3. **Choose Dynamic Elements⇨Dynamic Check Box.**

   The small dialog box shown in Figure 5-5 opens.

   The check box that you're dealing with should be correctly identified in the Check Box drop-down list. It's conceivable but very unlikely that you may need to select a different line.

4. **Click the lightning-bolt icon to the right of the Check If text box.**

   The Dynamic Data dialog box shown in Figure 5-6 opens. This dialog box is common to all the Dynamic Elements behaviors.

Part II: Bringing Data to Your Pages

Figure 5-5:
The Dynamic Check Box dialog box.

Figure 5-6:
The Dynamic Data dialog box that all Dynamic Element behaviors share.

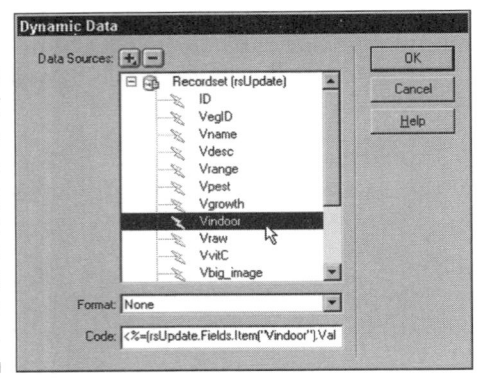

5. **Expand the recordset in the main window and scroll (if necessary) so that you can select the field that you need to bind to the check box.**

   The inline code appropriate to your server model appears in the Code text box down at the bottom. There's no conceivable use for formatting options for a check box, so ignore that drop-down list.

6. **Click OK to close this dialog box and return to the Dynamic Check Box dialog box.**

   All it needs you to tell it are the circumstances under which you want this check box to be checked.

7. **Type the word true in the Equal To text box and click OK.**

Now on the Update page the check box will be checked if the data field the check box is bound to is On, Yes, 1, or true.

WARNING! Here's an example of when you need to know about the underlying database: Check box binding won't be successful unless the field that you bind to is defined as binary. If there's any doubt, close UltraDev and go look at the actual database in its native application. If that field is simply a text field hoping to be fed either a Y or an N, it's not qualified for binding to a check box.

Making radio buttons dynamic

Your Great Aunt Bertha may be a little hazy about the function of radio buttons and how they differ from check boxes, but I'm sure you know. Chant it together. Yes or no: Check box. One choice from many: Radio buttons.

In HTML, form input elements of the radio type are grouped together by having the same name but different values. You can have as many as you like in a group, but only the value of the unique selected radio button is inserted into the data stream when the form's submitted. Figure 5-7 is a pretty good guide as to how to use the Property inspectors for a set of radio buttons to set them up as a group. To insert the actual button on your form, fetch it from the Forms panel of the Objects palette.

Figure 5-7: A set of radio buttons and one Property inspector.

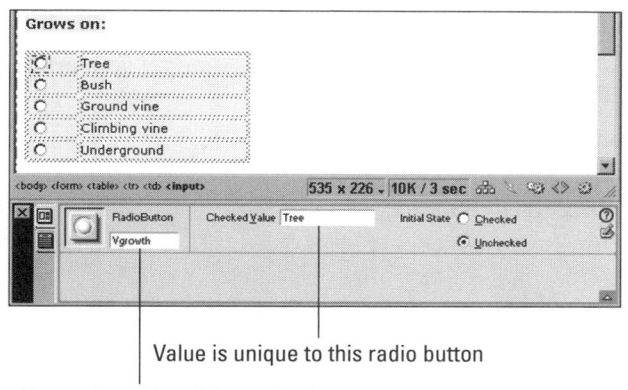

Value is unique to this radio button
Name shared by all five radio buttons

The set of radio buttons shown in Figure 5-7 deals with the type of plant each veggie in the database grows on. The name of the corresponding data field is $Vgrowth$, and its five possible values are Tree, Bush, Ground vine, Climbing vine, and Underground.

It's up to you to set up your radio button groups correctly by using their Property inspectors. But after you've done that, UltraDev is very clever at helping you to bind them to the data. Here's how:

1. **In the Server Behaviors inspector, click the plus (+) button and choose Dynamic Elements⇨Dynamic Radio Buttons from the pop-up menu.**

    The Dynamic Radio Buttons dialog shown in Figure 5-8 opens. You probably don't need to change any of the boxes. Just take a look to see that UltraDev has correctly identified all the members of the radio button set (if not, you may have made a typo in one of their Property inspectors). You can change the value of any button, if need be, by using the Value text box.

Figure 5-8: The Dynamic Radio Buttons dialog box.

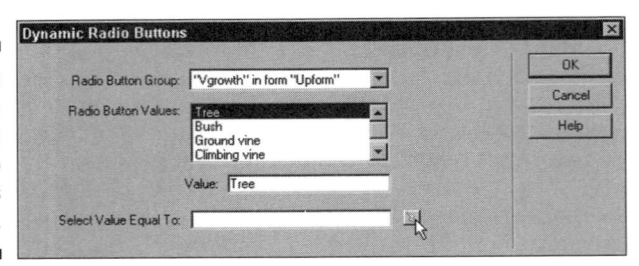

2. **Click the lightning-bolt icon to the right of the Select Value Equal To text box.**

   The Dynamic Data dialog box opens.

3. **Expand the recordset in the main window and scroll (if necessary) so that you can select the field that you need to bind to the radio button set.**

   The inline code appropriate to your server model appears in the Code text box down at the bottom.

4. **Close both dialog boxes.**

   Now, when this page is published, the radio button set will reflect the value in the current data record.

Dynamic list and menu elements

Lists and menus are extremely common in online forms. You might say that they pop up everywhere, har har. The official HTML tag for a list is <SELECT>; so many people in the biz refer to them as *select* lists. The attributes SIZE and MULTIPLE turn a list into a multi-select list. To Dreamweaver and UltraDev, an ordinary select list is a menu, and a multi-select list is a list. Take it or leave it.

Suppose that one field of a vegetable gardening database contains the most common pest that growers of this veggie need to defend against. Well, there are way more pests than a set of radio buttons could conveniently cope with. My goodness — aphids, slugs, snails, caterpillars, borers, beetles, weevils, leafhoppers . . . I can hardly bear to continue.

For such choices, a menu is what you need. On both Insert and Update pages, it's common to have the menu made up — *populated,* in the jargon — from a data table. On an Update page, the list has to be bound to the main data table so that when it appears, it's set with the appropriate item selected. On an Insert page, the equivalent list wouldn't need to be pre-selected at all.

When the form's submitted, a list or menu element doesn't necessarily submit the content the user actually sees. It submits a list *value,* which defaults to the same as the content but which is commonly just a boring old number. This makes sense — in the example I'm suggesting here, the master data table of veggie facts and the subsidiary data table of creepy-crawlies are *relational,* meaning that a complete picture of the data can be obtained only by relating one to another.

Although a human user needs to see an understandable (if, in this case, gruesome) word, a database management system is far happier with a number — so a relationship between the labels and values of a menu is established, as shown in Table 5-1.

Table 5-1   Labels and Values of a Typical Menu Element

Label (PestName)	*Value (PestID)*
Aphids	1
Beetles	2
Borers	3
Cabbage worms	4
Caterpillars	5
Hornworms	6
Leafhoppers	7
Leaf miners	8
Maggots	9
Slugs	10
Snails	11
Weevils	12

The master data table and the subsidiary pest data table are connected by the PestID, not by the more verbose PestName. So successful management of a list element requires you to consider two things: populating it and binding it to data. UltraDev's Dynamic List/Menu dialog box takes care of both. Here are the steps for managing a list element:

1. **Place a recordset on the page representing the data table from which the list will be populated (pests, in this example).**

   I'm assuming that you've also stuck in a master recordset representing the main data table. (Details for creating and managing recordsets are in Chapter 4.)

2. **From the Forms panel of the Objects palette, deploy a list element on the page wherever you need it.**

 3. **In the Server Behaviors inspector, click the plus (+) button and choose Dynamic Elements**⇨**Dynamic List/Menu from the pop-up menu.**

    The Dynamic List/Menu dialog box opens.

 4. **In the Recordset drop-down list, select the recordset from which the menu will be populated.**

    In the example, it's rsPests, the pest list in Table 5-1.

 5. **Choose the sources of labels and values independently by using the Get Labels From and Get Values From drop-down lists.**

    In the example, the labels come from the PestName field and the values from the PestID field.

 6. **Click the lightning-bolt icon to the right of the Select Value Equal To text box.**

    The Dynamic Data dialog box opens.

 7. **Expand the main recordset and scroll (if necessary) so that you can select the field that you need to bind to the list (Vpest in this example).**

    The inline code appropriate to your server model appears in the Code text box down at the bottom. Now when this page is published, the list will reflect the value in the current data record. Figure 5-9 shows this dialog box in its finished state.

Figure 5-9: The completed Dynamic List/Menu dialog box.

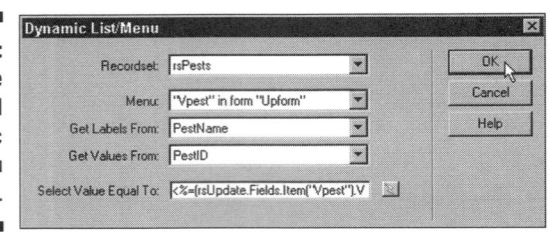

TIP: If you need to add a so-called *static option* to the top of a menu on an Insert page — an extra line with the words "Please make a selection," for example — you can do that by first populating the menu from a recordset, and then clicking the List Values button in the menu's Property inspector and manually adding that line. You can move it to the top using the little up-arrow button.

In data-driven pages, the value given to the static option is normally 0, and form validation routines can be imposed to inhibit form submit if the user has made no selection. Databases tend to go into a sulk if fed unexpected zeros.

Hidden form fields

Hidden form fields convey data without the user of the page being aware of them (unless the user is a nosy type, in the habit of inspecting source code). They're often used to pass data from page to page, or to provide a value to a recordset that's not under the user's control.

When you place a hidden form field on a page, a little *H* icon appears on the design-time page so that you can get a hold of it to inspect and modify its properties. You can select a hidden form field icon and bind it to data just like you bind a text box.

UltraDev operates in two modes where hidden things are concerned. It calls them *invisible elements,* and they can either be seen or not seen. To toggle invisible elements on and off, choose View⇨Visual Aids⇨Invisible Elements or choose the equivalent command starting from the View Options button on the toolbar.

Insert (New Stuff) and Update (Old Stuff)

UltraDev expects you to create Update and Insert pages using whatever form elements are appropriate to your data and then apply the Update Record or Insert Record server behavior to actually do the heavy lifting.

The dialog boxes that UltraDev provides for inserting or updating a data table are very similar. Here's a handy summary of the differences between an Insert and Update page:

- You use an Insert page to create a completely fresh record; an Update page displays an existing record for revision.

- An Update page needs a recordset representing the main underlying data table; an Insert page does not.

- On an Update page, each form element is bound to one field in the recordset; on an Insert page, the form elements are free.

- List elements on Insert pages often have static options; on Update pages they don't need them.

- On Update pages, radio button sets are checked appropriately; on Insert pages, the first button of the set is designated as checked to make it impossible for the user to submit the form without any being checked.

Hand-crafting the Insert/Update server behaviors

Figure 5-10 shows the Update Record dialog box for an imaginary Veggie-facts Web page. This and the Insert Record dialog box are invoked by clicking the plus button in the Server Behaviors inspector and then making the appropriate choice from the pop-up menu.

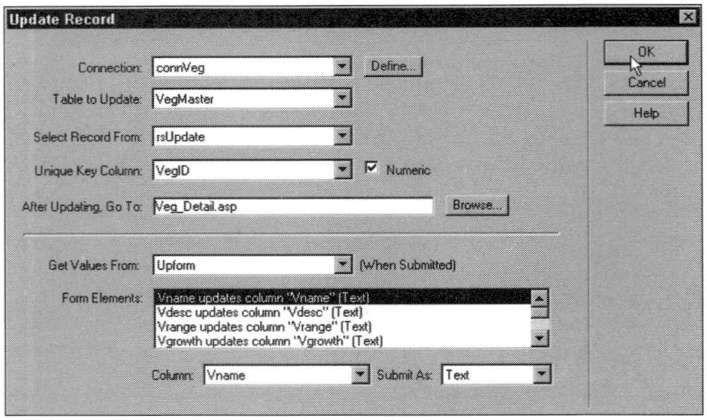

Figure 5-10:
The Update Record dialog box, which matches form elements and data fields.

You don't need to select any particular element on the page to invoke the Update Record or Insert Record dialog box: The philosophy of the Insert/Update behaviors is that they depend on submission of a form, and there's normally only one form on a page. In cases where you have more than one form on the page (as is the case when a page has both update and delete options), you can still select the correct one in the dialog box.

The main task in the Update Record dialog box is to select which form elements on the page correspond to which fields of the data table — and you may notice that it's a good idea to give your form elements the same names as the data fields they correspond to. If the names match, UltraDev basically does all the work for you. If the names are different, you have to select each form element in the Form Elements option list, one by one, and then scroll through the Column drop-down list to select the appropriate fieldname. Because of the way both the Form Elements and Column lists return to the top after every selection, this process can be *very* tedious.

To the right of the Column drop-down list in the Update Record dialog box is another drop-down list labeled Submit As. From this list, you may have to choose a data format for a column, even though the basic matchup of form element to data field has been done for you. Here are the types of formats from which you can choose:

Chapter 5: Making Server Behaviors Work for You

- ✔ Text
- ✔ Numeric
- ✔ Date
- ✔ Date MS Access
- ✔ Checkbox Y,N
- ✔ Checkbox 1,0
- ✔ Checkbox -1,0

The format of each field has to correspond with whatever format is defined within the database itself, or you'll soon be gazing at cryptic error messages.

TIP

Correct choice of the three possible check box data formats is imperative, or the data bind will not be successful. The best way to find out what your database is expecting in the way of a binary format is to click the Test button in a recordset dialog box and take a look at that column. The Test button is a quick and efficient way to examine all the data the recordset represents.

A browse-time view of the veggie Update page is shown in Figure 5-11. It shows the various types of form elements displaying current data.

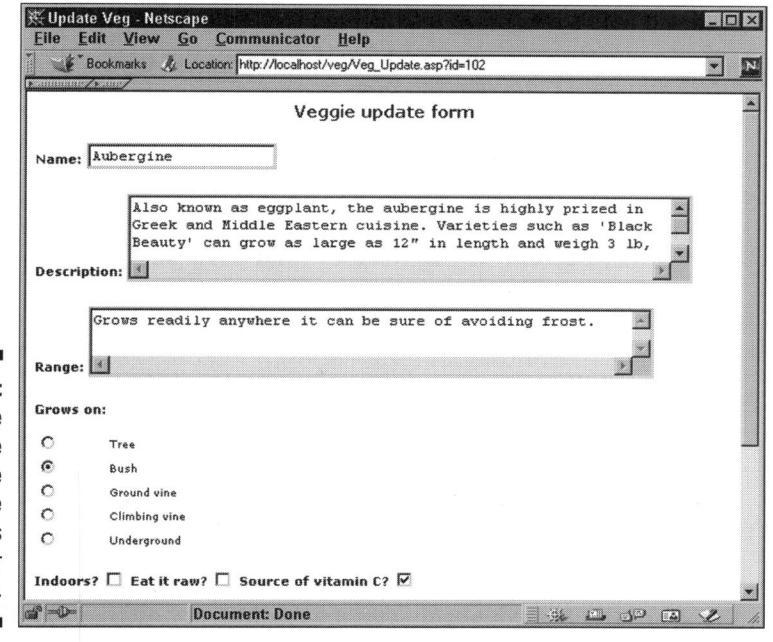

Figure 5-11: An Update page in the veggie database example, as the end user will see it.

An Insert page working with the same database would probably look very similar, and the Insert Record dialog box is like Figure 5-10 but without the recordset information.

Live objects short cuts

Click the header of UltraDev's Objects palette and the menu that pops up displays a class of objects called *Live*. Hmmm, does that mean that the others are all dead? Or prerecorded for your viewing pleasure?

Neither, actually. Live objects are prepackaged combinations of server objects and design tasks that Macromedia thinks are so commonplace that you may want to use them generically.

The Record Insertion Form and the Record Update Form Live objects open dialog boxes having some features in common with the Record Insert and Record Update dialog boxes described in the preceding section. But these Live objects do more. They actually design the page for you as well — so not surprisingly, the dialog boxes are a lot more complex.

To make use of one of these Live objects, follow these steps:

1. **Make a new page (press Control+N). Give it a name, and save it.**

2. **If this is an Update page, put a recordset on the page representing the data table that you need to update.**

    If it's an Insert page, you don't need a recordset for the data table that you're updating. You do, however, need a data connection.

3. **If you intend to create any menus or radio button groups as part of the page, and populate them from recordsets, make or copy over any subsidiary recordsets you need for that purpose.**

    In the example, a menu is needed for the list of pests, just as I describe in the "Dynamic list and menu elements" section earlier in this chapter. I call the pest recordset rsPests.

4. **Click the Live object that you need in the Live panel of the Objects palette.**

    The appropriate dialog box opens, either Record Insertion Form or Record Update Form.

5. **Set the top two drop-down lists to the appropriate data connection and update table.**

    In the example, my data connection is connVeg and the main data table is VegMaster.

6. **If this is the Record Insertion Form dialog box, set the Select Record From drop-down list to the main recordset and check that the Unique Key Column box defaults correctly.**

   A unique key column is a field in the data table that's guaranteed to be different in every record.

7. **Click the Browse button and browse to find and insert the redirect page.**

8. **Now take a look at the lower panel of this dialog box.**

   The main window is a list of all the fields in the data table that you're updating or inserting, with these features:

   - You can delete any fields that are not needed on the page using the minus button. The VegMaster table has an auto-number field, for example, which *must not* be made available for editing.

   - You can reinstate deleted fields using the plus (+) button.

   - You can change the order of fields by selecting one you want to move and using the up and down arrow buttons.

   - In the list, each field has columns for Column name, Label (this is the text of the label that will appear on the page), Display As (this is the type of form element that you want to put the field in) and Submit As (this is the data format, which you won't usually need to edit).

   - When you select a field, its properties are available for editing. The Label appears in a text box, Display As and Submit As appear in drop-down lists, and a Default Value appears in a dynamic text box (meaning a text box with a lightning bolt to access the Dynamic Data dialog box). On an Update page the default value is the value of that field in the main recordset. On an Insert page there's normally no default value.

9. **Work carefully down the list, editing the page labels and setting up the form elements that you need.**

   In the VegMaster example, I had to edit all the page labels and select several different form elements.

   - If you choose a Text Field, you'll get a text box 32 characters wide.

   - If you choose a Text Area, you'll get a multiline text box 50 characters wide and 5 lines high. The VegMaster data table needed a couple of these.

   - If you choose a Menu, click the Menu Properties button that then appears and set up your menu list in a dialog box similar to the Dynamic List/Menu dialog box. Figure 5-12 shows this dialog box as I set it for the pests' menu. Note that you can make up the list of labels and values manually if you like, or if no recordset is available.

Figure 5-12: Menu Properties dialog box used within the Record Update Form and Record Insert Form Live objects.

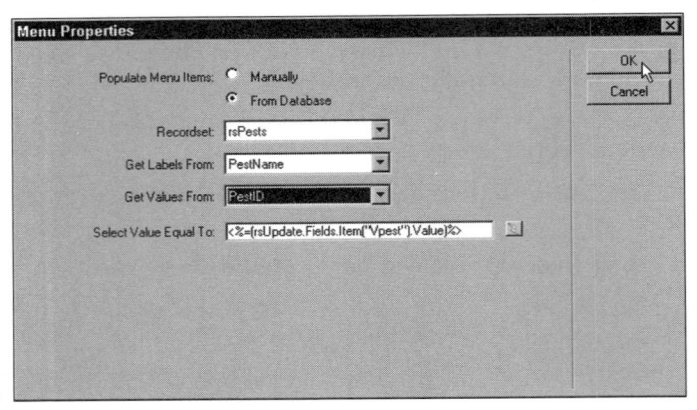

- Check boxes are automatically assigned to binary fields.
- If you choose a Radio Group, click the Radio Group Properties button that then appears and set up your group of radio buttons in a dialog box similar to the Dynamic Radio Buttons dialog box. Figure 5-13 shows this dialog box as I set it, manually, for the Vgrowth field. The labels will appear on the page; the values will end up in the database (in this case they're the same but often they would not be). Note that you can configure a radio group from a recordset if you have a suitable one.

Figure 5-13: Radio Group Properties dialog box used within the Record Update Form and Record Insert Form Live objects.

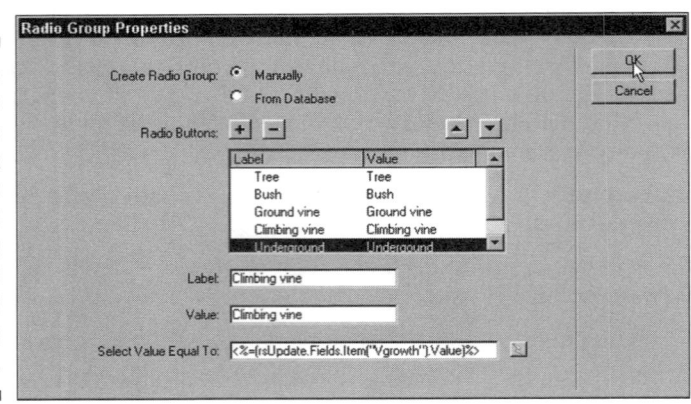

- If you choose Text, the field will not be editable at all but will appear on the page for information only as ordinary text.

Figure 5-14 shows the complete Insert Record Update Form dialog box.

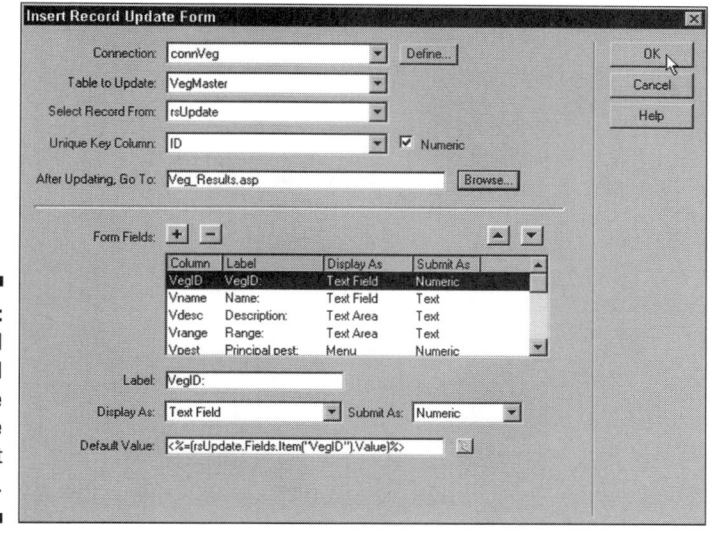

Figure 5-14:
Completed Record Update Form Live object dialog box.

> On no account should you press your Enter key until you've completely finished. If you do, it will prematurely close this complex dialog box. Unlike most of UltraDev's dialog boxes, these big Live object dialog boxes cannot be recalled later for editing. Only the Update Record or Insert Record dialog box can be recalled.

When you click OK, the server behavior is applied and a basic tabular form is automatically generated.

Figure 5-15 shows an Update page made with the Record Update Form Live object (after I compressed things a bit to fit more into the figure). Compare it with Figure 5-11, and see that it's a pretty good start. If you use one of these Live objects, you'll no doubt have a few ideas about enhancing the page design.

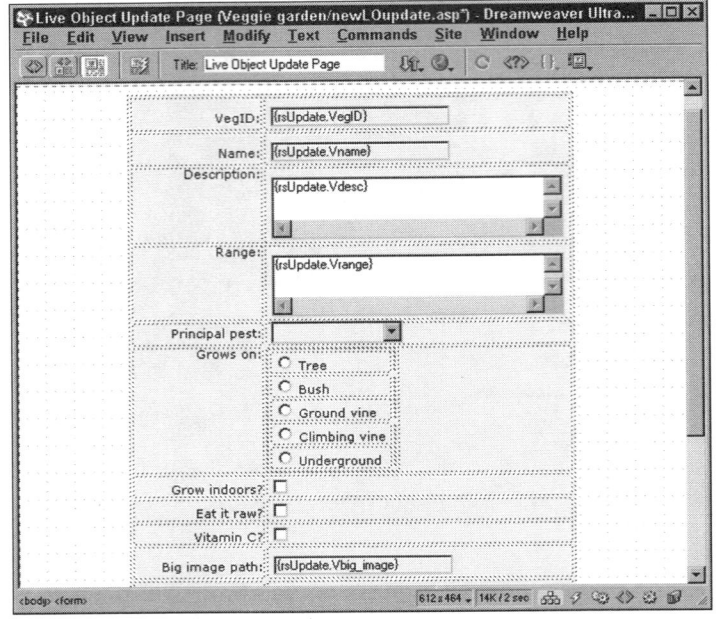

Figure 5-15: An Update page from the veggie database made with the Record Update Form Live object.

Making a Repeat Region

You often need to display more than one data record on a page — or more often, just bits and pieces of more than one data record. These multiple records are displayed in parts of the page that automatically repeat as many times as necessary. They're called *repeat regions* and they're often used on a Results page. Simple data-driven Web sites get away with just letting users browse through the Detail pages; but full-service sites allow users to search the data and then provide the results of the search on a *Results page*. "Show me all veggies I can grow indoors" or "Show me all veggies that can grow in Florida AND that can be eaten raw" are hypothetical search criteria. I cover search strategy in Chapter 4 — all I'm concerned with here is showing you how to use server behaviors to make an intelligent Results page.

A Results page is normally neither a set of complete Detail pages nor a simple list of veggies that meet the criteria, but something in between. Figure 5-16 shows an example of a Results page showing just enough data for the user to know whether he or she wants to see more info about one item.

In the figure you can see that just the name and description of each item in the database are listed. Much more information could be displayed by clicking the name, and the next group of four items can be displayed by clicking the Next button.

Chapter 5: Making Server Behaviors Work for You   121

Hyperlinks to Detail page

Figure 5-16: Browse-time view of a Results page showing four results.

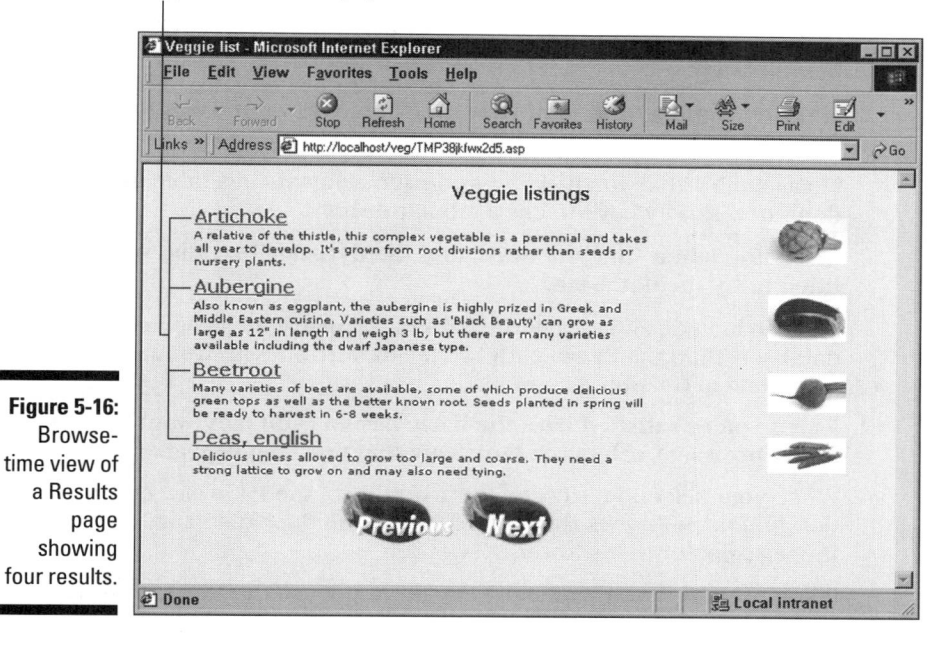

Figure 5-17 is the design-time view of the page shown in Figure 5-16, and you can just see the little gray `Repeat` flag indicating a repeat region.

Repeat region flag

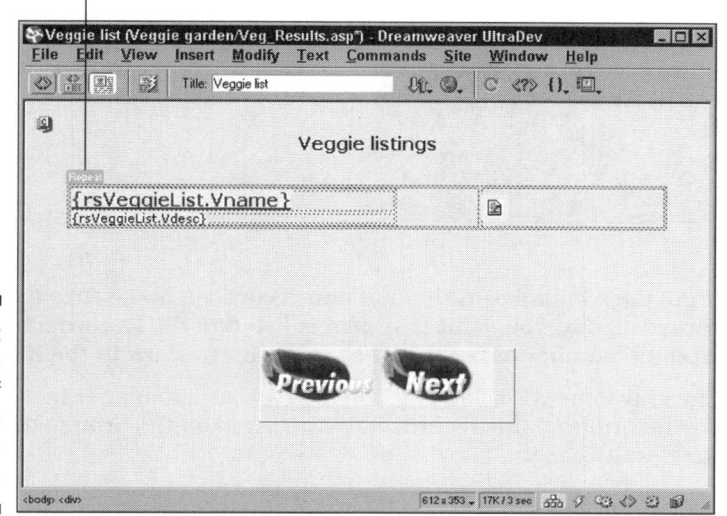

Figure 5-17: Design-time view of the page shown in Figure 5-16.

This is how you arrange for several records to appear on each Results page:

1. **Create or copy the recordset that you'll need to display live data at browse time.**

2. **Make a complete design of whatever data you want users to see on the Results page.**

   I'm assuming that you have these design elements in a table, but you don't necessarily have to use a tabular design.

3. **Insert the labels that you need, and the dynamic text that will be filled in by the database.**

   You can include an image if the path to the image file is defined in the database. Bind the image path to the SRC attribute of the image, as described in Chapter 4.

4. **When you're satisfied with the basic design (you may want to preview it in a browser), select the table row that needs to repeat.**

   When your selection is correct, the outline of the table row on the design-time page goes thick and dark, and so does the <table> tag in the tag selector in the lower-left border.

   If your design doesn't include a table, simply use the marquee-select technique to select all the text fields in the region that you want to repeat. You marquee-select a group of fields by clicking somewhere just outside the group and then holding down the mouse button as you sweep out a rectangle containing all items that you want to select.

5. **In the Server Behaviors inspector, click the plus (+) button and choose Repeat Region (it's the first item on the list of server behaviors).**

   The Repeat Region dialog box shown in Figure 5-18 opens.

Figure 5-18: The Repeat Region dialog box.

6. **If the page includes more than one recordset, make sure that the recordset that you want to repeat is listed in the Recordset box; then type the number of records that you want to show in the Records box.**

   The gray Repeat flag appears on the page as a reminder that more than one record from this recordset will be listed on the browse-time view of the Results page.

That's all there is to it.

Chapter 5: Making Server Behaviors Work for You   **123**

Linking to a Detail Page

Typically, a Results page looks up several records in a data table and only displays enough for the user to know whether an item is worth looking at further. So an important component of a Results page is a hyperlink that the user can click to see more detail of one data record — everything there is to know about rutabagas, for instance. The hyperlink source is usually the name of the thing.

So the data management problem is to know which record is being clicked and then to carry over a unique identifier of that record to the next page — the *Detail page* — so that the recordset on that page can be filtered accordingly. That's exactly what UltraDev's Go To Detail Page makes possible.

Setting up the hyperlink source

Here's how to apply the Go To Detail Page server behavior:

1. **In the document window, select the text (or image) that you want to use as the source of the hyperlink that's linking to the Detail page.**

   In the veggie database example, that's the dynamic text representing the veggie name.

2. **In the Server Behaviors inspector, click the plus (+) button and choose Go To Detail Page from the pop-up menu.**

   The Go To Detail Page dialog box opens.

3. **Examine the Link box to see that it shows the correct link.**

   You'll likely see a server expression, which overflows the width of the box. In Figure 5-16 it's just that, but I can see it's correct because it includes the Vname field value from my recordset.

4. **Click the Browse button to find the Detail page that will be the hyperlink destination.**

   Now look carefully at the Recordset and Column drop-down lists. They should show the master recordset that contains the data to be used on the Detail page and the field in that recordset, which is a unique identifier (key field) of the record to be displayed.

5. **Choose a label to enter in the Pass URL Parameter text box.**

   It defaults to the same as the Column drop-down list, but I usually change it to the simpler *id*.

   In most cases, the check boxes for passing existing URL and form parameters should be left unchecked. You could use these if, for example, you didn't want to lose some original search criteria.

124 Part II: Bringing Data to Your Pages

Figure 5-19 shows the completed Go To Detail Page dialog box.

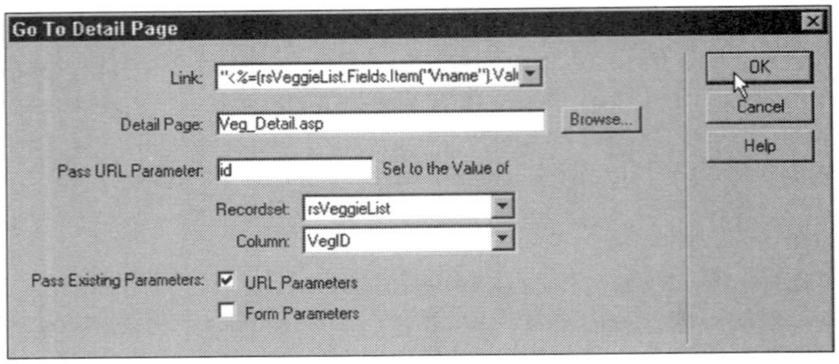

Figure 5-19:
The Go To Detail Page dialog box completed for the Veggie list.

What happens on the other side?

After setting up the hyperlink source, you've still only solved half the problem. Now you have to find some way of using that parameter id to ensure the correct record is displayed on the Detail page. Fortunately, that's pretty easy.

Figure 5-20 is a reminder of the Recordset Builder that's discussed in detail in Chapter 4. The four Filter boxes are there to enable you to do what's needed — pick up the incoming parameter that was sent over from the Results page and use it to display the right record.

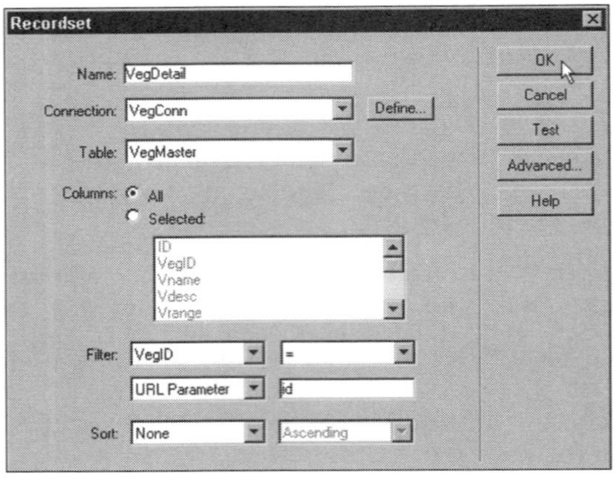

Figure 5-20:
A Recordset Builder with filtering imposed.

Design your Detail page with a recordset using data bindings to create all the dynamic text that you need (and very likely a pretty picture as well). Then open the recordset builder in its simple mode, and do this:

1. **In the lower-right Filter box, type the incoming parameter — id, in this example.**

   UltraDev is pretty clever with parameters, so it may well be there by default.

2. **Set the upper-left drop-down list to the recordset field that must match the id.**

   Select VegID, in this example.

3. **Make sure that the lower-left drop-down list is set to URL Parameter (also known as a *query string*).**

   This is how the parameter is exchanged between the two pages. Notice that you can filter recordsets by many other parameter types, including cookies.

4. **Set the upper-right Filter drop-down list to = for a Detail page.**

After completing these steps, try transferring the Results page and the Detail page to the server and giving them a thorough test run! The Results page will work perfectly okay whether or not it's filtered by search criteria.

> **WARNING!** The filtering procedure described here is only available for recordsets that use the Simple mode of the Recordset Builder — recordsets based on a single data table, in other words. This method also risks conflicting with navigation behaviors on the Detail page.

For filtering a Detail page that has to use the Advanced mode of the Recordset Builder, you have two choices:

- Use the Move to Specific Record server behavior
- Filter with a Request variable (as described in Chapter 8)

I recommend the Move to Specific Record behavior if there are also navigation behaviors on the Detail page.

Doing it on autopilot with a Live object

UltraDev has a Live object that not only applies the link from a Results page to a Detail page, but designs both pages for you, including (on the Results page only) navigation behaviors and signposts. It's clever, quick, and crude. Here's how you use it:

1. **Make a new page (press Control+N) for the Results page. Give it a name, and save it.**

   If you like, you can also make a new page for the Detail page as well — but it isn't required. UltraDev creates it for you if it doesn't exist.

2. **On the Results page, make or copy a recordset representing the data you want to present on these pages.**

 3. **Click the header of the Objects palette and select Live from the pop-up menu.**

 4. **Locate and click the Live object called Master-Detail Page Set.**

    It's at the top-left corner of the panel. The Insert Master-Detail Page set dialog box appears with selection panels allowing you to specify which data fields you want to display on both pages and how you want the two pages to communicate. The upper half of the dialog box is concerned with the Master page — this is what I've called the Results page — and the lower half with the Detail page.

 5. **Use the Master Page Fields plus, minus, up, and down buttons to select and order the list of fields that you want to display on the page.**

    UltraDev starts off showing you the complete list of fields, and it's up to you to whittle it down. Normally the list is greatly reduced for this type of data page.

 6. **Set the Link To Detail From drop-down list to the field that you want to make into a hyperlink whose destination is the Detail page.**

    Normally, this is the main name of whatever you have in the recordset — rutabaga, perhaps, in the example.

 7. **Set the Pass Unique Key drop-down list to the data field that's guaranteed to be unique in every record.**

    This data field is known as the *key field*. If your data table doesn't have one, the table needs to be redesigned.

 8. **Set the radio buttons and text field underneath to show as many records as you want on the Master page — up to all fields.**

 9. **If you've already created a page for the Detail page, click the Browse button and locate it. If you haven't created a page, type the name that you want for this page in the Detail Page Name text box and UltraDev creates a page on the fly.**

10. **Use the Detail Page Fields plus, minus, up, and down buttons to select and order the list of fields that you want to display on the page.**

    Figure 5-21 shows a complete Insert Master-Detail Page Set dialog box. Figures 5-22 and 5-23 show the resulting Master and Detail pages.

Figure 5-21:
The Master-Detail Page Set dialog box.

Figure 5-22:
A Master page created by the Live object.

It goes without saying that quite a bit of extra design work needs to be accomplished to make these pages presentable.

> **WARNING!** This complex procedure actually creates 13 separate server behaviors plus some data bindings on the Master page, a recordset and many data bindings on the Detail page — not to mention the page itself. You cannot retrieve this dialog box later for editing. Edits have to be carried out on the individual server behaviors.

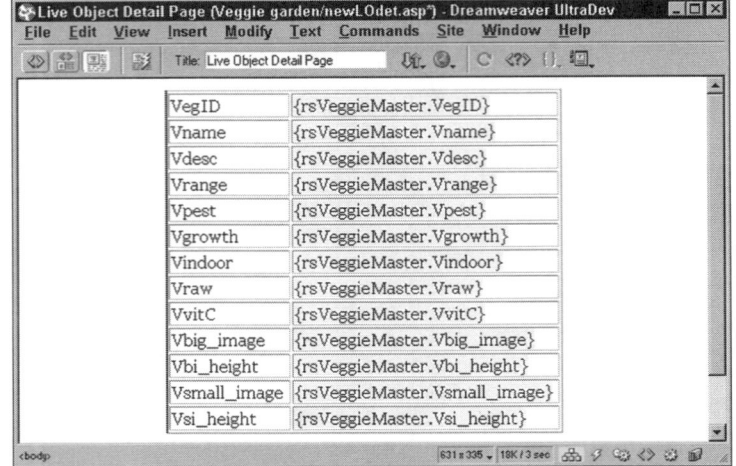

Figure 5-23: A Detail page created by the Live object.

Using Server Behaviors for Navigation

Whether you want to allow your site users to conduct simple searches, complex searches, start from Results pages, or just browse Detail pages, you're going to need navigation. At a minimum, you need some text saying "Go to next veggie" or whatever. But these days, Web designers love to make pretty arrays of mouseover buttons for complex navigation. UltraDev provides the logic that makes those pretty arrays do something useful.

Moving around the recordset, one behavior at a time

Figure 5-24 shows a whimsical set of buttons somebody made for me to navigate around a set of Detail pages (wish you could see the mouseover effects — they're awesome).

Here's how to activate a navigation button using server behaviors:

1. **Select the button in the document window.**

2. **In the Server Behaviors inspector, click the plus (+) button and choose Move To Record from the pop-up menu.**

3. **Now choose whichever movement is appropriate for this button in the submenu.**

   The dialog box that pops into view is very simple and its defaults are almost always correct.

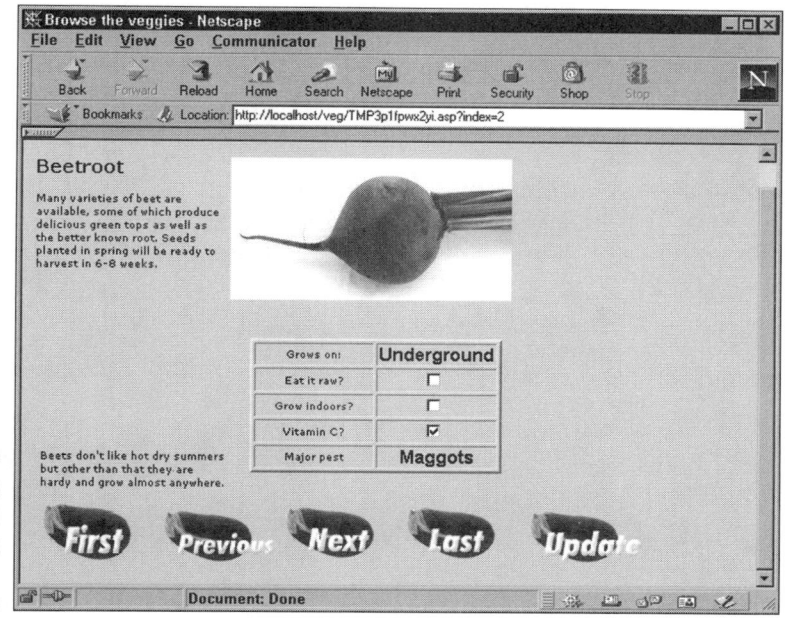

Chapter 5: Making Server Behaviors Work for You   *129*

Figure 5-24: Navigation by eggplant — nice!

Instant navigation with a Live object

If you don't have whimsical artwork like aubergine-shaped navigation buttons, and you just want quick and dirty First/Previous/Next/Last navigation options, the Recordset Navigation Bar Live object is your friend. It comes in two flavors — text and images, and here's how to deploy it (I'm assuming the page is already equipped with a recordset):

1. **In the document window, place your cursor where you want the navigation behaviors.**

   I recommend placing them on a layer.

2. **Click the header of the Objects palette and select Live from the pop-up menu.**

3. **Locate and click the Live object called Recordset Navigation Bar.**

   The Recordset Navigation Bar dialog box opens.

4. **Use the radio buttons to select whether you want Text-style navigation or Images.**

   The navigation bar drops on to your page fully functional, with a complete set of eight server behaviors — four Move To Record behaviors, and four Show If behaviors (see the "Hide-and-seek buttons" section later in this chapter).

Figures 5-25 and 5-26 show the browse-time appearance of the text and image instant navigation bars.

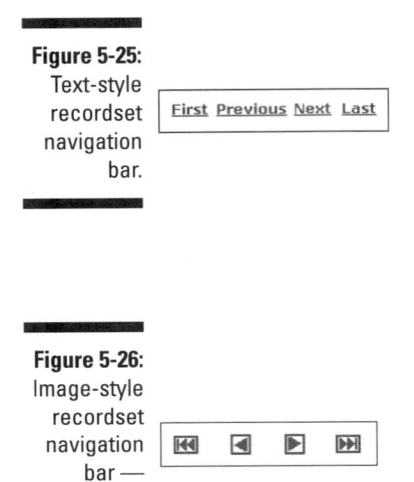

Figure 5-25: Text-style recordset navigation bar.

Figure 5-26: Image-style recordset navigation bar — remind you of anything?

> **WARNING!** If you have chosen an image-style navigation bar, you'll find four image files have been automatically added to your site folder — First.gif, Previous.gif, Next.gif, and Last.gif. In the Site window, select all four and transfer them to the server.

Record signposting

Have you noticed that when you expand a recordset in the Data Bindings inspector, you see three extra lines down at the bottom, beneath the field name list? They're labeled [first record index], [last record index], and [total records]. If you haven't, find a handy recordset and take a look now.

These numerical indices are there to help you make your data-driven pages user-friendly. Particularly when browsing through a larger set of pages, users love to know where they are in the whole scheme of things. Little signposts like "This is vegetable no. 16 of 44" make your users smile and walk with a spring in their step — and that's good.

Chapter 5: Making Server Behaviors Work for You   131

What do those indices mean? Well, [total records] should be obvious. As for [first record] and [last record], they refer to the first and last records *on this page*. So if you're *signposting* (it should really be called *indexing*) a Detail page with just one record per page, you can use first and last interchangeably.

UltraDev's most useful Live object takes all the drudgery out of record indexing. It's called the Recordset Navigation Status Live object, and it's so handy that you'd be insane to do your indexing any other way. Follow these steps and your page will be indexed in a jiff (I'm assuming that the page is already equipped with a recordset):

1. **In the document window, place your cursor where you want to place the indexing behaviors.**
2. **Click the header of the Objects palette and select Live from the pop-up menu.**
3. **Locate and click the Live object called Recordset Navigation Status.**

    A dialog box pops up just to check on the identity of the recordset. (I think Macromedia should inhibit this if there's only one recordset on the page. Maybe they will.)

    The indexing string deploys on to the page fully formed, and you can then select it and impose any text style on it you wish.

Figures 5-27 and 5-28 show the design-time and browse-time views of a signposted Results page.

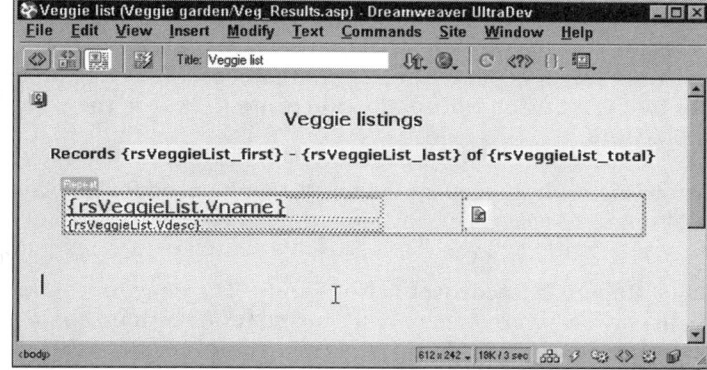

Figure 5-27: The Recordset Navigation Status Live object as it appears at design time.

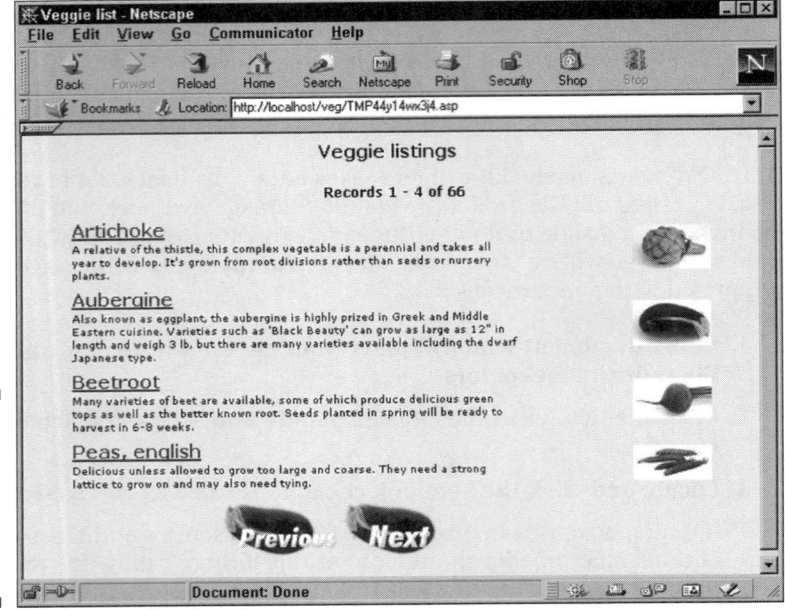

Figure 5-28: The page shown in Figure 5-27 at browse time.

Hide-and-seek buttons

Having meaningless buttons floating around on the page is considered poor Web page design. Two obvious examples of meaningless buttons are Go to First Record and Go to Previous Record if the dataset is already looking at the first record.

UltraDev offers a set of server behaviors that start Show Region If, which are great for hiding a button whose function is moot. Here is the complete set of these behaviors:

- **Show Region If Recordset Is Empty.** Can be used for displaying a layer containing a message saying something like `Sorry, no records matched your search criteria` if a search comes up empty.

- **Show Region If Recordset Is Not Empty.** The converse of the first, used to display search results only if a search does turn up some matching records.

- **Show Region If First Record.** In a hierarchical search, may be used to display a layer containing a message such as `These ten records best matched your search criteria.`

- **Show Region If Not First Record.** Apply this one to First and Previous buttons.

Chapter 5: Making Server Behaviors Work for You **133**

> ### Drummies, please don't panic
>
> Did you know I was a mind reader? No? Well I'm going to prove it. I know what you Drummies thought when you first opened UltraDev: "AAAaaaarrrgggghhhhhhhhh . . . WHERE'S THE INTERACTION CENTER????????"
>
> No, I'm not a genius; I just know it because I've been there. When you've gotten used to 400 or so contracts that handle problems from reading and writing server objects to DHTML effects and everything in between, it's not surprising that opening UltraDev for the first time gives you a severe case of separation anxiety.
>
> All I can say is, it's gone, it's history — get used to it. Learn to live with the 30-odd standard server behaviors that UltraDev supplies, plus the Live objects. Better still, take your bow and arrows into the deep dark forests of the Macromedia Exchange at `http://dynamic.macromedia.com/bin/MM/exchange/ultradev/main.jsp`, and see if you can bag a succulent young SBX or two. Chapter 9 is a guide to extending UltraDev, and Chapter 14 points out some of the tastiest game in the Macromedia forest.

- ✔ **Show Region If Last Record.** It's hard to know how to use this. Display of an animated message saying `That's All, Folks!` perhaps. . . .
- ✔ **Show Region If Not Last Record.** Apply this one to Next and Last buttons.

A *region* in this context can be anything — an image, a layer, a form element, a table row, even a selected piece of text.

The Show If Not First and Show If Not Last behaviors are built in to the Recordset Navigation Bar Live object; they come along as part of the kit and caboodle of that object (what's a *caboodle* anyway?). But if your page requires fancier navigation buttons than the built-in images (which remind me of a 1960s-era tape recorder console), you need to impose those behaviors individually.

Line your fancy-schmancy navigation buttons up in a row, First-Previous-Next-Last-Update, and proceed:

1. **Select the First button.**
2. **In the Server Behaviors inspector, click the plus (+) button and choose Show Region⇨Show Region If Not First Record from the pop-up menu.**

   A dialog box pops up just to check on the identity of the recordset.
3. **Repeat Steps 1 and 2 for the other three navigation buttons.**

TIP

The end result is more pleasing if you place navigation buttons in groups of two on layers and then apply the Show Region behaviors to the *layers* rather than the individual buttons. But why take all the trouble with layers, instead of hide-and-seeking the buttons themselves? The answer is that it ensures the buttons stay in the same place on the screen in all situations. If you apply the Show Region behavior to the buttons themselves, when the user navigates to the first record, the absence of the First and Previous buttons causes the remaining buttons to jump to the left — an effect I personally find annoying.

Drummies will recognize the hide-and-seek behaviors as another incarnation of a set of Drumbeat interactions that all began "Do not create if. . . ." Yes, it's the same idea.

Trash This!

UltraDev's Delete Record server behavior, like the Update and Insert behaviors, depends on submitting a form. If your data query is very simple, simply attaching a form and delete button to your Detail page works just fine.

More commonly, though, a complete Detail page brings in data from more than one table. In that situation, the delete function isn't allowed by the rules of the underlying database. Personally, I don't see the point of creating a special page for the delete function — I invariably add it to the Update page, like this:

1. **Complete the Update page as described in the "Insert (New Stuff) and Update (Old Stuff)" section earlier in this chapter.**

   At the very bottom of the design-time page, you see the end delimiter of the Update form. It's a broken red line stretching the entire width of the page. You may need to turn on invisible elements to see this. Use the View Options button on the toolbar and choose Visual Aids⇔Invisible Elements.

2. **Place your cursor beneath this line — in other words, outside the form.**

3. **Open the Forms panel of the Objects palette and insert a second form on the page.**

   The icon for a new form is usually in the top-left portion of the palette.

4. **In the Form's Property inspector, give the form a name (DelForm, for example).**

   You don't need an ACTION attribute. The method can default to POST.

5. **With your cursor between the upper and lower delimiters of the new form, click the Button icon on the Forms panel of the Objects palette.**

Chapter 5: Making Server Behaviors Work for You   **135**

6. **Name the button something suitable and give it a nice label** (Trash This Veggie!, **for example).**

    The Property inspector and part of the layout at this point are shown in Figure 5-29.

Figure 5-29: The Property inspector of a Delete button should look something like this.

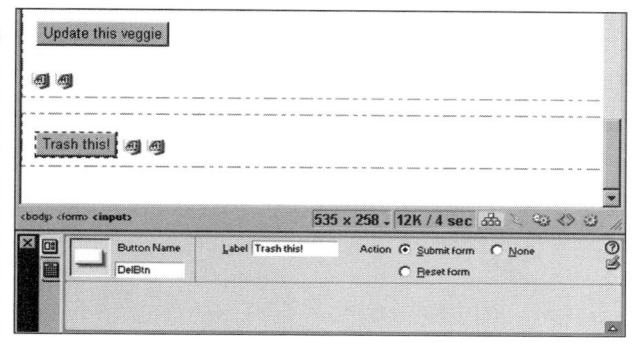

7. **In the Server Behaviors inspector, click the plus (+) button and choose Delete Record from the pop-up menu.**

    The Delete Record dialog box opens.

8. **Use the top four drop-down lists to set up the Connection, the data table to delete from, the recordset that holds the data, and the key field in the recordset.**

9. **Now that you have two forms on the page, you definitely need to change the fifth drop-down list, labeled Delete by Submitting Form.**

    Switch it to the delete form that you just created.

10. **Browse to find the page to redirect to after deleting.**

    Usually you direct the reader either back to the Detail page or to a search page.

    You should see a pair of hidden form fields inserted alongside the Delete button (you can see them in Figure 5-26). *Do not delete* these fields. If you ever want to remove the delete behavior from the page, open the Server Behaviors inspector, select the delete behavior, and use the minus button to remove it.

Chapter 6

Live Data View

In This Chapter

▶ Introducing Live Data View
▶ Working with query strings
▶ Changing LDV settings

The view of your Web pages in the document window is not what your users will finally see in their browsers — unless your pages are incredibly simple. The design-time view in the document window is only a useful approximation of the browse-time view — what you see in a browser. After you bring information to your page from a data table, that approximation can easily become more vague and less useful.

This chapter describes a very ingenious UltraDev invention called *Live Data View* (LDV). LDV offers a view of your page design — right there in the document window — that comes much closer to simulating browse-time view when live data is involved. What's even better, you don't have to stop designing while you check out your work in a browser!

Designing in the Browser: They Said It Couldn't Be Done

When you're working with dynamic pages, it doesn't take long to get just a little bit miffed about how badly the placeholder text often represents the real thing. Figure 6-1 shows an example of this misrepresentation. On this online newspaper page, layers have been created for data fields that represent the main title of a news article and for back and forward references on either side of the title. The actual data is very brief and will fit, but because the text style chosen is quite large and the recordset field names are long, the placeholders overlap each other, making redesign extremely difficult. It's very hard to visualize this page as it will actually appear.

Figure 6-1: Placeholders make a mess of this design-time news page.

People who know a great deal more than me about server technologies have said that it's impossible to have a true WYSIWYG design environment when parts of your page come from a database. The classic solution is to shrug and say, "If you want to design, work with design-time placeholders. If you want to see a Web page, look at it in a browser." The makers of UltraDev challenged this conventional wisdom and came up with Live Data View, a mode in which you can actually carry out design on genuinely representative data rather than on those funky placeholders.

Drummies are probably thinking, "Ha! Big Deal! Drumbeat has Preview mode." True, but did you ever try to do design work in Preview mode? It's impossible. Drumbeat's Preview mode is really just an insert of Internet Explorer's view of your page — slightly more convenient than publishing and viewing in the full browser window, but not much. Plus Preview mode is notorious for crashing when the going gets tough.

LDV may seem like a miracle, but really it's a compromise of a different kind. Here's a mixed bag of LDV features — some good, some bad:

- **Dynamic text placeholders are replaced with actual data** — by default, the data from the first record in the recordset.
- **Almost all standard Dreamweaver design capabilities are available in LDV.** You can add or delete elements, edit text, adjust the geometry of tables and layers, and so on.
- **Hyperlinks, including navigation within the dataset, are not live.**

Chapter 6: Live Data View   139

> ✓ **By default, invisible elements not seen at browse time are seen in LDV.** You can, however, turn them off on the toolbar by choosing View⇨Visual Aids⇨Invisible Elements. Note that turning off invisible elements also turns off the highlight that normally identifies the live data elements on your page.

Figure 6-2 shows how LDV cleans up the page shown in Figure 6-1. You can now see that the overlap of the back and forward references (<<E and G>>) was an illusion.

Figure 6-2: Live Data View of the same page shown in Figure 6-1.

So How Good Is Live Data View?

To fairly evaluate Live Data View, you need to give it a try. With your document open in design view, switch to Live Data View using any of the following methods:

> ✓ **Toolbar:** Click the Live Data View button (4th from left)
> ✓ **Keyboard:** Press Ctrl+Shift+R
> ✓ **Menu:** Choose View⇨Live Data

The view switches (it may take a few seconds), the data placeholders are replaced with typical data, and the LDV toolbar appears at the top of the page.

All of these actions are toggles, so repeat the toolbar or keyboard action or menu command to return to normal page view.

Part II: Bringing Data to Your Pages

The Live Data View of your page is sometimes virtually identical to the browser view. However, there can be some important layout differences.

Figures 6-3 to 6-6 are four views of the same page. Figures 6-3 and 6-4 are the design-time and browse-time versions of a search results page from a vegetable gardener's information site. Figure 6-5 is the Live Data View with invisible elements made visible, and in Figure 6-6 the invisible elements are turned off. All windows were the same width when these screen captures were made.

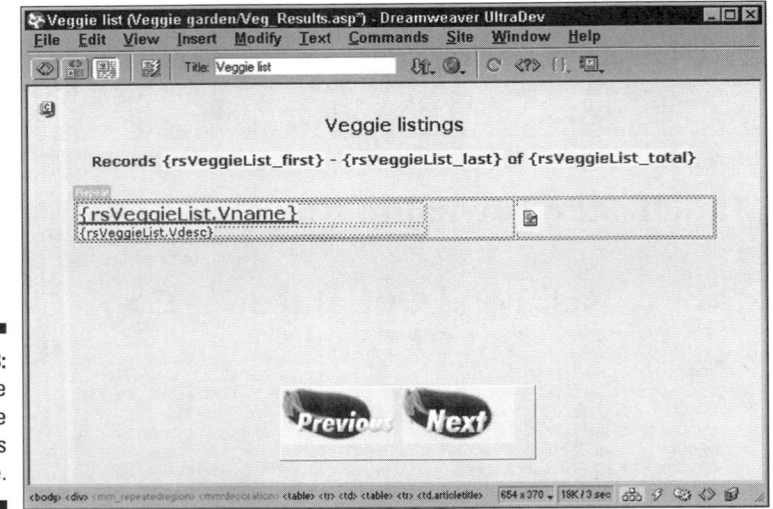

Figure 6-3: Design-time veggie results page.

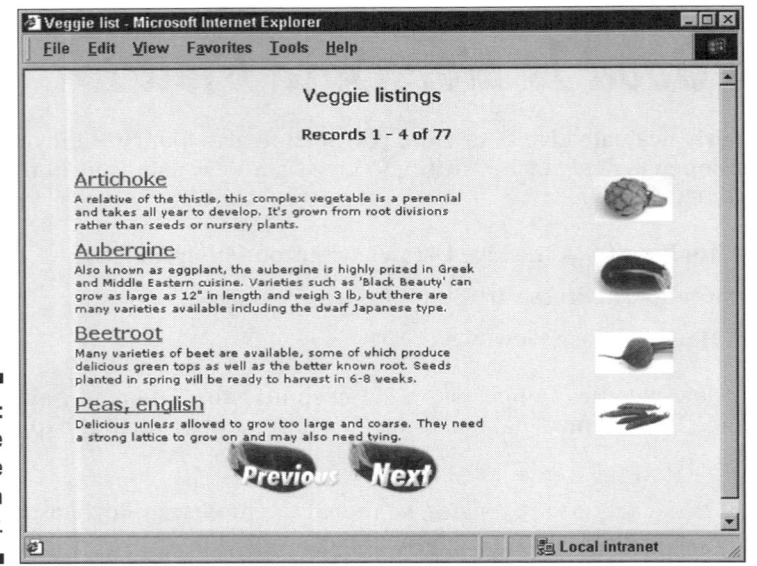

Figure 6-4: The veggie results page seen in a browser.

Chapter 6: Live Data View *141*

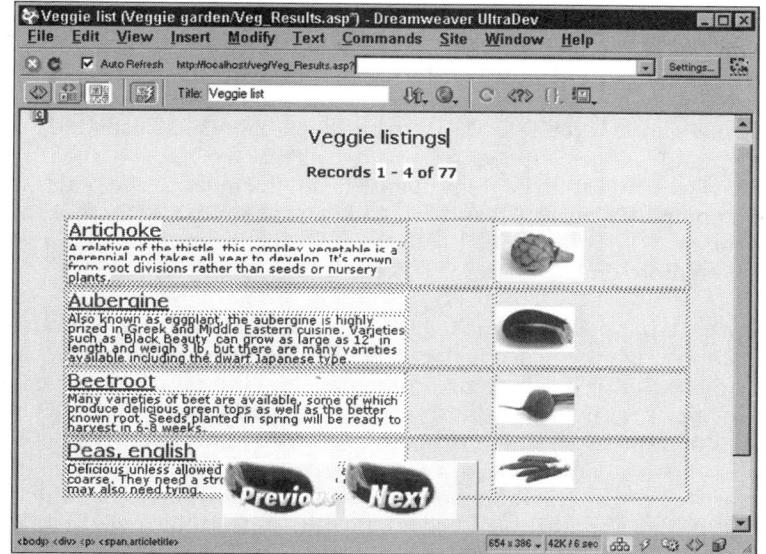

Figure 6-5: Live Data View of the same page with invisible elements made visible.

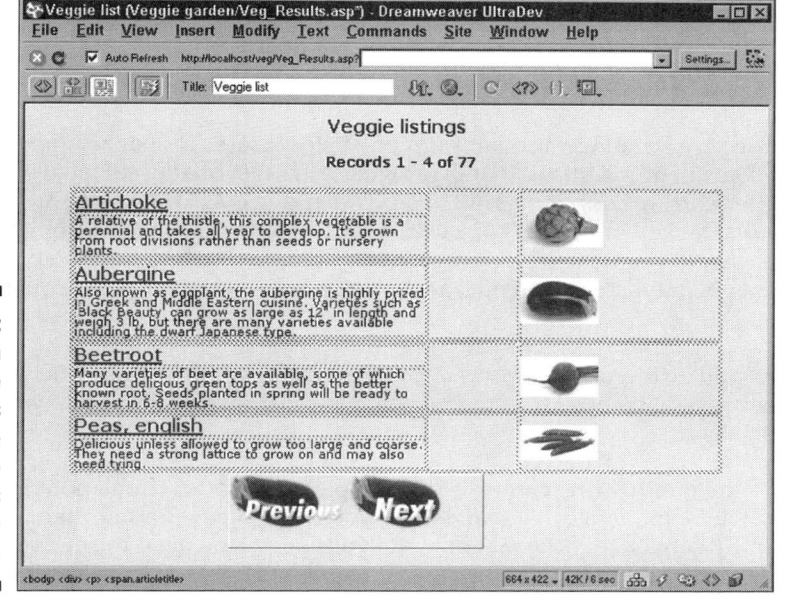

Figure 6-6: With invisible elements gone, the LDV page looks a lot like Figure 6-4.

See how LDV struggles to represent the page as it would appear in the browser, particularly with invisible elements made visible (refer to Figure 6-5). The highlighting of each line of text in the cramped style I chose for the descriptive text partially obscures the line above. The relationship between the main table and the navigation layer at the bottom has been badly miscalculated.

The view without invisible elements is much closer to the real thing. But if you compare Figures 6-6 and 6-4, you can see quite plainly that the line length of the text is not quite right, and the placement of the small thumbnail images is even more off the mark.

So what's happening to make LDV possible? Unlike Preview mode in Drumbeat, what you see is *not* an embedded browser page. Instead, the page is sent to the Web server for processing, and the raw data served up is run through UltraDev's own interpreter to create the page layout. That's why getting into LDV can take a few seconds for a complex page.

Figure 6-6 shows the table borders left in, but you can toggle them on and off by choosing View⇨Table Borders. Positioning of table cells is unaffected, however. Netscape's presentation of this page is nearly identical to that of Internet Explorer.

Adding the Query

The Live Data View toolbar normally incorporates a small window in which you can enter a query string, bringing extra information to a page just as a query string added to a URL in a browser does. As you may know, a *query string* tacked on the end of a URL conveys extra information from page to page and can be used to represent anything — the brand of motorcycle the user is interested in buying, a map reference, a clothing size, a quiz answer, and so on.

As you also probably know, one extremely common use of a query string is to convey an index so that the receiving page knows which of many records to display.

So the query string can resolve an apparent contradiction about LDV. The whole point is to bring real data to your design page rather than placeholders. To check that the real data fits your page, you need to see the complete range of data records — or at least enough of it to be pretty sure that you've seen the worst it has to offer. Obviously, if some fields are unexpectedly large, some adjustment will be needed. And yet, navigation doesn't work in Live Data View. So how on Earth are you supposed to flip through the data records, checking to see if there are any surprises?

Take a look at Figure 6-7, which is a design-time view of a detail page from the same veggie-dedicated site.

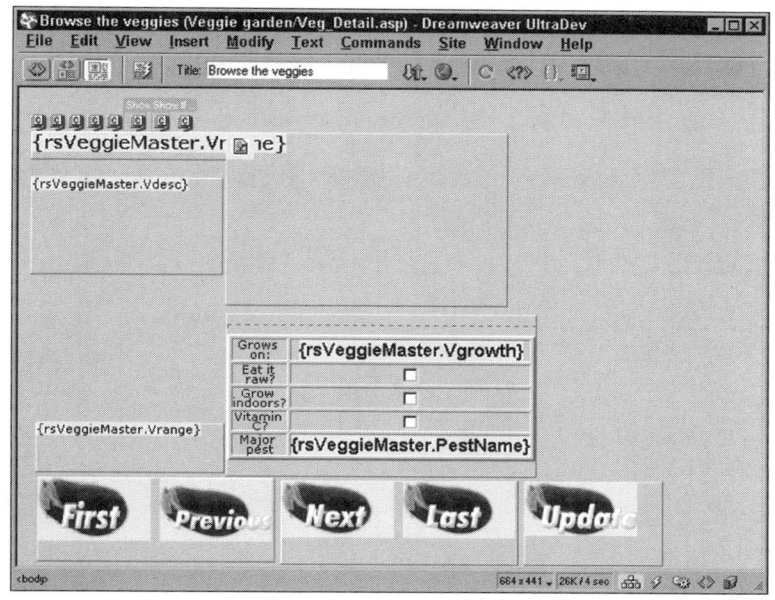

Figure 6-7: A design-time view of a detail page from the veggie site.

The page is made up in a series of layers, and an inexperienced designer may worry about the overlap between the main title layer and the image layer. But the Live Data View shown in Figure 6-8 makes it plain that there's no overlap in reality — the data placeholder is longer than the veggie's name.

Or is it? Artichoke, aubergine, and beetroot may be fine — but who's to say that there aren't veggies in the database with embarrassingly long names? (You say tomato, and I say *Lycopersicon esculentum* — let's call the whole thing off!)

The resolution of the data-browse problem in LDV is in the Query String window, embedded in the LDV toolbar and seen in Figure 6-8. To see a different data record (and possibly a longer veggie name) in LDV, follow these steps:

1. **Enter, for example,** index=3 **in the Query String window.**

    This invokes the fourth data record because data indexing starts at zero.

2. **Click the Refresh icon in the LDV toolbar.**

3. **The Working icon animates (charmingly) and, after a while, the fourth data record pops into the page.**

    Simple.

Part II: Bringing Data to Your Pages

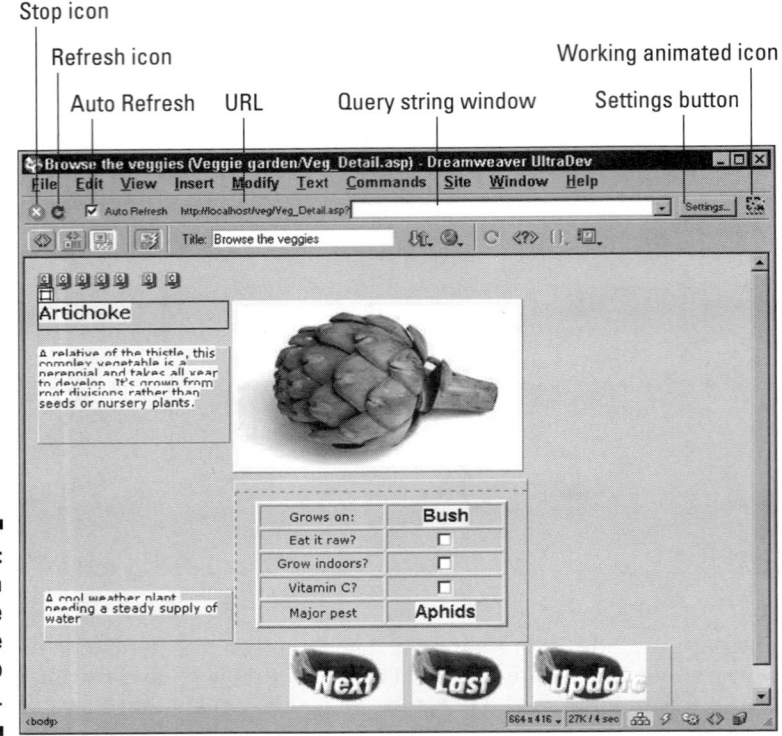

Figure 6-8:
A Live Data View of the detail page with no overlap.

The preceding steps assume that you have some arrangements for navigation on the browse-time page. Data indexing with a query string won't be recognized if there is none. To place temporary navigation on the page, follow these steps:

1. **Somewhere on your page, insert a forward chevron (>>) by typing two "greater than" symbols.**
2. **Select the chevron by sweeping your mouse over it.**
3. **In the Server Behaviors inspector, click the plus (+) button and choose Move To Record**⇨**Move To Next Record from the pop-up menu.**
4. **Save the page and transfer it to the server.**

After you add navigation to the page, you can use the LDV query string window to check any or all of your data records.

In Figure 6-9, an unexpectedly long name, *Minnesota Midget Cantaloupe,* pops out of the database. Mmmm, sounds delicious. The name, however, doesn't overlap the image because the layer containing the name is constrained in width (even though the placeholder text can stretch beyond its boundary). Instead, the name wraps to a second line and overlaps the *description* layer.

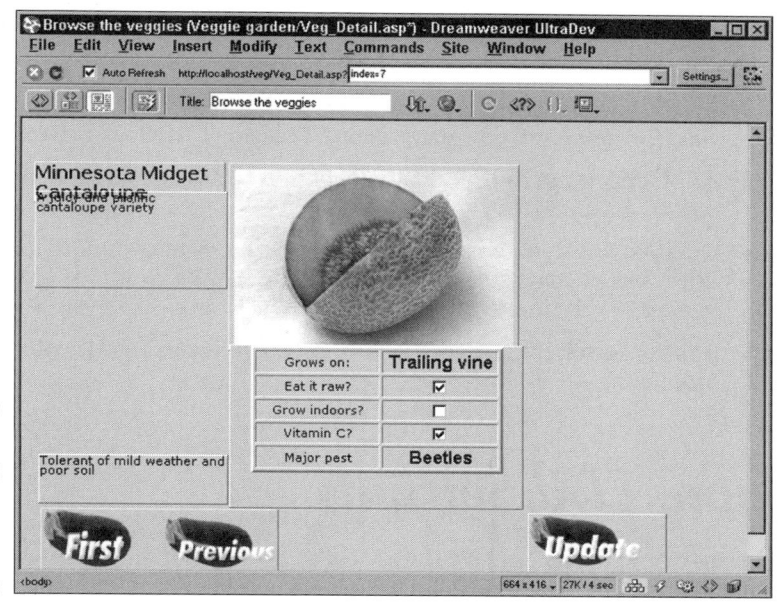

Figure 6-9: Oops! Didn't expect a long name like this.

The designer of this page blesses Live Data View and simply moves the description layer down a little, as shown in Figure 6-10. Now everything is hunky-dory.

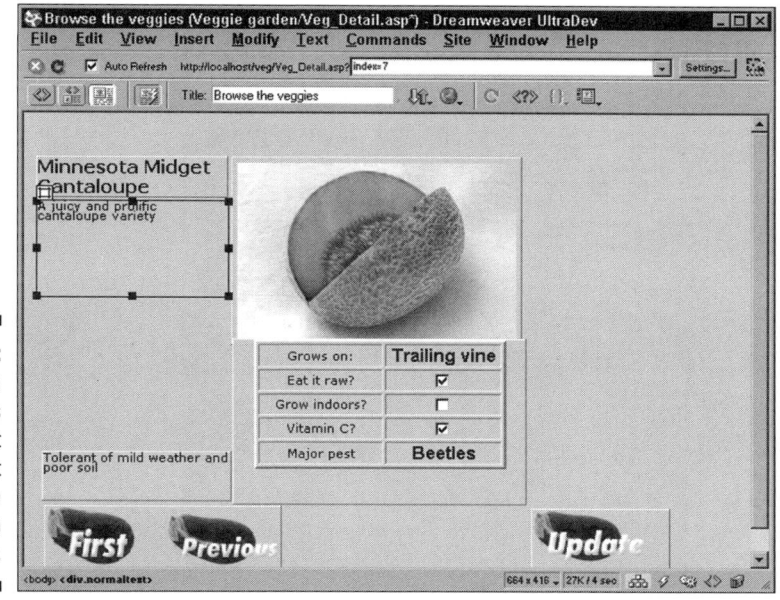

Figure 6-10: Live Data View allows instant adjustment of the description layer.

Here are a few more things to think about when you type a query in the Query String window on the LDV toolbar:

- Every time you write in a new query string, click the Refresh icon to make UltraDev fetch the new data record. Pressing Ctrl+R also refreshes LDV.
- If you check the Auto Refresh check box, UltraDev fetches the new data record automatically.
- Query strings you enter in the Query String window build up into a drop-down list so that you can recall them later with your mouse instead of having to retype them.
- If the data refresh process gets hung up, you can stop it with the red Stop icon.

Modifying LDV Settings

You may open a page in Live Data View at some point and discover that your Query String window is missing. Here's the explanation: If the incoming data is coming by POST rather than GET, UltraDev doesn't expect a query string and, therefore, doesn't provide a Query String window. To see if that's the case, click the Settings button on the LDV toolbar (you can also choose View⇨Live Data Settings) to open the Live Data Settings dialog box. If the Method drop-down list in the middle of this dialog box displays POST (see Figure 6-11), you have your answer.

Data transmitted by the GET method creates a query string. That's what GET means. POST data does not become part of the destination URL.

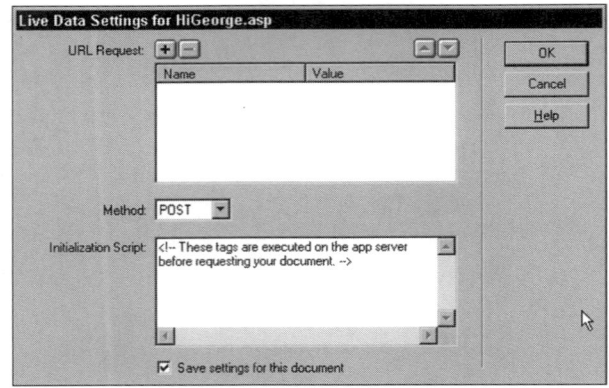

Figure 6-11: The LDV Settings dialog box set for the POST data method.

So who set this up as a POST page? Ah, that's a tricky question. The tooth fairy? Your eight-year-old daughter? You did while poking around aimlessly, clicking things late last night? It's got to be something along those lines because UltraDev *always* defaults the data method to GET.

In fact, setting the data transfer method to POST is a choice that you make yourself, as site designer, for whatever reason. Maybe your data is sensitive and you don't want it to appear in a public URL window for prying eyes to see. Maybe you think it may be over 255 characters long, and Unix browsers could chop off the end.

You can still insert test data into UltraDev's Live Data View, even if the method is POST, by using the list manager shown in Figure 6-11.

Suppose that you want to test a page that displays data about a butterfly species. The name of the species is supplied as POST data by some other Web page as the value of a variable named Bname. The test value is the word *Monarch*.

The Live Data Settings dialog box allows you to provide this test data as something called a *request variable*. Here's the step-by-step:

1. **Close the LDV Settings dialog box for now, and open the Data Bindings inspector.**

   If you happen to have the Data Bindings inspector on your launcher, you can open it simply by clicking that part of the launcher. If not, you can choose Window⇨Data Bindings or press Ctrl+F10.

2. **Click the plus [+] button and select Request Variable from the pop-up menu.**

   The small Request Variable dialog box opens.

3. **Change the request type to Request.Form in the drop-down list.**

   This is necessary because everything defaults to the GET method.

4. **In the Name box, type the variable name (Bname in this example) and click OK.**

   The Request Object appears in the Data Bindings inspector.

5. **Place a cursor on the page where you want to place the variable (the butterfly species, in this example).**

6. **In the Data Bindings inspector, expand the Request Object (if necessary) and select the request variable.**

   In this example, it is Form.Bname.

7. **Click the small Insert button in the inspector.**

   The placeholder, {Form.Bname} in my example, appears on the page. Now switch to LDV and proceed.

Part II: Bringing Data to Your Pages

8. **Click the Settings button on the LDV toolbar.**

    The Live Data Settings dialog box appears.

9. **In the Method drop-down list, select POST.**

10. **Click the URL Request plus [+] button.**

11. **In the Name column, type the name of a new variable (**Bname **in this example) and in the Value column type a value (**Monarch **in this example), and then click OK.**

12. **Unless the Auto Refresh check box is checked, click the Refresh icon on the LDV toolbar.**

    The value, Monarch, appears where the placeholder was on the page.

TECHNICAL STUFF

The preceding steps are for the ASP server model. Procedures for JSP and Cold Fusion are similar but not identical.

Part III
Advanced UltraDev

The 5th Wave — By Rich Tennant

"What do you mean you're updating our home page?"

In this part . . .

If you read Part II, I hope you appreciate that there's almost no actual computer language in it. I wanted to keep those four chapters as a totally code-free zone. But I couldn't avoid including a little SQL in Chapter 4. In general, though, there's enough functionality and flexibility in UltraDev's prepackaged data interfacing to take you a long way without ever seeing source code.

Because this part is unashamedly advanced, I felt free to delve deeper than UltraDev's point-and-click functions, extending the basic capabilities of the software in directions I hope you find helpful and practical.

Inevitably, some source code editing plays its part — but I've restrained myself. You find only about a dozen instances of code hacking, and they take you into territory I believe you'll find worthwhile — multidimensional searching, cookies, login validation, and site security are some examples.

Part III also includes a solid chapter on extending UltraDev in a different sense. Macromedia's policy is to be entirely open about how to get at the logic of Dreamweaver and UltraDev and to encourage the development of third-party, snap-on extensions that do anything HTML, JavaScript, and the server languages can achieve. The result is that enthusiasts — most of whom are more clever than you or I — have come up with a wonderful array of extension objects called exchange packages, which you can download for free. In Chapter 9, I tell you how to get and install exchange packages, and even how to make a few simple extension objects of your own.

Chapter 7

SQL Variables: The Answer to Problems of Many Sorts

In This Chapter
- The basics of SQL variables
- Simple searching
- SQL variables in multidimensional searches
- Static options and wild cards

Searching though data is one of the most common requirements of database-driven Web sites. Users of the Web probably aren't willing to scroll through page after page of your database data, winnowing for what they consider interesting. Unless you have an exceptionally small inventory of ideas or products, you're going to need to put in quite a bit of effort devising strategies for sorting your data. Sooner or later, you're going to find out how useful SQL variables can be.

SQL — Structured Query Language — is the formal language in which you need to address most databases in order to get them to yield relevant information. A sensible enough question in plain language, such as "How many orders has Juanita Gonçalves placed with this company?" needs to be translated into SQL before the database can respond with something like "Fourteen, and the last order was 12 days ago."

The question becomes even more useful if the name of the customer is not actually specified but is represented at design time by a token, called a *SQL variable,* that can ultimately be replaced with any name in the customers data table. The statement is then usable at runtime to interrogate the database about customer ordering history in a general sense. It's a formal way of saying, "I can't specify every detail of this SQL statement right now, but here's the gist of it, and I'll fill in the rest later."

In this chapter, you discover a number of ways in which you can use SQL variables to make searching your Web page data more efficient.

Giving Your Users a Way to Search

Perhaps after you've read this chapter you'll have the confidence to attempt a search that would respond in the smart-aleck way I suggested in the beginning of this chapter, but for now I'll take you through a less ambitious search — one that simply extracts from a data table the orders placed by a given customer and lists some details of each order. You need two pages — a search page and a results page.

Because the name of the customer is eventually going to be provided by whomever types something in the search page, it's completely unknowable at the time you design these pages. A SQL variable is the token you insert in the recordset to represent this unknown name at design time — UltraDev's Recordset Builder makes this pretty easy and even lets you try out a default name for testing your setup.

ON THE CD

In this chapter, I use the Down To Earth pottery site for my search strategy examples. You can find all the components of the Down To Earth site — site files, images, CSS style sheets, and data tables — on the accompanying CD. I have supplied files for both ASP/JavaScript and ColdFusion server models. See Appendix D and the README files for information on how to set up the sites provided on the CD.

Setting up a simple search page

The search page you need is really very simple, and its design is whatever you fancy. To function, though, it must include these elements:

- A form, whose ACTION points to the results page
- A form text element
- A submit button

All three of these elements are easily deployed from the Forms panel of the Objects palette.

Figure 7-1 shows the search page that I included on the CD, to search the records of the Down To Earth pottery business. The figure also includes the Property inspector of the form, and you'll see that the form's name is sform1 and its ACTION is `AllOrders.asp`. In other words, `AllOrders.asp` is the page to which it submits its data.

The name of the text element is Customer in this example. Keep that in the back of your mind.

Figure 7-1: The simple search page for the Down To Earth customer order history search.

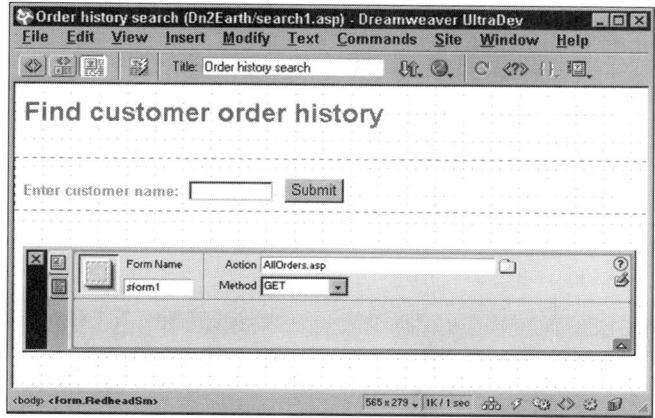

If you have some search project in mind, create a simple page such as this with whatever layout, labeling, and naming you feel like. If your grasp of UltraDev's page designing tools is really shaky, you can simply use or adapt my page from the CD.

The results page — a bit more demanding

With just a bit of effort, you can make a search results page really informative. By a results page, I mean the page that displays the outcome of the search in some sensible way. In the database of Down To Earth pottery (and in most commercial databases, too) there are separate data tables for customer information and ordering history. What relates one table to the other is a CustomerID — a cryptic number that appears in both tables. So what I needed was a SQL statement that pulls all orders out of the database, decodes the CustomerID by looking up the Customers data table, and then gives me only records in which the customer's name matches the name somebody has typed in to the search page.

How do I retrieve the name somebody entered? Fortunately, that's pretty simple. And no matter what actual search problem you're attempting, you need to know this. The name searched for appears on the results page as a *Request variable*.

Request variables offer many goodies to designers of dynamic pages (see Chapter 8 for goodie details), but the one you need to know about right now is the one that carries data from page to page. At least one Request variable is always created when a form on Page A submits data to Page B. The values entered into the form elements on Page A can be retrieved on Page B as `Request("elementname")`. In the example I'm following, Page A is the search page (`search1.asp`), Page B is the results page (`AllOrders.asp`), and the element name is *Customer*. So `Request("Customer")` is guaranteed to be the name somebody has decided to search for.

Figure 7-2 shows the recordset that does the job. You might need to refer back to Chapter 4 for a refresher on how to create a recordset, and also for a primer on the formal language SQL. In this example, I have to use the Advanced mode of the Recordset Builder because there are two separate data tables involved, and the Simple mode can only cope with a single table.

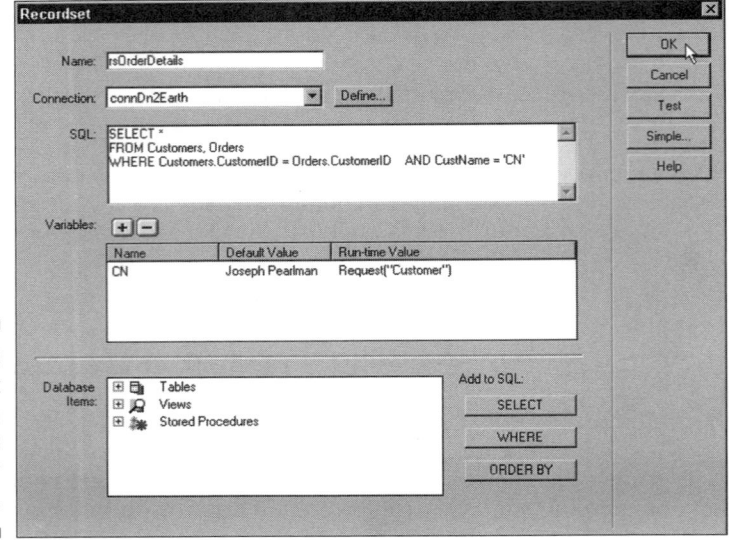

Figure 7-2:
A recordset that finds a customer's order history.

Now, here's where the SQL variable comes in, and here's how to use it. The first part of the SQL statement is

```
SELECT * FROM Customers, Orders
WHERE Customers.CustomerID = Orders.CustomerID
```

That's the part that pulls out complete customer information for every order on the books. Now to filter out only the orders for the customer being searched for, it would be nice to add

```
AND CustomerName = Request("Customer")
```

Unfortunately, you can't write that. SQL will honk, toot, blow whistles and klaxons, and perhaps revoke your executive washroom privileges for a while. It just ain't acceptable syntax.

Chapter 7: SQL Variables: The Answer to Problems of Many Sorts

You have to use a SQL variable to achieve what you want, and here's how you would duplicate the recordset in Figure 7-2:

1. **Add to the SQL statement** `AND CustomerName = 'CN'`.
2. **Click the plus (+) button above the SQL Variables window to create a new variable.**
3. **In the Name column, type** CN.

   Actually, CN is my variable name. You can choose what you like as long as you're consistent.

4. **In the Default Value column, type some name that you are sure actually exists in the data table.**

   This is the test value I mentioned a while back, and in my example I used *Joseph Pearlman* because I knew for sure that there was at least one order under that name.

5. **In the Run-Time Value column, type the name of the Request variable that's incoming from the search page.**

   In the example, it's `Request("Customer")` — remember?

6. **Test the SQL using the Test button.**

   In my example I had no trouble bringing Mr. Pearlman's order history into the Test SQL Statement window.

Figure 7-3 shows the skeleton design I decided on for the `AllOrders.asp` results page. All details of the customer go in the upper table, and the ordering history goes in the lower table, whose second row is a repeated region repeating all records. Repeated regions are explained in Chapter 4.

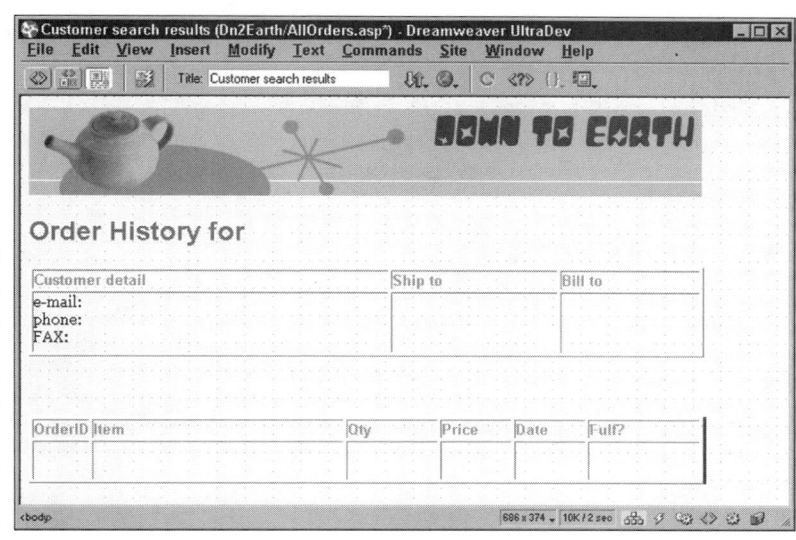

Figure 7-3: Skeleton layout of a proposed customer order history page.

Part III: Advanced UltraDev

If you want to follow along, here are the steps so far:

1. **Create your skeleton page to suit your data requirements.**

   Figure 7-3 shows the design I figured I needed.

2. **In the Data Bindings inspector, click the plus (+) button and select Recordset (Query) from the pop-up list.**

   The Recordset Builder opens.

3. **If necessary, click Advanced to get it into Advanced mode.**

4. **Create the SQL statement and the SQL variable(s) you need.**

   Figure 7-2 and the explanation is a guide to what I needed.

5. **Close the Recordset Builder, expand the recordset in the Data Bindings inspector, and flow the data fields onto the page as described in Chapter 4.**

   Figure 7-4 shows the Down To Earth AllOrders page with data placeholders inserted.

Now check out your search page and see what happens. Save both pages, transfer them to the server, and try entering a customer name in the search page (or whatever equivalent search you're creating). It should correctly find any customer who has an ordering history. The name must be spelled correctly, but the search is not case sensitive.

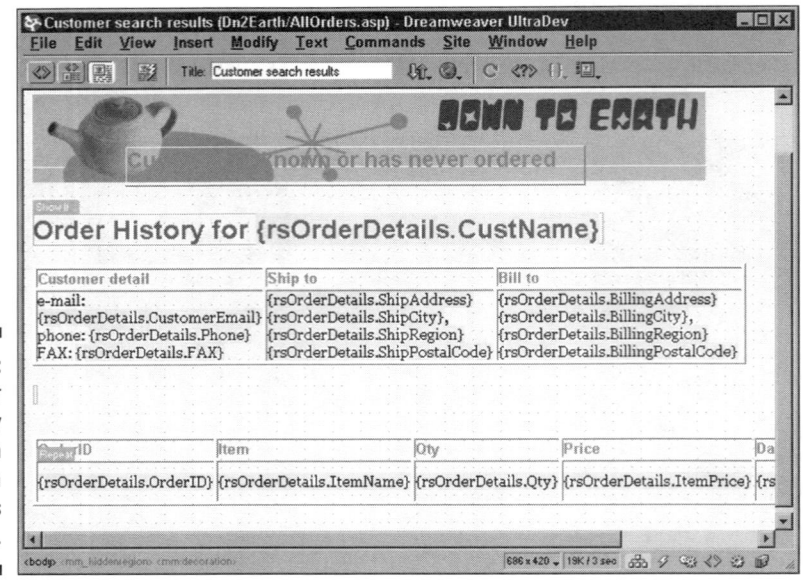

Figure 7-4: Customer order history page, with data placeholders inserted.

Chapter 7: SQL Variables: The Answer to Problems of Many Sorts *157*

The name supplied by the user of the search page provides the actual value of the SQL variable, which completes the SQL statement and generates useful data.

Figure 7-5 shows the result of an actual search for a customer's order history.

What if the search comes up empty?

A problem arises if someone enters a nonsense search criterion or, in the case of the Down To Earth example, perhaps a customer who is in the database but has never ordered anything. In either event, the recordset on the results page comes up empty and error messages are the very likely outcome.

UltraDev has an answer for this, and it's a pair of server behaviors very similar to the behaviors I describe in Chapter 5. The behaviors detect whether or not a recordset is empty, and show or hide selected regions of the page accordingly.

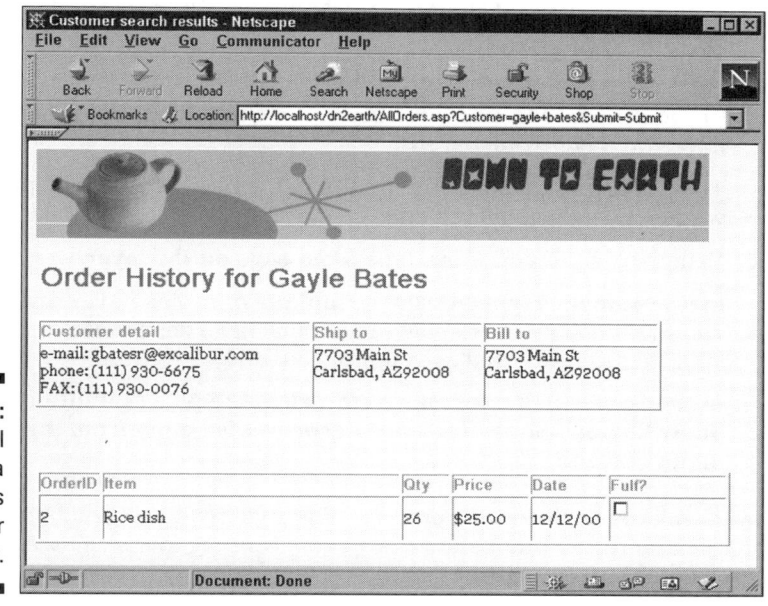

Figure 7-5:
Successful search for a customer's order history.

Well, that sort of behavior is exactly what you need to sense a null search result and do something graceful rather than let the server pop up its own error message and spoil your page. You need to create two alternative regions of the page, one of which is revealed if the search comes up with something and the other of which is seen only if the search is null (and therefore the recordset is empty). Step by step, here's how:

1. **Using your mouse, with a sweeping movement, select all the elements of the page that you do not want shown if the search is null.**

   Referring to Figure 7-4, that would include the headline and both tables. Most of the page, in other words.

2. **In the Server Behaviors inspector, click the plus (+) button and choose Show Region**⇨**Show Region If Recordset Is Not Empty from the pop-up menu cascade.**

   A dialog box pops up just to check on the identity of the recordset. (I think they should inhibit this if there's only one recordset on the page. Maybe they will.)

3. **In the Common panel of the Objects palette, click the Layer object and sweep out a wide rectangle over your page suitable for holding a text message.**

   A layer appears at the place you drew it.

4. **In the Property inspector of the layer, click the BgColor button and make the layer transparent.**

   The transparent color is the button in the head of the color picker that's white with a diagonal red line.

5. **Using any style you want, type a message on the layer.**

   In my example, I typed **Customer unknown or has never ordered.** The message ends up overlaying the original page design. Make sure the layer remains selected as you proceed.

6. **In the Server Behaviors inspector, click the plus (+) button and choose Show Region**⇨**Show Region If Recordset Is Empty from the pop-up menu cascade.**

Now check the behavior in a browser. The page renders normally if there's some search result, but it shows just your "Nothing found" message if the search comes up empty.

TIP

If your database is pretty small, you may have the option of using menu lists for things like customer names. It's a great convenience because users of the search page don't have to get the spelling right. If you use this method, you can also clean up the message you display if the search comes up empty-handed. You can be sure the customer exists, so there's no need to offer that possibility as a reason for search failure. A customer menu page is included on the CD as `search2`.

Chapter 7: SQL Variables: The Answer to Problems of Many Sorts   159

Searching by category

Narrowing a customer search by searching for a customer *category* isn't really practical, but that type of searching goes on all the time in employee databases. HR data managers may call it *Department* or *Position,* but it amounts to a category.

One category search that would make a lot of sense for the Down To Earth site, however, is a *product* search by category. Only a limited number of categories exist, and they are

- Art
- Bowls
- Jars
- Jugs
- Mugs
- Planters
- Plates
- Teapots
- Vases

Figure 7-6 shows the skeleton of a table intended to list the results of a category search. The page is called SearchResults. The lower table row is a repeated region, which means that it will repeat itself as many times as necessary to hold the complete search results. (To find out how to make a repeated region, see Chapter 5.)

Figure 7-6: Skeleton of a search results page.

Figure 7-7 shows the recordset on the SearchResults page. It extracts data from a Products data table, selecting only the fields that are going to be needed to populate the form shown in Figure 7-6.

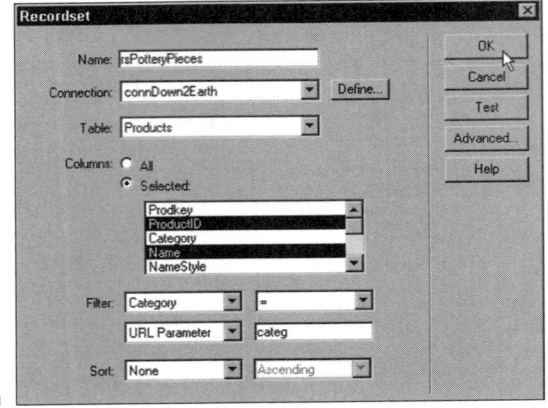

Figure 7-7: A filtered recordset on the results page.

This recordset shown in the example in Figure 7-7 was created in the Simple mode (as opposed to the Advanced mode) of the Recordset Builder. (To find out more about Simple and Advanced modes, see Chapter 4.) Even the Simple mode of the dialog box has filter options that you can use to filter out certain data. Here, records that don't match the URL parameter named *categ* have been filtered out by setting the Filter options to

```
Filter Category = URL Parameter categ
```

So what is this URL parameter? It's just another variety of Request variable — an incoming piece of data from a search page, like the Customer parameter I describe earlier in this section. If the incoming query string is *categ=vases*, only vases will get to step onto the page.

> **TIP:** Note that you can use Live Data View (press Ctrl+Shift+R or choose View⇔Live Data) to test this page. Type **categ=vases** in the Query String window and click the Refresh icon. (See Chapter 6 if you want to know more about Live Data View.)

Just like the simple search page shown in Figure 7-1, the actual design of this page is up to you. The one I used for the Down To Earth site (and included on the CD as `search3.asp`) has essentially the same features as the simple page, including the form whose ACTION points to the results page, but in place of the text element it has a menu element. Here's how to set that up:

Chapter 7: SQL Variables: The Answer to Problems of Many Sorts   *161*

1. **Inside the form, place a menu element by clicking the List/Menu button in the Objects palette.**

   It's polite to add some prompt text to guide users, such as **Pick a category:**.

2. **Give the menu element a name.**

   You enter the name of the menu element in its Property inspector. If the Property inspector isn't already open, open it by choosing Window⇨Properties or by pressing Ctrl+F3.

3. **Still in the Property inspector of the menu element, click the List Values button to open the List Values dialog box.**

4. **In the Item Labels column, type the categories you want to make available as search criteria.**

   In the Down To Earth example, I entered the nine categories displayed in the list at the beginning of this section.

   You don't need anything in the Values column because list values default to the same as the labels. The completed List Values dialog box is shown in Figure 7-8.

Figure 7-8:
The Completed List Values dialog box for a category menu.

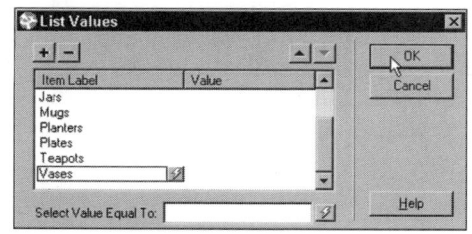

Transfer the search page and the SearchResults page to the server and check them out. You should be able to filter any of the nine categories by selecting one from the menu. Figure 7-9 illustrates the search page, and Figure 7-10 shows the result of the search in Internet Explorer.

To make this results list really useful, each item should be linked to the *detail page,* which describes it in full and displays its picture. This would be a catalog page similar to the one I showed you how to create in Chapter 4, but filtered for the particular item of interest. (See Chapter 5 to find out how to link and filter a detail page.)

Figure 7-9:
A search page in action.

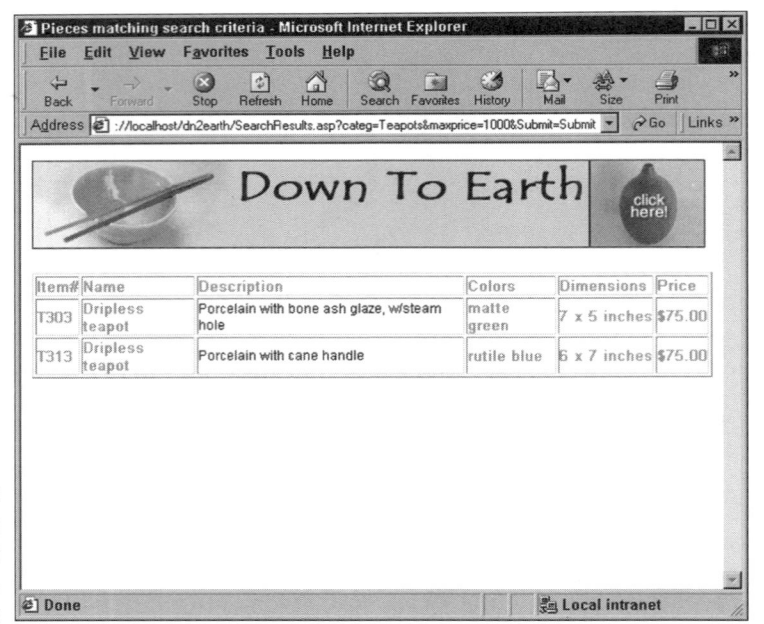

Figure 7-10:
The result of the search.

Double Your Fun: Searching by Two Criteria

Users may want to search your database using more than one criterion. A search page offering multiple ways of searching is known as *multidimensional*. For example, a user who's interested in a teapot may also want to see those that fall within a specific price range.

This section uses the Down To Earth site (which you can find on the CD accompanying this book) to guide you through setting up a Web page for a multidimensional search. After you complete the next set of steps, users who visit your Down To Earth site will be able to search by category as well as maximum price.

To provide two-dimensional search capability, add a second menu list to your search page:

1. **Click the Menu button on the Forms panel of the Objects palette to add another menu element to the page.**

2. **Give the menu element a name (maxprice would be appropriate in this example).**

   You enter the name of the menu element in the Property inspector. If the Property Inspector isn't already open, open it by choosing Window⇨Properties or pressing Ctrl+F3.

   It's also polite to add some prompt text such as **Pick a maximum price:**.

3. **Select the new menu element in the page window.**

4. **In the Property inspector, click the List Values button to open the List Values dialog box.**

   If you created the category search page earlier, you may remember that I told you not to add anything in the Values column. This time, the item labels and values do need to be a bit different. You're going to offer options of $200, $100, $50, and $25 as the price ceiling. For the user's benefit, you want to include the dollar sign in the display — but the recordset that handles the price data won't want that dollar sign. The recordset filters the data by using the WHERE clause of a SQL statement, which looks something like

   ```
   WHERE ... UnitPrice <= maxprice
   ```

and `maxprice` needs to be a pure number. (For more on SQL, see Chapter 4.)

Figure 7-11 illustrates how you fill out the menu list. Dollar signs on the left, none on the right.

Figure 7-11: A completed List Values dialog box for the maximum price menu.

5. **Save the page and transfer it to the server.**

6. **Reopen whatever page you made to display search results and open its recordset by double-clicking the recordset in either the Data Bindings inspector or the Server Behaviors inspector.**

   In the Down To Earth example, the name of the recordset is rsPotteryPieces.

   Remind yourself that the recordset filters the Category field with the value of the URL parameter categ.

7. **Click the Advanced button.**

   The Simple mode of the Recordset Builder can't deal with a multidimensional search. When the Advanced mode appears, notice that UltraDev has invented a SQL variable name, MMColParam, to achieve the category filter. (Actually, it was there all the time, you just didn't see it.) Clever, huh? The default value is 0 and the run-time value is `Request.QueryString("categ")`.

8. **Click the plus (+) button beside the Variables window to add a new variable.**

9. **In the Name column, type a variable name.**

   For the Down To Earth example, I typed **MAX**.

10. **In the Default Value column, type a reasonable figure for maximum price.**

    In this example, I typed **50**.

Chapter 7: SQL Variables: The Answer to Problems of Many Sorts   *165*

11. **In the Run-time Value column, type the name of whatever Request variable you want to substitute for the default value at run-time.**

    For example, if you're expecting a value for maximum price to come from a menu named `maxprice` using the `GET` method, the Request variable is

    ```
    Request.QueryString("maxprice")
    ```

12. **Change the default value of MMColParam to something representing your actual data.**

    In this example, I changed the 0 in the Default Value column to bowls.

13. **To filter the data by the new criterion, add something to the existing SQL statement.**

    For example, if you're expecting a value for maximum price to replace a SQL variable called `MAX`, add

    ```
    AND UnitPrice <= MAX
    ```

    to the SQL statement displayed in the SQL window of the dialog box.

    Figure 7-12 shows the completed Recordset Builder.

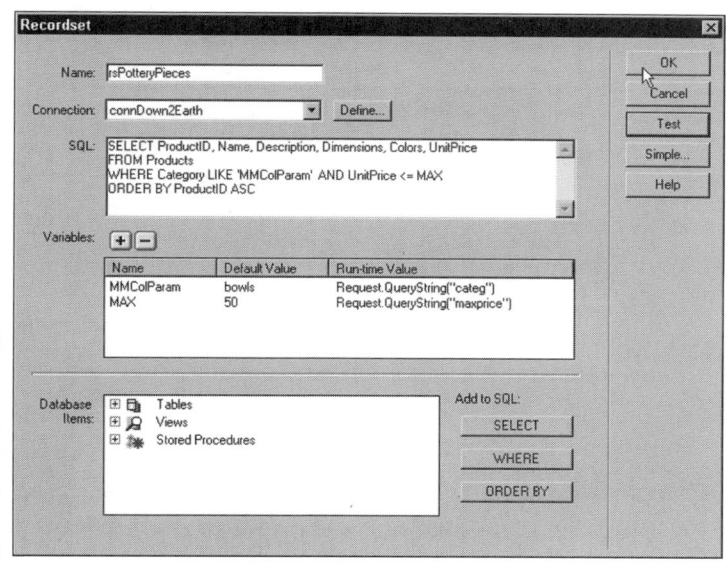

Figure 7-12: Finished recordset with two SQL variables.

Part III: Advanced UltraDev

14. **Click the Test button.**

    The Test SQL dialog box (see Figure 7-13) appears showing three bowls that meet the price criterion.

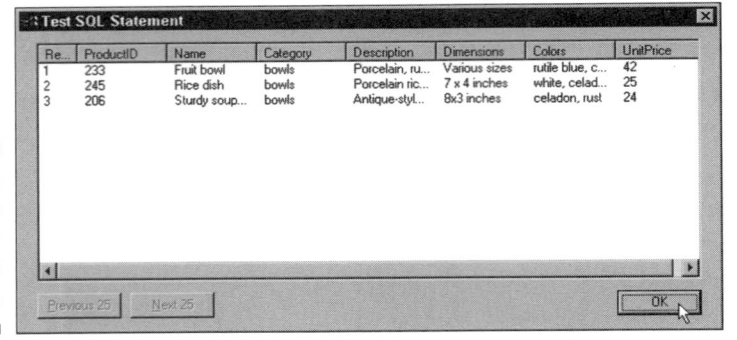

Figure 7-13: The results of a multi-dimensional search.

Figure 7-14 shows an even more advanced search page for Down To Earth, with a third option: to search by color. The color list element is named *Color* and contains a list of 12 colors that Down To Earth uses regularly.

Figure 7-14: Getting really daring — three search options.

There's a trick to the way the search for color is set up, however. In the Down To Earth example, colors are not listed individually but are grouped in an "Available in . . ." field. So a search for green, for example, has to be able to locate the color from within a field that may be `orange, green or rust`.

Chapter 7: SQL Variables: The Answer to Problems of Many Sorts

The SQL way of finding a substring is to use the symbol % before and after the search term, as in

```
WHERE ... Colors LIKE '%COL%'
```

You can see this code in the SQL box in Figure 7-15.

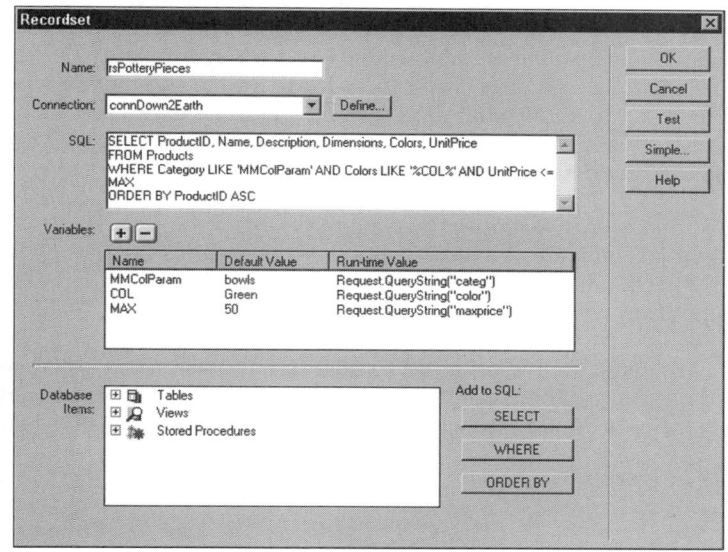

Figure 7-15: This SQL statement finds a single color from a whole sentence.

Filtering Multidimensional Searches with Static Options and Wild Cards

Multidimensional searches (discussed in the preceding section) can be quite useful, but they can also cause problems when you're dealing with a small inventory. If the user tries to search using too many criteria, the search generally results in very few items (sometimes none) that meet the criteria. There's a lesson here. Devising multidimensional searches is not useful if you force users to make a choice in every dimension. You must give users a way to say, "I don't care about this option." This section explains how to do that.

Throughout this chapter, I introduce you to increasingly more sophisticated options for searching a database. In this section, I discuss the most complex search so far — one using three criteria. You can offer your users the opportunity to search by these criteria by providing three drop-down menus on your search page (refer to Figure 7-14).

When you give users the opportunity to perform a three-way search, you also have to give them the option of *not* selecting a particular criterion in any of the three drop-down menus. Suppose a user wants to search for a particular category of product in a certain price range but isn't concerned with the color. That user needs to be able to choose an entry such as Any Color from the Color menu.

On the search page in my Down To Earth pottery Web site example, I want to add Any Category, Any Price, and Any Color to the three drop-down menus. Because these options aren't variable — they never change — they're known as *static options*, and they aren't too hard to add to the menus. The trick is for the recordset to know what data to send when the user leaves a list set at, say, Any Category. It's no good passing along the words Any Category — no way is the recordset going to interpret that correctly.

It's just a matter of knowing the right SQL variable jargon. For this situation, the right jargon is the % symbol, which — more or less — means "match anything" in SQL-talk. Symbols like the percent sign (and the * in DOS) are known in computer programming as *wild cards*.

There are just a couple of things to bear in mind when using SQL wild cards. First, you can use them only when you're matching *text* fields in a data table. Numeric fields don't match wild cards. Second, this SQL clause is illegal:

```
WHERE Category = '%'
```

You have to use

```
WHERE Category LIKE '%'.
```

In the following steps, I assume that you created a three-dimensional search page similar to my Down To Earth example. Then follow these steps to add static options and wild cards to your search operation:

1. **Open the three-dimensional search page you created.**
2. **In the page window, select the category menu element.**
3. **In the Property inspector, click the List Values button to open the List Values dialog box.**
4. **Click the plus (+) button and add a list item whose label is something like** Don't care **and whose value is** %. **Use the tab key to switch from the label column to the value column.**

   The new list item ends up at the bottom of the list.

5. **Click the up-arrow button as many times as necessary to move it to the top of the list; then close the list manager.**

Chapter 7: SQL Variables: The Answer to Problems of Many Sorts

6. **Do the equivalent to the color menu, adding a label such as** Any color with a value of % (see Figure 7-16).

Figure 7-16: Adding a static option to the color menu.

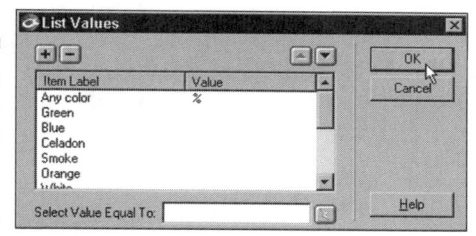

That's fine for category and color, but a static option for the maximum price has to be a bit different. The % wild card works only in text fields, remember, and the price is formatted as a currency field. The solution to this dilemma, however, is very simple. The value of the static option is set beyond the most expensive item you sell. In this enterprise, $1000 is more than enough to guarantee that you'll match anything price-wise. Figure 7-17 shows the List Values dialog box for the price.

Figure 7-17: Breaking the bank to create a static option for price.

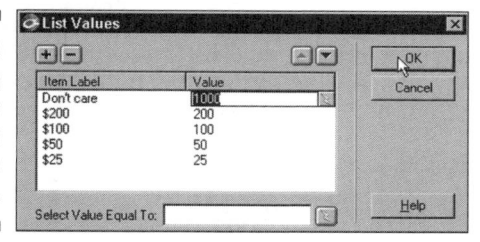

You don't need to amend the recordset on the results page, as long as it looks like Figure 7-14, but you can test the wild cards if you like by inserting them as default values for the SQL variables.

Figure 7-18 shows a successful search for cobalt blue vases at any price.

What if nothing matches the user's search criteria?

Even with static options and wild cards, there's always the possibility that a user will opt for search criteria that produce no result. As in the case of the order history search at the beginning of this chapter, you need to provide something graceful and polite if the search comes up empty.

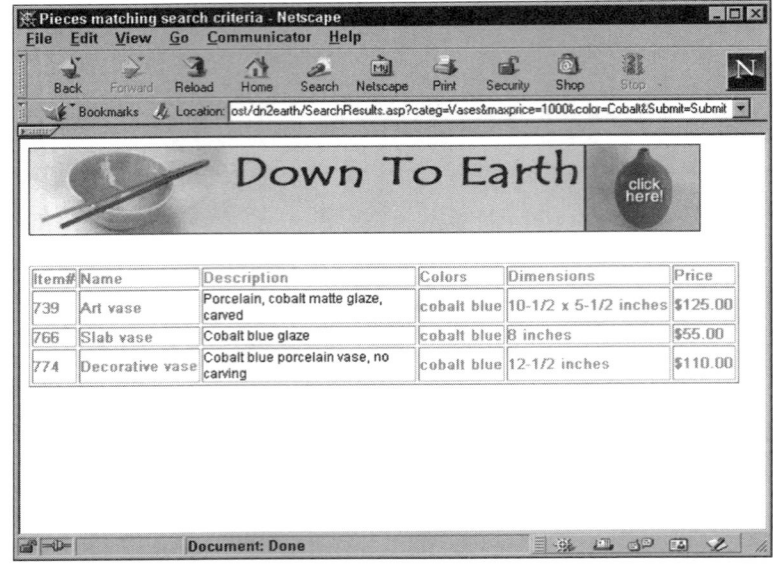

Figure 7-18: Found some nice-sounding vases.

The results page included on the CD, `SearchResults.asp`, includes a layer with the message `No pieces matched your search`, arranged to reveal if the recordset is empty, signaling a null search. The procedure and the server behaviors involved are exactly like the ones I describe in the section "What if the search comes up empty?" earlier in this chapter.

Reminding your users what they're looking for

You can remind users what search terms they used by inserting a statement at the head of the results page that says something like Result of search for green vases maximum price $150. But static options and wild cards introduce a slight complication to this process.

Ignoring the wild card problem for the moment, here's how to add a result statement to your results page:

1. **Open the SearchResults page.**

   You do this by double-clicking it in the Site window.

2. **In the Data Bindings inspector, click the plus (+) button and choose Request Variable from the pop-up list.**

   The Request Variable dialog box appears.

3. **Set the request type to Request.QueryString in the drop-down list.**
 4. **Type a name for the variable in the Name box** (categ, in my example).
 5. **Repeat Steps 2, 3, and 4 for the other variables** (color and maxprice in my example).
 6. **At the head of the page in the page window, using some suitable type style, add the text** Result of search for**, color**, maximum price $ **(replacing** color **and** maximum price $ **with the names of your variables, if they're different).**

    The asterisks represent nonbreaking spaces, which you can insert by pressing Shift+Ctrl+Spacebar.

 7. **Drag each of the three request variables from the Data Bindings inspector to its appropriate position in the statement shown in Step 6.**

    In the Down To Earth example, I place them as follows:

    - I drag the variable *categ* between the two spaces following the word *for*.
    - I drag the variable *color* between the two spaces following the word *color*.
    - I drag the variable *maxprice* immediately after the *$* (dollar sign).

    The statement now reads

    ```
    Result of search for {QueryString.categ}, color {QueryString.Color},
          maximum price ${QueryString.maxprice}.
    ```

If you save the page and transfer it to the server, you'll see that it works. But it needs fixing so that it doesn't end up saying

```
Result of search for %, color %, maximum price $1000.
```

Here's how to fix the category variable, and the other two are similar:

Select the category placeholder in the page window and expose its HTML source. After perhaps a little scrolling, you see the code shown in Figure 7-19 (ASP version).

172 Part III: Advanced UltraDev

Figure 7-19: HTML source code that needs fixing up.

Your mission, should you choose to accept it, is to manually edit that snippet so that it looks like the code shown in the following source code sample.

Source Code Sample 7-1

```
Result of search for
<%
var ct = Request.QueryString("categ");
if (ct == "%") {
  Response.Write("any category");
}
else {
  Response.Write(ct);
}
%>
```

The expression `Request.QueryString("categ")` evaluates to whatever is passed to this page as the categ variable. The code basically says "write the value of the categ variable unless its value is %, in which case write any category." The finished search results page is shown in Figure 7-20.

Now your users should be fully content. They have the option of three search criteria, but they won't be obliged to use all of them, and the reminder message makes sense for all searches. Time to brush up your award acceptance speech, perhaps?

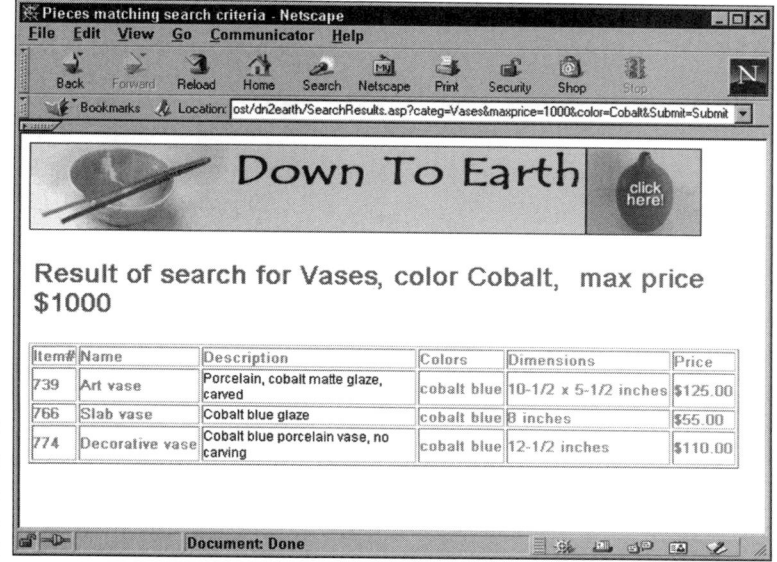

Chapter 7: SQL Variables: The Answer to Problems of Many Sorts

Figure 7-20: Final search result page.

Result of search for Vases, color Cobalt, max price $1000

Item#	Name	Description	Colors	Dimensions	Price
739	Art vase	Porcelain, cobalt matte glaze, carved	cobalt blue	10-1/2 x 5-1/2 inches	$125.00
766	Slab vase	Cobalt blue glaze	cobalt blue	8 inches	$55.00
774	Decorative vase	Cobalt blue porcelain vase, no carving	cobalt blue	12-1/2 inches	$110.00

Chapter 8

Server Objects and Cookies

In This Chapter

▶ Making use of the Request Object

▶ Reading and writing cookies

▶ Utilizing Session Objects

▶ Previewing server objects in Live Data View

▶ Working with ColdFusion

*A*ctive-server conventions such as ASP and JSP can enhance your Web sites enormously by playing logical tricks HTML could never learn — not even with the help of client-side Javascript. This book contains many examples of database manipulation using UltraDev's suite of server behaviors and data bindings, all of which are out of the reach of HTML and client-side scripting.

A very powerful feature of server technologies is the ability they offer you, as the site designer/programmer, to create and manipulate variables that persist on the server as your users move from page to page in your site.

A *server variable,* just like an algebraic variable, can represent anything. To be useful, a variable has to have a *name* and a *value.* As site designer, you get to name your variables whatever you like. Sometimes you get to give them values, too — more often values arise from the interaction of users with your Web site. A user's choice of music to download, for instance, might create the value *jazz* for the variable *genre.*

Unlike variables embedded permanently in a Web page — client side JavaScript variables, for instance — server variables don't evaporate when the user has finished looking at the page. The choice represented by a server variable *genre=jazz* is still there to be used after the page on which the user actually made that choice is long gone. That's what is meant by persistence.

Server variables exist within any of four or five constructs known as *server objects,* and this chapter illustrates some of the most common server objects that you can use to transform a simple Web site into a full-fledged Web application. They are

- **The Request Object:** Retrieves information from the server.
- **The Response Object:** Writes information to the server.
- **Cookies:** A special case of both a Request and Response Object.
- **The Session Object:** Stores data for the entire time a user is browsing your site.

Using the Request Object

The most common use of a Request Object is to retrieve form data entered by the user on a previous page. You can find several examples elsewhere in this book — notably a search of an arts-and-crafts database by type, color, and price in Chapter 7.

Suppose that Web page A has three form elements on it, named element1, element2, and element3. The form submits its data to Web page B. On page B, you can retrieve the values entered for the three elements by the user of Page A as Request("element1"), Request("element2"), and Request("element3"). The three variables are known as *request variables.*

That type of request variable is persistent for one page only. Page B can read values from page A, but those values evaporate if the user moves on to page C. Yet not all request variables are so short-lived. Request variables actually come in five types, known as *collections,* as discussed in the following list:

- **Request.QueryString.** Data submitted by the GET method. Because this is the default type, it may be abbreviated to simply Request.
- **Request.Form.** Data submitted by the POST method.
- **Request.Cookies.** Cookie data read from the user's computer.
- **Request.ServerVariables.** Data that's inherent to the server and its processes.
- **Request.ClientCertificates.** Data that can be read from a security certificate.

The first four types are explained in this chapter.

Making a page for listing approval

You often need to give users of your site an opportunity to see the data that they submit formatted as it will be finally presented. Auction sites, classified ad sites, and keypal/penpal sites are all examples of sites that have this need. The user fills out an online form on a submit page with details of his auction item, objêt d'art, or personal need and submits it.

GET or POST? Why do I care?

Although you know about HTML forms and how to submit them, you could be forgiven for being a bit vague about GET and POST and why on earth you should care. So here's a primer — it's optional; there will be no test on it at the end of the chapter.

The two principal attributes of the HTML `<FORM>` tag are `ACTION` and `METHOD`. `ACTION` simply states where the form's data is being submitted to. A music selection site, for example, may have successive selection pages for genre, artist, and year. The form on the genre page may have the attribute `ACTION="artists.asp"`, and the form on the artists page may have the attribute `ACTION="recyear.asp"`.

The `METHOD` attribute is a two-way choice of how you want the data submitted. The two methods to choose from are GET and POST, with GET as the default.

GET data is appended to the URL specified by the `ACTION` attribute as a query string, which itself is a series of name=value pairs representing the values entered by the user of the submitting page. `User=233476&genre=jazz` might be an example, turning the complete URL into `artists.asp?User=233476&genre=jazz`. If you want to see spectacular query strings, go shopping at Amazon.com or Lands End (`www.landsend.com`) and watch 'em grow as you make your way down the decision tree.

POST data is exactly the same data, but you don't see it attached to the URL. Because it does not appear in a browser's URL window, security is one reason that you may want to use POST rather than GET. POST data is read by different servers in different ways, but it all ends up looking the same.

You only care, in the context of server variables, because you need to know which Request object to use to read the data. GET data appears in the Request.Querystring object and POST data appears in the Request.Form object. If you look in the wrong one, you won't find your data — that's the bottom line on GET and POST.

The form on the submit page can be as boring as you like — it's a purely functional request for information. But when you're giving users a chance for a final approval, it's only fair to format it as it will eventually be displayed on an approval page. Request variables are ideal for retrieving information from the submit page to display on the approval page.

Figure 8-1 shows the home page of a fictitious Web site called KeyPalNation. Both the Submit Your Ad and Edit or Erase Your Ad pages are online forms that submit data to an approval page. The user can then either accept the listing as is or hit a Back button to revise the data.

The KeyPalNation site, including a very small starter database, is on the CD accompanying this book — in both ASP/JavaScript and ColdFusion versions — in the folder `\Demo sites\KeyPalNation`. Check Appendix D and the on-disc README files for how to install the site. Although the creation of this site is not described in detail in this chapter, the figures do illustrate the KeyPalNation site.

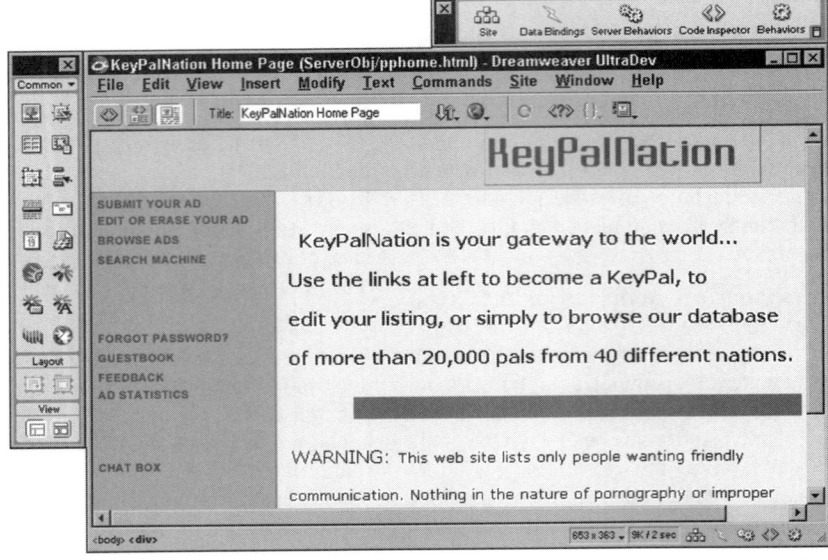

Figure 8-1: A fictitious KeyPal-Nation Web site.

As an example of using request variables, think about the user's name that he or she enters on the submit page in a form text element called, say, *name*. The act of submitting the page creates a request variable Request("name") on the approval page, which is used to display the name as it will appear on a finished Web page, and so on for any other data that may be collected on the submit page. The complete KeyPalNation submit page is shown in Figure 8-2.

Now think about the page that receives the submitted data — the approval page. Its main purpose, remember, is to display the data entered by the user as it will appear on the site. But the data itself is in limbo, as it were, waiting to be added to the database. If and when the user clicks a button signifying approval, the data is added at that time using UltraDev's Insert Record server behavior (see Chapter 5).

Because the Insert Record behavior can only insert the content of a form field, data for approval needs to be placed in a hidden form field as well as within the main page design. So you'll need to create a form area somewhere on the page by clicking the form object in the Forms panel of the Objects palette. Add some kind of approval button, clicking the button object in the same panel.

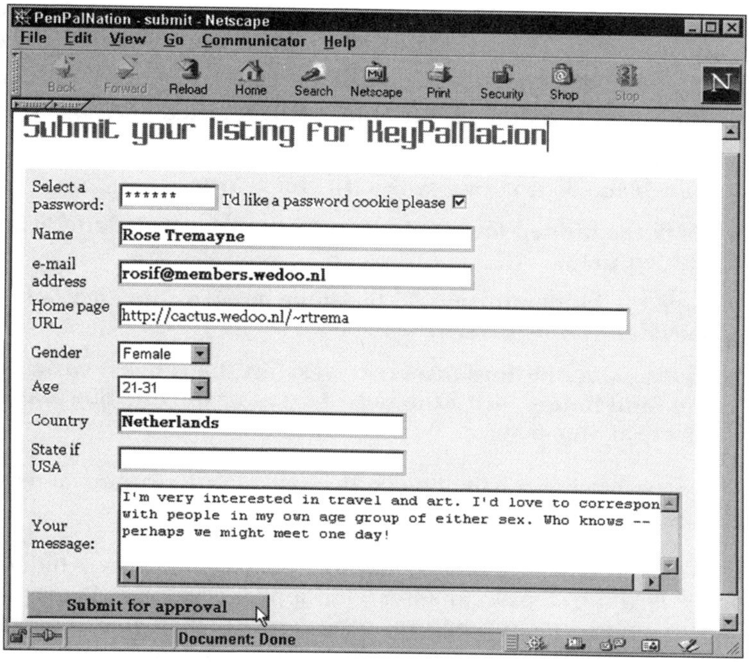

Chapter 8: Server Objects and Cookies

Figure 8-2:
A draft of the info submit page for the KeyPal-Nation Web site.

The actual design of the approval page, and the data it handles, depends entirely on the kind of site you're building. But generically, here's how to handle one request variable on an approval page:

1. **Open the Data Bindings inspector (normally by clicking your Launcher).**

2. **Click the plus (+) button in the Data Bindings inspector and choose Request Variable from the pop-up menu.**

    The Request Variable dialog box opens.

3. **If the incoming data is POST, set the Type menu to Request.Form. Otherwise, leave it at the default setting.**

    You set the Type menu by clicking the little down arrow at the right end of the menu box. A menu list drops down from which you then make your choice.

4. **Type the name of the variable in the Name text box and click OK.**

    The new request variable appears in the Data Bindings inspector list.

5. Place your cursor in the document window where you want this data to appear for approval and set any style your overall design requires for this field.

6. Make sure the request variable is still selected and click the Insert button at the base of the Data Bindings inspector.

7. Now place your cursor within the form area.

8. Click the hidden form field icon on the Objects palette to add a hidden field.

9. Give the hidden form field the same name as the data field in which its value will be placed.

10. In the Data Bindings inspector, reselect the request variable and click the Bind button — it's the same button as the one that was labeled Insert at Step 6.

The process is shown half done on the KeyPalNation approval page in Figure 8-3.

When all your data is deployed both on the page and also in hidden form fields, follow the steps in Chapter 5 for applying an Insert Record server behavior, redirecting to whatever page comes next in your sequence. Figure 8-4 shows the Insert Record dialog box I filled out when I was building the KeyPalNation approval process, redirecting to a simple thanks page.

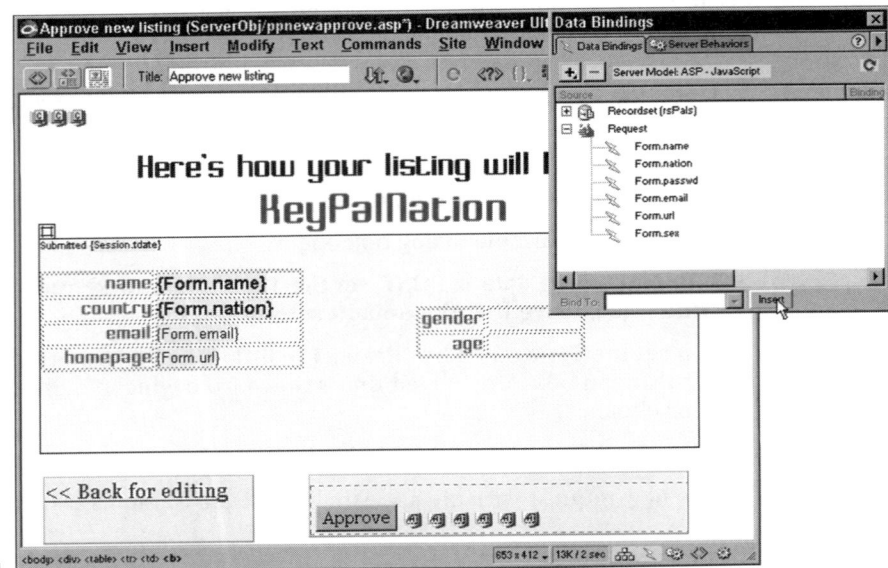

Figure 8-3: Entering request variables on an approval page.

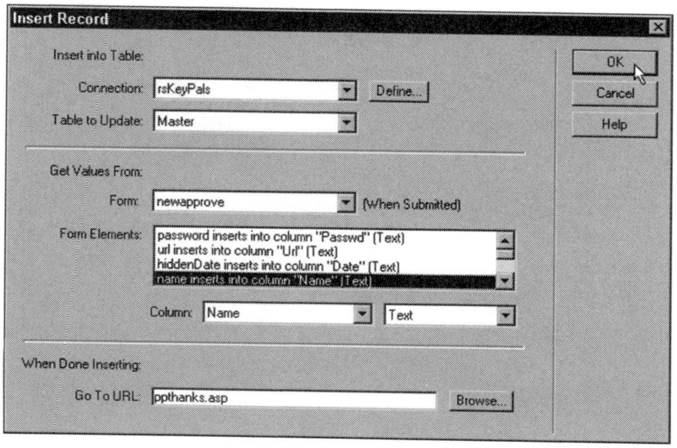

Figure 8-4: The Insert Record dialog box on the approval page.

Revising a listing

A request variable comes into play when users of a site like the KeyPalNation example want to retrieve an existing listing record for revision. Users normally enter a password in some login page. Assuming the name of the password form field is *passwd,* the request variable Request("passwd") would appear on the next page in sequence, which is an update page. The Request variable is then used to filter a recordset and display the correct record for update.

The recordset filtering is essentially identical to the single-dimension search procedure described in Chapter 7.

The procedure for approve/submit of an edited listing is identical to that for a new listing except that the final server behavior needed is Update Record, not Insert Record. The difference is explained in Chapter 5.

Searching for keypals — or anything else

Users wishing to search a data site should be offered some kind of search page on which they can set drop-down lists to initiate the search. Figure 8-5 illustrates the KeyPalNation search page, which allows a two-dimensional search by age and gender.

Request variables are also used in that search, which is functionally identical to the two-dimensional search described in Chapter 7.

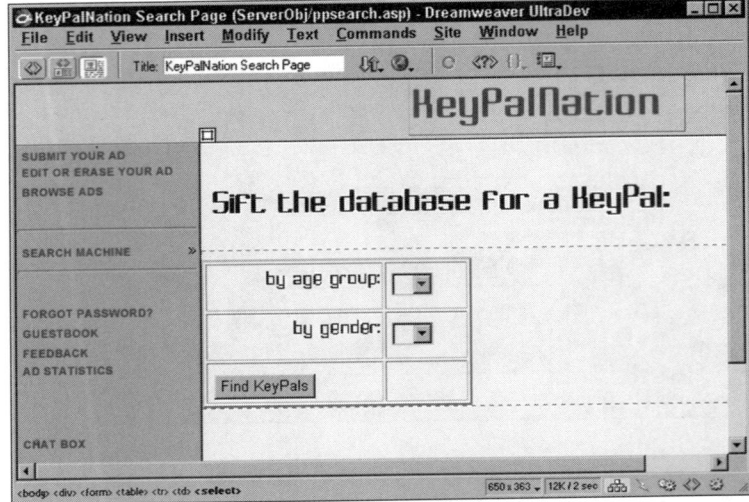

Figure 8-5: An age/gender keypals search page.

Server variables

A server variable isn't the temperature of soup by the time it reaches your table. It's a special collection of Request Objects that describe the server environment — in fact, in another context these same variables are known as environment variables.

To be perfectly honest, the animals in this menagerie are not all very interesting. Some, like GATEWAY_INTERFACE and INSTANCE_META_PATH, you may never want to come across in a dark alley. Others help you find out about your users, and can be quite informative. What page they just came from (HTTP_REFERER), what browser they're using (HTTP_USER_AGENT), even (but not very reliably) their own host name (REMOTE_HOST).

Sorry, advertisers — there's no such thing as a server variable called ANNUAL_INCOME.

The generic syntax for retrieving a server variable and displaying it on your page is `<%= Request.ServerVariables("SERVER_VARIABLE_NAME") %>`. You don't have to code that by hand, because UltraDev has a built-in data object for server variables.

Chapter 8: Server Objects and Cookies 183

Suppose you want to place a message on a page that proclaims "Hi there! I see you're connected from <REMOTE_HOST>, using <HTTP_USER_AGENT>, and you just came from <HTTP_REFERER>." You need three server variables, which you can set up like this:

1. **Click your Launcher to open the Data Bindings inspector, or choose Window⇨Data Bindings.**

2. **In the Data Bindings inspector, click the plus (+) button and choose Request Variable from the pop-up menu.**

   The Request Variable dialog box opens.

3. **In the Type drop-down box, select Request.ServerVariables.**

4. **Type the name of the variable in the Name text box and click OK (see Figure 8-6).**

   The new server variable appears in the Data Bindings inspector list.

5. **On the page on which you want the variable value to appear, using some suitable text style, type a sentence omitting the server variable.**

6. **Place your cursor in the sentence where you want the variable to appear, select the variable in the Data Bindings inspector, and click the Insert button.**

   A possible (and whimsical) result using three server variables is shown in Figure 8-7.

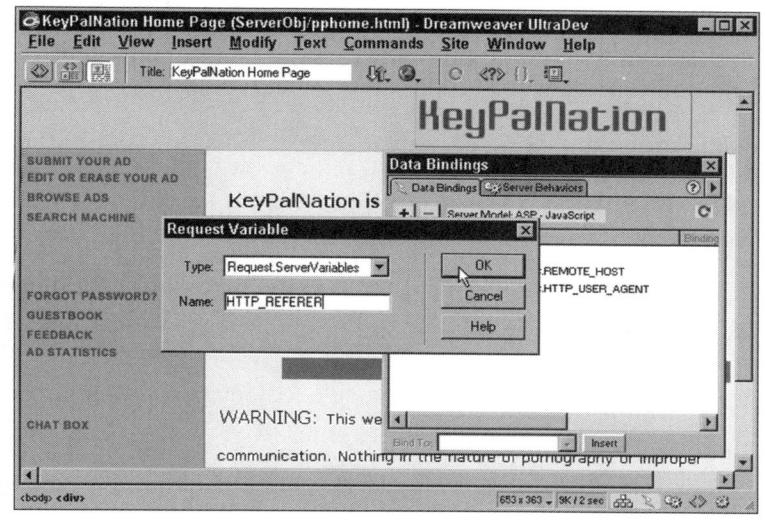

Figure 8-6: Placing a server variable on an ASP page.

Part III: Advanced UltraDev

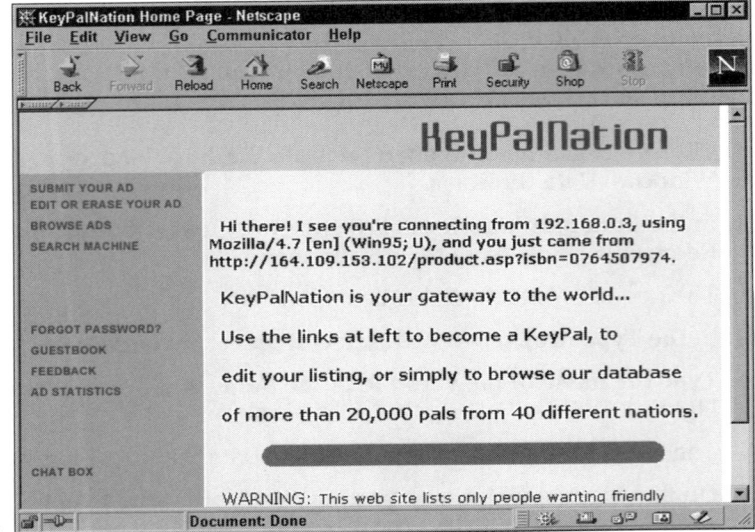

Figure 8-7: Browse-time view of a page using server variables.

Cookies: Request Objects and Response Objects

A *cookie* in the jargon of the Internet is a line of text written to a file in a user's computer for the express purpose of reading it back later. It contains information about the server that wrote it, its name and value, and its time of expiration calculated in seconds since January 1, 1970.

Cookies are commonly used, for example, to hold the name of the user (derived from a login procedure) and the date of the user's last visit. They enable a page to say things like "Welcome back, Jack Klesko. We haven't seen you since April 4."

The actual cookie allowing a page to say that would be something like:

```
Username=Jack+Klesko;Lastvisit=4+April
```

It would also quite likely contain some gobbledygook generated by the ASP parser.

One way of reading a cookie is to treat it as a special type of Request Object. To make a Username cookie available to your page, follow these steps:

1. **Click your Launcher to open the Data Bindings inspector or choose Window**➪**Data Bindings.**

2. **In the Data Bindings inspector, click the plus (+) button and choose Request Variable from the pop-up menu.**

    The Request Variable dialog box opens.

 3. **In the Type drop-down box, select Request.Cookies.**

 4. **Type** Username **in the Name text box and click OK.**

    The new cookie request variable appears in the Data Bindings inspector list.

You can now insert it anywhere you like on the page to display the name of the person visiting your site.

Who put the cookie in the jar?

Reading a cookie as a request variable begs the question of how the cookie information came to be written to the user's computer in the first place.

UltraDev is pretty good about letting you read server objects like cookies on a point-and-click basis. You can insert their values into your pages, bind them to form fields, or use them to filter recordsets. UltraDev is less effective when it comes to placing a value in a cookie — in fact, you're pretty much on your own for that. And if you can't write a cookie, you can't read one back. Fortunately, writing the server-side code isn't hard.

Because the Request Object is entirely concerned with information flow from the server to your Web page, there's a semantic problem with writing a cookie as a request variable. The semantic problem arises because, by definition, request variables *read* data, but don't *write* it. To get around this, every cookie can also belong to a whole different server object, the *Response Object*. The Response Object is the converse of the Request Object — it sends information from the page to the server. You can write a Username cookie correctly if you include a line of raw ASP code like this:

```
<% Response.Cookies("Username")="Jack Klesko" %>
```

Still, a couple of slight complications exist. You knew it couldn't be quite that simple, didn't you? Calm down, this is no big deal, it's just that:

- ✔ Response.Cookies declarations must be at the head of the document, even before the <HTML> tag.

- ✔ Unless you also declare an expiration time, your cookie will melt and disappear in approximately 20 minutes. A cookie with no specific expiration date is indistinguishable from a Session Object (see the sidebar "How long is a session?" in this chapter).

Declaring an expiration date is very simple if you have a specific date in mind. If you want Jack's cookie to last until February 14, 2009, just add this line of code:

```
<% Response.Cookies("Username").Expires = "14 Feb 2009" %>
```

Typically, however, you want to make a cookie persist for a set number of days, and that gets you into some calculations so that you don't end up with a nonsense date like February 31. I get to that shortly.

Letting keypals (or other users) put their passwords in the cookie jar

A common use of cookies is the storage of username/password data, so that users have the option of having that stuff filled in automatically. I don't know about you, but I sometimes have trouble remembering which of dozens of my favorite passwords I used for any given site.

Figure 8-8 shows the login page I built for the KeyPalNation site (it's on the CD), with the option for users to store a password in a cookie. I kept it simple — a more usual login page would need both a username *and* a password.

Using the four steps in the "Cookies: Request Objects and Response Objects" section, I created a Request.cookies data object called kppassword. I selected the password form field in the document window and bound the cookie to it using the Bind button in the Data Bindings inspector.

The password field now contained the placeholder `{Request.Cookies ("kppassword")}`. If you view a page like that in a browser right now, the password field is empty because no such cookie exists on your system (unless by some quite extraordinary coincidence). And that's fine.

Now, between the password field and the submit button, I added a line of text saying, "I'd like a password cookie please" followed by a check box called cookierequest. The checked value of the check box is "yes."

Next I made a page for the login page to submit to. The actual content and design of the page is of no consequence for understanding the cookie-making process — in the KeyPalNation site, it's the page that retrieves the user's listing for edit, but I expect you're thinking of building something quite different. No matter — I'll just call it the second page.

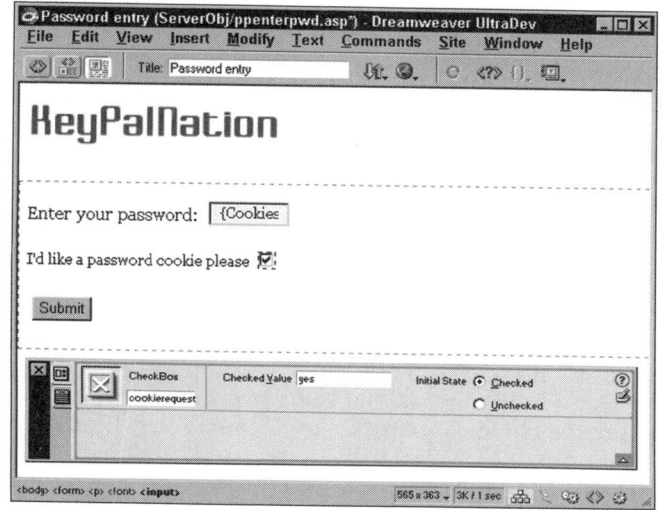

Figure 8-8: Gearing up an ASP page to write a password cookie.

I decided to call my password cookie kppassword, and the value to set it at is given by whatever the user entered for a password. Since the name I gave to the password form field on the login page was *passwd,* and since I was using the POST method for security, I could retrieve that value as `Request.Form("passwd")`.

Here's the code I inserted manually on the second page, complete with the JavaScript calculation needed to set the date forward 60 days:

Source Code Sample 8-1

```
<%
var cr = String(Request.Form("cookierequest"))
if (cr == "yes") {
  var expdays = 60; // Number of days we want cookie to persist
  var today = new Date();
  var expirecookie = new Date(today.getTime() + expdays*24*60*60*1000);
  Response.Cookies("kppassword") = String(Request.Form("passwd"));
  Response.Cookies("kppassword").Expires =
            expirecookie.toGMTString().substring(4,16);
}
else {
  Response.Cookies("kppassword").Expires = "01 Jan 1980";
}
%>
```

REMEMBER

All cookie writing must be completed before the <HTML> tag signaling the start of the document.

Here's how to check the functionality of a pair of pages like I just described:

- On the login page, enter a valid password, check the cookierequest check box and submit the page. Now use the browser back button to go back and refresh the login page. The password should remain in the password field.
- Uncheck the cookierequest check box and resubmit the page. Now go back and refresh the login page again. The password should disappear from the password field.

If you like, you can make a slight refinement to a cookie login page. If the user already has a password cookie, it looks silly for the login page to say, "I'd like a password cookie please." You can arrange to suppress that line completely if you detect that a cookie exists. But to be really user-friendly, you should give your users the choice of refreshing the cookie or getting rid of it.

You need to respond to the presence of a cookie by changing the text to "Refresh my password cookie please" and by arranging for the check box to appear already checked.

The existing portion of the HTML source is

```
I'd like a password cookie please
    <INPUT TYPE="checkbox" NAME="cookierequest" VALUE="yes" CHECKED>
```

Edit it manually to this:

Source Code Sample 8-2

```
<% if (Request.Cookies("kppassword") == "") {%>
    I'd like a <% } else { %>
    Refresh my <% } %>
    password cookie please
    <INPUT TYPE="checkbox" NAME="cookierequest" VALUE="yes"
<% if (Request.Cookies("kppassword") != "") {%>
 CHECKED
<% } %>
>
```

For code editing, you need to expose the HTML source. You can either launch the HTML Source window or bring the source code into the page window by using the Code View button on the UltraDev toolbar. Obviously, substitute your own element names for mine.

More Response Objects

Some Response Objects are highly technical, and if you're lucky they will never cross your path. Two that you should be interested in, however, are the *Redirect* object and the *Write* object.

The Response.Redirect object must have a value (called an *argument*) appended to it. The value is a URL, which you want the user of the page to be redirected to. Redirects are used for all sorts of reasons — here's the ASP/JavaScript code you'd need if you wanted to redirect users with Netscape browsers to a special page:

```
var browser = Request.ServerVariables("HTTP_USER_AGENT");
if (browser.indexOf("MSIE",0) == -1) {
  Response.Redirect("netscape_page.asp");
}
```

The Response.Write object simply displays its argument on the page, at whatever position it occupies in the document. The argument may be a predefined variable or a literal, hard-wired value. For example, either:

```
<% var str = "The value of element1 is " + Request("element1") %>
:
:
<% Response.Write(str) %>
```

or

```
<% Response.Write("The value of element1 is " + Request("element1")) %>
```

The often-used notation <%= is simply shorthand for Response.Write.

Using the Session Object

The Session Object is a wonderful, miraculous thing because it's completely free form and it doesn't evaporate on the next page. You can put anything in there and it'll still be there after the user of your Web site has scrolled through 20 of your pages.

In other words, unlike the Request Object, the Session Object remains available with useful stuff in it for the duration of a user's experience of your site (but see the sidebar "How long is a session?" for how vague the term *session* actually is).

The useful stuff is any number of so-called *session variables* that you define, assign values to, and then presumably retrieve at a later time. If by some means you obtain the current price per kilogram of cauliflower in the wholesale vegetable market in Paris, and you think you may need that number again, you merely have to write this variable assignment in your source code:

```
<% Session("ParisCauli") = "7.5Fr" %>
```

Any time you need to retrieve the magic number, the following code displays it on a page:

```
Cauliflower today costs <%= Session("ParisCauli") %>
```

I realize that Web sites featuring the price of cauliflower are not really in high demand. My point is that it's entirely up to you what you decide to define as a session variable. It can be a string, an integer, a real number, and even a member of an array. What could be friendlier than that?

Session variables in UltraDev

Typically, UltraDev has help to offer when reading a session variable but none at all for writing one. So if you need to create a session variable, you're in for some simple hand coding.

Here's how to create a session variable:

1. **Click your Launcher to open the Data Bindings inspector or choose Window⇨Data Bindings.**
2. **In the Data Bindings inspector, click the plus (+) button and select Session Variable from the pop-up menu.**

   The small Session Variable dialog box opens.
3. **Type a name for your variable in Name text box. Click OK.**

   That's all there is to it.

Well, okay, I lied — that's not really all there is to it. That just sets up a pigeonhole, as it were, to store your variable. You also need to set its value and then, at some later time, make use of that value.

Setting the value for your session variable requires inserting a small piece of code somewhere at the top of the document. Click your Launcher to open the HTML Source window (or use the Code View button), scroll to the top and insert the session variable definition.

For example, to create a session variable representing a timestamp, this would be the appropriate code:

Source Code Sample 8-3

```
<%
var today = new Date();
Session("tdate") = today;
%>
```

Timestamps are very useful when recording new data entered by users. I may even say they're necessary, but that would be going a bit far. In the KeyPalNation site on the CD, every new and revised keypal listing is time-stamped, and the timestamp is displayed as part of the published listing. You can see the placeholder `Session.tdate` in Figure 8-3.

Using session objects to set user access levels

UserID and UserGroup are very often fields in a database of known users. When somebody logs on to the site, the database is scanned and, if they're identified, the site designer arranges to copy their UserID and UserGroup into a pair of session variables. The UserGroup variable usually determines the status of the user. In particular, what privileges does he or she have on this site?

Suppose, for example, that you're building a commercial site that will be visited by a mixture of customers (low privilege, level 0) and administrators (higher privilege, up to level 4). You could make a two-tier site — one set of pages for the low-level user, another for the administrators who have added privileges like deleting, updating, and adding records. But that would be twice as difficult to maintain as a single site.

Instead, as long as you have knowledge of the user's status, you can hide things like delete buttons from those who can't be trusted not to abuse them. You have to write a little code by hand, but it's really simple.

When you place a delete button on a page and apply the server behavior for record delete, UltraDev creates the HTML for the button plus some hidden form fields.

```
<INPUT TYPE="submit" NAME="delrec" VALUE="Delete this record">
: [hidden form fields here]
```

You just wrap a conditional statement (`if`) around the whole thing like this:

Source Code Sample 8-4

```
<% if (Session("UserGroup") == 4) {%>
<INPUT TYPE="submit" NAME="delrec" VALUE="Delete this record">
: [hidden form fields here]
<% } %>
```

Now only level 4 administrators are able to see and use the delete button.

UltraDev's built-in server behavior for login validation is designed to retrieve user group information (see Chapter 10).

Personalizing your pages using session objects

Once a UserID is sitting in the Session Object, you know everything about the user of your site. Well — perhaps not the name of his secret high school sweetie, but whatever's in the database. You almost certainly know his real name, for a start.

Personalizing Web pages, such as for sordid commercial reasons (directed advertising), to be friendly, or just to prove you can do it, is common these days.

Figure 8-9 shows a recordset that filters a Users data table with the UserID session variable. Any information that the data table contains, personalized for that user, can now be placed on the page to which the recordset belongs. For example, if you want your page to read `Bye, William Crow, thanks for shopping here!`, proceed to the following steps:

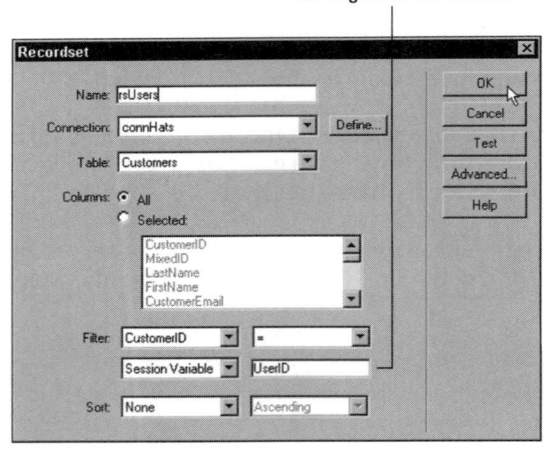

Figure 8-9: Filtering a recordset with a UserID from the Session Object.

1. **Using some suitable text style, type** Bye, thanks for shopping here! **on the page.**
2. **Place your cursor where you want the user's name to appear in that text.**
3. **Open the Data Bindings inspector and expand the recordset. Select the Customer Name field.**

   In the example, the recordset is `rsUsers` and the field name is `CustName`. Substitute your own recordset and field names, obviously.

4. **Click the Insert button in the lower-right corner of the inspector.**

   The placeholder {rsUsers.CustName} inserts into the text. At run time, it will be replaced by the user's name.

I assumed that the user's full name is in a single field in the data table. Some databases store the user's first and last name separately; some are more formal and use a salutation plus a last name. If two fields are required, just do two inserts with a space between them.

Using Session Objects to create a simple login validation technique

Now it's time to explain how to get variables such as UserID and UserGroup into the Session Object in the first place.

You can only derive that kind of data about the user in one of three ways:

- From cookies (see the "Cookies: Request Objects and Response Objects" section earlier in this chapter)
- From registration of a new user for the first time
- From login of an existing user, in a process called *login validation*

I want to show you the last process, because it's a good example of using session variables. And even though UltraDev has a built-in server behavior for login validation (explained in Chapter 10), you'll grasp the idea better if you hand-build the logic. It's not too hard.

Figure 8-10 shows a very simple login page. The login form field is called Login, and the password field is called Pword.

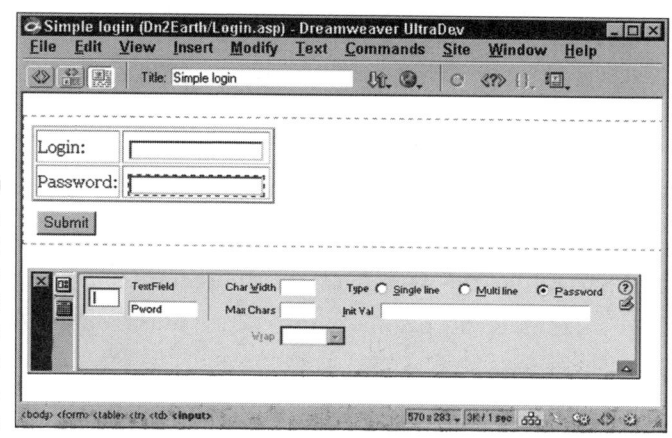

Figure 8-10: Login information here will generate a session variable.

Figure 8-11 shows a recordset that's applied to the page, using SQL variables (see Chapter 7) to compare the values entered by the user with the Username/Password values in the Customers data table.

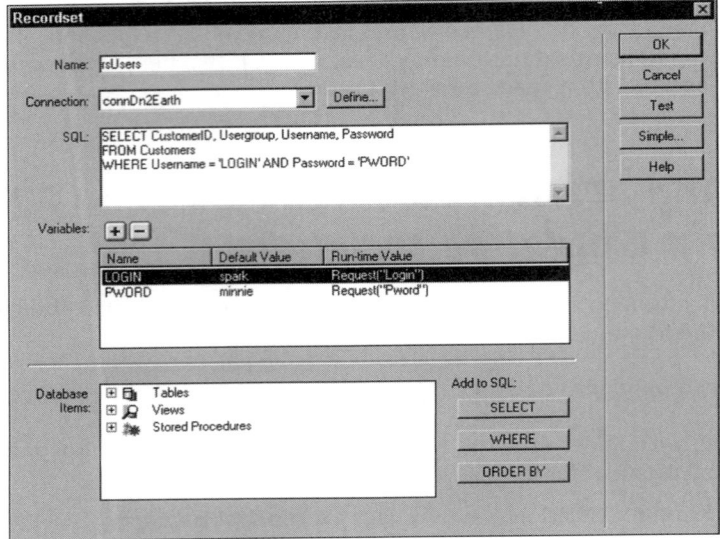

Figure 8-11: Filtering a recordset with a user-supplied login and password.

Decoding the SQL statement a bit, the SQL selects the unique data record for which the user-submitted value for Login matches the Username field in the data, and the user-submitted value for Pword matches the Password field in the data.

Hang on a minute . . . user-submitted? The recordset is *on the same page* as the Login and Pword form elements? How can their user-submitted values appear in the Request object?

The answer is that this page uses a favorite trick of active server technologies. The form on the page is made to submit data to the very same page. So the page loads twice — once to display the form input elements for the user, and a second time to take a look at what the user entered and decide what to do about it.

To identify the user and redirect to some other appropriate page in the site, some hand-made code needs to enable two decisions:

1. **Is this the first time the page loads, or the second?**
2. **If it's the second, is there a matching record in the data table?**

The first decision can easily be made by asking the question "Does the variable `Request("Login")` have any value at all, or is it undefined?" The second decision is made by asking whether `rsUsers.EOF` is true or false. If no record was found, the recordset will be End Of File — EOF for short.

In pseudo-code, the logic looks like this:

IF the Login request variable has some value

    IF the recordset is EOF

        User unknown, go to login fail page

    OTHERWISE

        Identified user, go to site start page

END

Pseudo-code is a sort of jargon that's neither straight English nor any actual computer language. Its intent is to lay out the logic of a useful piece of coding for the benefit of non-programmers, and the indentations help to follow the branching of the logic.

In ASP/Javascript, the code (plus an extra bit) goes like this:

Source Code Sample 8-5

```
<%
if (String(Request("Login")) != "undefined"){ //i.e. on 2nd pass
  if (rsUsers.EOF) { //i.e. no matching record found
    Response.Redirect("LoginFail.html");
  }
  else {
//*********************************
    Session("UserID") = String(rsUsers.Fields("CustomerID"));
    Session("UserGroup") = String(rsUsers.Fields("UserGroup");
//*********************************
    Response.Redirect("search1.asp");
  }
}
%>
```

Now comes the *ta-dah!* moment you've been waiting for. Once you're sure you know who this user is, you can take anything you like out of the data table and make a session variable out of it.

The two lines between the rows of asterisks are the extra bit that creates session variables from the CustomerID and UserGroup data fields. Once those lines are executed, those values are available whenever you need them.

> ### How long is a session?
>
> That's the kind of question you may ponder when you get your first invoice from a psychiatrist, right? But it's also a fair question in relation to the Session Object. Just how long *do* those session variables stay in the system?
>
> One answer you'll hear is that the session ends and all session variables cease to exist when the user leaves the site. But that cannot be true because there's no way of knowing for sure that the user has left your site. A better answer is that the session ends if the user has not requested anything from the server for 20 minutes — the default timeout. Another answer is that you can decide how long the server will sit tapping its fingers before it concludes that the user has wandered off. If 60 minutes is what you prefer, use this code:
>
> `<% Session.Timeout = 60 %>`

To summarize, what you need to do to set up user-specific session variables is as follows:

1. **Make a login page in which the form submits to the same page.**
2. **Place a recordset on the page, which pulls the CustomerID, UserGroup, Username, and Password fields from the Customers data table and uses SQL variables to compare the Username and Password fields with request variables (see Figure 8-11).**
3. **Make a page with which to redirect users whose logins fail.**
4. **Click HTML Source in your Launcher to open the HTML Source window, and scroll to the top.**
5. **Add the code in 8-4 by hand.**

   You should insert the code right above the `<HTML>` tag.

> **WARNING!** It's pretty obvious that if the user has disabled cookies — which is an option on all modern browsers — cookies can neither be set nor read. What's not so obvious is that session variables also fail if the user is refusing cookies.

Doing it All in Live Data View

Live Data View (LDV) is an extra-special UltraDev feature that enables you to display a very close approximation of the browse-time view of your page right there in the document window, and also allows you to continue design work on the page.

Server objects can be displayed in LDV, but you have to know how to assign values to them. The key to the procedure is the LDV Settings dialog box.

LDV is explained in much more detail in Chapter 6.

Session variables in Live Data View

Suppose that you're building an online auction. You've led your user through a series of lists so as to zero in on exactly what sub-sub-sub-section of your auction contains the stuff he or she is interested in. Having done that — if you're wise — you've probably generated session variables called `ArticleName` and `ArticleCode` so that you can refer to them at any time.

Now you're interested in testing a page that needs to display the `ArticleName` session variable, using LDV. Suppose that you want to simulate the situation where the user has followed the path Music⇨Instruments⇨Other⇨Accordions (Hey, *someone* must be interested in accordions). The following steps guide you through using the LDV Settings dialog box to make that easy:

1. **Open the Data Bindings inspector.**

2. **Click the plus (+) button and select Session Variable from the pop-up menu.**

3. **In the Name box, type the name of the variable you're interested in and then click OK.**

    The Session Object appears in the Data Bindings inspector (see Figure 8-12).

4. **Place a cursor on the page where the session variable belongs.**

5. **In the Data Bindings inspector, expand the Session Object (if necessary) and select the variable you want to place on the page.**

Figure 8-12: The Data Bindings inspector with Session Objects available for insert.

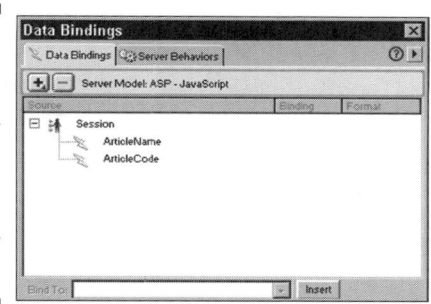

6. **Click the small Insert button at the base of the Inspector palette.**

    The placeholder {Session.ArticleName} appears on the page. Now switch to LDV and open the Settings dialog box. Because there's no handy-dandy list manager for session variables, you need to use the free-form initialization script window down at the bottom of the dialog box. This window takes any server-side script that may be necessary to set the page up as it expects to be in a live situation. Type the following in the initialization script box:

    ```
    <%
    Session("ArticleName") = "Accordions"
    %>
    ```

7. **Close the dialog box and refresh LDV.**

    The page looks like Figure 8-13.

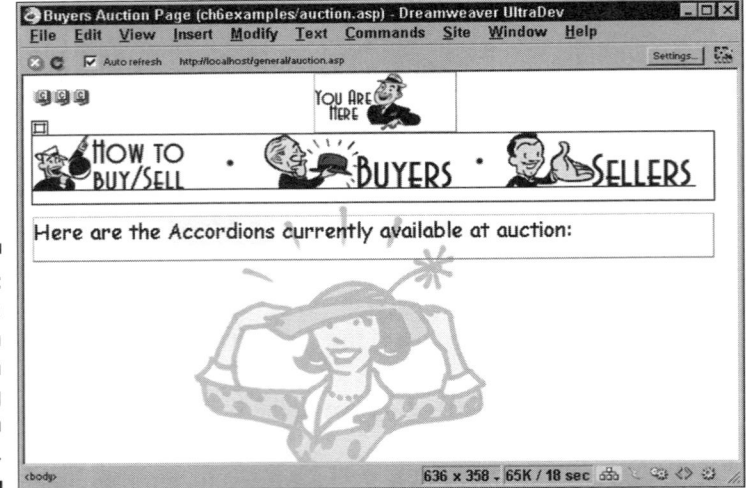

Figure 8-13: Live Data View of an auction page using a Session Object.

Cookies in Live Data View

Another data type that you may need to test in LDV is cookie information. A *cookie* is a small data file that was written to the user's computer on some previous visit to your Web site. You then read back and make use of that file.

A typical cookie is the date of the user's last visit, so you can display cheery stuff like "Hiya George, we haven't seen you since 2/21/00."

Cookies belong to the Request Object when they're being read, and the Response Object when they're being written. To test for a cookie, follow these steps:

A ColdFusion tip you need right now

Are you a ColdFusion user? This is as good a moment as any to tell you what nobody else will — most versions of the CF server can't handle server objects by default. Sooner or later you're going to need session objects for things like user logins and shopping carts. Teaching CF how to deal with these exotica is actually quite simple. Create a text file called `Application.cfm` with the following content:

```
<CFAPPLICATION NAME="TestApp"
    SESSIONMANAGEMENT="Yes">
```

Place this cute little file at the server root of the site that's going to need to deal with session objects. For example, if you've defined your site so that server-side files go in `C:\Inetpub\wwwroot\model_rockets`, put the `Application.cfm` file right in there.

If you snoop around a bit, you may find several other versions of the `Application.cfm` file. Pay them no heed. They're innocent until proved guilty.

A good up-to-date reference on ColdFusion in general is *ColdFusion 4 For Dummies* by Alexis D. Gutzman and John Paul Ashenfelter (IDG Books Worldwide, Inc.).

---

1. **Open the Data Bindings inspector.**

2. **Click the plus (+) button and select Request Variable from the pop-up menu.**

3. **Change the request type to Request.Cookie.**

4. **In the Name box, type the name of the cookie you're testing for and click OK.**

   The Request Object appears in the Data Bindings inspector.

5. **Place a cursor on the page where the cookie info belongs.**

6. **In the Data Bindings inspector, expand the Request Object (if necessary) and select the appropriate request variable.**

7. **Click the small Insert button at the base of the Inspector palette.**

   The placeholder {Cookies.LastVisit} appears on the page. Now switch to LDV and proceed.

8. **Click the Settings button on the LDV toolbar.**

   The Live Data Settings dialog box opens.

9. **Type this in the initialization script box:**

   ```
   <%
   Response.Cookies("LastVisit") = "2/21/00"
   %>
   ```

10. **Close the dialog box and refresh LDV.**

ColdFusion Specials

The ColdFusion server technology makes all the server objects described in this chapter available, but the terminology is a little different. ColdFusion does not refer to the Request Object as such, but the variables that ASP places in the Request Object appear in either the FORM object or the URL object in CF notation. For example, the CF equivalent of `Request.Form("element1")` is `FORM.element1`.

Cookies are also written and read differently in CF. Refer to Appendix C for translations of the ASP code used in this chapter to ColdFusion.

Chapter 9

UltraDev Extensions and Tricks

In This Chapter

▶ Messing around with the Object Palette
▶ Working with the Macromedia Exchange
▶ Using the Extension Manager
▶ Creating do-it-yourself UltraDev menus
▶ Making images (and other things) stay where you drop them
▶ Uncovering additional extension resources

"UltraDev is Extensible!" has been Macromedia's slogan, mantra, disclaimer, escape clause, call-it-what-you-will ever since UltraDev first launched in June 2000. What that phrase means is that UltraDev menus, palettes, inspectors, and dialog boxes are not shrouded in secrecy. Files describing these features are readily accessible and readable — you can edit them and add your own features if you like. Sometimes all you have to do to customize these files is add some pure techno-text; others require a little knowledge of JavaScript.

This chapter describes some of the games that you can play with UltraDev to extend and customize it. It helps if you know a little about JavaScript, but it isn't necessary for understanding the chapter.

Dreamies may know this stuff already because nearly all of it applies to Dreamweaver — the latest versions of Dreamweaver, anyway — as much as to UltraDev.

Drummies will find this all very unfamiliar because there's no equivalent in Drumbeat (unless you count the Contract Manager). Have fun!

Customizing the Objects Palette

Click the header of your UltraDev Objects palette to see the pop-up menu of eight object groups, starting at Characters and ending at Special (see Figure 9-1).

Part III: Advanced UltraDev

Figure 9-1:
The eight groups you can access from the Objects palette.

Figure 9-2:
The nine sub-folders of the \Configuration\Objects folder.

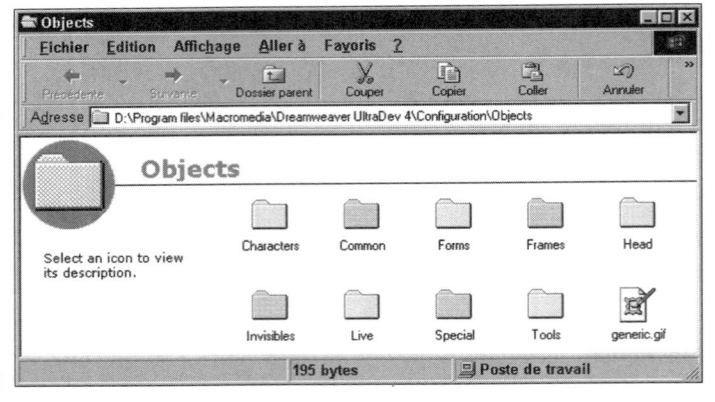

Now use your Windows Explorer (or Mac equivalent) to examine the folder structure at \Dreamweaver UltraDev\Configuration\Objects (see Figure 9-2). Well, how about that! Apart from the Tools folder, which contains stuff for the lower part of the Objects Palette, the list matches exactly!

UltraDev is like that. When it launches, it looks around the directory structure to see what's around and configures according to what it finds. Look, for example, at the files in the \Configuration\Objects\Common subfolder and you see a lot of familiar names. All the "common" objects have a GIF file and an HTM file associated with them — some also have a JS (external JavaScript) file.

The scheme isn't hard to figure out. The GIF files are the icons, or buttons, that actually appear on the Objects palette. The HTM files contain the instructions for inserting whatever the object is supposed to insert, such as an image or a table. A JS file is needed if parameter information needs to be collected from the user — the location of an image to insert, or the details for an e-mail link, for instance.

That set of two or three files (GIF, HTM, and possibly a JS file) *is* the object. If you delete these files, the object essentially disappears from UltraDev.

Regrouping the Objects palette

If you know what you're doing, you can perform a partial or total makeover of the Objects palette. To create your own object group:

1. **Set your Windows Explorer (or Mac equivalent) to** \Dreamweaver UltraDev\Configuration\Objects.
2. **Make a new folder one level below and give it whatever name you want for the new object group (Favorites, for example).**
3. **Raid the other object group folders (Common, Forms, Head, and so on) and grab any files associated with the objects that you want to use as part of your new group.**

   Cut them from the folder they occupied by default and paste them into your new folder.

WARNING! You must take files in complete sets. If, for example, you want to move the image object from the Common folder to your Favorites folder, you *must* move all three files Image.htm, Image.gif, and Image.js.

Making your own simple objects

Besides letting you create a custom *group* of objects (see steps in preceding section), UltraDev also enables you to custom build individual objects. To do so, however, you need the following kit of parts:

- An HTM file containing whatever you want to insert on the page.
- A GIF file containing an 18-x-18-pixel icon to associate with the object (if you don't provide one, the Objects palette displays a generic "mystery" icon).
- If any parameters are required from the user, the JavaScript logic to request them and use them appropriately. This logic often goes into a separate JS file, but it works just as well if you include it in the head of the HTM file.

Put these two or three files in whatever subfolder below the Objects folder that you think is appropriate. Next time you load UltraDev, the object will be there in the equivalent panel of the Objects palette for your use.

Here's a simple example: Suppose that you're in the habit of putting an <HR> tag followed by a copyright line and company address at the bottom of your documents. You can easily make that text into a reusable object. This is the simplest type of object because it's hard-coded and requires no user interaction at the time it's placed on the page.

Create a file similar to the following example, substituting your actual company or personal details:

```
<HR>
<ADDRESS>
&copy; Company name<BR>
Address line 1<BR>
Address line 2<BR>
</ADDRESS>
```

Save the file as `Address.htm` and place it in whatever Objects subfolder you want.

Now make an 18-x-18-pixel icon for the object, call it `Address.gif`, and put it in the same folder. That's all there is to it. Next time you load UltraDev, the object will be available on the Objects Palette. Click the button, and the copyright and company address information are inserted into your document.

TIP: When developing object extensions, you don't need to close and relaunch UltraDev every time you add a new object or make an edit. You can press Ctrl+click on the header of the Objects Palette and choose Reload Extensions.

Making your own parameterized (how do you like that word?) objects

Besides the simple custom-built object discussed in the preceding section, you can also create a *parameterized* object. Here's an example of a custom-built object, which has to collect some user input (the *parameters* of the object) before it's deployed. In spite of its million-dollar adjective, this particular object is not terrifically useful. It earned its place in this chapter only because it's a great way to show you how the user-supplied parameters are collected and used. Have you ever felt the temptation to place the cosine of 52° on a Web page? I thought not.

The useless-but-instructive object in the following example pops up a dialog box in which the user enters an angle in degrees and chooses a trigonometry function (tan, sin, or cos). The result is then inserted on the page at the cursor position.

Here are the two simple rules that you need to remember when you want to make a parameterized object:

1. The title of the HTM file and anything contained between the `<FORM>` and `</FORM>` tags are used to create the user-interaction dialog box. The title is also used as a tooltip in the Objects Palette.

2. Anything returned by the Javascript function `objectTag ()` is inserted into the document at the cursor position. Any instructions in that function are also executed.

Bearing these rules in mind, here's the `Trig.htm` file for the object. As you can see, it's not at all complicated:

```html
<HTML>
<HEAD>
<TITLE>Insert a trig function</TITLE>
<SCRIPT LANGUAGE="JavaScript" SRC="Trig.js">
</SCRIPT>
</HEAD>
<BODY>
<FORM NAME="Trigform">
<P>Choose your trig function:
<P>
<SELECT NAME="trigfunc">
<OPTION>TAN
<OPTION>SINE
<OPTION>COSINE
</SELECT>
<P>Angle in degrees:
<INPUT NAME="angle" TYPE="text" SIZE=4 MAXLENGTH=4>
</FORM>
</BODY>
</HTML>
```

The JavaScript file, `Trig.js`, has to do this:

1. Retrieve the user-supplied parameters, *trigfunc* and *angle*.
2. Convert the angle variable from degrees to radians.
3. Do the math and truncate the result to 3 decimal places.
4. Return the result.

Here is the `Trig.js` file called by the `Trig.htm` file:

```javascript
function objectTag(){
   var a = document.Trigform.angle.value*Math.PI/180;
   var b = document.Trigform.trigfunc.selectedIndex;
   if (b == 0) return trunc(Math.tan(a));
   else if (b == 1) return trunc(Math.sin(a));
   else if (b == 2) return trunc(Math.cos(a));
   else return "";
}

function trunc(n) {
   j = n.toString().indexOf('.')
   return n.toString().substring(0,j+4);
}
```

Figure 9-3 shows the dialog box that pops up when you deploy the Trig function object.

Figure 9-3:
The Trig function object collecting its parameters.

On the CD, in the folder `\Extensions\Object` extensions, you'll find a custom object that's much more practical than the Trig function object. The Scroller object accepts two parameters — a text string and a choice of speed (fast, medium, or slow) — and inserts the text string in the browser status window, scrolling right-to-left at the chosen speed. The files for this object are `Scroller.htm`, `Scroller.gif`, and `Scroller.js`. Making the status bar scroller requires JavaScript skill beyond the level of this book, but I've included it for you to examine or use, as you see fit. The Scroller object illustrates how to use the UltraDev *Document Object Model* to insert source code into the document at appropriate places. Besides the status bar scroller, the CD contains a few other custom objects that you can play with.

The server behavior builder

UltraDev 4 includes a very clever module that enables you to build and edit your own server behaviors. Just like objects, behaviors can be either parameterized or not. The server behavior builder really isn't hard to use, but it definitely needs a good grasp of source coding, either server-side JavaScript, VBScript, JSP, or ColdFusion — so I've declared it off limits for this book.

If you want to sneak a peek (or maybe even try your luck), place some source code on your clipboard, pull down the list of server behaviors, and select New Server Behavior. It's hard to imagine how you could do any actual damage — the worst that would happen is that you'd create an unusable behavior.

Using the Macromedia Exchange

When you pull down the Insert menu in an UltraDev document, the last item is Get More Objects. Likewise, when you use the plus button in the Behavior inspector or the Server Behaviors inspector, you see the Get More Behaviors option. These options (plus a couple more) lead you to the same place — the Macromedia Exchange Web site at http://dynamic.macromedia.com/bin/MM/exchange/dreamweaver/main.jsp.

This site is a cornucopia of UltraDev extensions — several kinds in a number of categories. Figure 9-4 shows one screen of object extensions in the Productivity category. Notice that some of them have official Macromedia approval, indicated by an icon.

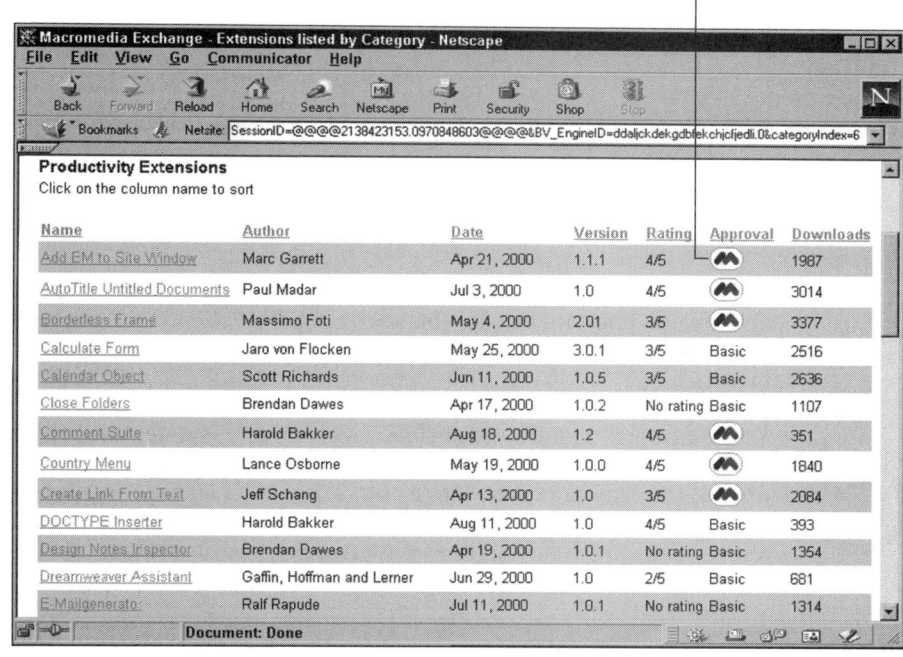

Figure 9-4: Some of the extensions available in the Productivity category of the Macromedia Exchange.

The Detail page of each extension (see Figure 9-5) includes descriptions, discussion threads, installation instructions, and other details in addition to the download links.

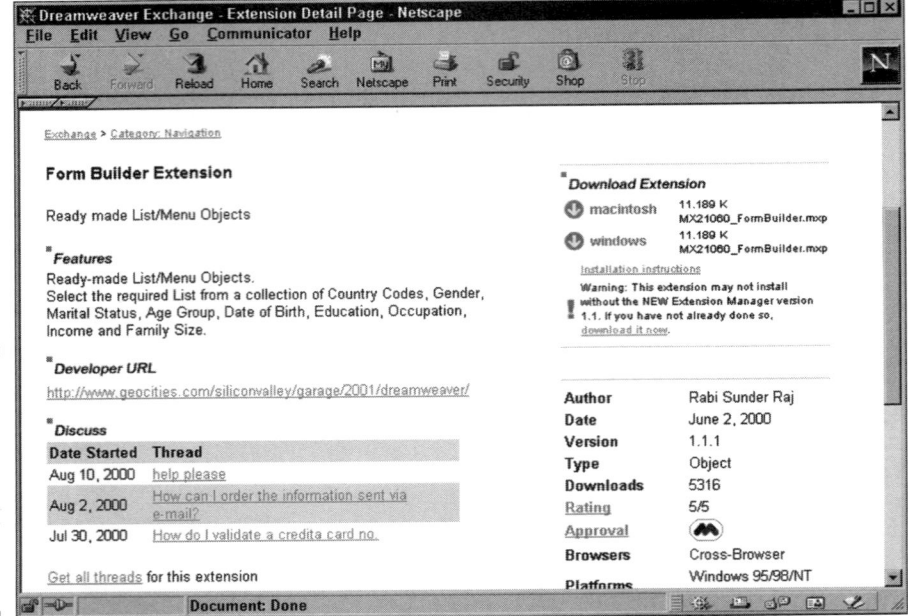

Figure 9-5: The Detail page for one downloadable UltraDev extension object.

When you download an extension, you can either install it on the fly or download it to the folder `Ultradev\Downloaded Extensions`.

All Extension files end in .mxp (Macromedia eXtension Package). The package file can contain, in addition to the source code for the extension, such things as help files, icons, description files, license terms, and menu tree inserts.

TIP: To get access to all the extensions, you need to register with the Macromedia Exchange and choose a username and password. Registration is easy, and by default the Exchange site sets a cookie so that you're recognized and greeted by name when you visit the site later. Fortunately, Macromedia doesn't assume registration is an invitation to send you an avalanche of trash e-mail.

Mastering the Extension Manager

When you select an object or behavior extension from the Macromedia Exchange, you have two choices: you can instant-install it, or you can download the MXP package file to your system and then use the Macromedia

Chapter 9: UltraDev Extensions and Tricks

Extension Manager to install it. The advantage of the latter method is that you then have the MXP file on your system. If you later upgrade UltraDev, you can reinstall the object or extension without having to search the Exchange for it again.

Here are the options for installing an extension from your own file system:

- Double-click the MXP file in your Explorer (Windows) or Finder (Mac).
- Launch the Manager by double-clicking `\Macromedia\Extension Manager\Extension Manager.exe`.
- In UltraDev, with a document window open, choose Commands⇔Manage Extensions.

One way or another, the Extension Manager opens, as shown in Figure 9-6, with a listing of whatever extensions you've already installed. An extension selected in the upper pane has its description text displayed in the lower pane.

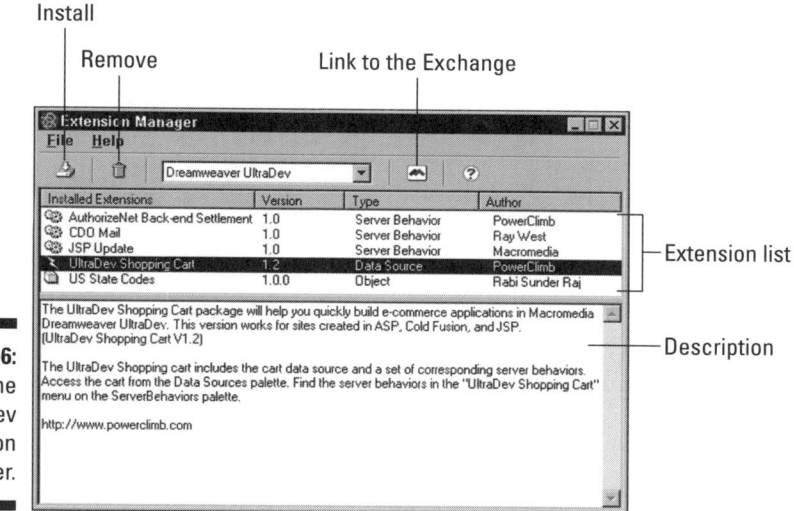

Figure 9-6: The UltraDev Extension Manager.

The Extension Manger includes a button for a direct link to the Macromedia Exchange, along with buttons for installing and deleting extensions. The File menu repeats these options.

Part III: Advanced UltraDev

To install an extension, you can click the Install New Extension button, choose File➪Install Extension, or press Ctrl+I. The Browse box opens on the `\Ultradev\Downloaded Extensions` folder. Select your extension package file and click Install.

A panel displaying license terms pops up. Unless you decline the terms, the extension installs. Most extensions install in seconds. You often need to close UltraDev and relaunch it for the extension to be fully available.

To uninstall an existing extension, either click the Remove Extension trash can, choose File➪Remove Extension, or press Ctrl+R. The extension is removed.

Cooking Up Your Own Insert Menu

If you ever build or download any extension objects (see instructions previously in this chapter) you may notice something weird about your Insert menu. Figure 9-7 shows my Insert menu after I created the object extensions Address, Simpledate, Scroller, and Trig and downloaded Rabi Sunder Raj's extension object, States — a list box populated with U.S. States.

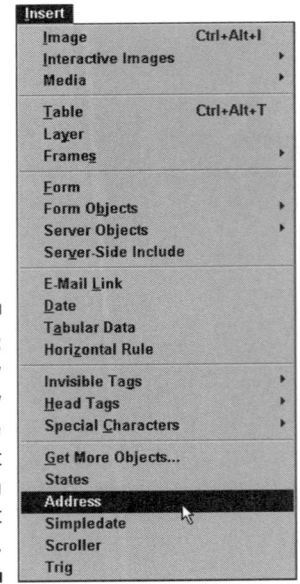

Figure 9-7: UltraDev sticks any spare objects at the bottom of the Insert menu.

I didn't think that looked very tidy, so I set about discovering how to customize UltraDev's menus. Here's what I found. . . .

When UltraDev loads into your computer, it configures according to what it finds in its environment. It looks at all the subfolders under `Ultradev\Configuration`, including all of the sub-subfolders under `Ultradev\Configuration\Objects`, where your objects are stored. But most of all, it reads and uses a big file called `Ultradev\Configuration\Menus\menus.xml`.

The `menus.xml` file is literally the blueprint for all of UltraDev's menus and keyboard shortcuts. It's a plain ASCII text file, so there's nothing to stop you from opening it in a text editor and poking around. It doesn't take long to figure out its structure (helped by the "Rearranging menus" section of Chapter 16 of the Dreamweaver manual). A straightforward menu of eight items with a couple of separators looks like this, in skeletal form:

```
<menu>
  <menuitem>
  <menuitem>
<separator />
  <menuitem>
  <menuitem>
  <menuitem>
  <menuitem>
<separator />
  <menuitem>
  <menuitem>
</menu>
```

You can nest menu blocks to create the cascading effect that keeps menu lists from overflowing the screen height.

After you get used to the simple structure, of course, you can tamper with it, but you have to learn the rules. The `<menu>` and `<menuitem>` tags have several attributes, some of which are required. In other words, if you don't put them in, the tag is ignored. Here are the required attributes:

- **name:** The label that appears on screen. Both `<menu>` and `<menuitem>` tags need a name.
- **id:** An identifier that's unique in the entire menu structure. Both `<menu>` and `<menuitem>` tags need an id.
- **file:** The name of the file that contains the principal instructions for creating the object. Objects need an HTM file, a GIF file, and sometimes a JS file. `<menuitem>` tags need the HTM file quoted as the file attribute.
- **key:** The shortcut key assigned to the object, if any. If you don't want a shortcut key, just type **key** ="" inside the `<menuitem>` tag.

Part III: Advanced UltraDev

The reason that the five object extensions are seen stuck on the end of the Insert menu in Figure 9-7 is that these objects are not present in the `menus.xml` file. After UltraDev reads `menus.xml`, it checks around to see if there are any objects, behaviors, and so on that haven't been mentioned. If it finds any, it just sticks them on the end of the menu.

Tidying up the Insert menu, then, is no big deal. I added a `<menuitem>` for the States object in the Form Objects section of `menus.xml`; then I built a complete submenu for the other four objects. Here it is:

```
<menu name="Object Extensions"  id="BM_extension">
     <menuitem name="Address"   id="BM_copyright"
         file="Address.htm"  key="">
     <menuitem name="Scroller"  id="BM_statusbar"
         file="Scroller.htm" key="">
     <menuitem name="Trig"      id="BM_trig" file="Trig.htm" key="">

</menu>
```

Figure 9-8 shows the successful submenu.

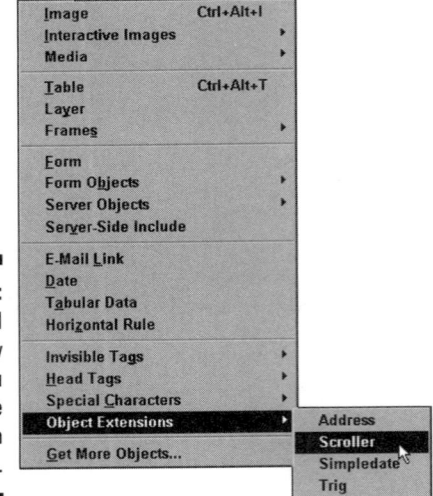

Figure 9-8: A brand new submenu for the extension objects.

Absolute Positioning à la Drumbeat

Drummies are going to love the absolute positioning feature. It's a way of teaching UltraDev to behave almost like Drumbeat when positioning objects in layout.

Chapter 9: UltraDev Extensions and Tricks

> ## Messing around with UltraDev
>
> This chapter mainly describes reconfigurations of UltraDev in relation to objects and object extensions. Many other aspects of UltraDev configuration are deliberately made available for inspection and editing by the user (that's you). All keyboard shortcuts, as well as all menu structures, can be edited in the `menus.xml` file. You can also edit keyboard shortcuts by choosing Edit➪Keyboard Shortcuts. Configuration of all property inspectors is governed by the editable file `\Configuration\TagAttributeList.txt`. You can even construct your own floating palettes if you feel so inclined (and if you're a JavaScript ace). Here are a few other config files of interest:
>
> **\Configuration\ActiveXnames.txt.** A list of nicknames for ActiveX objects in the format `Nickname/clsid:ClassID`. You can add your own downloaded ActiveX objects to this list.
>
> **\Configuration\SourceFormat.txt.** A guide to the precise formatting of HTML tags by UltraDev.
>
> **\Configuration\Startup\localTextUltraDev.htm.** A list of all warning and error messages used in UltraDev. If one of them drives you crazy, or if you find one impossible to understand, edit this file!
>
> . . . and finally, the file that sums up the whole UltraDev extensibility thing,
>
> **\Configuration\Configuration_Readme.htm.**
>
> **Note:** When editing any UltraDev config file, it's always wise to make a backup copy in some other folder. Then if you make some frightful mess, you can always revert to the original without needing to do a total UltraDev reinstall.

Some Web designers use layers a lot. Some don't like layers. I'm a layers fan, personally. It comes from using Drumbeat, which gives everything you place in layout its own layer. The effect is that you can drag assets into the document window — images, for example — and they stay where you drop them. This drag-and-drop-anywhere-you-like behavior doesn't come naturally to UltraDev, but it's a little-known fact that you can teach UltraDev this very Drumbeat-like behavior — and it's really, really easy.

As a matter of fact, you can position objects in the Document window in a couple of ways. I describe here what I think is the easiest method. I'm assuming that you want to drop images anywhere in the document window and have them stay where they're placed because they have a layer to sit on.

A *layer* — which is more often a `<div>` . . . `</div>` HTML element than a `<layer>` . . . `</layer>` — is an element that occupies a fixed absolute position on a Web page. Among the attributes of a `<div>` are its width, height, and position in x, y, and z coordinates, its visibility, and its background color or image.

The way to position layers, believe it or not, is to add just three lines to the JavaScript file that controls the placement of an image in UltraDev. The file that you want to add these lines to is `\Ultradev\Configuration\Objects\Common\Image.js`.

If you really want every single image that you place to import its own layer, like a slice of smoked salmon lying on its canapé of toast, you can modify that actual file. Or, you can create a new object by making a copy of the original file and calling it something like `Layerimage.js`. (You must also copy `Image.htm` to `Layerimage.htm` and invent a new icon called `Layerimage.gif`).

Simply open the JS file in a text editor (Notepad's fine), and you'll see that it's not the world's most complicated bit of programming. All you need to do is add the following three lines after the `objectTag(assetArgs)` function:

```
function objectInsertLayer() {
  return true;
}
```

Save the file and relaunch UltraDev. Presto! After you select an image from the Browse box, your cursor changes to the cross shape. Sweep out a rectangular area for the image position — guided by the rulers if you've made them visible — and when you release the mouse button, the image pops into the layer and stays there.

This layer-attachment trick applies not only to images but to form elements such as buttons, check boxes, radio buttons, and text fields — pretty much everything. (See Chapter 13 to find out how to size and align layers.)

Extensionology Resources

There's a lot more that I can say on the subject of extending UltraDev — much, much more! But the point of this chapter is just to let you know how accessible UltraDev's bits and pieces are and perhaps — considering how easy some of the simple extensions are to create and install — give you some confidence to experiment. Entire newsgroups and mail lists are devoted to the topic — some people seem to do nothing with their lives other than think up UltraDev extensions.

Other than the Macromedia Exchange Web site, three other sites are worth a look:

Macromedia's 10-step tutorial

www.macromedia.com/support/ultradev/behaviors/create_extensions/

Webmonkeys extensibility tutorial

www.hotwired.com/webmonkey/99/11/index2a.html?tw=design

Joseph Lowery's extensions database

www.idest.com/cgi-bin/database.cgi

Chapter 10

The UltraDev View of Site Security

In This Chapter

▶ Figuring out what information you need about your users
▶ Getting and storing information about your users
▶ Restricting access to whole pages

*I*n a nutshell, site security means knowing who your user is and reacting appropriately.

By knowing who your user is, I don't mean just knowing the user's IP address, which you can retrieve in ASP with a simple `Request.ServerVariables ("REMOTE_HOST")` statement — IP addresses are assigned dynamically and don't identify an individual user (or even an individual computer). By site security, I mean the whole process of creating and retrieving user identities and then storing them in a data table. After you have this knowledge, you can use it to

✔ Maintain a record of user activity on your page.
✔ Personalize your pages.
✔ Prevent unauthorized users from accessing parts of your site.

UltraDev provides a suite of four server behaviors for site security, grouped under the heading of User Authentication. They are Log In User, Log Out User, Restrict Access To Page, and Check New Username. These behaviors are the main topic of this chapter. Server behaviors in general are the subject of Chapter 5.

What You Need to Know about Your Users

How much do you need to know about your users? That entirely depends on the purpose of your site. If you're going to have site security at all, the one essential is that each user have a unique ID of some kind. You can arrange for those unique IDs to be supplied by the users themselves (as is the case with the KeyPalNation database supplied on the CD accompanying this book and described in Chapter 8). But that particular demonstration site is extremely poor from a security point of view because its users have no passwords.

Sites that take security seriously force their users to choose a username and password combination. When a new user registers, a logical routine checks to make sure the username is not already in use, and if not, a numerical User ID is automatically assigned. The most common method for generating User IDs is to use an auto-number field in a data table that increments to the next number every time a new record is added.

A users data table with passable security needs three fields as a rock-bottom minimum: user ID, username, and password. These three are sufficient to identify users with certainty, and track them economically. *Tracking,* also known as site logging, simply means recording what pages they request and when.

Table 10-1 presents an example of security data. Table 10-2 shows an example of the kind of information that you would expect to save in a database that logs site traffic.

Table 10-1   Minimal Users Data Table

User ID	Username	Password
515	Bear	ty667do
516	salixe	magenta
517	Flopoto	121266

Table 10-2   Minimal Site Traffic Log

Date/Time	Page	User ID
Mon Aug 28 15:23:23 PDT 2000	search.asp	515
Mon Aug 28 15:23:28 PDT 2000	results.asp	515
Mon Aug 28 15:24:11 PDT 2000	prodpage.asp	515
Mon Aug 28 15:24:13 PDT 2000	search.asp	517
Mon Aug 28 15:24:55 PDT 2000	colors.asp	515

A slightly more complete users data table would include a timestamp field to record when the user record was generated, and fields for the user's real (or assumed) names. You can make use of such a table to personalize pages by displaying the user's name.

If you're selling something to your users, you need to know a whole lot more information than just a username and password. You also need a shipping address, a billing address, and the user's credit card details — all of which is stuff that customers expect to give you only once.

Figure 10-1 shows the design view of the Customers data table of the Hatstore database. This Access 2000 database is supplied on the CD accompanying this book and described in Chapter 12.

The data table in Figure 10-1 was originally created by using the Microsoft Access Order Entry wizard — the CustomerID field is auto-numbered, generating unique IDs by incrementing the number every time a record is added.

Your first step in any site security scheme is to create the basic users data table, whether simple (like the one described in Table 10-1) or complex (like Figure 10-1), and seed it with one test record.

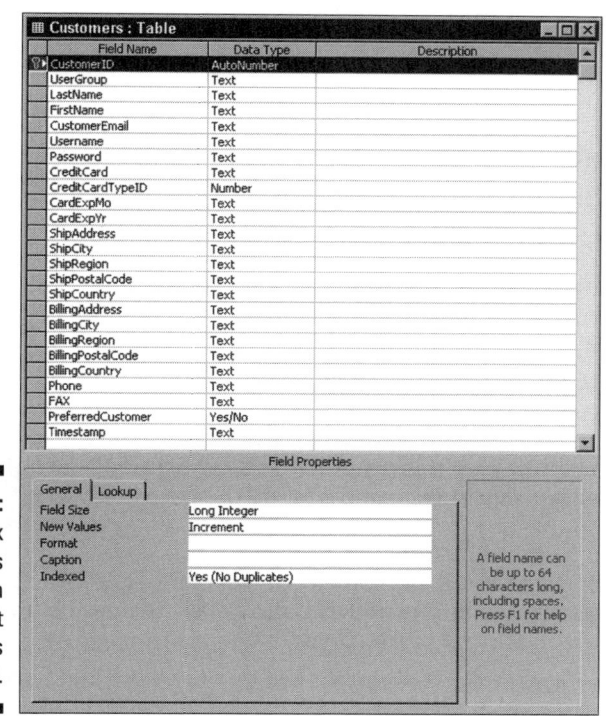

Figure 10-1: A complex Customers data table in Microsoft Access 2000.

How to Get Information from Your Users

At some point, you're going to have to collect information from your users. Unless you're running a super-secure encrypted site, that info is going to be collected from an online form. The process of gathering information from a new user is known as *registration*.

New user registration

Figure 10-2 shows part of a typical new user registration form that's designed to create a new record for the data table that I show you in the previous section (refer to Figure 10-1).

Figure 10-2: Part of a new user registration form built in UltraDev.

When you design a new user registration form, it's a good idea to give the form elements on the page the same names as the data fields that they correspond to. For example, my form text boxes have the names: FirstName, LastName, CustomerEmail, Username, Password, and so on, corresponding to field names in the database. If the names are the same, then UltraDev saves you time in creating associations between the database and the form by guessing at the associations for you. Neat.

After you complete the basic design of a form, you can activate it by following these steps:

1. **Make a data connection to the database containing your users data table.**

   Instructions for making data connections are in Chapter 3.

2. **Make sure all the form elements are inside a form and add a submit button (also inside the form).**

   You can fetch all form elements, including the submit button, from the Forms panel of the Objects palette.

   Don't assign any ACTION to the form. If you do, the ACTION risks conflicting with UltraDev's built-in server behavior.

3. **In the Server Behaviors inspector, click the plus (+) button and choose Insert Record.**

   The Insert Record dialog box opens.

4. **Set the top two drop-down lists to your data connection and the users data table in the database, whatever they are.**

5. **Scroll through the Form Elements list slowly and carefully, checking that the associations between form elements and data fields are all correct.**

   Here's where using the same names for form elements and data fields comes in handy. If you do, UltraDev guesses all the associations for you. If you don't, you need to make every one of these associations manually by using the Form Elements and Columns lists.

6. **Place the redirect page in the Go to text box in the middle of this dialog box, either by typing it in or by using the Browse button.**

   This is the page that the user of the online form will see immediately after submitting the form.

A completed Insert Record dialog box is shown in Figure 10-3.

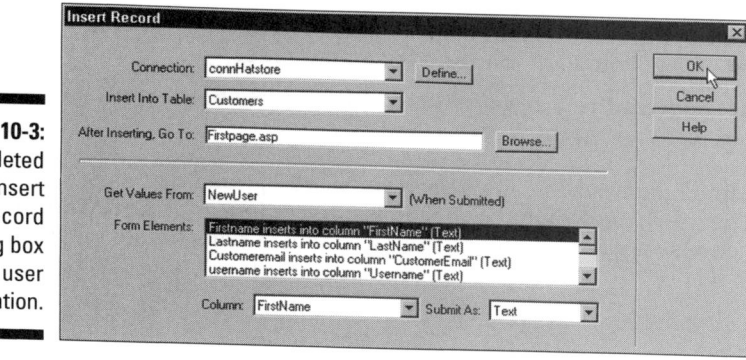

Figure 10-3: A completed Insert Record dialog box for new user registration.

Part III: Advanced UltraDev

On The CD

The page shown in Figure 10-2, `NewUser.asp`, is on the CD accompanying this book, as part of the Hatstore site in the `\Demo sites\HatsGalore\Asp` folder. It has one useful little gimmick (done with client-side JavaScript) — a check box for the user to select if the billing address is the same as the shipping address. If the user checks the box, address details are copied from shipping to billing instantly.

UltraDev's Check New Username server behavior

I can't imagine any security gaffe more serious than allowing two different users to have the same username and password combination. Although it isn't likely that two people would make that choice independently, it's possible — and a mischievous user may try to make it happen deliberately, just to see if you're on your toes.

Theoretically, there's no harm in having more than one person with the same username, as long as they don't also have the same password. But prudent data managers don't like to see two occurrences of a username in one table, so they reject a new user registration if the chosen username already exists.

The first of UltraDev's security-minded server behaviors is concerned with just that. It's called *Check New Username*, and it scans the users data table checking to see if a username already exists. To apply this server behavior, follow these steps:

1. **Apply the Insert Record server behavior as described in the preceding section.**

   This is an essential step. The security server behavior won't open unless there's an Insert Record behavior already applied.

2. **In the Server Behaviors inspector, click the plus (+) button and choose User Authentication⇨Check New Username.**

   The Check New Username dialog box opens.

3. **Use the Username Field drop-down list to define which field in the data table you want scanned for a duplicate.**

4. **Place the redirect page in the text box at the bottom, either by typing it in or by using the Browse button.**

The redirect page is basically a page you need to build that says something like, "The username you have chosen is already in use by a previous user. Please choose a different name." Still, a couple of refinements are in order.

First, it's polite to provide a link back to the registration page, but it must be done in such a way as not to reload the form and obliterate everything the user already entered. I don't know about you, but it would drive me crazy to enter all my address and credit card information, have my username rejected, and then find out that I have to enter everything all over again.

The way to ensure that the information will still be there after the user follows a back link is to link to this:

```
javascript:history.back()
```

Type some words on the redirect page, such as **Return to registration form**, select them, and enter the Javascript back-link in the Property inspector (see Figure 10-4).

Figure 10-4: Making sure the registration form is still filled when the user links back.

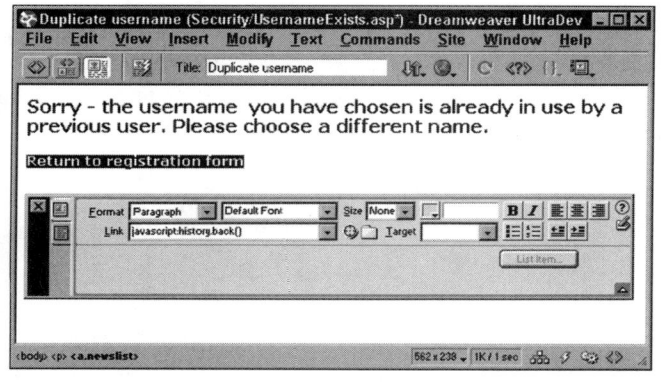

The other refinement to the redirect page is to make use of the fact that UltraDev's server behavior provides the rejected username as a request variable (request variables and other server objects are covered in Chapter 8).

The page is just a bit richer if you can make it say something like, "Sorry, the username Manowar is already in use by another user." It's a piece of cake, really. The username is available on the page as the request variable rqusername. Here's how to make use of it:

1. **In the Data Bindings inspector, click the plus (+) button and choose Request Variable.**

   The small Request Variable dialog box opens.

2. **Leave the Type drop-down list at its default setting and type in the name** rqusername.

   The variable appears in the Data Bindings inspector.

Modifying the UltraDev server behavior

Suppose that you don't like the idea of rejecting a duplicate username, and you'd prefer to scan username and password combinations. After all, a duplicate username is a very low security risk as long as it's matched with a unique password.

UltraDev doesn't provide a server behavior for this, but it isn't hard to modify the source code so that it scans both fields in the data table. Switch to code view by clicking the Code View button on the toolbar, and locate these lines:

Source Code Sample 10-1

```
var MM_dupKeyUsernameValue =
    String(Request.
    Form("username"));
var MM_dupKeySQL = "SELECT
    Username FROM Customers
    WHERE Username='" +
    MM_dupKeyUsernameValue +
    "'"
```

Add a new variable for the requested password, and a second term to the SQL WHERE clause. You should now have three lines like this:

Source Code Sample 10-2

```
var MM_dupKeyUsernameValue =
    String(Request.
    Form("username"));
var MM_dupKeyPasswordValue =
    String(Request.
    Form("password"));
var MM_dupKeySQL = "SELECT
    Username FROM Customers
    WHERE Username='" +
    MM_dupKeyUsernameValue + "'
    AND Password='" +
    MM_dupKeyPasswordValue +
    "'"
```

Now locate the line that passes the request variable:

Source Code Sample 10-3

```
MM_dupKeyRedirect =
    MM_dupKeyRedirect +
    MM_qsChar + "requsername="
    + MM_dupKeyUsernameValue;
```

Edit it to add a second request variable for the password:

Source Code Sample 10-4

```
MM_dupKeyRedirect =
    MM_dupKeyRedirect +
    MM_qsChar + "requsername="
    + MM_dupKeyUsernameValue +
    "&reqpassword=" +
    MM_dupKeyPasswordValue;
```

Now, on the redirect page, you have the option of including the rejected password in the text as well as the rejected username. At design time the text may be "Sorry the username and password combination {Request.rqusername} and {Request.rqpassword} are already in use."

3. **Click and drag it into position on the layout page.**

    The actual rejected username now appears in that position at browse time.

Keep Out!

There are many reasons why you might want to rope off certain pages in your Web site and admit only VIPs. In the corporate world, personnel files are considered very secret. In science, prepublication notes are shared only with the workgroup. In the software world, not everyone gets access to free downloads or beta versions. In commerce — possibly the most common reason for security — you usually have to keep the customers out of pages that add, delete, and edit records in your database. Only administrators get to do that stuff.

The problem is this: How do you know who are the VIPs?

Setting up user access levels

The security status of everybody in your database must be part of the database itself. In addition to fields for username and password, it's very common to have a field containing information about *user access level*. Because the user access level (sometimes known as user group) doesn't really need to be human-readable, it can just be a number (zero for casual callers, up to whatever number you like for VIPs). But UltraDev expects this field to be a readable string, so I oblige it — and make this section more intelligible — by using the access levels *guest, customer,* and *admin*.

Security by access levels depends on every user being defined as a member of one of the groups. Then either a login procedure or a cookie identifies the user, and the user's access level is retrieved from the data table and placed in the Session Object. The steps in that process are covered in Chapter 8.

I take you step-by-step through the UltraDev authentication procedure shortly. But first you need to know how to write the access levels to the database. Surely you can't allow anyone who registers to choose his or her own access level, can you? No you can't.

Access level is never a part of a registration form, at least not overtly. You have several options when dealing with this issue:

- Access levels are not set by registration. All editing of user access levels is done in the database application.
- The database is set to default to the lowest access level. Editing to a higher level is done in either the database application or on a special Web form accessible only to administrators.
- Separate registration forms are provided for users at each access level. URLs of the higher-level registration forms are given only to trusted users. The access level is then a hidden form field in each case.

✔ Administrative passwords are issued that set user access level as the new record is written to the data table.

Identifying the user's access level at login

Using UltraDev's User Authentication server behaviors to restrict access to pages starts with the login procedure. Here's how to apply it:

1. **Build a login page.**

    Figure 10-5 shows an example — a form containing a 2-x-2 table featuring Login and Password text boxes. You don't need a recordset on the page.

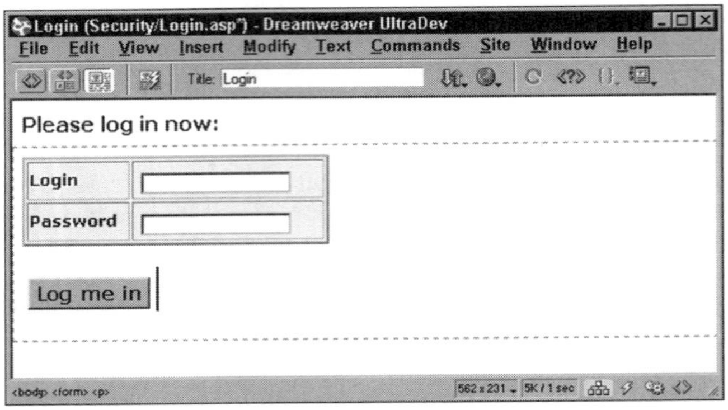

Figure 10-5:
A login page built in UltraDev.

2. **Make sure all the form elements are inside a form, and add a submit button (also inside the form).**

    You can fetch all form elements, including the submit button, from the Forms panel of the Objects palette. In the figure, you can see the start and end of the form as broken horizontal lines.

3. **Do not assign any ACTION to the form.**

    It's useful but not essential to give the form a name, however — Loginform, perhaps.

4. **In the Server Behaviors inspector, click the plus (+) button and choose User Authentication**⇨**Log In User.**

    The Log In User dialog box appears, as shown in Figure 10-6. It's a complex dialog box divided into four sections.

5. **In the top section of the dialog box, set the three drop-down lists to provide information about how the user's information is collected.**

    In the example, the form is Loginform, the Username Field is login and the Password Field is password.

6. **In the second section of the dialog box, set the four drop-down lists to identify the data connection that accesses your database, the data table containing user info, and the username and password columns in that table.**

   These are the columns (or fields) that the behavior will scan, attempting to match the user-supplied information specified in Step 5. If you don't have a data connection set up, you'll have to cancel out of this dialog box and make one. Chapter 3 tells you how.

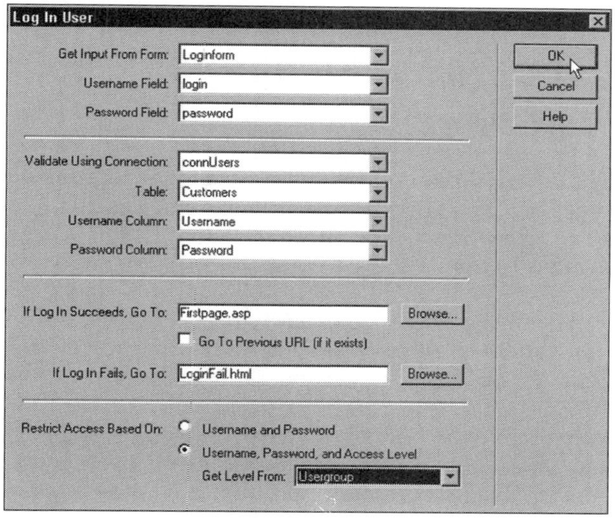

Figure 10-6:
The Log In User dialog box.

7. **In the third section of the dialog box, specify how you want users redirected when login succeeds or fails.**

   Normally, successfully logged-in users are redirected to whatever page is next in their natural progress through your site. Login failures are redirected to a special page letting them know that the database doesn't seem to know them and giving them a chance to try again. You need to build the login fail page, of course.

8. **In the bottom section of the dialog box, click the Username, Password, and Access Level radio button. In the Get Level From drop-down list, select the field in your data table that contains the user access level information.**

After you build the login page and the login fail page, you can save them, transfer them to the server, and test both good and bad logins.

What happens behind the scenes is that UltraDev scans the users data table looking for a match of both username and password. If the scan is successful, the username is stored as the session variable `MM_Username`, and the access level of that user is retrieved from the data table and stored as the session variable `MM_UserAuthorization`.

> **REMEMBER:** A session variable remains available for use on your site as long as the user keeps requesting pages from your server. For more details on session variables, see Chapter 8.

Setting up the checkpoint on a restricted page

If you apply the Log In User server behavior on a login page, as described in the preceding section, then you can use the powerful Restrict Access To Page server behavior to allow only users with a sufficiently high access level to see a page that you want to restrict.

The behavior relies on the existence of a `MM_UserAuthorization` session variable to decide whether the user has the credentials to see the page. The special login behavior creates this session variable.

> **WARNING!** The authentication behavior will fail if the user's browser is set to refuse cookies, or if the user requests no pages for a time of (by default) 20 minutes. See the sidebar "How long is a session" in Chapter 8 for an explanation.

To restrict access to a page, follow these steps:

1. **In the Server Behaviors inspector, click the plus (+) button and choose User Authentication➪Restrict Access To Page.**

    The Restrict Access To Page dialog box appears, as shown in Figure 10-7.

Figure 10-7: The Restrict Access To Page dialog box.

2. **Click the Username, Password, and Access Level radio button to restrict based on access level.**
 3. **If this is the first time you've used this behavior on this site, the Select Level(s) window is empty.**

    If this is not the first time, skip to Step 7.
 4. **Click the Define button.**

    The Define Access Levels dialog box opens, as shown in Figure 10-8.

Figure 10-8: Defining the access levels.

 5. **In the Name text box, type all the access levels that you want to create for this site. Click the plus (+) button after each entry to add them.**

    In Figure 10-7, I created the guest, customer, and admin access levels. The names (or numbers) of user levels are not chosen at random — they must correspond with user levels actually referenced in your database.
 6. **When done, click OK to close the dialog box.**

    The access levels you defined now appear in the Select Level(s) window.
 7. **In the Select Level(s) window, select all access levels you want to have access to this page.**

    You can click a single entry, Shift+click to select a contiguous range, or Ctrl+click to multiselect.
 8. **In the If Access Denied, Go To text box, type the name of the redirect page. You can also add it by using the Browse button.**

The redirect page is a special page announcing (politely, I hope) that the user doesn't have access privileges to this page and offering a hyperlink to somewhere appropriate to the user's access level. You need to build this page.

After you apply the server behavior and build the authorization fail page, you can save both pages, transfer them to the server, and test the behavior by logging in twice — first as a user with a sufficient access level, and again as a lower-level user to make sure you get the brush-off as intended.

Lackadaisical security

Both the Log In User and Restrict Access To Page server behaviors include an option to authenticate users based on username and password only.

That type of authentication is your only option if you have no user access levels in your database. The effect of placing this type of restriction on a page is that anybody who successfully logged in gets to see the page. Only people that enter the page's URL directly into their browser's location window — thus bypassing the login process — get the brush-off.

To use this type of authentication, follow the procedures in the two preceding sections of this chapter. The only difference is that when you reach the Restrict Access Based On (Log In User dialog box) or Restrict Based On (Restrict Access To dialog box) radio buttons, you must click the Username and Password option. The Select Level(s) window in the Restrict Access To Page dialog box is then irrelevant.

Logging out

UltraDev provides a server behavior for logging a user out. This server behavior isn't essential, but if you're the kind of person who likes to tie up all loose ends in a nice pink bow, you may opt to use it. The server behavior's only effect is to delete the session variables that are created as a result of a successful login. Proper logout prevents the same user from returning to the site 19 minutes later and still being considered logged in (session variables expire after 20 minutes of inactivity).

The Log Out User server behavior can be activated either by the user clicking a link, or by the loading of a page (the "Bye-bye" page, presumably).

To apply it to a link, open up whatever page links to the final exit page of the site (this could apply to more than one page). Create the text or image that will be the hyperlink source and select it. Then apply the User Authentication➪Log Out User behavior, putting the hyperlink destination in the box labeled When Done, Go To in the dialog box (see Figure 10-9). You do not also need to create a conventional hyperlink destination in the property inspector.

Figure 10-9:
The Log Out User dialog box.

To apply the logout behavior to a page, simply click the radio button for Log Out When Page Loads in the behavior's dialog box. It's unlikely that you'll need a redirect page in this case, but you can put one in.

Part IV
E-commerce with UltraDev

The 5th Wave — By Rich Tennant

"Since we began online shopping, I just don't know where the money's going."

In this part . . .

I suppose you could say that no modern Web-authoring software would be complete without e-commerce capability. If that's so, then strictly speaking, UltraDev is incomplete because there's no e-commerce in the out-of-the-box version. But you can easily snap on interesting (if a bit limited) e-commerce functionality in the form of an exchange package called UltraDev Shopping Cart, which I write about in Part IV.

No book about modern Web-authoring software is complete without some account of e-commerce, so I've devoted this part to the subject. Chapter 11 tells you how to develop an effective catalog page for selling your stuff online, and Chapter 12 gets down to the nitty-gritty of the shopping cart and all of its complex functions. Both chapters use an example of a fictitious e-commerce business with some millinery to sell.

Hang on to your hats!

Chapter 11

Setting Up Shop with UltraDev

In This Chapter

▶ Checking out the UltraDev Shopping Cart extension
▶ Starting small: No database required
▶ Expanding the enterprise: Setting up a dynamic catalog with a shopping cart

*I*f you're astute — which is the businessperson's equivalent of *intelligent* — you'll notice one important feature missing from the example databases in this book and on the accompanying CD. There's no way to actually buy anything online!

And yet, these days it seems that pretty well everybody is ready for e-commerce. If you build Web sites professionally, you know that what everyone wants is a *shopping cart.* As soon as you develop an e-commerce site with more than one sales page, you encounter the problem of how to store your shoppers' purchases as they browse your site. You certainly don't want to force them to go through the whole checkout procedure after every purchase.

The kind of temporary database for storing shopping decisions, pioneered by businesses like Land's End and Amazon.com, quickly became known as a shopping cart. Drummies will be familiar with the cart as the main feature of Drumbeat's e-commerce edition.

UltraDev is not e-commerce-capable, but a kind of plug-in, called an *extension,* does the job just fine. This extension, called UltraDev Shopping Cart and created by Powerclimb of San Diego under contract to Macromedia, makes no claim to being a complete e-commerce package. It just does what shopping carts are supposed to do, and very efficiently.

The UltraDev Shopping Cart extension is on the accompanying CD. You can find it as `UC_Cart_V12_Beta2.mxp` in the `\Extensions\SBXs\Win` folder. The demonstration Web site Hats Galore that's used as an example in this chapter and Chapter 12 is also on the CD, in ASP version only, in the folder `\Demo sites\HatsGalore\Asp`.

Unwrapping the Cart Extension

Installing the UltraDev Shopping Cart extension is a quick piece of work. First, you need the extension, which you can download from the Macromedia Exchange (http://dynamic.macromedia.com/bin/MM/exchange/ultradev/main.jsp) or get from the accompanying CD. (For the most up-to-date version, you should download it from Macromedia Exchange.) See Chapter 10 for instructions on downloading extensions.

To install the shopping cart:

1. **Launch UltraDev.**
2. **With any page open, choose Commands➪Manage Extensions.**

   The Extension Manager opens.
3. **From the Extension Manager menu, click the Install button or choose File➪Install Extension.**
4. **In the file finder that appears, navigate to the folder where you saved the extension, select it, and then click Install.**

   Accept the license terms, sit back, and watch it happen.

> **TIP:** If your file associations are properly set up (as they should be by the UltraDev installation process), you can double-click MXP file on your desktop or in Windows Explorer to unpack it. The Extension Manager automatically pops up and does all the work for you.

To see if your shopping cart was installed:

1. **Close and reopen UltraDev.**
2. **Open the Data Bindings inspector (usually by clicking your Launcher).**
3. **Click the plus (+) button and notice that UltraDev Shopping Cart has been added to the menu.**

The shopping cart acts much like a data source for your site. In order to use it, you only need to add it to a page and define the columns for the cart. You need to consider just a few caveats:

- You can have only one shopping cart on a site.
- Just like a recordset, you must add a shopping cart to every page where you want to use one.
- The shopping cart has to be identical on every page on the site. If you change it on one page, you must change it on every page.

Chapter 11: Setting Up Shop with UltraDev 235

> **TIP:** The easiest way to be sure that the cart is identical on all your pages is to copy and paste it from one page to another.

When you install the shopping cart, you get the shopping cart data source, along with an array of server behaviors that can be used with it.

To see the server behaviors that go with the cart:

1. **Open the Server Behaviors inspector.**
2. **Click the plus (+) button; then select the UltraDev Shopping Cart menu item.**

   The pop-up menu shows eight server behaviors in addition to the cart itself, as shown in Figure 11-1.

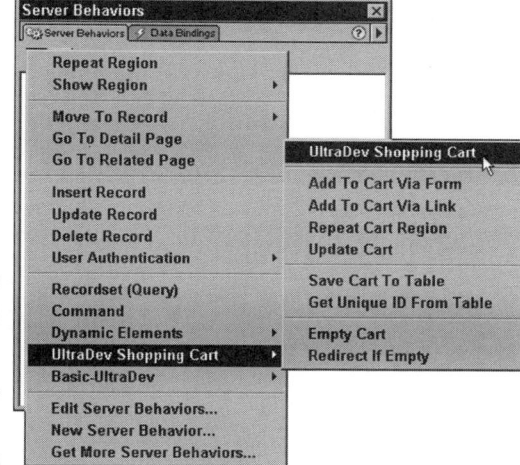

Figure 11-1: The shopping cart's bag of tricks.

If you try to choose one of these server behaviors right now, you get a message telling you that you first have to put an UltraDev shopping cart on the page. So here's the first rule of using the shopping cart extension: *You have to put the shopping cart on the page first.*

After you put a shopping cart on a page, you have to make a few easy decisions to define it. They're explained in the next section, "Defining the Shopping Cart."

The shopping cart actually contains a lot more than these eight behaviors. There are behaviors specifically tailored for ASP, JSP, and ColdFusion. You don't need to do anything special to use the version you want. You just need to define the site to use the right server technology. (See Chapter 1 for more about defining your site and selecting a server model.) The cart takes care of the rest, creating the proper matching code for your server model.

But — and here's the nifty part — you don't really need a database at all. You can make a quick and easy shopping cart with just a form, a few form elements, and a button. The "Look Ma! No Database!" section shows you how shortly.

Defining the Shopping Cart

To start your shopping cart site, you first create a new site for your online store venture, create your first page and give it a name, and then add a shopping cart to the page.

To add a shopping cart to the page:

1. **Open the Data Bindings inspector.**
2. **Click the plus (+) button and choose UltraDev Shopping Cart.**

   The UltraDev Shopping Cart dialog box opens, as shown in Figure 11-2.

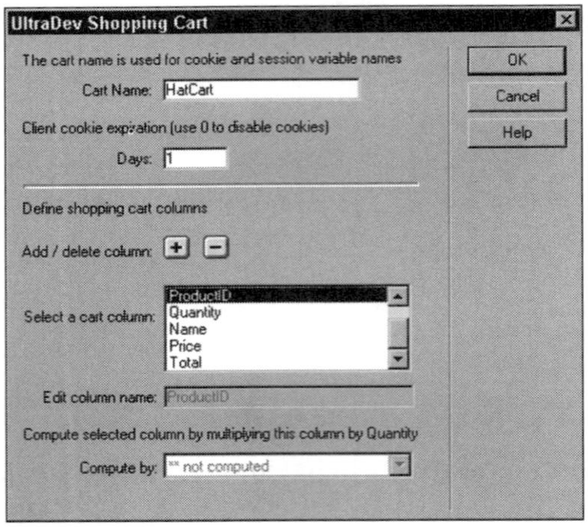

Figure 11-2: Setting up the shopping cart.

3. **Type a name for your cart in the Cart Name text box.**
4. **Type the number of days you want for cookie expiration in the Days text box.**

   The cookie expiration timer allows wishy-washy shoppers who can't make up their minds to come back later and retrieve the contents of their cart and head straight to checkout — kinda like putting your items on hold (with no guarantee they'll still be there when you come back). A reasonable setting is one day for cookie expiration.

The options in the Select a Cart Column list box are the five default columns. The only one of these that you can edit is the Name column. You can change the name of this column to something else (like HatType or ProductName) if you want by clicking the Name column and entering a new name in the Edit Column Name box.

It's always advisable to avoid using spaces when you're naming things that involve code. Spaces probably won't break the shopping cart, but they may upset other add-ons you use later. You can at least eliminate that as a potential problem if you just say no to them now. You can use an underscore character (as in Hat_Type) instead of a space, if you like.

If you select the Total column, the Compute By text box near the bottom of the dialog box tells you that this column is computed by multiplying Quantity times Price.

  5. Click OK to finish setting up the cart.

The five options in the Select a cart column list box are all you need to set up your first shopping cart. You can come back to this dialog box later if you want to add new columns or change your cart in some way.

Some things to keep in mind about the columns in the shopping cart:

- You cannot delete any of the default columns except for Name.
- You don't have to use all the columns. The only one you have to use is ProductID. It's the equivalent of a key field in a conventional data table.
- You can add new columns if you need them for your grand merchandising scheme.

Look Ma! No Database!

If you just want to sell a few items online, there's no reason you have to go for overkill. You can use the shopping cart extension to build a simple little e-commerce site with no database at all. This section guides you through setting up a database-free shopping cart site. The example I use here is a site to sell hats. This modest enterprise sells just one hat design, but the hat comes in three sizes and three colors. All I need to know to fill an order is how many, what size, and what color.

Setting up the display page

You can use your Web design talents to create the page to display your wares. You probably want to include a picture and a description of what you're offering, along with lots of little disclaimer text in tiny unreadable print at the bottom.

> If you're going to use a form on the page — that is, edit boxes, drop-down lists, or radio buttons for choices, and a form button for submitting selections — you can make your life a lot easier by putting the form on the page first and then adding your elements within it.

From the Forms panel of the Objects palette, add the form itself and then a menu list or two to the page for any options you want users to select. For example, the hat I'm selling on my site comes in three sizes (S, M, L) and three colors (sage, bluegrass, and eggplant).

In the Property inspector, click the List Values button and type the values that you want to include in the menu from which users will make their selection (see Figure 11-3). If you're not using a database, you can ignore the dynamic data buttons and just type in the text of each entry, clicking the plus (+) button after each one to add the entry.

Figure 11-3: Nobody sells things in plain, dull colors any more!

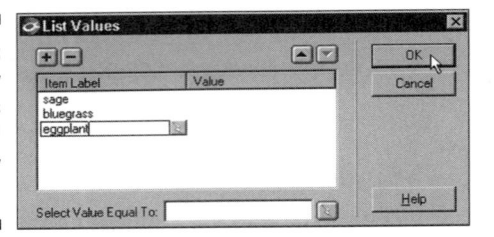

In my example, Size and Color are two important things that I want to be able to retrieve from the shopping cart when shoppers submit their orders. So I need to add two new columns to the shopping cart to hold these values.

To edit the shopping cart and add new columns:

1. **In the Data Bindings inspector, double-click the UltraDev Shopping Cart.**

    The UltraDev Shopping Cart dialog box appears.

2. **In the UltraDev Shopping Cart dialog box, click the plus (+) button to add a column.**

3. **In the Edit column name text box, type a name for the column.**

    For my hat site, I added two columns to the shopping cart: Size and Color.

4. **Click OK to save your changes to the cart.**

Adding the Buy Me button

To get shoppers to buy, you've got to have something for them to click so that their selection can be added to the shopping cart. You can use a standard form button, a simple text link, or a fancy rollover image button. You can choose from two different server behaviors to add items to the cart. Which server behavior you use depends on what you provide for the user to click.

You can choose from these two server behaviors:

- Add to Cart Via Form (use for a form button only)
- Add to Cart Via Link (use for a text link or an image link)

To apply the server behavior that adds an item to the cart:

1. **Add a form button to the page or add the text or image you want to use for the link.**

   If you already have form elements like menu lists on the page, you already have a form. Be sure to put the form button inside the existing form (that is, inside the red dotted lines, which show the form on the page). If you don't have a form on the page, click Yes to add a form when you add the form button.

   Note that to see the red dotted lines that indicate the boundaries of a form, you must have Invisible Elements made visible. Choose View⇨Visual Aids⇨Invisible Elements or the equivalent starting from the View Options button on the toolbar.

   If you use a text link, you can enter the text on the page first and then select it, or you can simply add the behavior and enter the link text in the dialog box.

2. **Select the form button, the text, or the image button. In the Server Behaviors inspector, click the plus (+) button and choose UltraDev Shopping Cart ⇨Add to Cart Via Form or Add to Cart Via Link.**

   The Add to Cart dialog box appears. The name of the form or link is shown in the first (Form or Link) drop-down list box. You shouldn't need to change this if you selected the right element in the first place.

3. **From the Cart Column list box, select each cart column and choose what you want to save in the cart for each one.**

   Your choices are

   - **Nothing:** You don't want this column to be saved.
   - **Literal:** You want a specified value to be saved.
   - **Form element:** The value of a form element (such as the user's choice from a menu).

Part IV: E-commerce with UltraDev

- **Recordset:** This option is disabled if you have not defined any data sources for the site. (See the "Going Big-Time: Bring That Database Right Over Here" section in this chapter for information on using a data source.)

In my hat site, I set up each column as follows (see Figure 11-4).

- Color: Form element, Color
- Size: Form element, Size
- ProductID: Nothing
- Quantity: Literal, 1
- Name: Literal, Trusty Explorer Hat
- Price: Literal, 15.95

Figure 11-4: The Add to Cart dialog box.

> **WARNING!** Be careful not to enter a dollar sign ($) in the price field. It conflicts with the code and makes your shopping cart behave peculiarly.

4. **In the Go To URL text box, type the name of your cart display page or click the Browse button to select it.**

5. **Click OK to finish.**

Now when a user wants to add an item to the shopping cart and clicks the button or link to do so, the value of each of the columns is saved to the shopping cart where you can retrieve it as needed on other pages in the site. The shopping cart actually works as temporary data storage for the site. Figure 11-5 shows a completed product page.

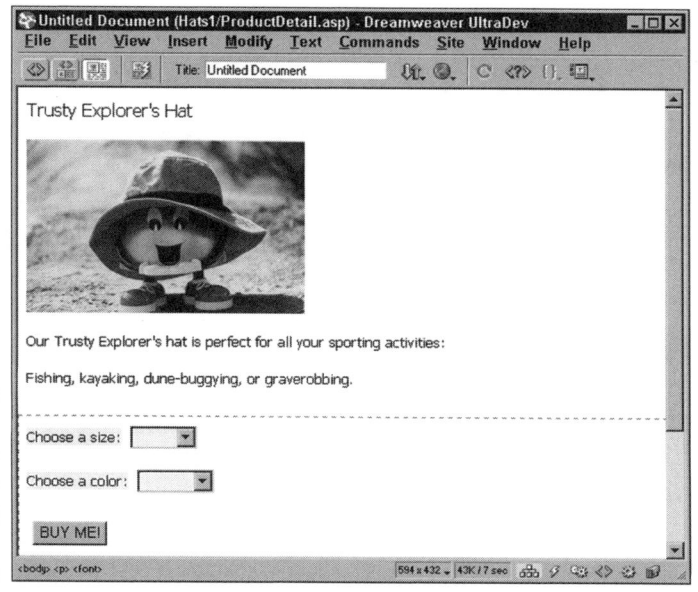

Figure 11-5:
Get your trusty explorer hat here.

Testing the cart

Naturally, you want to test the cart to prove that it's working. To set up a simple cart display for testing:

1. **Create a page named** CartDisplay.
2. **Copy the shopping cart that you defined earlier (in the "Defining the Shopping Cart" section) to the CartDisplay page.**

   To copy the shopping cart, select the page on which you defined the shopping cart. Then in the Data Bindings inspector, select the shopping cart line and click the arrow button at the top-right of the palette and choose Copy from the pop-up menu. Select the CartDisplay page and choose Paste from the same pop-up menu.

   The shopping cart must be identical on every page on the site. The easiest way to ensure this is to copy the shopping cart (after you define it). If you change the cart on one page, you have to change it on the other pages, too.

3. **Put an HTML table on the page.**

   Choose two rows for the table, one for headings and one for display. Choose as many columns as you need. The number of columns you need depends on how many shopping cart fields you want to show on this page.

For example, to display the name, size, color, quantity, and price, you have to choose five columns for the table.

4. **Type the headings in the first row of the HTML table.**
5. **Expand the cart in the Data Bindings inspector, and insert the appropriate field into each cell of the table's second row.**

Publish your pages and view them in a browser. You can now try adding an item to your cart. Figure 11-6 shows the results of adding a hat to the cart.

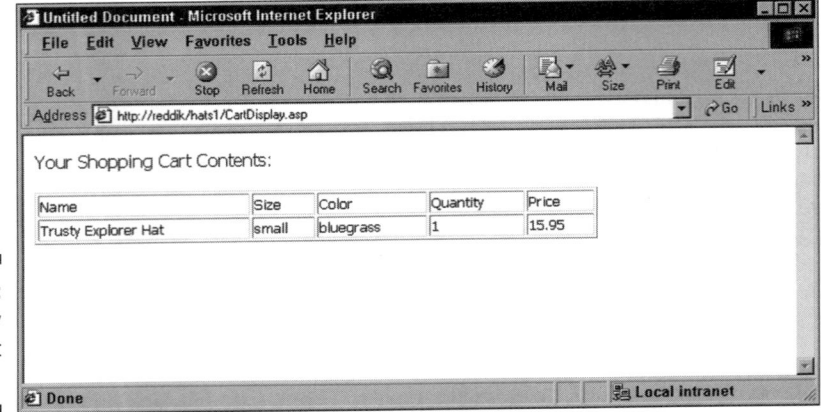

Figure 11-6: Well fancy that — it works!

After you prove to yourself that you can make it work, you can skip to setting up a much fancier shopping cart display (explained in detail in Chapter 12), or you can dive into making a site that uses a database with the shopping cart.

Going Big-Time: Bring That Database Right Over Here

Enough of this small-time biz — you gotta start thinking big if you're ever going to make any real money at this e-commerce game.

My hat store enterprise is going big-time. Through this site, I'm going to sell lots of different hats in different sizes and colors, with and without feathers, some with fancy custom sweatbands — Hats Galore, in fact. Who knows — maybe a big distribution deal with Wal-Mart is just around the corner. For this kind of thinking, a database is absolutely required.

What you need in the database

You can use any ODBC-friendly database for your online store. Your choice of database type depends on whether you use ASP, JSP, or Cold Fusion. The shopping cart extension works with all three server applications, with little difference between them. (See Chapter 3 to find out more about ODBC and Chapter 1 for more about choosing your server model.)

You have to set up your database schema carefully according to what your final objective is and to suit all the components you plan on using. It's worth spending some time figuring that out first before you get started.

A basic e-commerce database includes tables for product information, orders, and customer details. In the product table, you should include fields for any other product identifiers you need, such as size, color, and feathers. These are referred to in UltraDev as SKU modifiers. (If you've never worked in retail, you aren't expected to know that a SKU — pronounced *skew* — is a Stock Keeping Unit. It has something to do with those ubiquitous merchandise bar codes.)

If you're going to charge shipping, you have to figure out how that is calculated and whether you'll offer different options. Tax is another requirement you may have to calculate, based on your market area. You also want to think about quantity discounts for bulk orders. And don't forget about collecting credit card data. Maybe you want a quick checkout for registered customers, where their data is instantly retrieved. All these things require database support.

Typically, you might set up one table with four default fields to match the columns in the shopping cart:

- ProductID
- Product Name
- Quantity
- Price

The ProductID field is required. You probably need the others anyway, so you may as well put them in unless you've a good reason not to. A couple more useful fields that you might consider adding are

- **Product Picture:** If you want to display a product picture on the page, you need this field for an image path. (See Chapter 4 to find out more about including images.)
- **Product Description:** A field to add a little marketing hype to your display.

Part IV: E-commerce with UltraDev

If you're going to submit the contents of the cart to a database as the final checkout stage, you may want to set up a simple order ID table to use the shopping cart's native method. See Chapter 12 for what this entails.

Figure 11-7 shows a sample database structure set up in Microsoft Access. You don't need to start out with anything this complicated, but you can use it as a guide to think about what you may need down the road.

Hooking up the database

To use your product database with the shopping cart:

1. **Set up the DSN.**

    See Chapter 3 if you need help with this process.

2. **Define the site using the appropriate server technology.**

    You use ASP, JSP, or Cold Fusion depending on your server setup (see Chapter 1).

3. **Add the data connection by choosing Modify➪Data Connections and selecting the DSN for your database (see Chapter 3).**

4. **Define the recordset.**

    See Chapter 4 if you need help with defining the recordset.

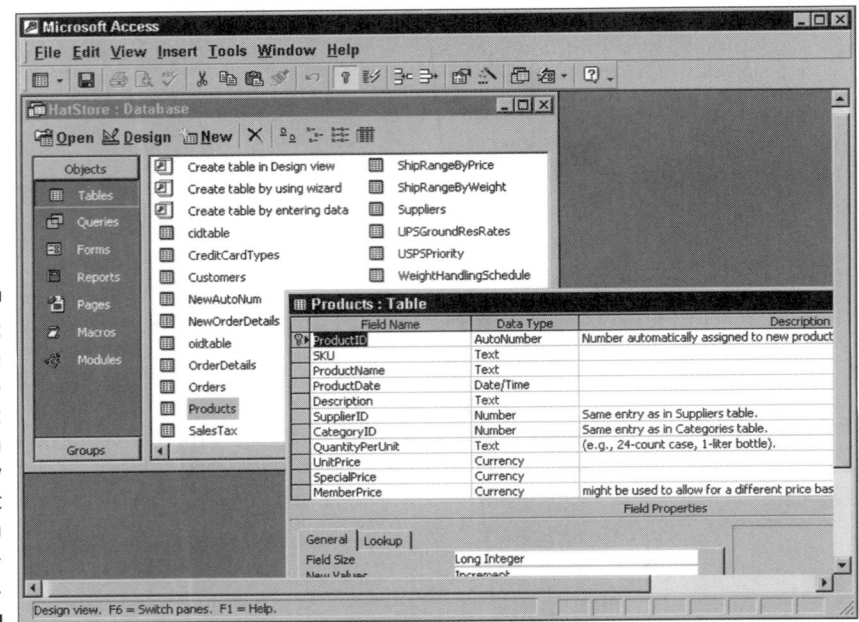

Figure 11-7: Sample database structure: More than you may need, but worth contemplating.

After your database is working in UltraDev, you're ready to go with the shopping cart.

Creating the catalog

The window display for your online store will be a browsable catalog of the items in your database. The details for the items in the catalog come from the records in your database.

To create this browsable catalog, your first setup tasks are to

- Create a page and give it a name such as ProductDetail.
- Add a recordset to the page (click the plus (+) button in the Data Bindings inspector). Choose the data source and the table that contains the product information.
- Add the shopping cart to the page. See "Defining the Shopping Cart" earlier in this chapter if you need a refresher.

Putting the goods on display

It's time to stock the virtual shelves of your store. You do this by mustering your UltraDev prowess to make a product display page. Keep in mind that the data for the product display page is dynamically generated from your product database. The page you create works more or less like a template to display each item.

To create the product display page:

1. **Add a layer to your page for each element that you want to display.**

   You probably want a layer for the product name, the description, the product picture, and the price. You can add additional layers for navigation buttons later.

2. **Place the cursor in the layer into which you want to insert the dynamic data.**

3. **Open the Data Bindings inspector and expand the products recordset.**

4. **Select the column that you want to display and click the Insert button in the border of the inspector.**

   A data placeholder appears on the page. Some examples of placeholders are visible in Figure 11-8.

   Repeat the steps for each column that you want to display.

You may also want to add a product picture. To do this, you must have a column in your database that contains the path to the image. The path should be the path from the root folder of your published site. If you place your images in an `images` folder off your root folder, the path in the database field is `images/picture.jpg`.

REMEMBER

You have to transfer all the images referenced in the database to an equivalent folder on the server. UltraDev does not publish these for you.

When designing your page, you may want to place one product image as a placeholder on your page so that you can design around it (as shown in Figure 11-8). When you're ready to publish, you can change the image source to a dynamic source. (See Chapter 4 if you need help in changing the image to a dynamic source.)

Figure 11-8: A catalog layout page in its preliminary setup. Screen-testing the model was the hardest part.

To see the results of your catalog page, publish the page or view it in Live Data View.

Flippin' through the catalog

You need to add a few navigation aids for your customers to view your wares. Navigation includes record signposting as well as the buttons that actually flip from page to page. You can do all this manually (as I did in this example), or make use of UltraDev's special Live Objects to make very quick work of it. Chapter 5 explains the whole deal.

Chapter 11: Setting Up Shop with UltraDev **247**

Publish the page and view it in the browser. Use the navigation buttons to cruise around the site — notice how the record counter keeps track of where you are.

Figure 11-9 shows the catalog for my Hats Galore site ready to go.

Feeding the buy impulse

The most important function of a shopping cart site from a commercial point of view is the button that says Buy or some more polite equivalent. In UltraDev, that function is brought to the site by a specialized server behavior.

To apply the server behavior that lets your customers add items to the shopping cart:

1. **Add a form button to your page, or add the text or image that you want to use for the link.**

    If you already have form elements on the page, you probably have already added a form tag to the page. Be sure that you add the form button inside the existing form. If you don't have a form on the page, click Yes to add a form when you add the form button.

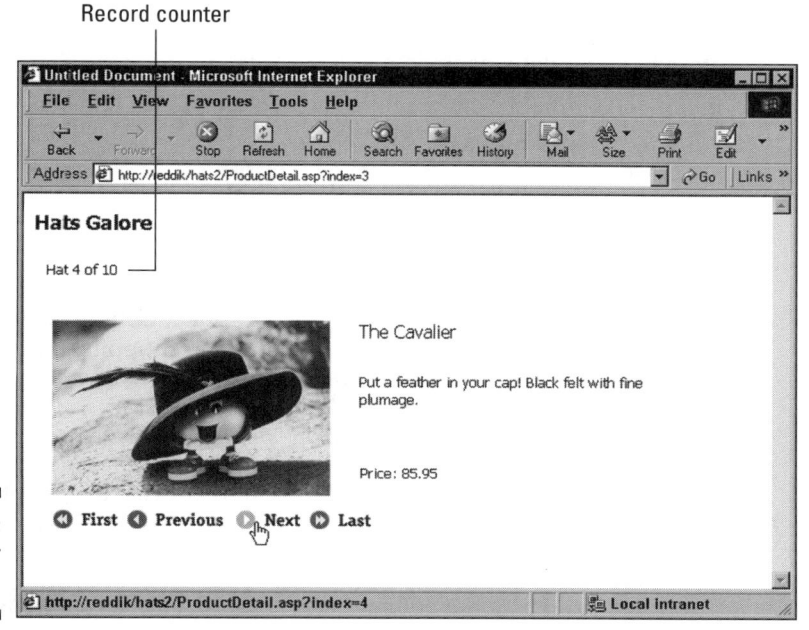

Figure 11-9: Ready for cruisin'.

2. **Select the form button, the text, or the image button. In the Server Behaviors inspector, click the plus (+) button and choose UltraDev Shopping Cart⇨Add to Cart Via Form or Add to Cart Via Link.**

   The server behavior that you apply depends on whether you use a form button or a link (text or image button). For a form button, use Add to Cart Via Form. If you use a text link or an image button, use Add to Cart Via Link.

   When the Add to Cart dialog box appears, the name of the form or link appears in the drop-down list at the top. You don't need to change this if you selected the right element in the first place.

3. **Select each cart column in the Cart Columns list box and bind it to the appropriate source column in your recordset.**

   For instance, select ProductID and click the radio button that says Recset col. In the Recset col drop-down list, choose the column that contains the product ID number. (This is normally a numerical identifier, which may be named ProductID, ProductNo, SerialNo, or SKU — any field used to identify the product in the database.)

   If you don't have a matching database column for a shopping cart column, and you don't think you need to use that column, you can select the Nothing button for that column. But remember: This column will not be added to the data stored in the shopping cart, so you can't retrieve it later. For example, the price of the item may be stored in the database and is fixed. You may want to display the price on the product detail page, but you don't need to add it to the shopping cart, because it's already in the database.

   In my juiced-up Hats Galore site, each column is set up as follows:

   - ProductID: Recset col: ProductID
   - Quantity: Recset col: QuantityPerUnit
   - Name: Recset col: ProductName
   - Price: Recset col: UnitPrice

   If you have drop-down lists on the page to select options like size, color, or other variables, you must store these in the shopping cart, too. In this case, the source is not coming from the database but from the selections users make on the page. You need to add the columns to the shopping cart first. (See "Setting up the display page" earlier in this chapter.) In the Add to Cart Via Form dialog box, you select the Form element button for the source and then select the name of the form element on the page.

4. **Choose a recordset and index column from the Recordset and Index Column drop-down list boxes.**

   The index column is the column in the recordset that functions as the primary key for the table.

The index column can be the same as the ProductID (as it is in my Hat database), or it can be a purely numerical database column that doesn't relate to the ProductID used to fill the order. Figure 11-10 shows the dialog box just about complete.

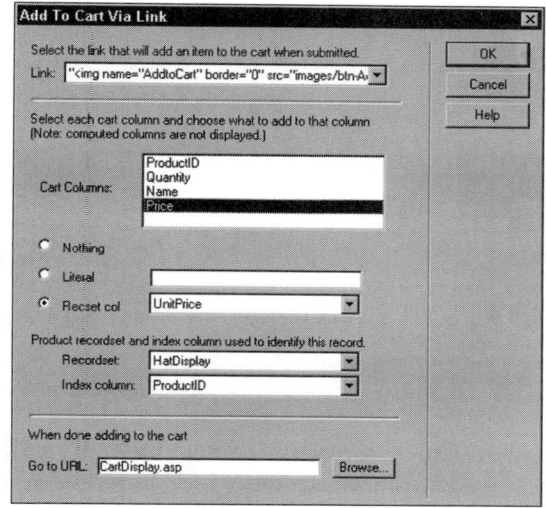

Figure 11-10: Got to get everything right here or you'll pull your hair out later.

> Be careful not to enter a dollar sign ($) in the Price field. A dollar sign conflicts with the code and makes your shopping cart behave peculiarly.

 5. **In the Go To URL text box, type the name of your cart display page or click the Browse button to select it from the site files.**

 6. **Click OK to finish.**

Now when a user wants to add an item to the shopping cart and clicks the button or link to do so, the value of the four columns is saved to the shopping cart where you can retrieve it as needed for other pages in the site.

The Total column, which is part of the original shopping cart setup, is not included in the Add to Cart dialog box. That's because the Total column is a computed column, which doesn't need to be stored in the cart. You can calculate the Total column's value in the database after the order gets submitted and stored as part of the order details.

Figure 11-11 shows my hat store site ready to go.

Figure 11-11: All ready for some fun in the sun.

There's just one thing left to do: Replace the placeholder image with the dynamic image source from the database. Refer to Chapter 4 if you need help with this task.

To test the shopping cart behavior, you can set up a simple test page (see "Testing the cart" earlier in this chapter). If you're satisfied that everything's working fine, blast ahead to Chapter 12 and to find out how to set up the full cart display.

Chapter 12

The Almost Complete E-store

In This Chapter
- Surveying your e-store
- Displaying the shopping cart contents
- Confirming an order
- Personalizing pages
- Sending automatic e-mail notification

In this chapter, you find out how to build an almost-complete e-commerce site by using the UltraDev Shopping Cart Server Behavior Extension (SBX) and another SBX for automatic e-mail.

I say "almost complete" because this chapter focuses primarily on the SBXs available off the shelf for UltraDev, and combined, they don't presently amount to a complete e-commerce solution. Most of this chapter is concerned with the behaviors of the shopping cart itself, which provide a flow of logic from choice of merchandise to review of cart contents to final checkout. Login of existing customers and registration of new clients are both covered in Chapter 10, which deals with the suite of server behaviors concerned with user authentication. You have to look elsewhere for the really tricky stuff like interstate sales tax calculations, shipping fees by the pound, online credit card, processing and so forth. I aim to keep it simple.

A *shopping cart* is nothing more than a temporary mini-database that the user can manipulate until it's time to confirm the order. At that point, the mini-database is transferred to the permanent database of merchandise orders, along with essential information about the customer.

What Your E-store Looks Like

No two e-stores are exactly the same, of course, but they have some essential features in common. You might say that a generic e-store includes these pages or sections:

- **Catalog.** This section allows users to browse the merchandise. A very simple T-shirt enterprise offering just eight different shirts might put all the items in its catalog on one page. A business like Land's End, however, with many product lines, needs to think hard about the search strategies its customers may want to use to zero in quickly on merchandise of interest. Two catalogs are fully described in Chapter 11.

- **Shopping cart display.** This essential page lets customers inspect the contents of the shopping cart before either returning to the catalog for more goodies or checking out. You can find detailed instructions for making this type of page later in this chapter.

- **Login section.** Customers need to identify themselves or there's no way to ship merchandise to them or accept payment from them. Pages in this section include a login for existing customers, registration for new customers, and a login fail loop. See Chapters 8 and 10 for more about login validation procedures.

- **Checkout.** Existing customers and newly registered customers come together on this page, which is a final review of the order before confirming checkout. It's polite to include some kind of "Bye-bye, thanks for shopping here" page just to round things off. You can find instructions for making these pages in this chapter.

You can find a complete demonstration e-commerce site, Hats Galore, in the `\Demo sites\HatsGalore` folder on the CD accompanying this book. It includes a database of products and customers.

E-store Preliminaries

The instructions in this chapter don't start from absolute scratch. To get to the point where they begin, you need to go through some procedures common to all UltraDev dynamic site setups, and you also must install the UltraDev Shopping Cart SBX.

Here's a checklist of your preliminary steps:

1. **Obtain a database of products and customers.**

   The Access 2000 database file `hatstore.mdb` provided on the CD is completely suitable for the purpose. If you want to use your own database, it needs to include the following data tables:
   - Products
   - Customers
   - Orders

- Order details
- OrderID — a one-record, one-field table designed to provide unique order ID numbers

  2. **Create a Data Source Name (DSN) to make the database file accessible.**

     See Chapter 3 if you need help with this procedure.

  3. **Create a data connection to the DSN.**

     The connection in the demonstration e-shop is called `ASPHatconn`. The data connection procedure is also described in Chapter 3.

  4. **Define a site for your e-shop.**

     The site definition procedure is described in Chapter 1.

  5. **Install the UltraDev Shopping Cart SBX and make a product catalog.**

     This procedure is described in Chapter 11.

The Shopping Cart Display Page

The purpose of a shopping cart display page is to allow your customers to inspect the current contents of the cart and then do any of the following four things:

- Vary the quantity of any line item, including setting the quantity to zero, thus effectively removing it from the cart.
- Empty the cart completely.
- Return to the catalog.
- Proceed to login/checkout.

The key design feature of the shopping cart page is a table that holds the detailed line-by-line cart contents, with dynamic data from the shopping cart data object inserted into table cells.

Here's the simplest way to create a shopping cart page (I assume that you already have a Catalog page with a cart on it, as described in Chapter 11):

  1. **Make a fresh UltraDev document.**

     If the Site window is open, choose File⇨New File and name the page in the local file list. If an existing document is open, choose File⇨New and use File⇨Save As to name the file.

     In the HatsGalore example, the page is named CartDisplay.asp.

2. **Title and decorate the page as you want.**

   Next, you need to copy the shopping cart data object from the catalog page to this page.

3. **Open the catalog page, open the Data Bindings inspector, and then select the Shopping Cart; then click the Cut/Copy/Paste arrow button and choose Copy.**

4. **Now return to the shopping cart display page, click the Cut/Copy/Paste arrow button, and choose Paste.**

   Next you make a layer to contain the shopping cart table and the user options listed in the bulleted list at the top of this section.

5. **Click the Layer button on the Common panel of the Objects palette and then sweep out an appropriate area on the page.**

   A good size to start with is 550 x 175 pixels — you can always adjust it later.

6. **Switch the Objects palette to the Forms panel and click to insert a form.**

7. **In the form's Property inspector, give the form a name.**

   In the example, I named it Hatform.

8. **Switch the Objects palette back to the Common panel and click the Table button to insert a table into the form.**

9. **In the Insert Table dialog box, set the table at 90% width with 3 rows and 5 columns.**

10. **Using any text style that you like, insert column headers for ID, Name, Qty, Unit Price, and Total.**

11. **Switch the Objects palette to the Forms panel and insert a text field in the table under the Qty header.**

    This is the item quantity box that the customer will be able to change.

12. **In the Property inspector for this text field, name it Qty and set its width at 5.**

13. **In the Data Bindings inspector, expand the Shopping Cart and insert the ProductID, Name, Price, and Total fields into the appropriate columns in the second row of the table.**

14. **Format the Price and Total fields as currency, using the Format drop-down menus in the Data Bindings inspector.**

    You now need to bind the Quantity field of the Shopping Cart to the Qty text box in the table.

15. **Select the Quantity field in the Data Bindings inspector, and the Qty text box in layout, and click the Bind button in the Data Bindings inspector.**

Chapter 12: The Almost Complete E-store **255**

16. **Insert the sum(Total) field in the lower-right table cell, formatting it as currency.**

    This cell will display the grand total of the value of the items in the cart.

Figure 12-1 shows a page completed to this point, with data placeholders visible.

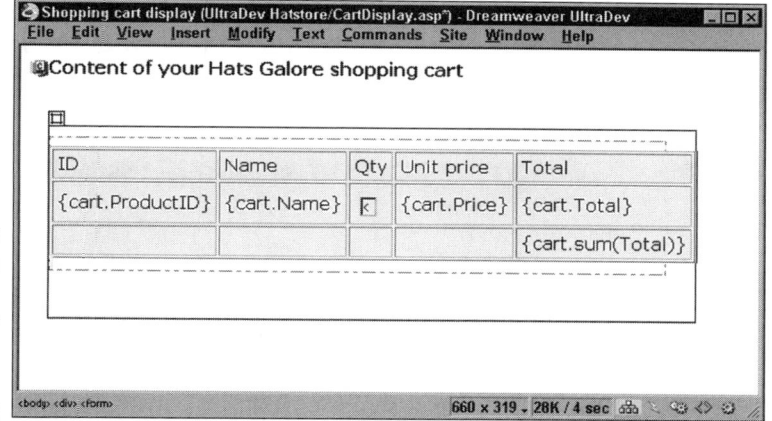

Figure 12-1: A shopping cart display page in progress.

Using the special repeat region server behavior

In designing the table on your shopping cart page to display cart content, you assign only one table row for the actual product details. But, of course, the cart may contain any number of products depending on how much the user wants to buy.

You can't predict how many table rows will be needed, but you can use a special server behavior called a *repeat region* to cause the table to adjust automatically. Chapter 5 discusses the use of a repeat region on a Results page, but the behavior you need here is a special one that's part of the UltraDev Shopping Cart SBX.

Here's how you apply the repeat region behavior:

1. **Select the table row that will hold purchase details.**

    This can be tricky with the mouse — perhaps the easiest way is to click the `<tr>` tag in the tag selector, as shown in Figure 12-2.

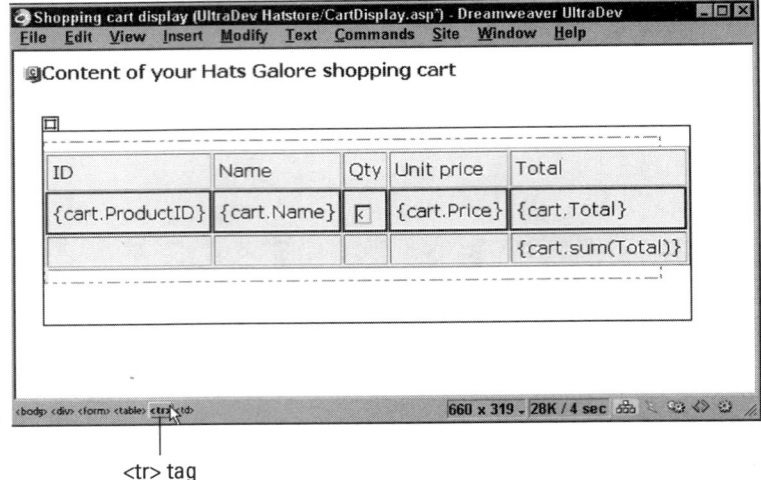

Figure 12-2: Selecting the purchase row for repeat.

2. **In the Server Behaviors inspector, click the plus button (+) and choose UltraDev Shopping Cart⇨Repeat Cart Region.**

   No dialog box appears.

   Now you need to arrange a link back from the cart display page to the catalog page.

3. **Place your cursor at the right margin of the table and press Enter. Using any text style that you like, type Continue shopping.**

4. **Select the words that you just typed and create a hyperlink to the catalog page in the Property inspector by clicking the little folder icon beside the word Target.**

Updating the cart

When a customer chooses something to buy and places it in the shopping cart, it appears in the cart in the default minimum quantity. If you're selling hats, for example, the customer's decision to purchase places one hat in the cart. If it's hardware items, the minimum quantity may be much more than one (if derived from a Quantity per unit field in your products data table).

This section shows you how to enable your customers to adjust the quantity on the cart display page by using the Update Cart server behavior. Customers may want to buy four hats or two gross of faucet washers — or they may just be dithering. It's their right!

Chapter 12: The Almost Complete E-store

Adding the Update Cart behavior is really simple, but you need to provide a submit button for the purpose. (Remember to apply the behavior to the quantity text box, *not* to the button itself.)

Here are the details for adding the Update Cart behavior to your page:

1. **Place a cursor where you want your Update button.**
2. **From the Objects palette, choose the Forms panel and click the Button icon to insert a submit button.**
3. **In the button's Property inspector, give it a name, such as Update Cart.**
4. **Click to select the Qty text box in the table.**
5. **In the Server Behaviors inspector, click the plus (+) button and choose UltraDev Shopping Cart⇨Update Cart.**

    The Update Cart dialog box opens (see Figure 12-3).

6. **The Form and Form Element drop-down lists are certain to default correctly because only one form and one element currently exist.**
7. **Leave the Go to URL text box empty unless you have some good reason to take your customers to another page after updating the cart.**

    Normally, a customer expects to stay on the same page to confirm that the update has happened correctly.

Figure 12-3: The Update Cart dialog box.

That's all you have to do to add the Update Cart server behavior. You may, however, want to consider two other useful server behaviors available in the Shopping Cart submenu. One of these behaviors completely empties the cart and redirects the user back to the catalog. The other behavior automatically redirects the page if the cart is empty. It isn't considered "good form" to let customers see an empty cart.

Here's how to apply the two behaviors to redirect the page:

1. **Make a special page to redirect customers to if the cart is empty.**

   It can be quite simple, just containing an "empty cart" message and a hyperlink back to the catalog. In the HatsGalore example on the CD, the page is called BarrenCart.html.

2. **Wherever you want, using any text style that you like, type the words** Clear cart **and then select them.**

3. **In the Server Behaviors inspector, click the plus (+) button and choose UltraDev Shopping Cart➪Empty Cart.**

   The Empty Cart dialog box opens.

4. **Type the URL for the catalog page in the Go to URL text box to redirect back to the catalog page; then close the dialog box.**

5. **In the Server Behaviors inspector, click the plus (+) button and choose UltraDev Shopping Cart➪Redirect If Empty.**

   The Redirect If Empty dialog box opens. Note that you do not have to have anything selected on the page when you apply this behavior. It's applied to the page itself.

6. **Use the Go to URL text box in the dialog box to redirect to the BarrenCart.html page (or whatever you called it).**

Proceeding to checkout

Linking to checkout from a cart display page doesn't require any special server behavior — in principle, it's just a hyperlink. But it's at this point that you, as designer of the e-shop, need to find out who the customer is. If you don't know that, how do you know where to ship those lovely hats or boring faucet washers?

The UltraDev Shopping Cart extension to UltraDev leaves you to your own devices on this, assuming that you have time-tested methods for identifying customers. Chapter 10 covers the whole topic of identifying users.

One way or another, by the time the customers reach final checkout, a CustomerID should be in the Session Object (see Chapters 8 and 10).

TIP

One of the special UltraDev Shopping Cart server behaviors is also useful for registration of new customers. It's called Get Unique ID From Table, and its primary use is to generate new order numbers. (See the following section, "Closing the Deal.") You can, however, also use this behavior to generate a new CustomerID, using a special data table designed for the purpose (in the HatsGalore database, it's CIDtable). As for getting a new CustomerID into the Session Object, there's an option to do just that in the dialog box of the Get Unique ID from Table behavior.

Closing the Deal

When you build an e-commerce site, you need a page for customers to take a last look at their order details and confirm the order. After leaving the shopping cart display page, existing customers normally log in and new customers are diverted to a registration page of some kind. Old and new customers come back together on a page that lets them confirm the order and then — after they press the magic button labeled Confirm — actually writes the order to the database.

Building the order confirm page

The visual elements of the order confirm page are really simple. It's what goes on behind the scenes that really matters. Here's how to build the page:

1. **Make a fresh UltraDev document.**

    If the site window is open, choose File⇨New File and name the page in the local file list. If an existing document is open, choose File⇨New and use File⇨Save As to name the file. In the example, the page is named OrderConfirm.asp.

2. **Title and decorate the page as you want.**

    Now you need to copy the shopping cart data object from your catalog page to this page.

3. **With the catalog page open, open the Data Bindings inspector and select the Shopping Cart. Click the Cut/Copy/Paste arrow button and choose Copy.**

4. **Now return to the order confirm page, click the Cut/Copy/Paste arrow button, and choose Paste.**

    Next, you have to make a layer to contain the shopping cart table and an Order Confirm button.

5. **Click the Layer button in the Common panel of the Objects palette; then sweep out an appropriate area on the page.**

    A good size to start with is 550 x 175 pixels — you can always adjust it later.

6. **Switch the Objects palette to the Forms panel and click to insert a form.**

7. **In the form's Property inspector, give the form a name (orderform, in the example).**

8. **Switch the Object palette back to the Common panel and click the Table button to insert a table into the form.**

   In the Insert Table dialog box, set the table at 90% width, with 3 rows and 5 columns.

9. **Using any text style that you like, insert column headers for ID, Name, Qty, Unit price, and Total.**

   The text styles on this page can be quite small — the user will not be able to make any changes on the page.

10. **In the Data Bindings inspector, expand the Shopping Cart and insert the ProductID, Name, Quantity, Price, and Total fields into the appropriate columns in the second row of the table.**

    Format the Price and Total fields as currency, using the Format drop-down menus in the Data Binding inspector.

11. **Insert the sum(Total) field in the lower-right table cell, formatting it as currency.**

    This cell displays the grand total of the value of the items in the cart.

12. **Apply the Repeat Cart Region server behavior by selecting the middle table row.**

13. **In the Server Behaviors inspector, click the plus (+) button and choose UltraDev Shopping Cart⇨Repeat Cart Region.**

14. **Place your cursor at the right margin of the table and press Enter.**

15. **Switch the Objects palette to the Forms tab and click to insert a submit button.**

16. **Label the button Confirm Order.**

Figure 12-4 shows a complete order confirm page in a browser with three items in the shopping cart.

Transferring the contents of a shopping cart to a database

Transferring a shopping cart order to a database is far from easy, but this section breaks it down into easy-to-follow steps. What makes it a bit complicated is that you have to write new records in two separate data tables.

First, each line of the shopping cart — each item of merchandise — needs to be written to the OrderDetails table. You need to record, line-by-line, exactly how many hats (or books, or dried meat products, or whatever you're selling) make up the order.

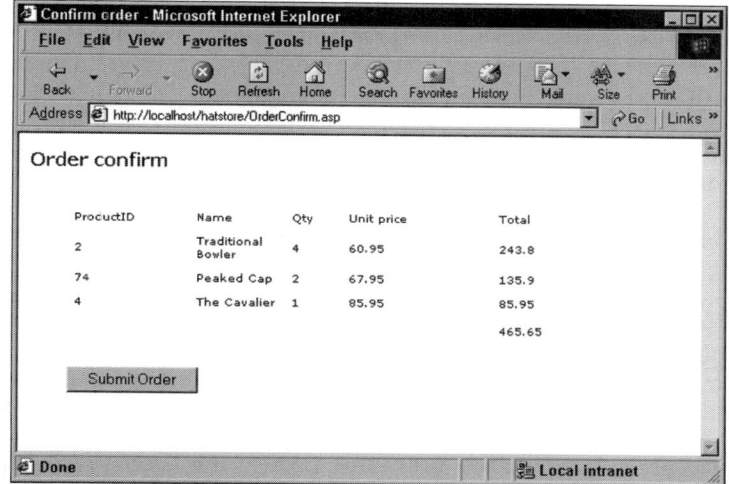

Figure 12-4: A completed order confirm page.

But you also need to record stuff like who the customer is, the current date and time, the total value of the order, and so on. It would be very wasteful to add all that to every single line of the shopping cart data, which may run 20, 30, or 40 lines.

For efficiency's sake, a single record is also written to a different data table called Orders. The relationship between the single Orders record and the who-knows-how-many OrderDetails records is maintained by tacking a unique OrderID number onto all the records you write.

So where does this OrderID come from? From a third data table (I'll call it OID) that you set up for this very purpose. This third table has but one record and one field, and that field is *not* auto-numbered. The special behavior you're going to use to access it takes care of incrementing it.

The big picture of the process that happens when the user presses the Confirm Order button is this:

- A unique OrderID is generated.
- A single record is written to the Orders data table that includes the OrderID and the CustomerID.
- The contents of the shopping cart are written to the OrderDetails data table, which also includes the very same OrderID on every line, and then redirects the customer to a thanks page.

I take you through the exact steps for this process shortly, but first some preparation is needed.

First you need a pigeonhole for the OrderID you're about to need. In the Data Bindings inspector, click the plus (+) button and make a session variable named OrderID. Just select Session Variable from the pop-up menu and type OrderID in the small Session Variable dialog box.

When you come to write the main Orders record, you'll be using UltraDev's standard Insert Record server behavior (see Chapter 5), and you can only insert data from form elements. The problem is that you don't actually have any form elements on this page, other than the submit button, and it's never going to yield any useful data no matter how nicely you talk to it.

The solution to the lack of form elements is to place a hidden form field on the page for each piece of data you need, and then bind the hidden field to whatever source of data you can find hanging around the page. Insert each hidden form field from the Forms tab of the Objects palette. You should probably have form fields for at least the OrderID and CustomerID (both from Session variables), and the total value of the order (from the Shopping Cart). A date and a timestamp are often added, too (see the sidebar "Generating dates and timestamps").

Having set up whatever hidden form fields you need, make a simple thank you page. All it needs is a text message. In the example, it's called ThanksBye.asp. Now you're ready for the step-by-step process of confirming the order.

1. **Click to select the Order confirm button.**

2. **In the Server Behaviors inspector, click the plus (+) button and choose Ultradev Shopping Cart⇨Get Unique ID From Table.**

    The Get Unique ID From Table dialog box opens (see Figure 12-5).

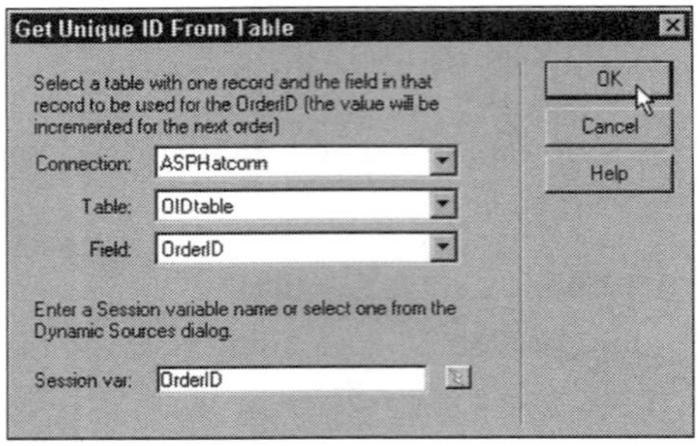

Figure 12-5: The Get Unique ID From Table dialog box.

3. **Select the Connection, Table, and Field where you keep your incrementing OrderID from the drop-down lists of the same name.**

    Note: The Get Unique ID From Table behavior takes care of incrementing the number as it fetches the ID for you.

4. **Click the lightning bolt icon to the right of the Session var box to open the Data Sources dialog box and select the session variable OrderID.**

 5. **Close both dialog boxes.**

    The OrderID automatically inserts into the session variable you prepared for it, and it's reflected in the hidden form field bound to that variable.

 6. **In the Server Behaviors inspector, click the plus (+) button and choose Insert Record.**

    The Insert Record dialog box opens, as shown in Figure 12-6.

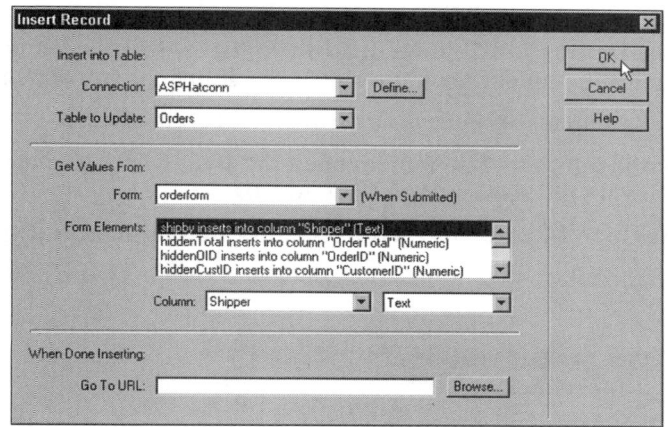

Figure 12-6: A complete Insert Record dialog box.

 7. **Select the correct data connection, if you have more than one, from the Connection drop-down list and select Orders in the Table to Update drop-down list.**

    The Form drop-down list is sure to be correctly set because there's only one form on the page.

 8. **In the Form Elements scrolling list, match the form elements on the page to the recordset fields they belong to.**

    If you took the precaution of giving all the hidden form fields the same names as the recordset fields they're associated with, UltraDev figures it all out for you, and all you need do is cruise through this list double-checking it. If not, select each line in turn and use the Column drop-down list to define the matching recordset field.

    Note: Do not put anything in the Go To URL text box at the bottom of the Insert Record dialog box. The redirect will be done at the next stage.

    Next, you need to write the contents of the shopping cart to the OrderDetails table:

9. **In the Server Behaviors inspector, click the plus (+) button and choose Ultradev Shopping Cart⇨Save Cart To Table.**

    The Save Cart To Table dialog box opens.

10. **Set the data connection and the data table (this time it's OrderDetails) and relate fields in the shopping cart to data fields in the table.**

    In the example, the names of the fields are nearly identical, so the match up is easy. The product name is not saved because in the OrderDetails table the product is identified by its ID.

    Next, you carefully set up the lower part of the dialog box to place the OrderID that you generated in Steps 1 through 5.

11. **Set the Destination Column drop-down list to the name of the column in your data table. Check the check box if the column is numeric.**

    In the example, the name is OrderID and it is Numeric.

12. **Click the lightning bolt icon to open the Dynamic Data dialog box and then locate the session variable OrderID.**

13. **In the Go to URL text box, type the name of your thanks page.**

    A completed version of this dialog box is shown in Figure 12-7.

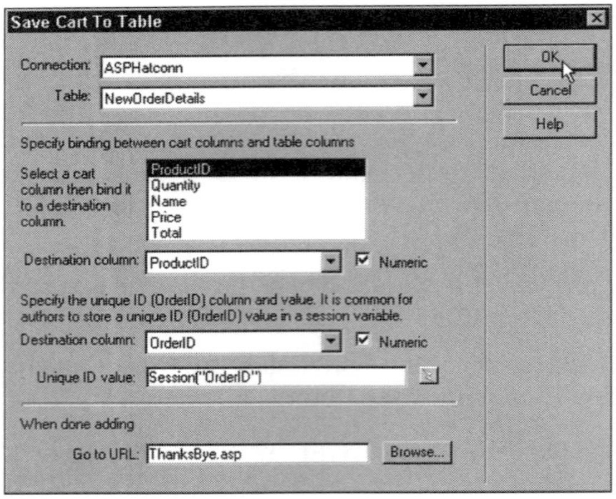

Figure 12-7: The completed dialog box for transferring the shopping cart to a database.

The e-shop is functionally complete once you get to this point. Order fulfillment is done within the database application itself, using data relationships to pull in the customer shipping/payment information required to match each order. In Chapter 4, you can find a suggestion on how to make an order-fulfillment Web page using UltraDev.

Generating dates and timestamps

Most merchandise ordering databases expect at least the date of the order to be recorded, if not also a timestamp, which can be checked, if necessary, to reveal the exact time the order was placed.

UltraDev has no built-in behaviors for generating dates or timestamps, but you can hand code to generate both and make them into session variables. Here's a suggested ASP/Javascript sample, using U.S. date conventions:

Source Code Sample 12-1

```
<%
today = new Date();
   var mm = today.getMonth() +1;
   if (mm < 10) mm = "0" + mm;
   var dd = today.getDate();
      if (dc < 10) dd = "0" + dd;
   var yy = today.getYear().toString().substring(3,4);
   var hh = today.getHours();    if (hh < 10) hh = "0" + hh;
   var nn = today.getMinutes();
   if (nn < 10) nn = "0" + nn;
   var ss = today.getSeconds();
   if (ss < 10) ss = "0" + ss;
   session("thisdate") = mm + "/" + dd + "/" + yy;
   session("ts") = mm + dd + yy + hh + nn + ss;
%>
```

After you make these values into session variables, you can bind them to hidden form fields and insert them into an Orders data table.

E-mail Notification of Orders

Larger e-enterprises have gangs of order fulfillment slaves working day and night checking the database for orders and gift-wrapping faucet washers — or whatever (personally I've never intruded upon a faucet-washer-wrapper's personal space). They don't need to be informed of incoming orders in any other way.

Smaller firms, though, may not look at their databases on a regular basis and would welcome e-mail notification of a new order. Some small merchants would even consider auto-e-mail an *essential* feature of their site. So, if you build e-commerce sites for a living, e-mail notification is a request — more like a *demand* — that you're going to get pretty soon, if you haven't already.

UltraDev has no built-in server behavior for firing off e-mail. Like the shopping cart itself, the e-mail module is an SBX — this one by Ray West of Basic Drumbeat. The extension makes use of the outgoing mail CDO (Collaborative Data Object) that's available for the NT server.

Part IV: E-commerce with UltraDev

> **WARNING!** CDO Mail won't run in any other Windows environment besides NT or on the Mac. The current version of the SBX is available for ASP only.

Configuring your NT server

The CDO mail object isn't something that's automatically available on your machine, like the Explorer or the Control Panel. You have to register a dynamic link library (DLL) and configure the SMTP (Simple Mail Transfer Protocol) server on your system.

So there's a little setup to be done, but it only takes a few minutes. Just follow these steps:

1. **Click the Start button and choose Run.**

   The Run dialog box appears.

2. **In the Open text box, type** regsvr32, **followed by the path to the library** cdonts.dll.

   The full command is normally `regsvr32 C:\WINNT\system32\cdonts.dll`, but you may need to find the correct path on your system.

3. **You get a message that the registration succeeded.**

4. **Open your Microsoft Management Console by clicking the Start button and choosing Programs➪Windows NT4 Option Pack➪Microsoft Internet Information Server➪Internet Service Manager (the one with the little hammer icon beside it).**

5. **Expand the directory tree in the left pane until you can see your Default SMTP Site (see Figure 12-8). Right-click this entry and choose Properties from the pop-up menu.**

   The multi-tab SMTP Site Properties dialog box opens.

Figure 12-8: Microsoft Management Console, expanded to show the default SMTP site.

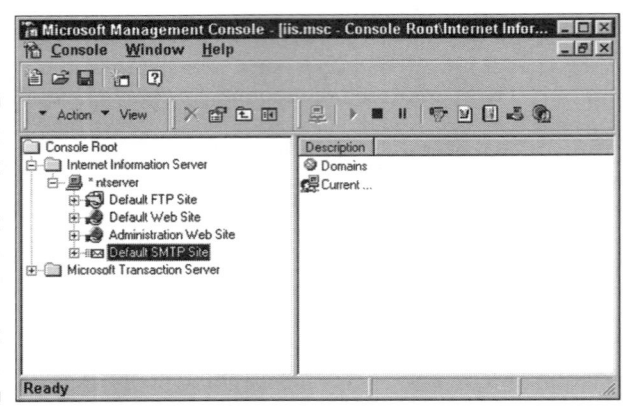

6. **Click the Delivery tab.**
7. **Check that the name of your server appears correctly in the Fully Qualified Domain Name text box.**
8. **Type the name of your SMTP server in the Smart Host text box.**

   What's required here is the hostname of whatever SMTP (outgoing e-mail) server that you have an account with. It makes no difference whether the server is on the same machine, on a network machine, or accessed by dialup. For outgoing mail, there's no need for a login/password — but if you dial in to more than one ISP, you should choose the one your server will be connected to when you make use of CDO mail. Figure 12-9 shows an example of the completed dialog box.

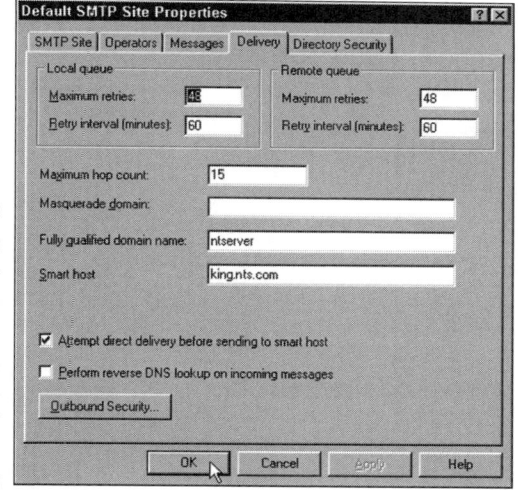

Figure 12-9: The Delivery tab of the SMTP Site Properties dialog box, set up for CDO mail.

9. **Click the Apply button and close the dialog box.**

TIP: You can find updated information on configuring `cdonts.dll` at `www.basic-drumbeat.com/articles/CDOSetup/`.

TECHNICAL STUFF: The SMTP Server normally installs as a subcomponent of the Internet Information Server (IIS) when you install NT Option Pack. If you find that you don't have the Default SMTP Server, run install again for the Option Pack, select the IIS component, click the Show Subcomponents button, and select the SMTP Service component. Then install.

Using the CDO Mail server behavior extension

If your NT server is correctly configured, you can download, install, and use the CDO Mail SBX.

First, get the extension. You can download it from the Macromedia Exchange or get it off the CD that accompanies this book. (For the latest up-to-date version, you should download it from the Macromedia Exchange.) Make sure that you have the Extension Manager installed. (See Chapter 10 for instructions on downloading and installing extensions.)

After you successfully install the extension, you should see it added to the pop-up menu of server behaviors when you click the plus (+) button in the Server Behaviors inspector (see Figure 12-10).

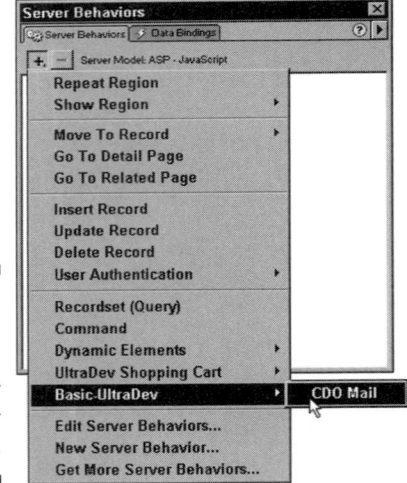

Figure 12-10: An extra option on the server behavior list.

When you use the CDO mail behavior, it simply inserts a block of ASP code that invokes the CDO mail object and fires off a message. The behavior assumes that a submit button named Submit has been clicked in order to activate the e-mail message. Either the submit button was on the previous page, or it's on the same page as the page that sends the e-mail and the form has been submitted to itself.

For an e-commerce site, I recommend applying the CDO mail behavior to a final "Thanks and Bye-bye" page. After all, you can't be certain the order has actually been placed until that page loads. The page preceding the thanks page is likely to be the type of order confirm page described in the section "Closing the Deal" earlier in this chapter. That page is likely to contain much of the information you need to construct your order notification e-mail message — order number, customer ID, and so on. This information will be automatically available in the Session Object or in the Request Object. If you've personalized the page by adding a filtered customer recordset, all the customer data is also close at hand. By default, a submit button named Submit is clicked to open the thanks page.

Here's an example of a typical e-mail message sent automatically to the merchant when a customer confirms an order.

```
Subject: Hats Galore -- Order received
Date: Tue, 19 Sep 2000 10:31:07 -0700

From: thehatstore@somesite.com
To: <merchant@someotherplace.com >

An order has been received from Francis Greene
Customer number 3343
Order number is 9665
Total value of order is $75.75
```

The components of the message body, and where they come from, are as follows:

Line 1: User name. Derived from a filtered recordset (see Chapter 8).

Line 2: Customer number. Assumed to have been placed in the Session Object by whatever login/registration procedure you use.

Line 3: Order number. In the Session Object, if you've generated it by using the UltraDev Shopping Cart server behavior described in the section "Transferring the contents of a shopping cart to a database" earlier in this chapter.

Line 4: Order total. Retrieved from the Request Object if the preceding page is the type of order confirm page described in the section "Transferring the contents of a shopping cart to a database" earlier in this chapter.

So, having got your thoughts in order, create or reopen your thanks page and proceed.

Part IV: E-commerce with UltraDev

1. **In the Server Behaviors inspector, click the plus (+) button and choose Basic UltraDev⇨CDO Mail.**

   The CDO Mail dialog box appears, as shown in Figure 12-11.

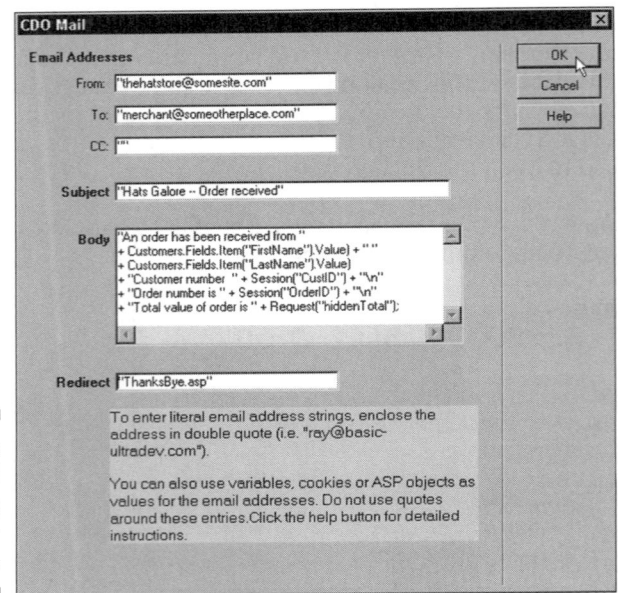

   Figure 12-11: Use the CDO Mail dialog box to auto-send e-mail.

2. **Type the From address between the double quotes in the From box.**

   This must be formatted as a genuine e-mail address and be an actual address of origin. Many SMTP servers check addresses of origin for security reasons and don't deliver mail whose origin cannot be verified.

3. **Type the To address between the double quotes in the To box.**

   This is the address of the merchant who needs to be alerted that an order has been received. For test purposes, you can address the e-mail to yourself.

4. **Type the CC address (or multiple comma-separated addresses) between the double quotes in the CC box.**

   If you have no CC addressee(s), leave the empty (double-double) quotes as they are.

5. **Type the subject of the message between the double quotes in the Subject box.**

   In the example, the subject is `Hats Galore -- Order Received`.

6. **Type the message in the Body box (Figure 12-11 shows the example).**

Literal strings are enclosed in quotes. Retrieved values are not. Strings are concatenated with + in JavaScript and with & in VBScript. Line endings are signaled with \n in JavaScript and chr(10) & chr(13) in VBScript. In JavaScript, don't terminate a line with a semicolon until the entire message body is built. In VBScript, don't use your Enter key but allow the text to wrap.

7. **If you want to redirect to another page after the mail message is sent, type the redirect URL between the double quotes in the Redirect box.**

   If you don't need a redirect, simply redirect to the same page. The behavior requires something in this box.

TIP: If, like the example, you're retrieving values from a recordset, inspect the source code to be sure the recordset is defined *before* the CDO mail code. If the CDO mail code ends up ahead of the recordset definition, you have to manually copy and paste it further down or the code will give errors.

TECHNICAL STUFF: Some e-commerce sites send e-mail to the customer, confirming the order and quoting an order number, in addition to alerting the merchant. It's possible to do this by using the CDO mail SBX — after all, the customer's e-mail address can surely be retrieved from a filtered recordset without any problem. But if you want to try this, I recommend that you build the second instance of the CDO object manually. You must allow the first instance to be killed and then create a duplicate server object. Example code follows, assuming a filtered customers recordset rsCustomers is on the page:

Source Code Sample 12-2

```
<% if (String(Request("Submit")) != "undefined")
{
var objCDO = Server.CreateObject("CDONTS.NewMail");
objCDO.From = "thehatstore@somesite.com";
objCDO.To = "themerchant@someotherplace.com";
objCDO.cc = "";
objCDO.Subject = "Hats Galore -- Order received";
objCDO.Body = "An order has been received from " +
            rsCustomers.Fields.Item("FirstName").Value + " " +
            rsCustomers.Fields.Item("LastName").Value + "\n"
+ "Customer number " + Session("CustID") + "\n"
+ "Order number is " + Session("OrderID") + "\n"
+ "Total value of order is " + Session("Total");
objCDO.Send();
objCDO = null;

var objCDO = Server.CreateObject("CDONTS.NewMail");
objCDO.From = " thehatstore@somesite.com ";
objCDO.To = rsCustomers.Fields.Item("CustomerEmail").Value;
objCDO.cc = "";
objCDO.Subject = "Your Order from Hats Galore";
objCDO.Body = "Thankyou for your order from Hats Galore\n"
+ "Your order number is " + Session("OrderID") + "\n";
objCDO.Send();
objCDO = null;
Response.Redirect("thanksbye.html");
}
%>
```

E-commerce plug-ins

Many e-commmerce packages claim to plug in to your Web site and add functionality that would take you a lot of effort to create independently. Most of them actually route your customers to their own site, and thus they invoice you for site hosting on a per-time, per-megabyte, or per-transaction basis. Additional costs are normally incurred in setting up a merchant account, subscribing to a payment processing service, and obtaining a security certificate.

Here are three companies that Macromedia recognizes as e-commerce partners.

- **Netstores.com.** Provides a set of Dreamweaver extensions, providing product search and credit card verification as well as purchase functionality. Setup is $595 plus $50 a month.

- **Catalog Builders** (catalogbuilders.com). An e-commerce database hosting service that features full shipping and tax calculation. Installation costs $200, and a monthly fee is calculated on the amount of traffic.

- **ICat.** A full-service e-commerce company that provides online payment processing and tax and shipping calculations. Hosting is split between ICat servers and your own ISP. Merchants don't sign up with ICat directly, but with one of their Commerce Service Providers to obtain the banking services they need.

Part V
The Part of Tens

In this part . . .

This part is the traditional grab bag that finishes off all books in the *For Dummies* series. I was grateful for the opportunity to bring together ten offbeat UltraDev features that wouldn't otherwise have found a place in this book, and ten server behavior extensions that I think are really worth having.

To call these items secrets is a slight exaggeration, but I do claim that it would take you a long, long time to discover them without this part.

Chapter 13
Ten Cute Things UltraDev Can Do

In This Chapter
- Using Layout View
- Converting tables to layers (and layers to tables)
- Aligning and sizing
- Binding a recordset field to attributes of a `DIV`
- Adding a `color` attribute to the Horizontal Rule tag
- Defaulting CSS attachments and other stuff
- Fooling your computer
- The poor man's database
- Turning `read-only` attributes on and off
- I changed my mind!

*H*ere's a small miscellany of interesting things I've learned as I've explored UltraDev like a cat in a new house, looking in every closet. In no particular order, and not guaranteed to be the *most* cute stuff, here are some features that you won't use often but you may have fun with.

Using Layout View

Sometimes UltraDev's standard table object isn't quite up to the task that you have in mind. Sure, it's fine for run-of-the-mill tables — and certainly all the menu options are available for merging cells, splitting cells, increasing and decreasing rowspan and columnspan. Some genius at Macromedia must have thought that we all need a special toy to make tables with, however.

UltraDev offers a whole new free-form way of making tables. Click the Layout View tool at the base of the Objects Palette (see Figure 13-1), and you get to use the Layout Table and Layout Cell tools to bring your own weird ideas about table cells to life.

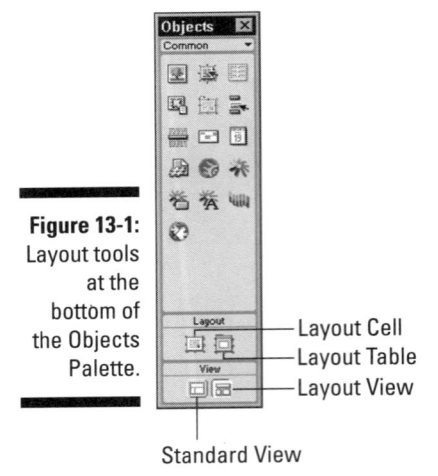

Figure 13-1: Layout tools at the bottom of the Objects Palette.

- Layout Cell
- Layout Table
- Layout View
- Standard View

Start by using the Layout Table tool to sweep out the outline of your table. You'll find it snaps to your guide grid (see Chapter 2). Then use the Layout Cell tool to create a cell anywhere within the table. (You can even put down a table cell before you have a table to put it in, but then you can't easily control the overall table size.)

Carry on building cells in whatever pattern you like. Figure 13-2 shows a finished table that would have been hard (but not impossible) to make using the normal table object.

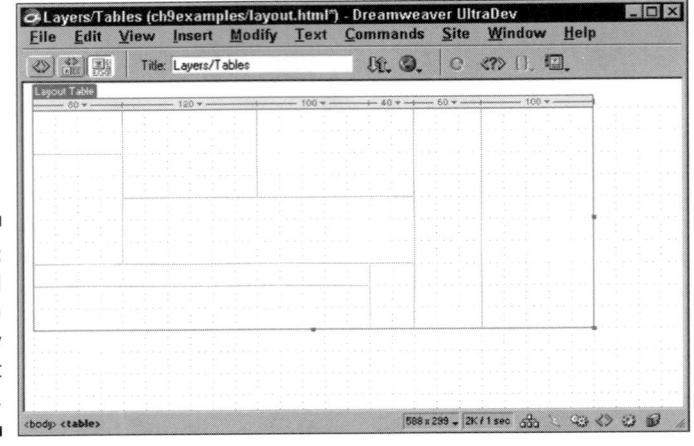

Figure 13-2: Unusual table made possible by Layout View.

Chapter 13: Ten Cute Things UltraDev Can Do 277

Selecting a table by clicking its title tab makes it acquire handles, which you can use to stretch it, creating grayed (undefined) areas.

You can even nest tables inside other tables. Simply draw a new table in the grayed area of an existing table.

TIP

While you're in Layout View, the standard table and layer objects are not available.

Converting Tables to Layers (And Layers to Tables)

Everybody knows that it's important to create Web pages that are compatible with the widest practicable range of browsers. Some people, however, are more conscientious about this than others. One of the most controversial techniques in modern page design is the use of layers, which cannot be interpreted by any pre-4.0 browser version.

Did you know that UltraDev makes it easy to convert a layer page into a table page? As long as layers aren't overlapping, you can choose Modify⇔Convert⇔Layers to Table, and UltraDev figures it all out. Figures 13-3 and 13-4 show a demonstration of before-and-after conversion.

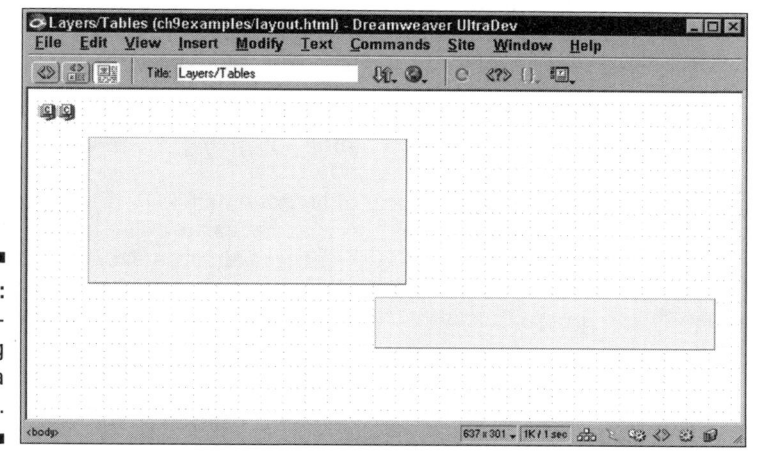

Figure 13-3: Nonoverlapping layers on a page.

Figure 13-4: Layers converted into a table.

UltraDev also features a converse option, to convert table cells to layers. It's kind of fun, but I can't think of any situation in which to use it.

Aligning and Sizing

This feature is especially for Drummies — I know how you must miss using Drumbeat's Aligning, Sizing, and Spacing menu options for getting your higgledy-piggledy labels and form fields to form fours, dress right, and stand at attention.

You can make groups of UltraDev objects in layout align left, right, top, or bottom, and snap to the same width or height — as long as they're on layers. The layers are what really do the aligning and sizing.

To perform this trick, select a group of layers by clicking the left-mouse button and pressing Shift as many times as necessary. The last layer that you click is the *reference layer* to which the others align or size.

Now use the menu options after choosing Modify⇨Align to call your layers to order.

Binding a Recordset Field to Attributes of a DIV

In Chapter 4, I tell you how to use the attributes of a DIV to bind a recordset field to the style of a piece of text. In this section, I introduce you to an even

Chapter 13: Ten Cute Things UltraDev Can Do   279

more offbeat binding technique involving the visibility or Z-index of the `DIV`. You can use this type of binding to, for example, make images or text pop onto the screen as users browse a catalog. Figure 13-5 shows an example of a prominent discontinued label that's been made to pop into the foreground of a product picture by this method.

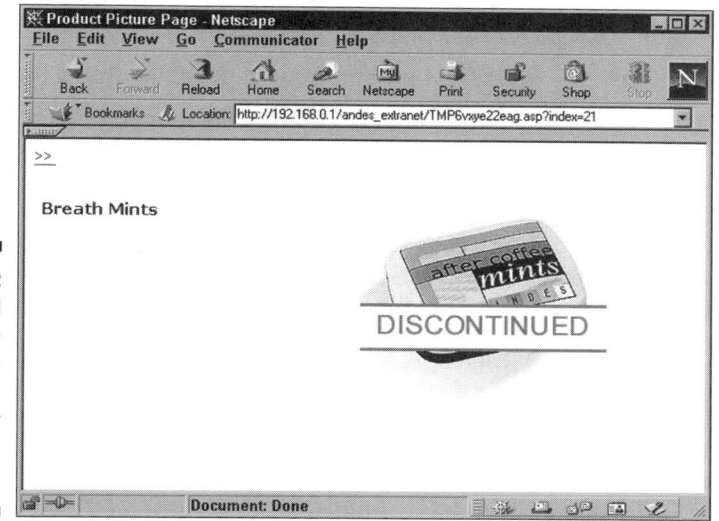

Figure 13-5: Special image brought into foreground under database control.

But you have to perform a trick to make this data binding happen. The snag is that visibility and Z-index are not independent attributes of a `DIV` — they're all wrapped up in the single attribute called `style`. A complete `DIV` tag might look like this:

```
<div id="ProductLayer" style="position:absolute; left:55px; top:45px;
       width:280px; height:130px; z-index:1; visibility:visible;
       background-color:#CCFFFF; layer-background-color:#CCFFFF; border:
       1px none #000000"></div>
```

If you want to bind the `style` attribute of the `DIV` to a recordset field, the recordset field would need to be mighty wide. But not if you do this:

1. **In the Property inspector of the `DIV`, select LAYER in the Tag drop-down list.**

    LAYER is a Netscape-only HTML element that functions exactly like a `DIV`. The difference is that the various components of the `DIV` style are all independent attributes in a LAYER.

2. **If you want to use the `visibility` attribute, select visible in the Vis drop-down list.**

3. **Click the List View tab on the left side of the Property inspector.**

    The list of attributes appears in the Property inspector. `Id`, `left`, `top`, `width`, `height`, `bgcolor`, and — yes — `z-index` and `visibility`.

 4. **Select which attribute you want to bind and click the lightning bolt icon at the extreme right of the selected line.**

    The Dynamic Data dialog box opens, with whatever recordset on the page that is available for binding.

 5. **Select the recordset field to bind to and close the dialog box.**

 6. **Click the Standard View tab in the Property inspector (see Figure 13-6) and reset the layer tag type to `DIV` in the tag drop-down list.**

    The binding of the attribute is still valid, even though it's now only one component of the `style` attribute.

If you're using the `z-index` attribute, make a data field for it in your data table with most records having the value 0, and records that deserve prominence having 2 or higher. In Figure 13-5, the DISCONTINUED image changes its Z-index from 0 to 2 when appropriate, moving into the foreground of a product picture whose Z-index is set to 1.

If you're using the `visibility` attribute, the data field must contain either the word visible or the word hidden.

Adding a Color Attribute to the Horizontal Rule Tag

If you click a horizontal rule tag (`<HR>`) in an UltraDev document and look at its Property inspector, you don't find anything enabling you to specify color. But Internet Explorer accepts a `color` attribute of the horizontal rule tag (although it isn't an official attribute in the HTML 4.0 specification). To make UltraDev accept a `color` attribute, follow these steps:

 1. **In the Property inspector, click the List View tab (see Figure 13-6).**

    The attribute list comes up empty (no attributes) and doesn't display any width, height, or alignment attributes that you may have previously set.

 2. **Click the plus (+) button to add a new attribute.**

    An empty attribute line appears.

 3. **Click the little down arrow in the new attribute line to pop up a menu of possible attributes (see Figure 13-6).**

4. **Select the** `color` **attribute.**

5. **Now you find a little color picker at the right end of the attribute line. Use it to select the color you want.**

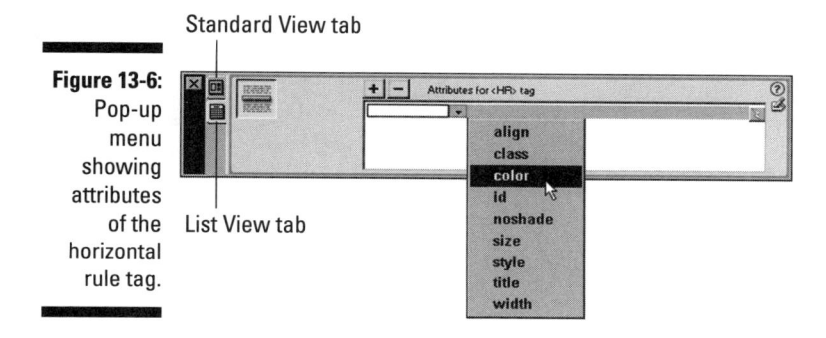

Figure 13-6:
Pop-up menu showing attributes of the horizontal rule tag.

Standard View tab

List View tab

Defaulting CSS Attachments and Other Stuff

Attaching a style sheet to a newly created UltraDev page is easy. Chapter 2 tells you how in just two steps (three if you count opening the CSS Styles palette first).

But what if you know that you need the same style sheet attached to page after page after page? Even those three steps are going to get tedious, right?

What if you want the same `<head>` tags on page after page? Suppose, for example, that you want a bunch of keywords. You can insert `<head>` tags by choosing Insert⇨Head Tags, and then selecting one of six options. Not too hard, but how about typing the same 25 keywords every time you create a new page?

Guess what? The page that pops into the document window when you create a new page is an actual file, and you can place anything in it you want. You can find it at

```
\Ultradev\Configuration\Templates\Default.htm
```

To default a link to a style sheet called `master.css`, open the `Default.htm` file in a text editor and add the following line between the `<head>` and `</head>` tags:

```
<link rel="stylesheet" href="master.css">
```

To default your 25 keywords, insert the following line between the `<head>` and `</head>` tags:

```
<meta name="keywords" content="keyword1 keyword2 keyword3...">
```

Actually, anything that you can write in HTML or any server-side language can be pre-set by inserting it in that file, appearing in every new page you create. When you no longer need the defaults, just delete them from `Default.htm`.

Fooling Your Computer

It's 2:00 a.m. and your computer knows where you are. Well, let me rephrase that — your Microsoft IIS Web server knows where *it* is. And that often comes to the same thing.

But suppose that you want to fool the server into thinking it's in Switzerland or Thailand? Perhaps you need to verify that date and currency formats work out okay.

You can do so by changing the value of a Session variable called `Session.LCID`. If you're in the U.S., `Session.LCID=1033` (see Chapter 8 for an explanation of Session variables).

If you want to pretend that you're in Thailand, put the following line of ASP at the head of your document:

```
<% Session.LCID = "1054" %>
```

The LCID for the U.K. (where currency is £ and dates are dd/mm/yy) is 2057. You can find a complete list of LCID codes at http://support.microsoft.com/support/kb/articles/q229/6/90.asp. On that same page is a chunk of code that you can use to test currency and date/time formats.

The Poor Man's Database

UltraDev is all about databases. You knew that, right? And if you've read Part II of this book, you're thinking of a database as something formatted as Microsoft Access, Paradox, Excel, FoxPro, or one of the other brand names in the data biz.

A data table, however, can be ASCII text. Here are the header and first three records of a data table belonging to a (fictitious) yacht charter company:

Chapter 13: Ten Cute Things UltraDev Can Do 283

```
BoatID,YachtType,YearBuilt,Berths,HighSeason,MidSeason,LowSeason
1,Sun Light 30,89/90,6,"$1,250 ","$1,150 ",$850
3,Gibsea 312,89/90,6,"$1,700 ","$1,600 ",$980
4,Atlantic 31,90/93,6,"$1,300 ","$1,250 ",$850
```

This type of openly readable file is known as a comma-separated values (CSV) file because the field values are delimited by commas. CSV files pop up all over — they're cheap and cheerful, truly the "poor man's database."

You can make a DSN for one of these files by using the Microsoft Text Driver, but UltraDev has its own super-convenient way of importing files like this directly into the document and formatting them as tables. Choose Insert⇨Tabular Data. Figure 13-7 shows the dialog box that lets you format the resulting table, and Figure 13-8 shows the complete charter yacht table inserted.

Figure 13-7: Dialog box for formatting tabular data.

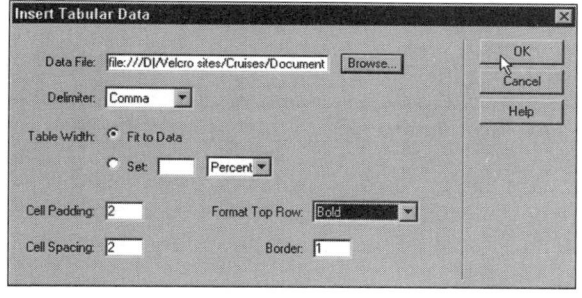

Figure 13-8: A complete CSV table inserted on a page.

Turning Read-Only Attributes On and Off

A minor annoyance is that some imported site files, especially those copied from a CD, are marked as read-only. Turning off the `read-only` attribute for a whole set of files is a chore if done manually. But UltraDev has a labor-saving option.

In the site window, you can tell if a file is read-only by a little padlock icon immediately to the left of the filename. To turn the `read-only` attribute off, select the file (or an entire folder). Either right-click and select Turn Off Read Only or choose File➪Turn Off Read Only from the site window menu.

I Changed My Mind!

Several UltraDev warning boxes include a check box that says `Don't show me this again`. A perfect example is when you place a form object in a document and there's no form on the page. The message you see says `Add form tag?`. The problem with those "Never again" options is that because you never see the message again, you never get a chance to change your mind. One reason you may want to is that you're training a newbie, and need those warnings back again.

The key to changing your mind is finding and deleting the note file that contains the instruction to inhibit the warning.

Note files generally have the double extension `.js.mno`. The one that governs the `Add form tag?` message, for example, is at `\Ultradev\Configuration\Objects\Forms\_notes\forminsert.js.mno`.

Chapter 14
Ten Extension Objects Worth Your Time

In This Chapter
- UltraDev shopping cart
- CDO mail
- Footnotes
- Form Button Fever!
- Right-Click Menu Builder
- Horizontal Looper
- Banner Builder
- Redirect if Cookie Exists
- Guest Book
- Upload File From Page

Extensions to UltraDev can be objects, commands, behaviors, or server behaviors. This chapter covers a small selection of the hundreds of extensions available, providing at least one example of each type of extension.

I've tested all these extensions on ASP sites, so I know they basically work in that server technology. The description text is copied directly from the extension author's "official" description, with just a very few edits for consistency.

The size quoted in each case is the size of the Macromedia eXtension Package (MXP) file that you download. After you install an extension, you can delete the MXP file if you wish.

Instructions for installing extensions are in Chapter 9.

You can find all ten of these extensions on the CD accompanying this book, in the folder Extensions\SBXs\Win or Extensions\SBXs\Mac, as appropriate to your system.

UltraDev Shopping Cart

Macromedia category:	e-commerce
Author:	Rick Crawford, Powerclimb
Size:	162K
Adds to:	Data Bindings inspector and Server Behaviors inspector

* Featured in Chapters 11 and 12 of this book

The UltraDev Shopping Cart package will help you quickly build e-commerce applications in Macromedia Dreamweaver UltraDev. This version works for sites created in ASP, Cold Fusion, and JSP.

The UltraDev Shopping cart includes the cart data source and a set of corresponding server behaviors. Access the cart itself either from the Data Bindings inspector or the Server Behaviors inspector. Find the server behaviors in the UltraDev Shopping Cart submenu on the Server Behaviors inspector.

CDO Mail

Macromedia category:	Productivity
Author:	Ray West, Basic-UltraDev
Size:	10.7K
Adds to:	Server Behaviors inspector

* Featured in Chapter 12 of this book

This behavior allows the user to add simple CDO e-mail functionality to their pages. It is an ASP extension that supports both VBScript and JavaScript as the server-side language.

Footnote

Macromedia category:	DHTML/Layers
Author:	Jed Hartman, `logos-footnote@kith.org`
Size:	4.7K
Adds to:	Objects palette (Common panel) and Insert menu
Demo at:	`www.kith.org/logos/things/footnotes.html`

This object allows you to easily add footnotes to an HTML page, viewable in any browser that supports showing and hiding layers. The footnote text appears when the person viewing the page moves the mouse to point to the footnote number, and disappears when the mouse pointer moves away.

The object also includes a primitive system for tracking the current footnote number, though it doesn't provide an automatic way to renumber existing footnotes.

After you've created a footnote, you may want to resize the layer to better fit the text (but beware of IE5/Mac issues regarding layers with colored backgrounds and specified heights; it may be best to adjust the width only). You may also want to choose Commands⇨Add/Remove Netscape Resize Fix; if you don't use that command, then resizing a page with footnotes in Netscape looks very ugly. Finally, you may want to move the footnote a little to avoid the pointer covering up part of the footnote text in the browser.

Note: The author of this SBX, Jed Hartman, disclaims compatibility with UltraDev 4. His code has been fully tested only with Dreamweaver 3. I've tested it (perhaps not quite *fully*) with UltraDev 4 and it worked fine.

Form Button Fever!

Macromedia category:	Navigation
Author:	Drew McLellan, `dreamweaverfever.com`
Size:	4.3K
Adds to:	Behaviors inspector

This behavior will make any object a Submit or Reset button for your form. The default Event will be set to *onClick* to help ensure maximum browser compatibility. This can, however, be changed in the Behaviors palette to an Event of your choice.

Select an object to apply the behavior to, and then locate and select Form Button Fever! in the behavior palette.

Right-Click Menu Builder

Macromedia category:	Navigation
Author:	Rabi Sunder Raj
Size:	11.4K
Adds to:	Commands menu

Creates a custom Right-Click Menu for Windows Internet Explorer 5 browser. Netscape and older browsers will ignore this feature.

Horizontal Looper

Macromedia category:	Productivity
Author:	Tom Muck
Size:	122K
Adds to:	Server Behaviors inspector

This is a Horizontal Repeat Region server behavior. You simply choose the number of rows and columns to display, and this behavior builds a table based on the number of rows and columns you chose. There's also an option to show all records, by clicking the radio button for All records. It will work with the standard Move To Record (next, previous, and so on) Server Behaviors. Works with ASP/VBScript, ASP/JavaScript, JSP, and Cold Fusion.

Apply this server behavior by highlighting an area that contains a database column or columns and choose "HLooper" in the Server Behaviors inspector.

Banner Builder

Macromedia category:	Rich Media
Author:	Rabi Sunder Raj
Size:	7K
Adds to:	Commands menu

Creates a sequence of images that changes at specified intervals. Each image can have its own unique hyperlink source.

This extension can also be used to create an animated JPEG, by assigning a sequence of JPEGs.

On the MSIE browser, the images change with a random transition effect.

Redirect if Cookie Exists

Macromedia category:	Security
Author:	Jag Sidhu
Size:	5K
Adds to:	Server Behaviors inspector

By adding this server behavior to a Web page, you can redirect the user to a different URL if a specified cookie exists.

Guest Book

Macromedia category:	e-commerce
Author:	mycomputer.com
Size:	1540K
Adds to:	Special panel in the Objects palette, and item on the Insert menu

GuestBook.com offers a fully customizable guestbook that gives you the option not to place banners or ad buttons on your page. Our service allows you to build and configure your guestbook to meet your unique preferences and requirements. For Windows only.

Upload File from Page

Author:	Jag Sidhu
Size:	6K
Adds to:	Server Behaviors inspector

This server behavior can be used to let users upload files to your Web site. Two pages are required: submit.asp and upload.asp. Submit.asp will have a form where you can browse for a file and submit the form to upload.asp. In upload.asp, apply this server behavior.

Enter the complete path for the directory that you want to upload the file to. The format should be similar to c:\inetpub\yourid\uploads. If you do not know the path for your uploads directory, ask your server administrator. The SA-FileUp component should be installed on the server. The upload directory should have RDW permissions.

SA-FileUp is an independent software package sold by Software Artisans. A 30-day evaluation copy is available.

For more information check out www.softwareartisans.com or www.magicfind.com/ultradev.asp.

You might also want to add the following code to the body of the uploads.asp page:

```
<p>Thank you for uploading your file.
<br>Total Bytes Written: <%=upl.TotalBytes %>
```

Part VI
Appendixes

The 5th Wave   By Rich Tennant

"OK, I think I forgot to mention this, but we now have a Web management function that automatically alerts us when there's a broken link on The Aquarium's Web site."

In this part...

A good appendix is like a good closet. It's a place to put useful stuff that doesn't fit anywhere else. In these appendixes, you find some installation instructions that you may use only once, but can't do without, along with some code samples that you can substitute for the ASP/JavaScript examples in the book, written for you VBScript, JSP, or ColdFusion mavens.

Finally, tucked way in the back, a laundry list of what's on the CD — a few old socks, a pair of beginner skis, a sack of kitty litter. . . . well, no, not really — have a look. You can keep anything you find.

Appendix A
Installing UltraDev for Windows

*T*he technical requirements I list here are what Macromedia recommends for installing UltraDev. What — do you think I invent this stuff? Personally I think they're somewhat over-generous. You could get by with a bit less RAM, a bit less hard drive space, and a few less MHz. But it's fair to say that this is a checklist of what you need for *optimal* performance.

Technical Requirements Checklist

To install UltraDev on a Windows machine, you need the following:

- Windows 95, 98, 2000, or NT 4 or later.
- 48MB available RAM.
- 30MB available hard drive space.
- 166 MHz (minimum) Intel Pentium processor (or equivalent).
- CD-ROM drive.
- Windows NT 4 users should have Service Pack 5 or greater installed.
- Microsoft Data Access Components (MDAC) 2.1 or greater. MDAC 2.1 is installed if you have installed Office 2000, and you can download the latest version from www.microsoft.com/data/download.htm. The installation follows standard Microsoft practice and it's pretty quick.
- If you're using JDBC, you need either of the following Java Virtual Machine (JVM) types:
    - Sun's Java Runtime Environment (JRE) or the Java Development Kit (JDK) version 1.1.8 or greater.
    - Microsoft Virtual Machine for Internet Explorer 5.01 or later.
- Netscape Navigator or Internet Explorer 4.0 or greater to view the Help system.
- Macromedia Shockwave 8 plug-in installed in your browser if you want to view the Help system Guided Tours and Show Me movies.

The Simplest Installation You Ever Did

Insert the UltraDev CD and, in either the Windows Explorer or the My Computer menus, double-click `UltraDev Installer.exe`. The program takes a little while to unpack, and then leads you through these eight screens:

1. **Welcome.**
2. **License terms.**

   Accept them (better read them first, perhaps?).

3. **Personal details.**

   Fill this screen out. The only thing you really must get right is the serial number — it's on the user service card, and also stuck on the CD sleeve. Be careful to use the one that begins UDW, not UDM. After you get it right, you're rewarded with a little red check mark to the right of the serial number box.

4. **Install folder.**

   Accept or change this.

5. **Default Editor.**

   UltraDev offers to be the default editor for six different file types (see Figure A-1). You should pay attention to this, because it may conflict with defaults you already know and love.

Figure A-1: Think carefully about UltraDev's default editor options.

6. **Start menu.**
7. **Current settings.**

   Click Next on this screen and the installation swings into action.

8. **Install confirm.**

   Click Finish.

Appendix B
Installing UltraDev for Macintosh

This appendix includes all the setup information that you need to make the required connections to a networked NT server machine. You only need to make this connection once. Data connections, which you need to do every time you bring a new database into service with UltraDev, are described in Chapter 3.

Technical Requirements Checklist

To install UltraDev on a Mac, you need the following:

- Mac OS 8.6 or later.
- QuickTime 3.0 or later.
- 64MB available RAM.
- 130MB available hard drive space.
- G3 or later recommended.
- CD-ROM drive.
- Netscape Navigator or Internet Explorer 4.0 or better to view the Help system.
- Macromedia Shockwave 8 plug-in installed in your browser if you want to view the Help system Guided Tours and Show Me movies.

Why Do I Need All This Setup?

If you intend to use UltraDev to create database-driven Web sites (and if you don't, you may as well just use Dreamweaver), as a Mac user you're in for some setup time. As explained in Chapter 3, the database and the final published site are unlikely to be on a Mac. Therefore, you must expect to work on a networked machine with permissions to access data and site folders on a Windows machine (an NT server is strongly recommended, but it's possible to get by with Win9*x* or Win2000).

You're likely to need the two machines to talk to each other in these three ways:

- **Database access.** The database is likely to be on the NT machine, so a connection to it needs to be established via TCP/IP. The Mac's TCP/IP settings need to be set for connection via Ethernet rather than PPP — Figure B-1 shows a typical TCP/IP settings dialog box set for the data access task, with an IP address allocated to the Mac. The actual data connection process is covered in Chapter 3.

- **Posting files to the server.** When you need to view UltraDev-created Web pages that have a dynamic data component, you need to post them to the server. The most convenient way is by an AppleTalk connection, and the (fairly complex) setup for that is described later in this appendix. You also have the option of posting to the server by FTP, avoiding the whole AppleTalk setup but incurring some performance penalty. You set that up in the Application server page of the Site definition — see Chapter 1 for details.

- **Previewing your sites in a browser.** On the same page of the six-part Site definition, you need to state a URL prefix to enable your local browser to load your pages for preview. This should be the network IP address of the server, and again the communication between the two machines is by TCP/IP.

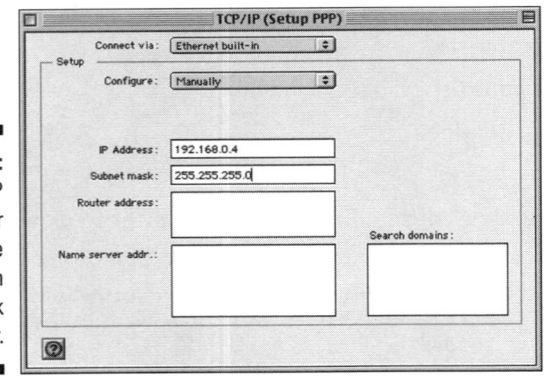

Figure B-1: Mac TCP/IP settings for a database connection to a network server.

If you're lucky enough to have a very cooperative ISP (or if the CEO is your brother, maybe), then it's possible to work direct to the remote site, accessing everything including the DSN as you design your pages. That's theoretically possible because UltraDev uses an HTTP call to access the DSN — but it requires file access permissions at the remote site that most ISPs would be reluctant to grant. You also need a high-speed connection (ISDN minimum).

Installing UltraDev

Now you can install UltraDev — just follow these steps:

1. **Insert the UltraDev CD and double-click the UltraDev icon that magically appears on your desktop.**
2. **Double-click the UltraDev Installer.**

   The Splash Screen appears.
3. **Click Continue.**

   The license terms screen appears.
4. **Read the terms and click Accept.**
5. **Click Install on the install screen.**
6. **Fill out the personalization screen.**

   The serial number is the one that begins UDM, not UDW, which is the Windows version serial number. The serial number appears on the user service card and also on a label on the installation CD.

Installation runs its course. Don't forget to remove the CD when you're done.

The next few sections are all about what has to happen on the server end of things. If your NT server administrator won't allow you near the precious machine, make him or her read this while you take a coffee break. Better make it an all-day break, actually....

Configuring the NT Server

You need to check on a few aspects of the NT server before you can start being hospitable to a Mac and allowing it access to your ODBC database.

Pre-flight checklist

Before configuring your NT server, you need to verify the following:

- Make sure the database itself is present and that permissions on both the file and the folder containing it are adequate for remote access. This is particularly important for Microsoft Access databases.
- Check your ODBC Data Source Administrator to see that a DSN has been created for the database. If not, refer to Chapter 3.

✔ Create a folder one level below server root (usually `C:\Inetpub\wwwroot\`) to accept published files, and set permissions on that folder as well.

Hosting the Mac

After checking the NT server connection, you can turn your attention to the Mac connection. First you need to install Services For Macintosh (SFM) on the server:

1. **On the NT server, open the Control Panel and double-click Network.**

   The Network dialog box opens.

2. **Click the Services tab, as shown in Figure B-2.**

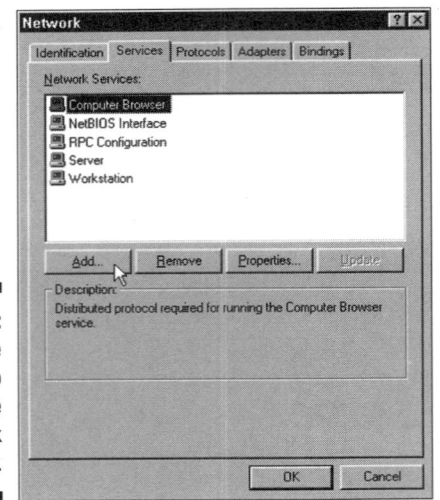

Figure B-2: The Services tab of the Network dialog box.

3. **Click the Add button.**

   The Select Network Service dialog box opens.

4. **Scroll if necessary and select Services for Macintosh.**

   The Windows NT Setup dialog box opens with a default directory from which to copy the necessary files. You may have to insert your Windows NT Server CD and direct the Setup to the I386 folder on that disk — many machines also have a copy of I386 on their C: drives.

5. **Allow the Setup to proceed and note that SFM now appears in the Services tab of the Network dialog box (see Figure B-3).**

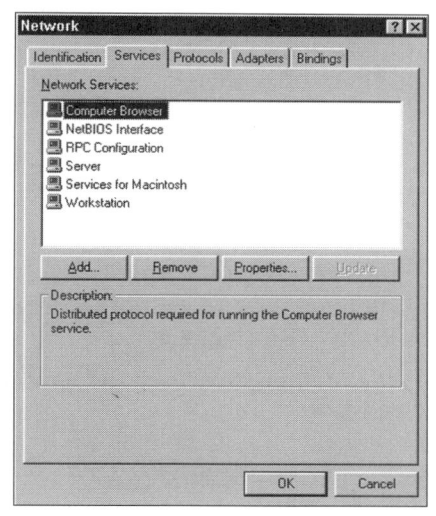

Figure B-3:
The Services tab with SFM now added.

6. **Click OK.**

   The Microsoft AppleTalk Protocol Properties dialog box opens (see Figure B-4). You don't need a share zone, and certainly have no use for the Routing tab.

7. **Close all dialog boxes and restart the server.**

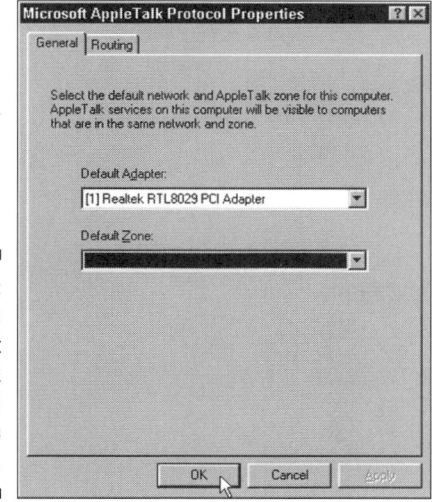

Figure B-4:
The Microsoft AppleTalk Protocol Properties dialog box.

Next you must facilitate the exchange of files between the Macintosh and the server by making a special Mac-accessible folder. The process is officially known as creating a *Mac volume*. The good news is that this folder can be identical to an existing NT subdirectory, although it must have a different name. I like to make `C:\Inetpub` appear on the Mac desktop by aliasing it to a Mac volume called IIS. That way I have instant access from the Mac side to the `wwwroot` and `ftproot` subdirectories on the Windows machine.

Here's how to create a Mac volume:

1. **Open the File Manager by clicking the Start button and choosing Programs➪Administrative Tools➪File Manager.**

2. **In the File Manager, select the Inetpub directory and choose Macfile➪Create Volume (see Figure B-5).**

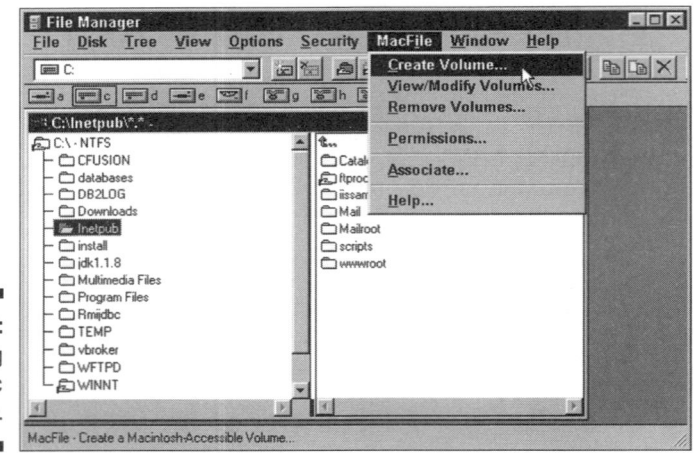

Figure B-5: Creating a Mac Volume.

The Create Macintosh-Accessible Volume dialog box appears, as shown in Figure B-6.

Figure B-6: The Create Macintosh-Accessible Volume dialog box.

Appendix B: Installing UltraDev for Macintosh

3. **In the Volume Name text box, type IIS.**

   The displayed path should be correct.

4. **Click to select the Guests Can Use This Volume check box (unless you have special security concerns).**

5. **Click the Permissions button.**

   The Macintosh View of Directory Permissions dialog box appears, as shown in Figure B-7.

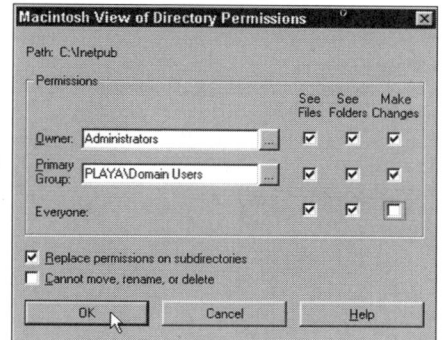

Figure B-7: Setting permissions for the Mac volume.

6. **Set all permissions except the permission for Everyone to change folders.**

7. **Click to select the Replace Permissions on Subdirectories check box.**

   Again, you may have special security concerns.

Meanwhile, Back on the Mac . . .

After you configure the NT server to host the Mac, you need to take care of the AppleTalk setup and the User Authentication Method (UAM):

1. **On the Mac, choose Apple➪Control Panels➪AppleTalk.**

   The small AppleTalk dialog box opens.

2. **In the Connect Via drop-down box, select Ethernet (see Figure B-8).**

Figure B-8: The AppleTalk connection method must be Ethernet.

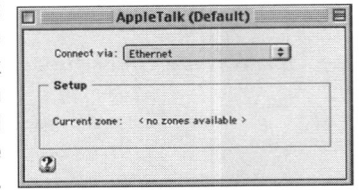

3. **Close the dialog box and open the Chooser. Double-click AppleShare to open the AppleShare window.**

   The name of the NT server should appear in the window, along with any other local networks the machine sees (see Figure B-9).

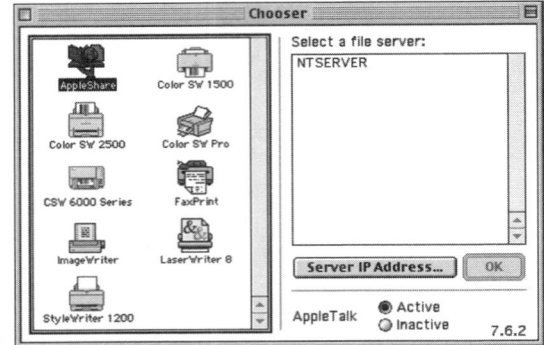

Figure B-9: Making a connection with the NT server.

4. **Double-click the NT server name to open the Connect dialog box, as shown in Figure B-10.**

Figure B-10: Setting up user authentication for a Mac-NT connection via AppleTalk.

Appendix B: Installing UltraDev for Macintosh   **303**

5. **Select the Connect as Registered User option and type a username and password in the Name and Password text boxes.**

   The name and password must have administrator privileges on the server.

6. **Click Connect.**

   The next dialog box shows the IIS volume you created for immediate access to wwwroot and ftproot, plus the Microsoft UAM Volume that is created by default.

7. **Click the check boxes beside both volumes (see Figure B-11) and click OK.**

   Icons for both volumes appear on the Mac desktop. You can close the Chooser.

Figure B-11: Mac volumes successfully acquired.

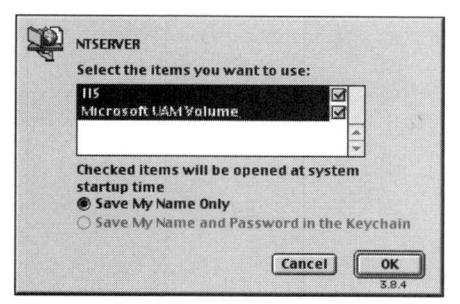

Now you've achieved what you need — a Mac desktop folder that is a mirror of the C:\Inetpub directory on the NT server. The UAM Volume contains a folder called AppleShare, which you can use to enhance the security of the Mac-NT connection. If enhanced User Authentication is not chosen, the username and password entered in Step 4 will be requested every time the Mac is powered on and sent unencrypted to the NT's Mac services handler.

Now you're — Phew! Finally! — in shape to move on to the Mac data connection tasks described in Chapter 3.

Appendix C
Source Code Translations

The source code you see embedded in the text of this book is the version appropriate for ASP/JavaScript sites. This appendix provides the equivalent source code for ASP/VBScript, JSP, and ColdFusion sites.

Source Code Sample 7-1 **Suppressing Display of the % Wild-Card Character**

ASP/VBScript
```
<p>Result of search for
<% ct = Request.QueryString("categ")
        If ct = "%" Then %>
        any category
        <% Else %>
        <%=ct %>
        <% End If %>
```

JSP
```
<p>Result of search for
<% String ct = request.getParameter("categ")
        if (ct.equals("%")){%>
        any category
        <% } else{ %>
        <%=ct %>
        <% } %>
```

ColdFusion
```
<p>Result of search for
<CFIF Form.categ EQ "%">any category
<CFELSE><CFOUTPUT>#Form.categ#</CFOUTPUT>
</CFIF>
```

Source Code Sample 8-1 **Setting or Killing a Cookie**

ASP/VBScript
```
<%
If (Request.Form("cookierequest") = "yes") then
  Response.Cookies("kppassword")= Request.Form("passwd")
  Response.Cookies("kppassword").Expires = Date + 60
Else
  Response.Cookies("kppassword").Expires =  Date - 1000
End if
%>
```

Part VI: Appendixes

JSP

```
<%
if ((request.getParameter("cookierequest")).equals("yes")){
            String cookieVal = request.getParameter("passwd") != null
            ? = request.getParameter("passwd") : "";
            int cookieExp = 60*24*60*60; //60 days
cookie = new Cookie("kbpassword",request.getParameter("passwd");
cookie.setMaxAge(cookieExp);
response.addCookie(cookie);
}
else {
            // first get the cookie from the request
            String cookieName = "kppassword";
            Cookie [] cookies = request.getCookies();
            if (cookies != null){
                    for (int i = 0; i< cookies.length; i++){
    // find the cookie, set age to zero, and 'add' the cookie back
                            if(cookies[i].getName().equals(cookieName)){
                                    cookies[i].setMaxAge(0);
                                    response.addCookie(cookies[i]);
                            }
                    }
            }
}
%>
```

ColdFusion

```
<cfif IsDefined("form.cookierequest")>
    <cfset expdays="60">
    <cfcookie name="kppassword"
        value="#form.passwd#"
        expires="#expdays#">
<cfelse>
    <cfcookie name="kppassword"
        expires="NOW">
</cfif>
```

Source Code Sample 8-2   **Changing Text If a Cookie Exists**

ASP/VBScript

```
<% If Request.Cookies("kppassword") = "" Then %>
    I'd like a <% Else %>
    Refresh my <% End If %>
    password cookie please
    <INPUT TYPE="checkbox" NAME="cookierequest"  VALUE="yes"
<% If Request.Cookies("kppassword") <> "" Then %>
CHECKED
<% End If %>
>
```

JSP

```
<%
String cookieName = "kppassword";
String cookieVal = "";
Cookie [] cookies = request.getCookies();
```

```
if (cookies != null){
        for (int i = 0; i< cookies.length; i++){
                if(cookies[i].getName().equals(cookieName)){
                        cookieVal = cookies[i].getValue();
                        break;
                }
        }
}
if (cookieVal == "") {%>
    I'd like a <%} else {%>
    Refresh my <% } %>
    password cookie please
        <INPUT TYPE="checkbox" NAME="cookierequest"   VALUE="yes"
<% if (cookieVal != "") {%>
CHECKED
<% } %>
>
```

ColdFusion

```
<cfif NOT IsDefined("Cookie.kppassword")>
   I'd like a
<cfelse>
    Refresh my
</cfif>
    password cookie please
       <INPUT TYPE="checkbox" NAME="cookierequest"   VALUE="yes"
<cfif IsDefined("Cookie.kppassword")>
CHECKED
</cfif>
>
```

Source Code Sample 8-3 — Setting a Timestamp Session Variable

ASP/VBScript

```
<%
Dim today
today = Date + Time
Session("tdate") = today
%>
```

JSP

```
<%
Long milliseconds = new Long(System.currentTimeMillis());
Session.putValue("tdate", milliseconds.toString());
%>
```

ColdFusion

```
<CFSET Session.tdate = #DateFormat(Now())# & " " & #TimeFormat(Now())#>
```

Source Code Sample 8-4 — Hiding a Delete Button from Unauthorized Users

ASP/VBScript
```
<% If Session("Usergroup") = 4 Then %>
<INPUT TYPE="submit" NAME="delrec" VALUE="Delete this record">
: [hidden form fields here]
<% End If %>
```

JSP
```
<% if (session.getValue("Usergroup") != null && ((String)
            session.getValue(Usergroup)).equals("4")){ %>
<INPUT TYPE="submit" NAME="delrec" VALUE="Delete this record">
: [hidden form fields here]
<%}%>
```

ColdFusion
```
<CFIF Session.Usergroup IS "4">
  <INPUT TYPE="submit" NAME="delrec" VALUE="Delete this record">
: [hidden form fields here]
</CFIF>
```

Source Code Sample 8-5 — Simple Login Validation

ASP/VBScript
```
<%
If Not rsUsers.EOF or Not rsUsers.BOF AND Request.Form("Login") = "true" And
            rsLogin.RecordCount = 1 Then
   Session("UserID")= rsLogin.Fields.Item("CustomerID").Value
   Session("UserGroup")= rsLogin.Fields.Item("UserGroup").Value
   Response.redirect "search1.asp"
ElseIf Request.Form("Login") = "true" then
   Response.redirect "LoginFail.html"
End If
%>
```

JSP
```
<%
// utilize the MM-created 'isEmpty' variable to test whether a JDBC result set
            is empty and the
if (!rsUsers_isEmpty && request.getParameter("Login") == "true"){
            // try and fetch next record; UltraDev fetches first record when
               recordset
//is instantiated.  If another record can be fetched, we have more
// than one record returned
if (!rsUsers.next()){
            String userID = rsUsers.getString("CustomerID");
            String userGroup = rs.getString("UserGroup");
            if (userID != null && userGroup != null){
                session.putValue("UserID", userID);
                session.putValue("UserGroup", userGroup);
                response.sendRedirect("search1.jsp");
            }
}
}
else if (request.getParameter("Login").equals("true")){
            response.sendRedirect("LoginFailed.html");
}
```

ColdFusion

```
<CFIF IsDefined("form.Login")>
<cfoutput query = "Login">
  <CFIF (form.username is Login.Username) AND (form.password is Login.Password)>
  <CFSET Session.userID = Login.CustomerID>
  <CFLOCATION URL="search1.asp">
  <CFELSE>
  <CFLOCATION URL="LoginFail.html">
  </CFIF>
</cfoutput>
</CFIF>
```

Source Code Samples 10-1 through 10-4 — **Adapting the Check New Username Server Behavior to Scan Both Username and Password Fields**

10-1: ASP/VBScript

```
MM_dupKeyUsernameValue = CStr(Request.Form("username"))
MM_dupKeySQL="SELECT Username FROM Customers WHERE Username='" &
          MM_dupKeyUsernameValue & "'"
```

10-2: ASP/VBScript

```
MM_dupKeyUsernameValue = CStr(Request.Form("username"))
MM_dupKeyPasswordValue = CStr(Request.Form("password"))
MM_dupKeySQL="SELECT Username FROM Customers WHERE Username='" &
          MM_dupKeyUsernameValue & "' AND Password='" &
          MM_dupKeyPasswordValue & "'"
```

10-3: ASP/VBScript

```
MM_dupKeyRedirect = MM_dupKeyRedirect & MM_qsChar & "requsername=" &
          MM_dupKeyUsernameValue
```

10-4: ASP/VBScript

```
MM_dupKeyRedirect = MM_dupKeyRedirect & MM_qsChar & "requsername=" &
          MM_dupKeyUsernameValue & "&reqpassword=" & MM_dupKeyPasswordValue
```

10-1: JSP

```
String MM_dupKeyUsernameValue = request.getParameter("username");
String MM_dupKeySQL = "SELECT Username FROM Customers WHERE Username='" +
          MM_dupKeyUsernameValue + "'";
```

10-2: JSP

```
String MM_dupKeyUsernameValue = request.getParameter("username");
String MM_dupKeyPasswordValue = request.getParameter("password");
String MM_dupKeySQL = "SELECT Username FROM Customers WHERE Username='" +
          MM_dupKeyUsernameValue + "' AND Password='" +
          MM_dupKeyUsernameValue + "'";
```

10-3: JSP

```
MM_dupKeyRedirect = MM_dupKeyRedirect + MM_qsChar + "requsername=" +
          MM_dupKeyUsernameValue;
```

10-4: JSP

```
MM_dupKeyRedirect = MM_dupKeyRedirect + MM_qsChar + "requsername=" +
            MM_dupKeyUsernameValue + "reqpassword=" + MM_dupKeyPasswordValue;
```

10-1: ColdFusion

```
<cfset MM_dupKeyUsernameValue=FORM.username>
<cfquery datasource=#MM_dupKeyDataSource# name="MM_rsKey" username=""
            password="">
SELECT Username FROM Customers WHERE Username='#MM_dupKeyUsernameValue#'
```

10-2: ColdFusion

```
<cfset MM_dupKeyUsernameValue=FORM.username>
<cfset MM_dupKeyPasswordValue=FORM.password>
<cfquery datasource=#MM_dupKeyDataSource# name="MM_rsKey" username=""
            password="">
SELECT Username FROM Customers WHERE Username='#MM_dupKeyUsernameValue#' AND
            Password='#MM_dupKeyPasswordValue#'
```

10-3: ColdFusion

```
MM_dupKeyRedirect_trigger = MM_dupKeyRedirect & MM_qsChar & "requsername=" &
            MM_dupKeyUsernameValue;
```

10-4: ColdFusion

```
MM_dupKeyRedirect_trigger = MM_dupKeyRedirect & MM_qsChar & "requsername=" &
            MM_dupKeyUsernameValue & "reqpassword=" & MM_dupKeyPasswordValue;
```

Source Code Sample 12-1   Creating Dates and Timestamps

ASP/VBScript

```
<%
MyDate = Date
MyTime = Time
mm = Month(MyDate)
if mm < 10 then
mm = "0" & mm
end if
dd = Day(MyDate)
if dd < 10 then
dd = "0" & dd
end if
yy = Right(Year(MyDate),2)
hh = Hour(MyTime)
if hh < 10 then
hh = "0" & hh
end if
nn = Minute(MyTime)
if nn < 10 then
nn = "0" & nn
end if
ss = Second(MyTime)
if ss < 10 then
ss = "0" & ss
end if
session("ts") = mm & dd & yy & hh & nn & ss
session("thisdate") = mm & "/" & dd & "/" & yy
%>
```

ColdFusion

```
<%<cfset mm = #Datepart('M',Now())#>
<cfif mm LT 10>
<cfset mm = "0" & #mm#>
</cfif>
<cfset dd = #Datepart('D',Now())#>
<cfif dd LT 10>
<cfset dd = "0" & #dd#>
</cfif>
<cfset yy = #Right(Datepart('YYYY',Now()),2)#>
<cfset hh = #Datepart('H',Now())#>
<cfif hh LT 10>
<cfset hh = "0" & #hh#>
</cfif>
<cfset nn = #Datepart('N',Now())#>
<cfif nn LT 10>
<cfset nn = "0" & #nn#>
</cfif>
<cfset ss = #Datepart('S',Now())#>
<cfif ss LT 10>
<cfset ss = "0" & #ss#>
</cfif>
<cfset Session.ts = #mm# & #dd# & #yy# & #hh# & #nn# & #ss#>
<cfset Session.thisdate = #DateFormat(Now())#>
```

Source Code Sample 12-2   Using CDONTS.NewMail to Send Two Separate E-mail Messages (ASP Only)

```
<% if (cStr(Request.Form("Submit")) <> "") Then
Dim objCDO
Set objCDO = Server.CreateObject("CDONTS.NewMail")
objCDO.From = " thehatstore@somesite.com "
objCDO.To = " themerchant@someotherplace.com "
objCDO.CC = ""
objCDO.Subject = "Hats Galore -- Order Received"
objCDO.Body = "An order has been received from "
            &rsCustomers.Fields("FirstName") & rsCustomers.Fields("LastName")
            & chr(10) & chr(13)& "Customer number " & Session("CustID") &
            chr(10) & chr(13) & "Order number is " & Session("OrderID") &
            chr(10) & chr(13) & "Total value of order is " & Session("Total")
            & chr(10) & chr(13)
objCDO.Send()
Set objCDO = Nothing
Set objCDO = Server.CreateObject("CDONTS.NewMail")
objCDO.From = " thehatstore@somesite.com "
objCDO.To = rsCustomers.Fields("CustomerEmail")
objCDO.CC = ""
objCDO.Subject = "Your Order from Hats Galore"
objCDO.Body = "Thankyou for your order from Hats Galore " & chr(10) & chr(13) &
            "Your order number is " & Session("OrderID") & chr(10) & chr(13)
objCDO.Send()
Set objCDO = Nothing
Response.Redirect("thanksbye.html")
End If
%>
```

Appendix D
About the CD

*H*ere is some of what you find on the *Dreamweaver UltraDev 4 For Dummies* CD-ROM:

- Trial versions of UltraDev for Windows and Mac
- Fireworks graphics-creation program from Macromedia
- Servers for ColdFusion and JSP
- Scads of interesting UltraDev objects and extensions
- Databases and demo sites to use to follow along with some of the examples in the book

System Requirements

Make sure that your computer meets the minimum system requirements listed here. If your computer doesn't match up to most of these requirements, you may have problems using the contents of the CD:

- A PC with a Pentium or faster processor (166 MHz or better), or a Mac OS computer with OS 8.6 or later.
- Microsoft Windows 95/98/00 or NT.
- At least 64MB of total RAM installed on your computer. For best performance, we recommend at least 128MB of RAM installed.
- At least 400MB of hard drive space available to install all the software from this CD. (You'll need less space if you don't install every program.)
- A CD-ROM drive — double-speed (2x) or faster.
- A monitor capable of displaying at least 256 colors or grayscale.

If you need more information on the basics, you can check out the following: *PCs For Dummies,* 7th Edition, by Dan Gookin; *Macs For Dummies,* 6th Edition, by David Pogue; *iMacs For Dummies,* by David Pogue; *Windows 98 For Dummies* or *Windows 95 For Dummies,* 2nd Edition, both by Andy Rathbone (all published by IDG Books Worldwide, Inc.).

Using the CD with Microsoft Windows

If you're running Windows, follow these steps to get to the items on the CD:

1. **Insert the CD into your computer's CD-ROM drive.**

   Give your computer a moment to take a look at the CD.

2. **When the light on your CD-ROM drive goes out, double click the My Computer icon (it's probably in the top-left corner of your desktop).**

   This action opens the My Computer window, which shows you all the drives attached to your computer, the Control Panel, and a couple of other handy things.

3. **Double-click the icon for your CD-ROM drive.**

   Another window opens, showing you all the folders and files on the CD.

4. **Double-click the file called** License.txt.

   This file contains the end-user license that you agree to by using the CD. When you finish reading the license, close the program (most likely NotePad) that displayed the file.

5. **Double-click the file called** Readme.txt.

   This file contains instructions about installing the software from this CD. It may be helpful to leave this text file open while you use the CD.

6. **Double-click the folder for the software that you are interested in.**

   Be sure to read the descriptions of the programs in the next section of this appendix (much of this information also shows up in the Readme file). These descriptions give you more precise information about each program's folder name and about finding and running the installer program.

7. **Find the .exe file, often called** Setup.exe, Install.exe, **or something similar, and double-click it.**

   The program's installer walks you through the process of setting up your new software.

To run some of the programs, you may need to keep the CD inside your CD-ROM drive. This is a good thing. Otherwise, the installed program would require you to install a very large chunk of the program to your hard drive, which could keep you from having the space to install other software.

Using the CD with the Mac OS

To install the items from the CD to your hard drive, follow these steps.

1. **Insert the CD into your computer's CD-ROM drive.**

    In a moment, an icon representing the CD you just inserted appears on your Mac desktop. Chances are, the icon looks like a CD-ROM.

2. **Double-click the CD icon to display the CD's contents.**

3. **Double-click the file called** `License.txt`.

    This file contains the end-user license that you agree to by using the CD. When you finish reading the license, you can close the window that displayed the file.

4. **Double-click the Read Me First icon.**

    This text file contains information about the CD's programs and any last-minute instructions you need to know about installing the programs on the CD. Some of this information may not be specifically covered in this appendix.

5. **If the program you want to open comes with an installer, you can simply open the program's folder on the CD and double-click the icon that displays the word Install, Installer, or sometimes sea (for self-extracting archive).**

    If you don't find an installer, just drag the program's folder from the CD window and drop it on your hard drive icon.

Software on the CD-ROM

The following sections tell you what software you'll find on the CD.

Shareware programs are fully functional, free trial versions of copyrighted programs. If you like particular programs, you can register with their authors for a nominal fee and receive licenses, enhanced versions, and technical support. *Freeware programs* are free, copyrighted games, applications, and utilities. You can copy them to as many PCs as you like — free — but they have no technical support. *Trial, demo,* and *evaluation* versions are usually limited either by time or functionality (such as being unable to save projects, or being limited to one single user).

Web-authoring software

Dreamweaver UltraDev 4

For Mac OS 8.6 or later and Windows 95, 98, 00, or NT 4.0 or later. Trial version.

Dreamweaver UltraDev is what this book is all about. Use this trial version to check out the features I describe in this book and perhaps decide to buy a full license. For more information and updates, visit the Macromedia Web site at www.macromedia.com/software/ultradev/.

Web servers

ColdFusion Enterprise Server 4.5.1

For Windows NT, works in conjunction with Microsoft IIS.

This powerful server adjunct from Allaire Corporation is remarkably easy to install and maintain. ColdFusion is one of the three special server technologies supported by UltraDev. For more information and updates, check out www.allaire.com/products/coldfusion/index.cfm.

JRun Server 3.0, Developer Edition

For Windows NT.

A complete JavaServer Pages (JSP) server package from Allaire Corporation, conforming to the new J2EE standard and including Enterprise Java Beans, Java Transaction API, Java Messaging Service and Java Servlets as well as the JSP Web server. JSP is one of the three special server technologies supported by UltraDev. For more information and updates, check out www.allaire.com/products/jrun/index.cfm.

Graphics program

Fireworks 4.0

For Mac OS 8.6 or later and Windows 95, 98, or NT (with Service Pack 3) or later. Trial version.

Fireworks is Macromedia's Web graphics-creation program. It includes both bitmap and vector graphic editing tools. 100MB disk space and 64MB RAM are needed for the installation. For more information and updates, check out www.macromedia.com/software/fireworks/.

Web browsers

Netscape Communicator 4.7
For Windows and Mac. Commercial version.

This free suite of programs from Netscape includes a full-featured browser (Navigator), e-mail program (Messenger), and an HTML editor (Composer). This program is updated frequently, so be sure to check out `home.netscape.com`.

Microsoft Internet Explorer 5.5 Web browser
For Windows and Mac. Commercial product.

This is the popular, powerful Web browser from Microsoft that's packed with all the latest features for today's cybertravels. It includes Outlook Express, Windows Media Player, Dial-Up Networking, and NetMeeting. The whole package is free, which makes it a true bargain. These programs are updated frequently, so check out the Microsoft Web site at `www.microsoft.com`.

Server behavior extensions

All of the server behavior extensions listed in Chapter 14 of this book are included in folders called `\Extensions\SBXs\Win` and `\Extensions\SBXs\Mac`. See Chapter 14 for the descriptions and authors. The actual MXP filenames are listed in Table D-1.

Table D-1	Server Behavior Extensions on the CD
SBX	**Filename**
Horizontal looper	MX50074_HorizontalLooper.mxp
US States menu	MX15708_stateCodes.mxp
Banner builder	MX35773_BannerImageBuilder.mxp
Right-click menu builder	MX34761_RightClickMenuBuilder.mxp
Form button fever	MX37468_FormButtonFever.mxp
Footnote maker	MX17667_Footnote.mxp
CDO Mail sender	MX50232_CDOMail.mxp
Guest book	MX16032_mcbook.mxp

(continued)

Table D-1 *(continued)*

SBX	Filename
Ultracart shopping cart	`UC_Cart_V12_Beta2.mxp`
Authorizenet interface	`MX61552_UC_AN_Authorize_B1.mxp`
Redirect on cookie	`MX92926_MB_CookieExists.mxp`
File Upload	`MagicBeatSBSuite170.mxp`

Template sets

Three template sets created by Juxt Interactive for Macromedia are on the CD (see Chapter 2). The sets are called E-zine, Club, and Design, and they can be found in these folders:

- `\Extensions\Templates\Ezine`
- `\Extensions\Templates\Club`
- `\Extensions\Templates\Design`

The files are the same for Windows and Mac users.

Files from the author

The following sections describe the files that I've thrown in to help you add some zing to your Web site.

UltraDev sites

Three complete UltraDev sites are provided on the CD. They are provided as HTML files in the start condition, with no dynamic data inserted, and also in the finished condition for all three server models — ASP, JSP, and ColdFusion. The files are the same for Windows and Mac users. Each site's file structure can be found in subdirectories under the main directory `\Demo sites`. The sites are:

- The DownToEarth ceramics site described in Chapter 4
- The KeyPalNation site described in Chapter 8
- Hats Galore described in Chapters 11 and 12

Databases

These three Access2000 databases are supplied, in the folder \Demo sites\ databases. They are the databases that match the three sites I provide. The files are the same for Windows and Mac users.

- DownToEarth.mdb
- Ppnation.mdb
- HatStore.mdb

Object extensions

Most of the custom-built objects I describe in Chapter 9 are included on the CD, in the folder \Extensions\Object extensions. The files are the same for Windows and Mac users. Table D-2 lists the filenames.

Table D-2	Custom UltraDev Objects on the CD
Object	**Filenames**
Scroller	Scroller.htm, Scroller.js, Scroller.gif
Trigonometry	trig.hm, trig.gif
Simple date	simpledate.htm, simpledate.gif

If You've Got Problems (Of the CD Kind)

I tried my best to compile programs that work on most computers with the minimum system requirements. Alas, your computer may differ, and some programs may not work properly for some reason.

The two likeliest problems are that you don't have enough memory (RAM) for the programs you want to use, or you have other programs running that are affecting installation or running of a program. If you get error messages like Not enough memory or Setup cannot continue, try one or more of these methods and then try using the software again:

- **Turn off any anti-virus software that you have on your computer.** Installers sometimes mimic virus activity and may make your computer incorrectly believe that a virus is infecting it.

- **Close all running programs.** The more programs you're running, the less memory is available to other programs. Installers also typically update files and programs. So if you keep other programs running, installation may not work properly.

> ✓ **Have your local computer store add more RAM to your computer.** This is, admittedly, a drastic and somewhat expensive step. But if you have a Windows 95 or later PC or a Mac OS computer with a PowerPC chip, adding more memory can really help the speed of your computer and allow more programs to run at the same time.

If you still have trouble with installing the items from the CD, please call the IDG Books Worldwide Customer Service phone number: 800-762-2974 (outside the U.S.: 317-572-3993).

Index

• Symbols •

% wild-card character, source code translations, 305

• A •

absolute positioning, 212, 214
Access (Microsoft)
  database structure sample, 244
  databases, 56
  setting up a DSN (ASP), 59–61
  setting up a DSN (ColdFusion), 63–64, 66
access levels
  setting up the checkpoint on a restricted page, 226–227
  setting up users, 223–224
  user login identification, 224, 226
Active Server Pages (ASP) Server. *See also* ASP/VBScript
  creating a data connection, 58–59
  getting connected, 61–63
  setting up a DSN, 59–61
admin, security access levels, 223–224
aligning layers, 278
Allaire Corporation
  Coldfusion Enterprise Server 4.5.1, 316
  Jrun 3.0, Developer Edition, 316
  Web site, 316
alt attribute, 97–98
AppleTalk setup, 301–303
Application Server page (Site Definition dialog box), 24–25
approval page
  request variables, 176–178, 180
  revising a listing, 181
arguments, described, 188–189
ASP/VBScript. *See also* Active Server Pages (ASP) Server
  adapting the check new username server behavior to scan both username and password fields, 309

changing text if a cookie exists, 306
  creating dates and timestamps, 310
  hiding a delete icon from unauthorized users, 308
  setting a timestamp session variable, 307
  setting or killing a cookie, 305
  simple login validation, 308
  Structured Query Language (SQL), 84–85
  suppressing display of the % wild-card character, 305
  using CDONTS.NewMail to send two separate e-mail messages, 311
Assets panel
  creating templates, 36–37
  described, 12
attributes
  alt, 97–98
  binding other attributes of the <IMG> tag, 96–97
  color, adding to the horizontal rule tag, 280–281
  DIV, binding to a recordset field, 278–280
  height, 97
  multiple, 110–112
  read-only, 284
  size, 110–112
  width, 97

• B •

Banner Builder extension, 289
Behaviors inspector. *See also* Server Behaviors inspector
  described, 12
  Form Button Fever extension, 287–288
Behaviors palette, Form Button Fever extension, 287–288
binary, described, 107–108
bindings (data)
  Delete Record server behavior, 134–135
  dynamic check boxes, 107–108
  dynamic elements, 103–104

bindings (data) *(continued)*
  dynamic images, 95–99
  dynamic lists and menus, 110–112
  dynamic radio buttons, 109–110
  hidden form fields, 113
  inserting and updating data, 113–116
  inserting text elements, 106, 107
  linking results page to a detail page, 123–127
  Live objects short cuts, 116–119
  making a repeat region, 120–122
  server behaviors for navigation, 128–134
  updating text elements, 104–106
Boolean field, described, 88
bridge (JDBC-ODBC translator), described, 67–68
browser view, compared to Live Data View (LDV), 139–142
browsers (Web)
  Microsoft Explorer 5.5, 317
  Netscape Communicator 4.7, 317

• C •

Cascading Style Sheets (CSS)
  applying styles, 47–48
  Attachments defaulting, 281–282
  described, 45–46
  editing a style, 51
  external style sheets, 48–51
  Styles, 12
  Styles palette, 46–47
catalogs
  creating the database, 245
  navigating through, 246–250
  online store feature, 252
  putting products on display, 245–246
category search, 159–161
CD with this book
  installing on Macintosh computers, 297
  installing on Windows computers, 294
  software included, 315–319
  system requirements, 313
  technical requirements for Macintosh computers, 295–296
  technical requirements for Windows computers, 293
  troubleshooting, 319–320
  using with Mac OS, 315
  using with Windows, 314
CDO Mail extension, 286
  configuring NT server, 266–267
  notification of online orders, 265
  using server behavior extension, 268–271
CDONTS.NewMail, using to send two separate e-mail messages, 311
CF Administrator, described, 63
check boxes (dynamic), 107–108
Check In/Check Out feature (File Transfer Protocol), 24
Check New Username server behavior, 220–222
checkout
  links, 258
  online store feature, 252
ClientCertificates, request variable, 176
Code Navigator icon (document toolbar feature), 30
Code View (document toolbar feature), 30
ColdFusion
  adapting the check new username server behavior to scan both username and password fields, 310
  CF Administrator, 63
  connecting Macintosh computers to a data source, 72
  creating a data source name, 63–64, 66
  hiding a delete icon from unauthorized users, 308
  Remote Development Services (RDS), 66
  Request object, 200
  setting or killing a cookie, 306
  Structured Query Language (SQL), 84–85
  suppressing display of the % wild-card character, 305
ColdFusion Enterprise Server 4.5.1, CD with this book, 316
collections (request variables), 176–178, 180
color attribute, adding to the horizontal rule tag, 280–281
columns. *See* fields
Commands menu
  Banner Builder extension, 289
  Right-Click Menu Builder extension, 288

Index

Common panel. *See* Objects palette
confirmation page (UltraDev Shopping Cart), 259–260, 261
connection string, described, 62
cookies
  changing text, 306–307
  described, 184–188
  Live Data View (LDV), 198–199
  request variable, 176, 185–188
  setting or killing, 305–306
creating Web sites. *See* Web pages; Web site creation; Web site design; Web sites
CSS attachments defaulting, 281–282
CSS Styles, described, 12
CSS Styles palette, 46–51
customer
  searches that come up empty, 157–158
  searching SQL statements and variables, 153–157
  security access levels, 223–224

• D •

data
  cursor, described, 76
  described, 55–56
  dynamic, formatting data using the Recordset Builder, 92–94
  filtering, Recordset Builder, 88–91
  formatting, 92–94
data bindings
  Delete Record server behavior, 134–135
  described, 15–16, 98–100
  dynamic check boxes, 107–108
  dynamic elements, 103–104
  dynamic lists and menus, 110–112
  dynamic radio buttons, 109–110
  hidden form fields, 113
  inserting and updating data, 113–116
  inserting text elements, 106–107
  linking results page to a detail page, 123–127
  Live objects short cuts, 116–119
  making a repeat region, 120–122
  server behaviors for navigation, 128–134
  updating text elements, 104–106

Data Bindings inspector
  described, 12
  inserting text elements, 106–107
  Recordset Builder, 76–80, 86–92, 94–97
  Sort drop-down lists, 82–83
  UltraDev Shopping Cart extension, 286
  updating text elements, 104–106
data filtering, Recordset Builder, 88–91
Data Source Name (DSN)
  described, 59
  getting connected (ASP), 61–63
  setting up access (ASP), 59–61
  setting up access (ColdFusion), 63–64, 66
  setting up access (JSP), 66–68
  setting up access (Macintosh computers), 71–73
data tables
  alphabetically sorting, 82–83
  check new username server behavior, 220–222
  data filtering using the Recordset Builder, 88–91
  flowing data from recordset to Web page, 79–80
  making a repetitive list, 81–82
  making data available to a Web page, 76–79
  new user registration information, 218–220
  products, 94, 160
  setting up user access levels, 223–224
  site security, 216–217
  user login identification, 224, 226
  using the advanced mode of the Recordset Builder, 85–87
database-free shopping cart sites, 237
  adding the Buy Me button, 239–240
  setting up the display page, 237–238
  testing the cart, 241–242
databases
  basics, 55–56
  CD with this book, 319
  creating a data connection for an ASP Server, 58–63
  creating a data connection on a Macintosh computer, 71–73
  creating a data hookup with a JSP Server, 66–69
  creating a data source name for a ColdFusion Server, 63–64, 66

databases *(continued)*
  local Web servers, 57–58
  Open Database Connectivity (ODBC), 57
  poor man's, 282–283
  recordsets, 75–83
  rows and columns (records and fields), 56
  setting up a Macintosh computer, 70
  shopping cart extension, 242–250
  Structured Query Language (SQL), 151
  transferring contents of shopping cart, 260, 262–264
dates, creating, 310–311
DB2 (IBM), creating a data hookup with a JSP Server, 68–69
defining Web sites, 16–17
delete icon, hiding from unauthorized users, 308
Delete page, described, 102
Delete Record server behavior, 134–135
Department search, 159–161
Design Notes page (Site Definition dialog box), 26
Design View (document toolbar feature), 30
design view, compared to Live Data View (LDV), 139–142
Detail page
  described, 102
  linking from a results page, 123–127
  navigation, 128–134
  search results, 159–160, 161
DIV attributes, binding a recordset field, 278–280
<DIV> tag, 279
Document Object Model, described, 206
document toolbar, features, 29–30
Dreamies, described, 4
Dreamweaver UltraDev
  absolute positioning, 212–214
  adding a color attribute to the horizontal rule tag, 280–281
  adding results statement on results page, 170–172
  aligning and sizing, 278
  binding a recordset field to attributes of a DIV, 278–280
  binding form elements, 103–113
  building database-driven Web sites on a Macintosh computer, 70
  CD with this book, 316
  changing your mind about reoccurring messages, 284
  converting tables to layers, 277–278
  Cookies, 184–189
  creating a data connection for an ASP Server, 58–63
  creating a data connection for Macintosh computers, 71–73
  creating a data hookup with a JSP Server, 66–69
  creating a data source name for a ColdFusion Server, 63–64, 66
  creating an insert menu, 210–212
  customizing, 43–47
  data filtering, 88–91
  database basics, 55–58
  defaulting CSS attachments, 281–282
  defining sites, 18
  defining styles with CSS, 45–51
  Delete Record server behavior, 134–135
  described, 1, 9
  dynamic images, 94–99
  extensions, 214, 233, 285
  filtering multidimensional searches, 167–169
  floating palettes, 10–14
  fooling your computer, 282
  formatting data, 92–94
  inserting and updating data, 113–119
  Launcher, 14
  Layout View tool, 275–277
  linking results page to a detail page, 123–127
  Live Data View (LDV), 196–199
  Macromedia Exchange Web site, 207–208
  Macromedia Extension Manager, 208–210
  making a repeat region, 120–122
  multidimensional searches, 163–167
  Objects palette, 201–206
  poor man's database, 282–283
  recordset basics, 76–83
  Request Object, 176–178, 180–183
  server behavior builder, 206

server behaviors for navigation, 128–134
Session Object, 189–196
setting up search pages, 152–161
site security, 215–229
Structured Query Language (SQL), 84–87
templates, 35–42
turning read-only attributes on and off, 284
UltraDev Shopping Cart extension, 234–250
driver (ODBC), described, 57
Drummies, described, 4
Dynamic Check Box, 107–108
dynamic data, formatting data using the Recordset Builder, 92–94
dynamic elements
  check boxes, 107–108
  described, 103–104
  inserting text elements, 106–107
  lists and menus, 110–112
  radio buttons, 109–110
  updating text elements, 104–106
dynamic images
  binding an image to a recordset, 95–97
  binding other attributes of the <IMG> tag, 96–97
  catalogs using Recordset Builder, 94
  data bindings, 97–99
Dynamic List/Menu, 110–112
dynamic pages, described, 15–16
Dynamic Radio Buttons, 109–110

• E •

e-commerce
  building a store site, 251
  closing the shopping deal, 259–260, 262–264
  preliminary store setup steps, 252–253
  shopping cart display page, 253–258
  shopping e-mail notification of orders, 265–271
  store features, 251–252
  UltraDev Shopping Cart, 233–250
editable regions
  described, 36
  templates, 38

elements (dynamic)
  check boxes, 107–108
  described, 103–104
  inserting text elements, 106–107
  lists and menus, 110–112
  radio buttons, 109–110
  updating text elements, 104–06
e-mail, using CDONTS.NewMail to send two separate messages, 311
e-mail notification of online orders, 265
  configuring your NT server, 266–267
  using the CDO Mail server behavior extension, 268–271
e-stores. See e-commerce; online stores
Extension Manager (Macromedia), 208–210
extensions
  Banner Builder, 289
  CDO Mail, 286
  creating an insert menu, 210–212
  Footnote, 287
  Form Button Fever, 287–288
  Guest Book, 289–290
  Horizontal Looper, 288
  Macromedia Exchange Web site, 207–208
  MXP files, 208–210
  objects, 319
  Redirect if Cookie Exists, 289
  resources, 214
  Right-Click Menu Builder, 288
  Server Behaviors, 317–318
  UltraDev Shopping Cart, 233–250, 286
  Upload File From Page, 290
external style sheets (CSS)
  creating, 48–49
  editing, 49–51
  linking to, 50–51

• F •

fields
  Boolean field, 88
  described, 56
  hidden form, 113
File Management icon (document toolbar feature), 30

File Transfer Protocol (FTP)
  Check In/Check Out feature, 24
  defining a Web site in UltraDev, 17
  Remote Info page (Site Definition dialog
    box), 23–24
files (author), CD with this book, 318–319
filters
  multidimensional searches, static options
    and wild cards, 167–169
  session variable, 192–193
Fireworks 4.0, CD with this book, 316
floating palettes. *See also* palettes
  described, 10–12
  graphics cards, 10
  making subgroups of palettes, 13–14
<FONT> tag, 39
Footnote extension, 287
Form, request variable, 176
Form Button Fever extension, 287–288
form buttons, UltraDev Shopping Cart,
    239–240, 247–250
<FORM> tag, 205
Frames inspector, described, 12

• G •

GET display, 146–148
graphics
  cards, dual-monitor support and double-
    wide screen resolution, 10
  program, Fireworks 4.0, 316
grid guide, described, 43–44
Grid Settings dialog box, 43
guest, security access levels, 223–224
Guest Book extension, 289–290
guidedots, customizing, 43–44
guidelines, customizing, 43–44

• H •

<HEAD> tag, 281–282
height attribute, 97–98
hidden form fields, 113
hide-and-seek buttons, 132–134
History inspector, described, 12
Horizontal Looper extension, 288
<HR> tag, 280–281
HTML code
  <DIV> tag, 279

<FONT> tag, 39
<FORM> tag, 205
<HEAD> tag, 281–282
<HR> tag, 280–281
<HTML> tag, 186–188
<IMG> tag, 96–97
<MENU> tags, 211–212
<MENUITEM> tags, 211–212
<SELECT> tag, 110–112
HTML Source Code inspector, described, 12
HTML Styles, described, 12
<HTML> tag, 186–188
hyperlinks, linking results page to detail
  page, 123–127

• I •

IBM, DB2, 68–69
image links, UltraDev Shopping Cart,
    239–240, 247–250
images (dynamic)
  binding an image to a recordset, 95–96
  binding other attributes of the <IMG> tag,
    96–97
  catalogs using Recordset Builder, 94
  data bindings, 97–99
<IMG> tag, 96–97
Insert menu
  creating, 210–212
  Footnote extension, 287
  Guest Book extension, 289–290
Insert page
  described, 102, 113
  dynamic check boxes, 107–108
  hand-crafting the Update server behavior,
    114–116
  inserting text elements, 106–107
  Live objects, 116–119
Insert Record server behavior
  dialog box, 114–116
  request variables, 176–178, 180
inspectors
  Behaviors inspector, 12
  Data Bindings inspector, 12–14, 76–80,
    82–83, 86–92, 94–98, 104–107
  Frames inspector, 12
  History inspector, 12
  HTML Source Code inspector, 12
  Property inspector, 11, 33–34, 109–110

Index

Server Behaviors inspector, 12–14, 79, 81–83, 102–103, 107–112, 114–116, 120–135, 255–256
UltraDev Shopping Cart extension, 255–256
Internet Explorer. *See* Microsoft Internet Explorer 5.5
Internet Information Server (IIS), described, 58–59

• J •

Java Server Pages. *See* JSP
JDBC (Java Database Connectivity)
  bridge to ODBC, 67–68
  connecting Macintosh computers to a data source, 73
  described, 66
  IBM's DB2, 68–69
Joseph Lowery's extensions database, 214
Jrun 3.0, Developer Edition, CD with this book, 316
JSP
  bridge to ODBC, 67–68
  changing text if a cookie exists, 306
  creating a data hookup, 66
  IBM's DB2, 68–69
  setting or killing a cookie, 306
  Structured Query Language (SQL), 84–85
  suppressing display of the % wild-card character, 305

• K •

key field, described, 126

• L •

Launcher
  customizing, 14
  described, 11
layer anchor, described, 32
layers
  absolute positioning, 212, 214
  aligining and sizing, 278
  converting to tables, 277–278
  described, 12
  reference, 278
  Show Region behaviors, 132–134
  Web page design, 30–32

Layout Cell tool (Objects palette), 276
Layout Table tool (Objects palette), 276
Layout View tool (Objects palette), 275–277
LDV. *See* Live Data View
library, described, 12
links. *See* image links; text links
lists (dynamic), 110–112
Live Data Settings dialog box
  GET display, 146–148
  POST display, 146–148
Live Data View (LDV)
  adding query strings, 142–146
  compared to design-time and browse time versions, 139–142
  cookies, 198–199
  described, 137–139, 196–197
  document toolbar feature, 30
  features, 138–139
  modifying settings, 146–148
  session variables, 197–198
Live objects
  described, 101–102
  linking result page to a detail page, 125–127
  navigation, 129–130
  short cuts, 116–119
Local Info page (Site Definition dialog box), 20–21
locked regions, 36
Log In User server behavior, 224, 226
Log Out User server behavior, 228–229
login
  creating a simple login validation technique, 193–196
  identifying user access level, 224, 226
  online store feature, 252
  page, cookies, 186–188
  simple validation, 308–309

• M •

Macintosh computers
  AppleTalk setup, 301–303
  configuring the NT server, 297–301
  connecting to a DSN, 71–73
  installing Dreamweaver UltraDev CD, 297
  setting up for building database-driven Web sites, 70

Macintosh computers *(continued)*
  technical requirements for CD installation, 295–296
  User Authentication Method (UAM), 301–303
  using the CD with this book, 315
Macromedia
  10-step tutorial, 214
  Dreamweaver UltraDev, 316
  Fireworks 4.0, 316
  Web site, 316
Macromedia Exchange
  MXP files, 208–210
  Web site, 207–208
Macromedia eXtension Package (MXP) file, 208–210
MDAC (Microsoft Data Access Components), 66
`<MENU>` tag, 211–212
`<MENUITEM>` tag, 211–212
menus (dynamic), 110–112
Microsoft
  Data Access Components, 66
  Web site, 317
Microsoft Access. *See* Access (Microsoft)
Microsoft Internet Explorer 5.5, CD with this book, 317
Mini-Launcher, described, 14
multidimensional search, 163–167
  adding results statement on results page, 170–172
  filtering with static options and wild cards, 167–169
`multiple` attribute, 110–112

• N •

navigation
  online stores, 246–250
  using server behaviors, 128–134
Netscape Communicator 4.7
  CD with this book, 317
  Web site, 317
Newbies, described, 4
noneditable regions, 36
NT server
  building database-driven Web sites on a Macintosh computer, 70–73

configuring, 297–301
configuring for e-mail notification of online orders, 266–267
Web servers, 58–59

• O •

objects
  absolute positioning, 212, 214
  extensions, CD with this book, 319
Objects palette
  creating objects, 203–204
  customizing, 201–203
  described, 11
  Footnote extension, 287
  Guest Book extension, 289–290
  layers for Web pages, 30–32
  Layout Cell tool, 276
  Layout Table tool, 276
  Layout View tool, 275–277
  Live objects, 116–119
  parameterized objects, 204–206
  radio buttons, 109–110
  regrouping, 203
online stores
  building a site, 251
  closing the deal, 259–260, 262–264
  creating the catalog, 245
  database-free shopping cart sites, 237–242
  databases, 242–245
  e-mail notification of orders, 265–271
  features, 251–252
  navigating through the catalog, 246–250
  preliminary setup steps, 252–253
  putting products on display, 245–246
  shopping cart display page, 253–258
Open Database Connectivity (ODBC)
  bridge to JDBC (Java Database Connectivity), 67–68
  described, 57

• P •

palettes. *See also specific palettes*
  floating, 10–14
  making subgroups, 13–14
parameterized objects, described, 204–206

Index

parsing, described, 22, 57–58
password
  cookies, 186–188
  site security, 215–220
Personal Web Server (PWS IIS), described, 58–59
poor man's database, 282–283
Position search, 159–161
positioning (absolute), 212, 214
POST display, 146–148
Preferences dialog box, 44–45
Preview/Debug in Browser icon (document toolbar feature), 30
product search, 159–161
product table, 243
Products data table, 160
programs, graphics, 316
Property inspector
  described, 11
  radio buttons, 109–110
  text format for Web page design, 33–34
pseudo-code, described, 195
publications
  Access 97 For Windows For Dummies, 58
  Access 2000 For Windows For Dummies, 58
  Database Development For Dummies, 58
  Dreamweaver 3 For Dummies, 35
  iMacs For Dummies, 313
  Macs For Dummies, 313
  Oracle8 For Dummies, 58
  PCs For Dummies, 313
  Windows 95 For Dummies, 313
  Windows 98 For Dummies, 313

• Q •

query string, Live Data View (LDV), 142–146
QueryString, request variable, 176

• R •

radio buttons (dynamic), 109–110
`read-only` attributes, turning them on and off, 284
Record Insertion Form, 116
record signposting, 130–131
Record Update Form Live objects, 116
records, described, 56

Recordset Builder (Data Bindings inspector), 76–80
  binding an image to a recordset, 95–97
  catalogs (dynamic images), 94
  data filtering, 88–91
  formatting data, 92–94
  linking results page to a detail page, 124–127
  Simple mode, 160–161
  Structured Query Langauge (SQL), 86–87
recordsets
  alphabetically sorting, 82–83
  binding a field to attributes of a `DIV`, 278–280
  binding an image, 95–97
  category search, 160–161
  data bindings, 97–99
  data filtering by using the Recordset Builder, 88–91
  described, 75–76
  flowing data to a Web page, 79–80
  formatting data using the Recordset Builder, 92–94
  making a repetitive list from ten data records, 81–82
  making data available to a Web page, 76–79
  multidimensional search, 163–167
  using for searches and results page, 153–157
  using the advanced mode of the Recordset Builder, 86–88
Redirect if Cookie Exists extension, 289
Redirect Object (response variable), 188–189
redirect page
  check new username server behavior, 220–222
  decline access to restricted page, 227
Reference icon (document toolbar feature), 30
reference layer, described, 278
Refresh Design View icon (document toolbar feature), 30
region, described, 133
registration
  check new username server behavior, 220–222
  described, 218
  new users, 218–220

Remote Development Services (RDS), 66
Remote Info page (Site Definition dialog box), 21, 23–24
Repeat Region Server Behavior, 81–82, 120–122, 255–256
repeat regions, described, 120–122
Request Object
 ColdFusion, 200
 cookies, 184–188
 described, 176–178, 180
 revising a listing, 181
 searching a data site, 181
 server variables, 182–183
request variables
 collections, 176–178, 180
 cookies, 185–188
 described, 153–157
 rejected usernames for site, 221–222
 revising a listing, 181
 searching a data site, 181
Request.Client Certificates, described, 176
Request.Form
 described, 176
 making a page for listing approval, 176
Request.QueryString, described, 176
resources, extensions, 214
Response Object
 cookies, 184–188
 Redirect and Write object, 188–189
Response.Redirect object, 188–189
Response.Write object, 188–189
Restrict Access To Page server behavior, 226–227
restrictions, access levels, 226–227
Results page
 adding results statement, 170–172
 category search, 159–161
 described, 102
 linking to a detail page, 123–127
 multidimensional searches, 163–167
 navigation, 128–134
 repeat regions, 120–122
 searches that come up empty, 157–158
 SQL statements and variables for a search, 153–157
resultsets. *See* recordsets

Right-Click Menu Builder extension, 288
rows, described, 56
rulers, described, 44

• S •

search page
 category search, 159–161
 filtering multidimensional searches, 167–169
 multidimensional searches, 163–167
 searches that come up empty, 157–158
 setting up a simple search page, 152–153
 two-dimensional searches, 163–167
 using SQL statements and variables for results page, 153–157
SearchResults page, 159–161
security (site)
 check new username server behavior, 220–222
 Log In server behavior, 224
 Log Out User server behavior, 228–229
 new user registration, 218–220
 Restrict Access To Page server behavior, 226–227
 server behaviors, 215–217
 setting up user access levels, 223–224
 user login identification, 224, 226
<SELECT> tag, 110–112
server behavior
 builder, 206
 Check New Username, 220–222
 Delete Record server behavior, 134–135
 described, 15–16, 101–102
 dynamic check boxes, 107–108
 dynamic lists and menus, 110–112
 dynamic radio buttons, 109–110
 hidden form fields, 113
 Insert Record, 176–178, 180
 inserting and updating data, 114–116
 inserting text elements, 106–107
 linking results page to detail page, 123–127
 Live objects short cuts, 116–119
 Log In User, 224, 226
 Log Out User, 228–229
 making repeat region, 120–122

Index

navigation, 128–131
Restrict Access To Page, 226–227
Show Region, 132–134
Update Record, 181
updating text elements, 104–106
Server Behavior extensions
 CD with this book, 317–318
 UltraDev Shopping Cart, 239–240, 247–250
Server Behaviors inspector, 102–103.
 See also Behaviors inspector
 CDO Mail extension, 268–271, 286
 Delete Record server behavior, 134–135
 described, 12
 Dynamic Check Box, 107–108
 Dynamic List/Menu, 110–112
 Dynamic Radio Buttons, 109–110
 Horizontal Looper extension, 288
 linking results page to detail page, 123–127
 navigation, 128–131
 recordsets, 79
 Redirect if Cookie Exists extension, 289
 Repeat Region Server behavior, 81–82, 120–122, 255–256
 separating from the Data Bindings inspector, 13–14
 Show Region behavior, 132–134
 Sort drop-down lists, 82–83
 UltraDev Shopping Cart extension, 255–256, 286
 Upload File From Page extension, 290
Server Object, Live Data View (LDV), 196–197
server variables, described, 175–176
 Request Object collections, 182–183
 request variable, 176
session, described, 189–190
Session Object
 described, 189–190
 login validation, 193–196
 personalizing Web pages, 192–193
 session variables, 190–191
 setting user access levels, 191
session variables
 changing the value, 282
 creating, 190–191
 creating a simple login validation technique, 193–196

described, 189–190
Live Data View (LDV), 197–198
personalizing Web pages, 192–193
setting user access levels, 191
shareware programs, described, 315
shopping cart. *See also* UltraDev Shopping Cart extension
online store feature, 252
transferring to a database, 260, 262–264
Show Region, server behaviors, 132–134
shutter arrow, described, 16
signposting (record), 130–131
Site Definition dialog box
 Application Server page, 24–25
 described, 18
 Design Notes page, 26
 Local Info page, 20–21
 preparing for a new site, 18–19
 Remote Info page, 21, 23–24
 Site Map Layout page, 27
Site Files view, 16
Site Map Layout page (Site Definition dialog box), 27
Site Map view, 16
Site window
 described, 11, 16–17
 Site Files view, 16
 Site Map view, 16
six degrees of site definition
 Application Server page, 24–25
 described, 19–20
 Design Notes page, 26
 Local Info page, 20–21
 Remote Info page, 21, 23–24
 Site Map Layout page, 27
size attribute, 110–112
sizing layers, 278
SKU modifiers, 243
software, CD with this book, 315–319
Sort drop-down lists (Server Behaviors inspector), 82–83
source code translations
 changing text if a cookie exists, 306–307
 creating dates and timestamps, 310–311
 hiding a delete icon from unauthorized users, 308
 setting a timestamp session variable, 307

source code translations *(continued)*
  setting or killing a cookie, 305–306
  simple login validation, 308–309
  suppressing display of the % wild-card character, 305
  using CDONTS.NewMail to send two separate e-mail messages, 311
SQL statements
  login validation, 194
  results page of a search, 153–157
SQL variable
  described, 151
  results page of a search, 153–157
  search pages, 152
  setting up a simple search page, 152–153
static option, described, 112
string (query), Live Data View (LDV), 142–146
Structured Query Language (SQL), 84–85
  adding results statement on results page, 170–172
  category searches, 159–161
  data filtering using the Recordset Builder, 88–91
  described, 151
  empty search results, 157–158
  filtering multidimensional searches with static options and wild cards, 167, 169
  multidimensional searches, 163–167
  results page of a search, 153–157
  search pages, 152
  setting up a simple search page, 152–153
  using the advanced mode of the Recordset Builder, 85–87
Style Definition dialog box, 51
style sheets. *See* Cascading Style Sheets (CSS)
Styles palette, 46–51. *See also* Cascading Style Sheets (CSS)
submit page
  request variables, 176–178, 180
  revising a listing, 181
system requirements for CD, 313

• T •

tables (data)
  alphabetically sorting, 82–83

  check new username server behavior, 220–222
  converting to layers, 277–278
  data filtering by using the Recordset Builder, 88–91
  flowing data from a recordset to a Web page, 79–80
  making a repetitive list, 81–82
  making data available to a Web page, 76–79
  new user registration information, 218–220
  products, 94, 160
  setting up user access levels, 223–224
  site security, 216–217
  user login identification, 224, 226
  using the advanced mode of the Recordset Builder, 85–87
tags. *See* HTML code
template sets, CD with this book, 318
templates
  adding content, 41–42
  Assets panel, 36–37
  creating new templates, 36–38
  described, 12, 36
  editable regions, 36, 38
  locked regions, 36
  modifying, 38–39
  saving pages as, 37–38
  using, 40–41
text formats, Web page design, 33–34
text links, UltraDev Shopping Cart, 239–240, 247–250
timelines, described, 12
timestamps
  creating, 310–311
  session variables, 190–191
  setting session variable, 307
Title text box (document toolbar feature), 30
toolbars, document, 29–30
tracking, described, 215–217
translations (source codes)
  changing text if a cookie exists, 306–307
  creating dates and timestamps, 310–311
  hiding a delete icon from unauthorized users, 308
  setting a timestamp session variable, 307
  setting or killing a cookie, 305–306
  simple login validation, 308–309

Index

suppressing display of the % wild-card character, 305
using CDONTS.NewMail to send two separate e-mail messages, 311
trig function, 205–206
troubleshooting, using the CD included with this book, 319–320
two-dimensional searches, 163–167

• U •

UAM. *See* User Authentication Method
UltraDev. *See* Dreamweaver UltraDev
UltraDev Shopping Cart extension, 286
  checkout links, 258
  closing the deal, 259
  database-free e-commerce site, 237–242
  databases, 242–250
  defining the shopping cart, 236–237
  described, 233
  display page, 253–255
  e-mail notification of orders, 265–271
  installing, 234–236
  order confirmation page, 259–260
  preliminary set up steps, 252–253
  repeat region server behavior, 255–256
  transferring order to a database, 260, 262–264
  updating the cart, 256–258
UltraDev sites, CD with this book, 318
Update Cart behavior, 256–258
Update page
  described, 102, 113
  dynamic check boxes, 107–108
  hand-crafting the Update server behavior, 114–116
  Live objects, 116–119
  updating text elements, 104–106
Update Record server behavior
  dialog box, 114–116
  revising a listing (request variables), 181
Upload File From Page extension, 290
URLs (Uniform Resource Locators), adding a query string, 142–146
user access level
  described, 223–224
  login identification, 224, 226
  using session objects to set, 191

User Authentication Method (UAM), 215–217, 301–303
UserGroup
  session variable, 193–196
  using session objects to set user access levels, 191
UserID
  session variable, 192–196
  site security, 215–217
  using session objects to set user access levels, 191
username
  check new username server behavior, 220–222
  cookies, 186–188
  logging out, 228–229
  login identification, 224, 226
  setting up the checkpoint on a restricted page, 226–227
  setting up user access levels, 223–224
  site security, 215–220
users
  logging out, 228–229
  login identification, 224, 226
  setting up the checkpoint on a restricted page, 226–227
  setting up user access levels, 223–224
  site registration, 218–222
  site security, 215–218

• V •

variables
  session, 282
  timestamp session, 307
View Options icon (document toolbar feature), 30

• W •

Web browser programs
  Microsoft Internet Explorer 5.5, 317
  Netscape Communicator 4.7, 317
Web pages. *See also* Web site creation; Web site design; Web sites
  adding a shopping cart, 236–237
  adding results statement on results page, 170–172

Web pages *(continued)*
  alphabetically sorting a recordset, 82–83
  binding an image to a recordset, 95–97
  cookies, 184–188
  creating the first page, 28–29
  data filtering using the Recordset Builder, 88–91
  database-free shopping cart page, 237
  database-free shopping cart site, 237–242
  document toolbar, 29, 30
  filtering multidimensional searches, 167–169
  flowing data from a recordset, 79–80
  formatting data using the Recordset Builder, 92–94
  layers, 30–32
  Live Data View (LDV), 137, 139–140, 142–148
  making a repetitive list from ten data records, 81–82
  making data available through recordsets, 76–79
  multidimensional searches, 163–167
  personalizing using session objects, 192–193
  request variables, 176–178, 180–181
  Response object, 188–189
  saving as templates, 37–38
  searching a data site, 181
  searching by category, 159–161
  server variables, 182–183
  shopping cart databases, 242–250
  Structured Query Language (SQL), 151
  text formats, 33–34
  using session objects to create a simple login validation technique, 193–196
  using the advanced mode of the Recordset Builder, 85–87
Web servers
  ColdFusion Enterprise Server 4.5.1, 316
  creating a data connection for an ASP Server, 58–59
  creating a data hookup with a JSP Server, 66–69
  creating a data source name for a ColdFusion Server, 63–64, 66
  described, 57–58
  Jrun 3.0, Developer Edition, 316
  setting up a DSN (ASP), 59–63
Web site creation. *See also* Web pages; Web site design; Web sites
  Application Server page, 24–25
  Design Notes page, 26
  Local Info page, 20–21
  preparing for a new site, 18–19
  Remote Info page, 21, 23–24
  Site Map Layout page, 27
  templates, 36
Web site design. *See also* Web pages; Web site creation; Web sites
  absolute positioning, 212, 214
  database-free shopping cart site, 237–242
  shopping cart databases, 242–250
  templates, 35–42
Web sites. *See also* Web pages; Web site creation; Web site design
  Allaire Corporation, 316
  binding form elements, 103–113
  defining, 16–17
  Delete Record server behavior, 134–135
  linking results page to a detail page, 123–127
  Live Data View (LDV), 196–199
  Live objects short cuts, 116–119
  Macromedia, 316
  Macromedia Exchange, 207–208
  making a repeat region, 120–122
  Microsoft, 317
  Netscape, 317
  results page of a search, 153–157
  search page, 152
  searches that come up empty, 157–158
  searching by category, 161
  security, 215–217
  server behaviors, 102–103
  server behaviors for navigation, 128–134
  Session object, 189–196
  setting hyperlink source, 123–124
  setting up a simple search page, 152–153
  site security, 218–224, 226–229
Web-authoring software, Dreamweaver UltraDev, 316

Index

Webmonkeys extensibility tutorial, 214
`width` attribute, 97
windows, Site window, 11, 16–17
Windows computers
  installing Dreamweaver UltraDev CD, 294
  technical requirements for CD
    installation, 293
  using the CD with this book, 314
Write Object (response variable), 188–189

IDG Books Worldwide, Inc., End-User License Agreement

READ THIS. You should carefully read these terms and conditions before opening the software packet(s) included with this book ("Book"). This is a license agreement ("Agreement") between you and IDG Books Worldwide, Inc. ("IDGB"). By opening the accompanying software packet(s), you acknowledge that you have read and accept the following terms and conditions. If you do not agree and do not want to be bound by such terms and conditions, promptly return the Book and the unopened software packet(s) to the place you obtained them for a full refund.

1. **License Grant.** IDGB grants to you (either an individual or entity) a nonexclusive license to use one copy of the enclosed software program(s) (collectively, the "Software") solely for your own personal or business purposes on a single computer (whether a standard computer or a workstation component of a multiuser network). The Software is in use on a computer when it is loaded into temporary memory (RAM) or installed into permanent memory (hard disk, CD-ROM, or other storage device). IDGB reserves all rights not expressly granted herein.

2. **Ownership.** IDGB is the owner of all right, title, and interest, including copyright, in and to the compilation of the Software recorded on the disk(s) or CD-ROM ("Software Media"). Copyright to the individual programs recorded on the Software Media is owned by the author or other authorized copyright owner of each program. Ownership of the Software and all proprietary rights relating thereto remain with IDGB and its licensers.

3. **Restrictions on Use and Transfer.**

    (a) You may only (i) make one copy of the Software for backup or archival purposes, or (ii) transfer the Software to a single hard disk, provided that you keep the original for backup or archival purposes. You may not (i) rent or lease the Software, (ii) copy or reproduce the Software through a LAN or other network system or through any computer subscriber system or bulletin-board system, or (iii) modify, adapt, or create derivative works based on the Software.

    (b) You may not reverse engineer, decompile, or disassemble the Software. You may transfer the Software and user documentation on a permanent basis, provided that the transferee agrees to accept the terms and conditions of this Agreement and you retain no copies. If the Software is an update or has been updated, any transfer must include the most recent update and all prior versions.

4. **Restrictions on Use of Individual Programs.** You must follow the individual requirements and restrictions detailed for each individual program in Appendix D of this Book. These limitations are also contained in the individual license agreements recorded on the Software Media. These limitations may include a requirement that, after using the program for a specified period of time, the user must pay a registration fee or discontinue use. By opening the Software packet(s), you will be agreeing to abide by the licenses and restrictions for these individual programs that are detailed in Appendix D and on the Software Media. None of the material on this Software Media or listed in this Book may ever be redistributed, in original or modified form, for commercial purposes.

5. **Limited Warranty.**

    (a) IDGB warrants that the Software and Software Media are free from defects in materials and workmanship under normal use for a period of sixty (60) days from the date of purchase of this Book. If IDGB receives notification within the warranty period of defects in materials or workmanship, IDGB will replace the defective Software Media.

    (b) IDGB AND THE AUTHOR OF THE BOOK DISCLAIM ALL OTHER WARRANTIES, EXPRESS OR IMPLIED, INCLUDING WITHOUT LIMITATION IMPLIED WARRANTIES OF MERCHANTABILITY AND FITNESS FOR A PARTICULAR PURPOSE, WITH RESPECT TO THE SOFTWARE, THE PROGRAMS, THE SOURCE CODE CONTAINED THEREIN, AND/OR THE TECHNIQUES DESCRIBED IN THIS BOOK. IDGB DOES NOT WARRANT THAT THE FUNCTIONS CONTAINED IN THE SOFTWARE WILL MEET YOUR REQUIREMENTS OR THAT THE OPERATION OF THE SOFTWARE WILL BE ERROR FREE.

    (c) This limited warranty gives you specific legal rights, and you may have other rights that vary from jurisdiction to jurisdiction.

6. **Remedies.**

    (a) IDGB's entire liability and your exclusive remedy for defects in materials and workmanship shall be limited to replacement of the Software Media, which may be returned to IDGB with a copy of your receipt at the following address: Software Media Fulfillment Department, Attn.: *Dreamweaver UltraDev 4 For Dummies*, IDG Books Worldwide, Inc., 10475 Crosspoint Blvd., Indianapolis, IN 46256, or call 800-762-2974. Please allow three to four weeks for delivery. This Limited Warranty is void if failure of the Software Media has resulted from accident, abuse, or misapplication. Any replacement Software Media will be warranted for the remainder of the original warranty period or thirty (30) days, whichever is longer.

    (b) In no event shall IDGB or the author be liable for any damages whatsoever (including without limitation damages for loss of business profits, business interruption, loss of business information, or any other pecuniary loss) arising from the use of or inability to use the Book or the Software, even if IDGB has been advised of the possibility of such damages.

    (c) Because some jurisdictions do not allow the exclusion or limitation of liability for consequential or incidental damages, the above limitation or exclusion may not apply to you.

7. **U.S. Government Restricted Rights.** Use, duplication, or disclosure of the Software for or on behalf of the United States of America, its agencies and/or instrumentalities (the "U.S. Government") is subject to restrictions as stated in paragraph (c)(1)(ii) of the Rights in Technical Data and Computer Software clause of DFARS 252.227-7013, or subparagraphs (c) (1) and (2) of the Commercial Computer Software - Restricted Rights clause at FAR 52.227-19, and in similar clauses in the NASA FAR supplement, as applicable.

8. **General.** This Agreement constitutes the entire understanding of the parties and revokes and supersedes all prior agreements, oral or written, between them and may not be modified or amended except in a writing signed by both parties hereto that specifically refers to this Agreement. This Agreement shall take precedence over any other documents that may be in conflict herewith. If any one or more provisions contained in this Agreement are held by any court or tribunal to be invalid, illegal, or otherwise unenforceable, each and every other provision shall remain in full force and effect.

Installation Instructions

The *Dreamweaver UltraDev 4 For Dummies* CD contains valuable information that you don't want to miss. The following sections tell you how to install the items from the CD.

Using the CD with Microsoft Windows

If you're running Windows, follow these steps to get to the items on the CD:

1. **Insert the CD into your computer's CD-ROM drive.**
2. **After the light on your CD-ROM drive goes out, double-click the My Computer icon (which is probably in the top-left corner of your desktop).**
3. **Double-click the icon for your CD-ROM drive.**
4. **Double-click the file called** License.txt.
5. **Double-click the file called** Readme.txt.
6. **Double-click the folder for the software that you're interested in.**
7. **Find the file called** Setup.exe, Install.exe, **or something similar, and double-click it.**

Using the CD with the Mac OS

If you're working on a Mac, follow these steps to install the items from the CD to your hard drive:

1. **Insert the CD into your computer's CD-ROM drive.**
2. **Double-click the CD icon to display the CD's contents.**
3. **Double-click the file called** License.txt.
4. **Double-click the Read Me First icon.**
5. **If the program you want to open comes with an installer, you can simply open the program's folder on the CD and double-click the icon that displays the word** Install, Installer, **or sometimes** sea **(for self-extracting archive).**

For more complete information, see Appendix D, "About the CD."

IDG BOOKS WORLDWIDE BOOK REGISTRATION

Register This Book and Win!

We want to hear from you!

Visit **http://my2cents.dummies.com** to register this book and tell us how you liked it!

- Get entered in our monthly prize giveaway.
- Give us feedback about this book — tell us what you like best, what you like least, or maybe what you'd like to ask the author and us to change!
- Let us know any other *For Dummies®* topics that interest you.

Your feedback helps us determine what books to publish, tells us what coverage to add as we revise our books, and lets us know whether we're meeting your needs as a *For Dummies* reader. You're our most valuable resource, and what you have to say is important to us!

Not on the Web yet? It's easy to get started with *Dummies 101®: The Internet For Windows® 98* or *The Internet For Dummies®* at local retailers everywhere.

Or let us know what you think by sending us a letter at the following address:

For Dummies Book Registration
Dummies Press
10475 Crosspoint Blvd.
Indianapolis, IN 46256

...FOR DUMMIES™
BESTSELLING BOOK SERIES